The "Last Post":

BEING

A ROLL OF ALL OFFICERS

(NAVAL, MILITARY OR COLONIAL)

WHO GAVE THEIR LIVES

FOR

THEIR QUEEN, KING AND COUNTRY,

IN THE SOUTH AFRICAN WAR, 1899—1902.

BY

MILDRED G. DOONER.

WITH A FRONTISPIECE BY W. L. WYLLIE, ESQ., A.R.A.

> "When Peace dawns over the country side,
> Our thanks shall be to the men who died;
> Oh! quiet hearts! can they hear us tell
> How Peace was won by the men who fell?"
> —ST. JAMES' GAZETTE.

LONDON:
SIMPKIN, MARSHALL, HAMILTON, KENT & CO., LTD.

To

THE MEMORY OF THOSE

WHO HAVE FALLEN.

―――

"PRO PATRIA NON TIMIDUS MORI."

PREFACE.

LAST autumn when our troops were returning from South Africa and were receiving the welcome they had so nobly earned, it occurred to me that the names of those officers who had lost their lives in the war should not be allowed to fade into oblivion, and that there should be some more fitting memorial of them than the bare mention of their names in the official casualty list.

The present volume represents an attempt at such a memorial. It contains what I trust is an accurate list of all those officers—Naval, Military, and Colonial—who were killed or died of wounds or disease in the recent South African War, together with such information regarding their careers and services as I have been able to collect. The difficulty of obtaining information, especially in the case of Colonial officers has been very great, and in some instances I have only been able to trace the notification of their deaths without any further particulars. Should therefore any omissions or errors be noticed, I shall be very grateful to any of my readers who will communicate with me.

I wish here to express my gratitude to all those who have written approving and thanking me for having undertaken this work. I shall indeed feel repaid for my efforts if in any way I have assisted in honouring the memory of such men as:—Roberts, Coulson, Younger, Egerton, Digby Jones, Lloyd, Cathcart; Chichester and Tabor dying where they stood to carry out their orders; Sutherland scorning to surrender; Holt attending the wounded under heavy fire; Weldon dashing forward to help his stricken servant; Kimber to save his wounded sergeant; the Marquis of Winchester with his reckless courage, and hosts of others who have died heroic deaths.

The title of this book seemed to me to be appropriate because in recent years at military and naval funerals it has become the custom to sound the bugle call the "Last Post" over the grave, and only a few weeks ago when the memorial to the Royal Marines in St. James' Park was being unveiled by His Royal Highness the Prince of Wales, this call was played with band accompaniment. The "Last Post" has sounded over the graves of those who sleep on the South African veldt and kopje, and this book, written in their memory, is only an echo of that bugle call; an epitaph to their bravery and heroism.

Preface. vii

I am indebted to my father, Colonel Dooner, late A.A.G. Thames District, for the advice and assistance he has given me in compiling these records: and I have to thank Sir A. Conan Doyle and his publishers, Messrs. Smith, Elder & Co., for their kindness in allowing me to quote from "The Great Boer War," also the Editor of *The Times* for a similar permission regarding "The History of the War."

In a short appendix I have added a few names of Nursing Sisters who have died in South Africa, and who have done so much for the sick and wounded. Field-Marshal Earl Roberts wrote concerning the Nursing Staff, "It was largely due to their unremitting devotion and skill that the wounded in many cases made marvellous recoveries," and Major-General Baden-Powell stated "The work done by the lady nurses was beyond all praise." Surely, then, those who have given their lives in the discharge of such a duty should have their names recorded in a book of this kind.

I have also in the appendix added a list of war correspondents of newspapers who have fallen in South Africa as far as they can be traced.

MILDRED G. DOONER.

SOUTHGATE, ROCHESTER,
August, 1903.

LIST OF ABBREVIATIONS.

Aide-de-Camp	*abbreviated*	A.D.C.
Assistant Adjutant-General	,,	A.A.G.
City Imperial Volunteers	,,	C.I.V.
Deputy Assistant Adjutant-General	,,	D.A.A.G.
Distinguished Service Order	,,	D.S.O.
Imperial Light Horse	,,	I.L.H.
Imperial Yeomanry	,,	I.Y.
London Gazette	,,	L.G.
Mounted Infantry	,,	M.I.
Orange River Colony	,,	O.R.C.
Passed Staff College	,,	p.s.c.
Royal Military Academy	,,	R.M.A.
Royal Military College	,,	R.M.C.

THE "LAST POST."

Abadie.—Lieut. Harry Bertram Abadie, 11th Hussars, died of enteric at Norval's Pont on Feb. 25th, 1901. He was the son of Major-Gen. H. R. Abadie, C.B., Lieut-Governor of Jersey, was born in June, 1872, educated at Winchester, and entered the 11th Hussars, in Oct., 1892, being promoted lieut. Sept., 1894. He served with the Chitral Relief Force under Sir Robert Low in 1895, receiving the medal with clasp. Lieut. Abadie afterwards served in the North-West Frontier Campaign of 1897-98 under the late Sir William Lockhart as Assistant Transport Officer, 2nd Brigade, Tirah Expeditionary Force; being mentioned in despatches, L.G., April 5th, 1898, and received the medal with two clasps. He was appointed A.D.C. to Lieut.-Gen. Sir Archibald Hunter in March, 1900, and was mentioned in despatches, L.G., Feb. 8th, 1901, as being "deserving of much praise" during the siege of Ladysmith, when he performed the duties of Staff Officer for Water Supplies. He was again mentioned in despatches, L.G., Sept. 5th, 1901, and was granted the D.S.O., and medal with five clasps.

Abraham.—Lieut. Thomas Oxenham Pollard Abraham, South African Constabulary, was killed at Syferfontein Farm, about nine miles north of Vaal Station on Feb. 8th, 1902. He was born in 1876, and first served in the Cape Mounted Rifles in which he rose to the rank of sergeant. In May, 1900, on the nomination of the Governor of Cape Colony, Lieut. Abraham was granted a commission as 2nd Lieut. in the King's Liverpool Regt., but this was afterwards cancelled at his own request. He then joined the South African Constabulary. He had served from the commencement of the war.

Adams.—Lieut. William Frederick Adams, Imperial Light Horse, was killed in action at Wagon Hill, near Ladysmith, on Jan. 6th, 1900. In this great struggle the Imperial Light Horse rendered gallant service; ten officers being killed or wounded, and the regiment came out of action commanded by a junior captain.

Adams-Wylie.—Lieut. Charles Henry Benjamin Adams-Wylie, Indian Medical Service, died of enteric at Bloemfontein on June 2nd, 1900. He was born Feb. 6th, 1871, and entered the Army Jan. 28th, 1899. He is understood to have been sent to South Africa in consequence of the good work he had done at Bombay during the plague there in 1899. Out of his private income he offered three days' provisions to each person who came forward to be inoculated. Over 8,000 accepted this charity. Lieut. Adams-Wylie sailed from India Jan., 1900, in medical charge of a party conducting remounts. There were many hundreds of natives under his charge, and it is stated that there was not one single death amongst them owing to his care and attention. He volunteered for sanitary work at Bloemfontein and it is supposed contracted fever in carrying out his duties.

Agnew.—Lieut. Herman Maitland Agnew, I.Y., was killed in action at Tweefontein in De Wet's attack on Christmas morning, 1901. He was the fourth son of T. F. A. Agnew, Esq., Bank of England, Liverpool, was twenty-five years of age, and educated at St. Edward's School, Oxford, where he rowed in the school four. Lieut. Agnew joined as a trooper early in 1900, and served throughout the war. He had been wounded, and for his services was awarded the Distinguished Conduct Medal, being appointed lieut. in March, 1901. He is buried at Tweefontein and his name is inscribed on an obelisk which has been erected there in memory of all who fell in this action.

Airlie.—Lieut.-Col. David Stanley William Ogilvy, tenth Earl of Airlie, and Lord Ogilvy of Airlie, of Alyth, and Lintrathen, in the Peerage of Scotland, was killed in action at Diamond Hill, June 11th, 1900. He was the eldest son of the ninth Earl by Henrietta Blanche, second daughter of the second Lord Stanley, of Alderley, born Jan. 20th, 1856, and educated at Eton (Dr. Warre's). He entered the First Royals June, 1874, being promoted lieut. in the 10th Hussars May, 1876, capt. Feb., 1884, brevet-major 1885, and major Aug., 1892. He was transferred to the 2nd Dragoon Guards in Jan., 1897, and was selected to command the 12th Lancers in Dec., 1897. Lord Airlie served with the 10th Hussars in the Afghan War 1878-79, and was present at the attack of Ali Musjid and in the engagement at Futtehabad, receiving the medal with clasp. He took part in the Soudan Expedition in 1884, as adjutant of the 10th Hussars, and was present at the engagement at Tamai, and was granted the medal with clasp, Khedive's star, and the Fourth Class of the Medjidie. He served in the Nile Expedition of 1884-85 as brigade-major under Sir Herbert Stewart, was present at the action of Abu Klea (slightly wounded) also at the engagements at Abu Klea Wells on Feb. 16th and 17th, 1885, and in the reconnaissance to Metammeh (slightly wounded) being twice mentioned in despatches. For these services he received the brevet of major and two clasps to his medal. Lord Airlie was specially mentioned in despatches for gallantry at Modder River and Magersfontein by Lieut.-Gen. Lord Methuen, who reported that Lord Airlie "did excellent work with two dismounted squadrons when good service was much needed." By Lord Arlie's action a threatened flank attack of the enemy was held back. In the beginning of May, 1900, he took an active part in the fighting around Brandford, where he was wounded, again assuming command of his regiment in a fortnight, after having been nursed at Bloemfontein by Lady Airlie. He was three times mentioned in despatches, L.G., Feb. 8th, 1901, F.-M. Earl Roberts expressing his regret at the loss of the "gallant Earl of Airlie" who fell at the head of his regiment. Lord Airlie was hon. colonel of the 3rd (Dundee Highland) V. Batt. of the Black Watch. He succeeded to the title in 1881, and was a Scottish Representative Peer. Lord Airlie married in 1886 Lady Mabel Frances Elizabeth Gore, eldest daughter of the Earl of Arran and sister of Viscountess Cranbourne and Lady Esther Smith; and left three sons and three daughters. The heir, David Lyulph Gore Wolseley-Lord Ogilvy was born in 1893.

Alderson.—Capt. James Beaumont Standly Alderson, 1st Batt. Royal Irish Regt., died of wounds received July 7th, 1900, in action at Bethlehem. He was born in July, 1869, educated at Highgate School, and entered the Royal Irish Regt. June, 1890, being promoted lieut. Aug., 1891, and capt. April, 1899. He took part in the operations on the North-West Frontier of India, 1897-98, with the Tirah Expeditionary Force, receiving the medal with clasp. Capt. Alderson had served with his battalion in South Africa from Jan., 1900.

Aldred.—Civil Surgeon J. W. Aldred died at Kroonstad on Jan. 1st, 1901. He volunteered for active service at the beginning of the war, and sailed for South Africa Nov. 7th, 1899. He was educated at the Grammar School, Manchester, where he was in the classical fifth, and among the first eleven reserves for cricket when he left in 1893.

Aldworth.—Lieut.-Col. William Aldworth, D.S.O., p.s.c., Duke of Cornwall's Light Infantry, was killed in action, near Paardeberg, Feb. 18th, 1900. He was the eldest surviving son of the late Col. Robert Aldworth, of co. Cork, and Claremont, Dorking (formerly of the 94th Foot and North Cork Rifles), was born Oct., 1855, and educated at Rossall and Clifton. Lieut.-Col. Aldworth entered the 16th Foot June, 1874, being promoted capt. March, 1881, major Feb., 1893, brevet-lieut.-col. May, 1898, and lieut.-col. to command the 2nd Batt. Duke of Cornwall's Light Infantry in the following Oct. He was adjutant of the 1st Batt. Bedfordshire Regt. from Oct., 1877 to March 1881, and held an interpreter's certificate in Russian. Lieut.-Col. Aldworth was an enthusiastic sportsman, and a first-rate rider. He served with the Burmese Expedition 1885-86 as A.D.C. and Acting Military Secretary to Sir Harry Prendergast, was mentioned in despatches, and received the D.S.O. and medal with clasp. He was also A.D.C. in Madras 1886-87, and served with the Isazai Expedition 1892, and with the Chitral Relief Force, under Sir Robert Low, 1895, with the 1st Batt. Bedfordshire Regt.; including the storming of the Malakand Pass, and the engagement near Kahr, receiving the medal with clasp. He also took part in the campaign on the North-West

Frontier of India, under the late Sir William Lockhart, 1897-98, with the Tirah Expeditionary Force, as D.A.A.G. 2nd Brigade, and with the Khyber Force, as D.A.A.G. 1898, was present at the forcing of the Sampagha and Arhanga Passes, in the operations against the Chamkanis in the Bazaar Valley; being mentioned in despatches, and granted the brevet of lieut.-col. and two clasps. Lieut.-Col. Aldworth fell near Paardeberg, while leading his battalion and calling to them "we will make the name of the Cornwalls ring in the ears of the world, boys," was struck down, but raising himself on his elbow he continued to urge his men forward, his last words being "go on men and finish it." He is buried close to where he fell. Maj.-Gen. Smith-Dorrien reported " he deeply deplored the loss of this gallant and distinguished officer." Lieut.-Col. Aldworth was mentioned in despatches by F.-M. Earl Roberts, L.G., Feb. 8th, 1901, as having "rendered conspicuously valuable services." A memorial has been erected in Cork Cathedral to the memory of Lieut.-Col. Aldworth.

Alexander.—2nd Lieut. John Alexander, South African Light Horse, was killed in action at Metz Farm, on May 15th, 1901. He was the son of Mrs. George Alexander, of Lidwells, Goudhurst, Kent, born in May, 1880, and educated at Cranbrook Grammar School. At the outbreak of the war, 2nd Lieut. Alexander was in the Argentine Republic where he had saved three men from drowning, and nearly lost his life in doing so. So anxious was he to serve in South Africa, that he managed to get a passage by attending to some horses, and on arrival at Cape Town, joined the South African Light Horse as a trooper. It is stated that of the whole troop of thirty, enrolled by Major Childe, only one survives the war. 2nd Lieut. Alexander was present at the actions of Acton Homes, Spion Kop, Vaal Kranz, Hussar

Hill, Monte Christo, Pieters Hill, and the Relief of Ladysmith. Having contracted severe enteric he was ordered home, but on recovering returned Nov., 1900, and in May, 1901, was given his commission. The day he was killed he was one of a party sent to surround two farm houses. He rushed into the farm at Metz, calling on the Boers to surrender, and was mortally wounded as he entered. Lieut.-Col. Byng, commanding the column reported that "had 2nd Lieut. Alexander lived, I would have recommended him for the V.C., he displayed the greatest coolness and valour in leading his men to the attack and on entering the building he offered the Boers a chance of surrendering before firing, it cost him his life." 2nd Lieut. Alexander is buried at Springfontein, near Philippolis. A Yorkshire cross has been erected over his grave.

Alt.—Lieut. W. Brian L. Alt, C.I.V., was killed in action at Diamond Hill, near Pretoria, on June 12th, 1900. He was the son of Col. W. J. Alt, commanding the 22nd Middlesex Volunteers, and one of the youngest officers in the C.I.V.'s, being only 22 years of age. He was educated at Clifton and New College, Oxford, and was an excellent athlete. Lieut. Alt went to South Africa Jan., 1900, and served in the north of Cape Colony, moving thence to Bloemfontein. He then took part in the advance on Pretoria, marching through Lindley, Heilbron, and Vredefort. The C.I.V.'s were afterwards present at the attack on Diamond Hill. Early in the day Lieut. Alt was wounded in the arm, but having got it dressed he returned to the firing line. Later on, when about to get his wound redressed, he was shot in the temple. He is buried at the foot of the kopje where he fell, near Kleinfontein Farm, not far from Van der Merwe Station on the Delagoa Railway. Lieut. Alt was the only officer of the C.I.V.'s who lost his life during the war.

Amedroz.—2nd Lieut. William Henry Amedroz, 3rd Batt. South Wales Borderers, died of enteric at Boshof on May 25th, 1900. He was educated at Elizabeth College, Guernsey, and joined his regiment Jan., 1900, accompanying it to South Africa in Feb.

Anderson.—Lieut. J. Anderson, Commander-in-Chief's Bodyguard (late Southern Rhodesian Volunteers), was killed in action at Clocolan Dec. 22nd, 1900.

Anderson.—Lieut. Rainy Anderson, 26th Co. Royal Engineers, was mortally wounded in action at Zeekogat, Transvaal, July 10th, 1901, and died on the following day. He was the only son of the late Staff-Surgeon James Rainy Anderson, R.N., and Mrs. Anderson (now Mrs. Darling Barker), and was born in Sept., 1873. He was educated at Neuenheim College and at Dr. Northcott's, Ealing, and entered the Royal Military Academy, Woolwich, soon after his sixteenth birthday; gaining his commission in the Royal Engineers in Feb., 1892, and was promoted lieut. Nov., 1895. He was fond of all sports and a good linguist. After serving at Chatham, Portsmouth, Ceylon, and Plymouth, he embarked for South Africa on Oct. 27th, 1899, and saw much service during the campaign. He served in the forces commanded by Lieut.-Gens. Sir J. D. P. French and Sir C. Tucker, and was in the advance on Bloemfontein and Pretoria. At the latter place he had for some time charge of the electric lighting. He was afterwards with Gen. Beatson's column, to which, shortly before his death, he was appointed Intelligence Officer. Lieut. Anderson was present at the capture of Jack Hindon's camp, ten miles north of Middelburg, and had his horse shot under him July 9th, 1901, the day before he received his death wound. On this occasion he is stated to have behaved with great gallantry, and owing to his dash a large capture of arms, ammunition, etc., was made. He rendered good service, "none more gallant than he," and was mentioned in despatches; Gen. Beatson stating he "deeply regretted his loss." Lieut. Anderson is buried in Middelburg Cemetery. A memorial tablet has been erected to his memory in the crypt of St. Paul's Cathedral.

Andrew.—Lieut. Henry Andrew, 70th Co. I.Y., died of dysentery at Salisbury Hospital, Rhodesia, July 9th, 1900. He was born in May, 1870, and was formerly a lieut. in the Royal Highlanders. Lieut. Andrew joined the I.Y. on March 21st, 1900. His name is engraved on a Latten Brass, placed in St. Paul's Cathedral in memory of all ranks belonging to the 18th, 21st and 23rd Batts. I.Y. who fell in the war.

Angell.—Lieut. John Charles Angell, Welsh Regt., was killed in action at Paardeberg Feb. 18th, 1900. He was born Feb., 1874, entered his regiment from the 3rd Batt. Royal Irish Fusiliers in 1897, being promoted lieut. Feb., 1899. When killed, Lieut. Angell was serving with M.I. His death is mentioned in the despatch of F.-M. Earl Roberts from Paardeberg, Feb. 28th, 1900.

Angus.—Lieut. William Gordon Angus, 19th Co. I.Y., was killed in action with Col. Pilcher's column on June 3rd, 1901. He was the second son of Col. William Mathwin Angus, of Framlington House, commanding 1st Newcastle-on-Tyne Volunteer Artillery, was twenty years of age, and educated at Rugby. He joined the I.Y. in Feb., 1901, from the 1st Newcastle-on-Tyne Volunteer Artillery: and when killed, was in charge of a flanking party which was suddenly attacked. Col. Pilcher wrote "deploring the loss" of Lieut. Angus.

Annett.—Lieut. J. W. Annett, Queensland M.I., was killed in action at Eland's River Aug. 4th to 6th, 1900. Sir A. Conan Doyle considers that this stand on the Eland's River "one of the very finest deeds of arms of the war." The force numbered 500, Victorians, New South Wales Bushmen and Queenslanders, with 130 Rhodesians. "2,500 Boers surrounded them, and most favourable terms of surrender were offered and scouted." During eleven days, 1,800 shells fell within their lines, but "neither the repulse of Carrington, nor the jamming of their only gun, nor the death of the gallant Annett, was sufficient to dishearten them." They were sworn to die before the white flag should wave over them and bravely held out till relieved by Brig.-Gen. Broadwood.

Annison.—Capt. A. J. Annison, Prince Alfred's Volunteer Guard, M.I., was killed in action at Buffelsfontein Sept. 30th, 1901.

Arbuthnot.—Lieut. F. Arbuthnot, 10th Batt. I.Y., was wounded near Mafeking on Dec. 7th, 1900, and died from his wounds at Lichtenburg on the 9th. He was educated at the Victoria College, Jersey, and gazetted in June, 1900, to the I.Y. with the rank of lieut. in the army.

Arbuthnot.—Capt. Reginald Ramsay Arbuthnot, Royal Irish Regt., died Sept. 3rd, 1900, at Mafeking, of wounds received Aug. 20th, in action at Ottoshoop. He was born in April, 1869, entered the Royal Irish Regt. Oct., 1891, promoted lieut. 1893, and capt. Oct., 1899. Capt. Arbuthnot served in the war from its commencement as a special service officer with the Rhodesian Field Force.

Arkwright.—Lieut. Cyril Arkwright, 5th Lancers, died of enteric March 9th, 1900, at Ladysmith. He was the third son of Lieut.-Col. and Mrs. A. C. Arkwright, of Thoby Priory, Brentwood, and was born in March, 1874. He was educated at Harrow, entered the 5th Lancers Oct., 1894, and was promoted lieut. July, 1896. Lieut. Arkwright was in Natal with his regiment when war was declared, and served in Ladysmith throughout the siege.

Armstrong.—Capt. H. M. Armstrong, 7th Batt. I.Y., was killed in action at Vlakfontein on May 29th, 1901. He was a son of Major Armstrong, late of 16th Lancers, of Morville, Warwick. Capt. Armstrong was born in Dec., 1868, educated at Stubbington School and on H.M.S. "Britannia," entered the Royal Navy in 1884, and retired as sub-lieut. 1890. He went to South Africa from Canada with Strathcona's Horse in Feb., 1900, and was granted a commission as lieut. in the Devon Co. of the 7th Batt. I.Y. May, 1900, being promoted capt. Aug., 1900. He served in Natal and O.R.C., and was present at the action at Belfast, being awarded the medal with three clasps.

Arnold.—Capt. H. M. R. Arnold, 2nd Batt. Royal Canadian Regt. of Infantry (Major 90th Winnipeg Rifles), died on the 23rd of wounds received Feb. 16th-18th, 1900, in action near Paardeberg. He was the first Canadian officer killed in the war.

Atkins.—Capt. William Atkins, Wiltshire Regt., was killed in action at Nooitgedacht Dec. 13th, 1900. He was born in June, 1861, and having served in the ranks six years was appointed 2nd lieut. Royal Irish Rifles in July, 1888, promoted lieut. Aug., 1889, and capt. in the Wiltshire Regt. July, 1896. He served in South Africa with M.I. from Oct., 1899.

Atkinson-Clark.—Lieut. Francis Maurice Augustus Atkinson-Clark, 1st Batt. Scots Guards, died of enteric at Bloemfontein April 21st, 1902. He was the eldest son of G. D. Atkinson-Clark, Esq., of Belford Hall, Northumberland. Lieut. Atkinson-Clark was born in Sept., 1874, educated at Eton (Mr. Hales'), entered the Scots Guards Dec., 1897, and was promoted lieut. July, 1899. He had served from the commencement of the war, and was present at the engagements of Belmont, Graspan, Modder River, and Magersfontein, the march to Bloemfontein and Pretoria, the engagement at Diamond Hill, the operations at Belfast, and the advance to Komati Poort.

Ashfordby-Trenchard.—Capt. George Augustus Ashfordby-Trenchard, 5th Batt. Royal Irish Regt., died of enteric at Elandsfontein. He was the son of George Ashfordby-Trenchard, Esq., of Bella Vista, Torquay. He was born in 1870, and appointed 2nd lieut. in the Lancashire Artillery Militia Feb., 1887. In 1890 he resigned his commission and went on the stage; where, under the name of George Hippisley, he had considerable success. When the war broke out he obtained a commission as lieut. in the 5th Batt. Royal Irish Regt. Soon after he was gazetted the batt. was embodied, and having spent the summer on Salisbury Plain, it moved to Aldershot in Oct., 1900. Here, as in the Lancashire Artillery, he was reported as an energetic and zealous officer. He was promoted capt. July, 1900, and when, in March, 1901, a detachment of M.I. for service in South Africa was supplied by the 5th Batt. Royal Irish Regt., Capt. Ashfordby-Trenchard was selected for the command. Since that time he saw much service, being on one occasion wounded. He contracted enteric in Jan., 1902, and after lying between life and death for many weeks passed away on March 21st.

OFFICERS WHO FELL IN SOUTH AFRICA. 13

Ava.—Archibald James Leofric Temple Blackwood, Earl of Ava, was wounded in the attack on Wagon Hill, Ladysmith, on Jan. 6th, 1900, and died on the 11th. He was the eldest son and heir of the Marquis and Marchioness of Dufferin and Ava, was born July 28th, 1863, and educated at Eton (Mr. Marindin's). He joined the 17th Lancers, in which as Lord Clandeboye, he served for some years in India as a lieut. during the Marquis of Dufferin's term of office as Viceroy. Later on Lord Ava retired from the army. When the war broke out he went to South Africa as a War Correspondent and proceeded to Ladysmith. Being a keen sportsman and a first rate horseman, adventure of all kinds attracted him. He had served previously in South Africa under Lieut.-Gen. Lord Methuen, and had also prospected in the North-West of Canada. At Wagon Hill he was wounded, shot in the temple while taking a message from Sir Ian Hamilton. He is buried in the cemetery, close to Cemetery Hill. He was a Fellow of the Royal Colonial Institute, and his name is inscribed on a Memorial Tablet in the hall of the building in Northumberland Avenue, S.W.

Awdry.—Lieut. Vere Henry Ambrose Awdry, Lancashire Fusiliers, was killed in action at Spion Kop Jan. 24th, 1900. He was born in June, 1875, and educated at Wellington, where he was in the Hardinge, a prefect, and in the football team. He was a son of the late Major Awdry, Royal Engineers, and entered the Lancashire Fusiliers from the Royal Military College, Sandhurst, Feb., 1895, being promoted lieut. April, 1898. He was mentioned in despatches, L.G., Feb. 8th, 1901. It was at first thought that Lieut. Awdry was not killed at Spion Kop, and he was promoted to the rank of capt. on Jan. 25th, 1900. Afterwards he was reported as missing, and finally in Nov., 1900, it was notified that he had been killed on Jan. 24th.

Bacon.—Capt. Arthur Henry Bacon, 1st Batt. Royal Dublin Fusiliers, was killed in action at the battle of Colenso Dec. 15th, 1899. He was a son of Major-Gen. E. A. Bacon, Bombay Staff Corps, was born in 1862, and educated at Wellington, where he was in the Blucher. He joined the Royal Dublin Fusiliers from the Hereford Militia 1883, and was promoted capt. 1892. He had been adjutant of the 4th Batt. Royal Dublin Fusiliers (Dublin City Militia) for a period of five years from Sept., 1892, to 1897.

Bailey.—Capt. Edward Burdon Bailey, 4th Batt. Derbyshire Regt., died from accidental injuries at Port Elizabeth Feb. 15th, 1901. He formerly belonged to this battalion and was promoted capt. in May, 1886, but had retired. On his old corps being embodied and placed under orders for South Africa, Capt. Bailey was re-appointed in Jan., 1900, and served with it during the war, and had been slightly wounded. He was mentioned in despatches, L.G. Sept. 10th, 1901, for his services.

Bailey.—Acting-Chaplain the Rev. G. C. Bailey, M.A., died during the war in the Dundee sub-district. He is buried at Dundee.

Baillie.—Capt. William Lyon Dennistoun Baillie, 2nd Batt. Royal Scots Fusiliers, was killed in action at Frederickstad Oct. 25th, 1900. He was a son of Mrs. Baillie, Victoria House, Blair Athol, N.B., was born Aug. 11th, 1872, and educated at Clifton College. He entered the Royal Scots Fusiliers March, 1894, being promoted lieut. Oct., 1896, and capt. Feb., 1900. He fell while leading his company under a heavy fire to attack some Boers. He was wounded twice, but staggered on until a third bullet struck him down—six of his men were found lying beside him. In writing concerning this attack Sir

A. Conan Doyle states: "There have been few finer infantry advances during the war, for the veldt was perfectly flat and the fire terrific."

Baines.—Lieut. Lancelot Oswald Talbot Baines, 1st Batt. East Lancashire Regt., died from enteric at Heilbron March 4th, 1902. He was the fourth son of L. T. Baines, Esq., of Bawtry, Yorkshire, was born July, 1877, and educated at Cheltenham. He joined the East Lancashire Regt. in May, 1900, from the 3rd Batt. York and Lancaster Regt. (3rd West York Militia), then embodied and in Ireland, and was promoted lieut. Oct., 1901. He served in South Africa during 1900, being invalided home in 1901. On recovering he returned in Dec., 1901, and served in the O.R.C. up to his death. His name is inscribed on the Eleanor Cross War Memorial at Cheltenham College.

Baker.—Lieut. and Quartermaster Joseph William Baker, Army Service Corps, died from lacerated wounds in the thigh and hip, at Pretoria, May 12th, 1902. As a private and non-commissioned officer he served for twelve years before being advanced to warrant rank, and after another six years' service received his commission July 17th, 1901. He was in his 42nd year, and went out to South Africa in 1899.

Ball-Acton.—2nd Lieut. Vere Annesley Ball-Acton, Oxfordshire Light Infantry, was killed in action Feb. 18th, 1900, near Paardeberg. He was the son of Mrs. Ball-Acton, Brooklands, Hemel Hempstead, Herts, born in April, 1879, and educated at Rugby. He entered the Oxfordshire Light Infantry Feb., 1899, and embarking with the 1st battalion for South Africa in Dec., 1899, was present at the relief of Kimberley and the action at Klip Drift. When killed he was entitled to the medal with four clasps. His death is mentioned in the despatch of F.-M. Earl Roberts of Feb. 28th, 1900, from Paardeberg.

Barber.—2nd Lieut. Arthur Barber, 50th Company I.Y., died of enteric at Springfontein on May 25th, 1901. He was at first a trooper in the 44th Co. I.Y. (Loyal Suffolk Hussars), and went out to South Africa in Feb. 1900. He was invalided home, but recovering, was granted a 2nd lieutenantcy in the 50th Co. Feb., 1901, and returned to the seat of war. He was, however, again taken ill a few weeks after his arrival, and died as stated.

Barclay.—2nd Lieut. Charles Roger Barclay, Northumberland Fusiliers, was killed in action near Reddersburg, April 4th, 1900. He was the only son of Charles Barclay, Esq., of Manor House, Bayford, was born Jan. 9th, 1878, and educated at Harrow. He entered the 2nd Batt. Northumberland Fusiliers from the 4th Batt. Bedfordshire Regt. Nov., 1899, and joined the former corps at East London in Jan., 1900.

Barker.—Lieut. E. H. Barker, South African Light Horse, was killed in action at Kaliesfontein March 5th, 1901, aged 32.

Barker.—Lieut. Francis Oswald Barker, 5th Batt. Lancashire Fusiliers, attached to the Army Service Corps as 2nd lieut., died of enteric Feb. 2nd, 1900, at Pietermaritzburg.

Barnett.—Lieut. Richard Charles Barnett, King's Royal Rifle Corps, was killed in action at the battle of Talana Hill, Natal, Oct. 20th, 1899. He was the second son of Charles Edward Barnett, Esq., of Edge Grove, Watford, by his marriage with the Hon. Augusta Rose Benn-Walsh, daughter of John, first Lord Ormathwaite. He was born in Dec., 1875, and educated at Winchester.

He joined the King's Royal Rifle Corps in April, 1896, and was promoted lieut. Dec., 1898. Lieut. Barnett is buried at Talana.

Barningham.—Veterinary-Lieut. Darnley C. Barningham, M.R.C.V.S., 20th Batt. I.Y., died suddenly of enteric and heart complications in Pretoria Dec. 7th, 1900. He joined the I.Y. in March, 1900, as veterinary officer with the temporary rank of lieutenant.

Barrett.—Capt. Rushland T. Barrett, Thorneycroft's M.I., was killed in action at Florence, O.R.C., Sept. 21st, 1901. He was mentioned in the despatch of Gen. Lord Kitchener, Oct. 8th, 1901, for conspicuous gallantry in the attack on Wessel's commando, charging a donga from which the enemy was firing heavily.

Barrow.—Lieut. Stephen Douglas Barrow, Royal Engineers, died of enteric at Modder River, March 9th, 1900. He was the son of F. H. Barrow, Esq., late Bengal Civil Service. Lieut. Barrow was born in July, 1876, educated at Clifton, and entered the Royal Engineers from the Royal Military Academy in March, 1896, being promoted lieut. in March, 1899. He embarked for South Africa, in Oct., 1899.

Barter.—Lieut. J. St. A. Barter, Johannesburg Mounted Rifles, died of enteric at Johannesburg, Feb. 5th, 1901.

Barton.—Lieut.-Col. Crosbie-Barton, formerly of the Princess of Wales's Own Yorkshire Regt., and latterly of the 18th Batt. (Sharpshooters) I.Y., died March 25th, 1902, at the Lodge, Frampton-on-Severn, Gloucestershire. Lieut.-Col. Barton was the third son of the late S. W. Barton, Esq., of Rochestown, Cahir, co. Tipperary, and was born June, 1845. He entered the Army in 1863, was promoted lieut. 1868, capt. 1878, major 1881, being placed in the Reserve of Officers as hon. lieut.-col. Oct., 1886. In 1900-01, he served in South Africa as 2nd-in-command of the 18th Batt. I.Y., and was mentioned in despatches, L.G., Sept. 10th, 1901, and in recognition of his services was promoted lieut.-col. in the Reserve of Officers, from Nov. 29th, 1900. Lieut.-Col. Barton's name is engraved on a Latten Brass placed in St. Paul's Cathedral in memory of all ranks belonging to the 18th, 21st and 23rd Batts. I.Y. who fell in the war.

Barttelot.—Capt. Sir Walter George Barttelot was killed in action at Retief's Nek, July 23rd, 1900. He was the son of the first Baronet by Harriet, daughter of Sir Christopher Musgrave, of Edenhall, Cumberland. He was born in 1855, educated at Eton (Mr. Joynes'), and served for some years in the 5th Dragoon Guards, in which he attained the rank of capt., retiring in 1879. In 1880, he was appointed capt. of the first Devon Yeomanry Cavalry, and in 1886, capt. and hon. major of the second V.B. Royal Sussex Regiment, being appointed temporarily capt. in the army, March, 1900. He married in 1879, Georgiana Mary, only daughter of G. E. Balfour, Esq., of the Manor, Sidmouth. He was a J.P. and D.L. for Sussex, a J.P. for Devonshire and a County Councillor for the Western Division of Sussex. He is succeeded by his son, Walter Balfour Barttelot, born in 1880.

Basche.—Lieut. C. O. Basche, New South Wales M.I., died of enteric at Bloemfontein on Oct. 16th, 1900.

Bate.—Lieut. Roger Whitley Bate, 3rd Batt. Royal Welsh Fusiliers, was killed in action at Rostpan near Boshof, Dec. 5th, 1901. He was born Oct., 1882, and educated at Eton (Mr. Austen Leigh's) also at Bayonne,

OFFICERS WHO FELL IN SOUTH AFRICA.

and Altenhage, Hanover. He was the eldest son of Thomas Bate, Esq., of Kelsterton, Flint, in which county his family have resided since 1266. He excelled in swimming and fencing, and was a fine horseman. When war broke out, although only 17 years old, Lieut. Bate joined the Royal Welsh Fusiliers, and early in 1901, left for South Africa with the 22nd Co. M.I. He saw considerable service and was awarded the medal with three clasps. When killed he was in command of a section of the rearguard protecting a convoy, and was shot dead while endeavouring to prevent some Boers pressing forward, which he succeeded in doing by his skilful handling of his men. Lieut. Bate is buried at Boshof. Had he lived it is stated that he would have been granted a commission in the regular army.

Bayley.—2nd Lieut. Melville Gordon Bayley, 3rd. Batt. Royal Lancaster Regt., died at St. Leonard's, Jan. 25th. 1901. He was the son of Sir Stewart Colvin Bayley, K.C.S.I., late Lieut.-Governor, Bengal, of 8, Barkston Gardens, Kensington, was educated at Blundell's School, Tiverton, and entered the Royal Lancaster Regt. Jan., 1900. He accompanied his battalion to South Africa in Feb., 1900; but after much service was invalided home and died.

Baynes.—Lieut. J. T. Baynes, 12th Batt. I.Y., was drowned at Kroonstad Nov. 30th, 1901.

Begbie.—Capt. Alfred Richard Glynn Begbie, Royal Field Artillery, was killed near Holspruit, O.R.C., Feb. 24th, 1902. He was the eldest son of Lieut.-Col. Begbie, Royal Engineers (retired) and grandson of the late Col. Lloyd-Phillips, of Dale Castle, Pembrokeshire, and Mabws, Cardiganshire, was born in April, 1875, and educated at Haileybury. He entered the Royal Artillery in June, 1895, being promoted lieut. June, 1898, and capt. April, 1901. He left for South Africa with the 75th Battery Royal Field Artillery, shortly before the war broke out. He was present at the actions of Belmont, Graspan, Modder River (mentioned in despatches), and Magersfontein, and also at the capture of Jacobsdal, and the battle of Paardeberg. At Modder River, the seniors being wounded, he was suddenly placed in command of his battery, and Lieut.-Gen. Lord Methuen reported he brought it into action with great coolness. After Driefontein he was transferred to T Battery Royal Horse Artillery, in which he served at the taking of Johannesburg and in the actions at Diamond Hill and Belfast. When promoted capt. he was put in charge of a Pom-Pom section. In July, 1901, Capt. Begbie joined Rimington's column with which he served continuously until his death. He died whilst endeavouring to rally some men, and was mentioned in despatches, L.G. July, 18th, 1902, "for very marked gallantry in action."

Belcher.—2nd-Lieut. William Greaves Belcher, 38th Battery Royal Field Artillery, was killed in action near Lindley, July 3rd, 1900. He was born in July, 1878, educated at Harrow and entered the Royal Artillery in Feb. 1898. (*See Major Oldfield.*)

Bell.—Lieut. Reginald William Bell, Royal Engineers, died of enteric Feb. 11th, 1900, at De Aar. He was the eldest son of Rev. W. Bell, vicar of Cranbrook, late Headmaster of Dover College. Lieut. Bell was born in April, 1874, and educated at Dover College, where he was captain of the Football XV. At the Royal Military Academy, Woolwich, he played for the Academy, and also for the R.E. at Chatham. He was a keen sportsman and a good horseman. He entered the Royal Engineers, July, 1893, being promoted lieut. 1896. He was stationed at Gibraltar in 1899, and went from there to South Africa in Nov., and served in Cape Colony.

Bellew.—Capt. Robert Walter Dillon Bellew, 16th Lancers, was killed in action at Fourteen Streams, Piquetberg Road, Oct. 16th, 1901. He was born July, 1872, entered the 16th Lancers in March, 1892, was promoted lieut. March, 1895, and capt. Oct., 1899. He served with the 16th Lancers in India, and during the later months of the Tirah Campaign, 1897-98, he was attached to the late Sir William Lockhart's Staff as an extra orderly officer. While in South Africa, Capt. Bellew contracted enteric fever, and when convalescent was appointed Assistant Press Censor at Bloemfontein, which post he held for a short time, afterwards rejoining his regiment.

Bennet.—Capt. Arthur Buckley Bennet, 2nd. Batt. Royal Warwickshire Regt., died of peritonitis, April 24th, 1900, at Bloemfontein. He was born in June, 1866, educated at Cheltenham, and entered the Cheshire Regt. in Aug. 1886, being promoted into the Royal Warwickshire Regt. as capt. in April, 1898. He served in the Burmese expedition 1887-89, with the 2nd Batt. Cheshire Regt. receiving the medal with clasp. His name is inscribed on the Eleanor Cross War Memorial at Cheltenham College.

Benson.—Lieut. A. E. Benson, Kitchener's Fighting Scouts (late New South Wales Bushmen), was dangerously wounded at Klip Kraal, near Richmond, and died subsequently at Deelfontein.

Benson.—Col. George Elliott, Benson, p.s.c., Royal Artillery, died Oct. 31st, 1901, of wounds received in action near Brakenlaagte, twenty miles north-west of

Bethel. He was the son of the late William Benson, Esq., of Allerwash, Northumberland, was born in May, 1861, and educated at Harrow. He entered the Royal Artillery as a lieut. in 1880, being promoted capt. July, 1888, brevet-major March, 1896, major Feb., 1898, brevet-lieut.-col. Nov., 1900, and col. May, 1901. He served in the Soudan Campaign, 1885, and was present at the engagement of Hasheen (slightly wounded), and at the destruction of Tamai, receiving the medal with clasp, and the Khedive's star. His next experience of active service was with the expedition to Ashanti, under Sir Francis Scott, in 1895, when he received the brevet of major and the star. He also served with the Dongola Expeditionary Force under Lord (then Sir Herbert) Kitchener, in 1896, as Brigade-Major, Mounted Corps, until invalided, including the engagement at Firket and the operations at Hafir, being mentioned in despatches, and receiving the Fourth Class of the Order of the Osmanieh, and the Khedive's medal with two clasps. He was also in the Nile Expedition of 1898, in command of a force on special service in Kassala district, and was awarded the medal. He was Brigade-Major Royal Artillery at Aldershot from Jan. 1st, 1892, to Dec. 31st, 1894. Col. Benson was selected for special service in South Africa, and served with the Kimberley Relief Force under Lieut.-Gen. Lord Methuen. After the battle of Modder River, he took the place of Lieut.-Col. Northcott —who had been killed—as D.A.A.G., was present at the action of Magersfontein, and the relief of Kimberley. At Magersfontein he guided the Highland Brigade during the night march, and with unerring accuracy to the point of the hill he had previously at great personal risk reconnoitred. He was mentioned in despatches March, 1900, and Nov. of that year, and promoted to the rank of lieut.-col. Nov. 29, 1900. A few weeks later he was appointed staff officer to the Rustenburg command, and in May,

1901, was given local rank as colonel. The column which he commanded was attacked on Oct. 31st, in a deluge of mist and blinding rain. The Boers under Louis Botha, Grobler and Oppermann in overwhelming numbers, swept down on a ridge held by the rearguard of Col. Benson's force, and here 123 men out of a total of 160 fell. Col. Benson, who at once went to the point of danger, was twice wounded; but continued to give his orders directing and exhorting those under him to hold out. In this engagement, in addition to Col. Benson, twelve other officers were killed and sixteen wounded, but the main body and the convoy were saved. This action has been described as one of the most hotly contested and desperate of the campaign.

Benson.—Capt. Richard Arthur Starling Benson, 1st Batt. Coldstream Guards, died in Wynberg Hospital, on Feb. 19th, 1900, from dysentery, contracted on the Modder River. He was the only son of Col. Starling Benson, late commanding the 17th Lancers, was born in Dec., 1869, and educated at Eton (College). He entered the Coldstream Guards from the 3rd Batt. Essex Regt., in July, 1890, being promoted lieut. Jan., 1894, and capt. Feb., 1899. Capt. Benson, when war was declared, belonged to the 3rd Batt. Coldstream Guards, and was undergoing a course of instruction at the Ordnance College. He volunteered for active service, and being accepted, was posted to the 1st battalion, and joined it in South Africa.

Bentley.—Lieut. Oliver Tyser Bentley, 2nd Batt. Worcestershire Regt., was killed in action at Bethlehem, Dec. 29th, 1900. He was born in March, 1880, entered the Worcestershire Regt. from the 4th Batt. Somersetshire Light Infantry, April, 1900, and was promoted lieut. the following Sept.

Berghuys.—Lieut. H. G. Berghuys, Kitchener's Horse, died of wounds received at Krugersdorp, in Feb., 1901.

Berney.—Capt. Thomas Hugh Berney, 2nd Batt. West Yorkshire Regt., was killed in action on Feb. 18th, 1900, at Monte Christo, during the advance to the relief of Ladysmith. He was the eldest son of Sir Henry H. Berney, of Barton Bendish, Norfolk, by his marriage with Jane Dorothy, daughter of the late Rev. Andrew Bloxam, rector of Harborough Magna, Rugby. Capt. Berney was born Oct., 1866, and educated at Hillside, Godalming, and the United Services College, Westward Ho, from 1880-85. He entered the West Yorkshire Regt. from the 3rd Batt. Royal Warwickshire Regt., in May, 1887, was promoted lieut. May, 1889, and capt. Sept. 1894. Capt. Berney served in the Ashanti Expedition of 1895-96, receiving the star awarded for that expedition. On Feb. 18th, 1900, he was the first man to reach the top at the storming of Monte Christo, where he was shot through the head. He was three times mentioned in despatches by Gen. Sir R. Buller, L.G., Feb. 8th, 1901, for his gallantry, as having led the assault on Monte Christo, and was "first man up." Capt. Berney left a widow and two sons. His name is inscribed on a tablet erected at the United Services College, Westward Ho, in memory of old pupils who fell in the war.

Berry.—Lieut. Charles Frederick Berry, Prince of Wales's Light Horse, was killed in action March 31st, 1901. He was 31 years of age and a native of Taunton. Several years ago he went to South Africa, and was one of the inhabitants of Johannesburg who took part in the Jameson Raid. When the South African War broke out Mr. Reitz refused him permission to stay in Pretoria, and he accordingly left for Cape Town, joined the Durban Light Infantry and took part in several engagements. When his regiment was disbanded Lieut. Berry joined the Prince of Wales's Light Horse and was given a commission in command of the cycle section.

Berry.—Lieut. W. J. Berry, New Zealand M.I., died of pneumonia on June 10th, 1900, at Johannesburg.

Berthon.—Lieut. Herbert Cecil Willoughby Berthon, of Cleeve Court, Somersetshire, 2nd Batt. Royal Highlanders (Black Watch), died on Dec. 15th, 1899, at Wynberg, Cape Colony, of wounds received at Magersfontein. He was the son of the late Major-Gen. T. P. Berthon, of West Mount, Ryde, Isle of Wight, and was born June 10th, 1865. Lieut. Berthon served in the ranks nearly seven years and gained his commission as 2nd lieut. in the East Yorkshire Regt., Jan., 1894; promoted lieut. Oct., 1896, and transferred to the Royal Highlanders, Oct., 1897. He served with the Kimberley Relief Force under Lieut.-Gen. Lord Methuen previous to being wounded at Magersfontein.

Besley.—2nd Lieut. Arthur Charles Gordon Besley, 4th Batt. Royal Fusiliers, was killed in action at Wedelfontein, June 23rd, 1901. He was the younger son of the late Charles Robert Besley, Esq., 14, Leinster Gardens, W., and of Mrs. Besley, 15, Palmeira Avenue, Hove, Sussex, and great grandson of the ninth Marquis of Huntly, his mother being a daughter of the late Lord Cecil Gordon. He was born April, 1881, educated at Wellington where he was in Bevir's, and joined his regiment from the Royal Military College in August, 1900. 2nd Lieut. Besley was a first-rate rider and good shot. He embarked for South Africa in March, 1901, and served with M.I., being present at many actions.

A tablet to his memory has been erected by his brother officers in St. John's Church, Hove.

Best.—Lieut. Alexander Archie Dunlop Best, Gordon Highlanders, was killed in action in an attack on a train four miles north of Naboom Spruit, July 4th, 1901. He was the only son of A. V. Dunlop Best, Esq., was born in May, 1879, and educated at Haileybury and Eton (Mr. Radcliffe's). He entered the Gordon Highlanders in April, 1899, being promoted lieut. in the following Oct. He had served from the commencement of the war. The party which he commanded was escort to a train travelling from Pretoria to Pietersburg, which was wrecked and all in it were killed or wounded.

Betty.—2nd Lieut. G. E. K. Betty, Army Service Corps, died of enteric at Bloemfontein, on Feb. 25th, 1901. He was educated at Brighton College.

Bickford-Smith.—Capt. George Percy Bickford-Smith, died at Heilbron from wounds received in action, on May 30th, 1901. He was the second son of the late Mr. W. Bickford-Smith, of Trevarno, Cornwall, educated at Leys School, Cambridge, 1884-90, and entered the 1st V.B. Duke of Cornwall's Light Infantry in 1893, being promoted capt. June 27th, 1900. He joined the I.Y. in March, 1901, with the rank of 2nd lieut., and served in Cape and Orange River Colonies.

Biddulph.—Capt. Charles Thomas Biddulph, 3rd Batt. Leinster Regt., died of enteric at Queenstown, South Africa, April 26th, 1900. He was the youngest surviving son of Lieut.-Col. F. E. Biddulph, late 9th Norfolk Regt., Marie Lodge, Dalkey, co. Dublin, was born in June, 1869, and educated privately. Capt. Biddulph, previous to going to South Africa, had been employed under the Colonial Office as Superintendent of Police in Gambia,

OFFICERS WHO FELL IN SOUTH AFRICA. 27

where he saw some service, but had to return to England owing to ill-health. When the 3rd Batt. Leinster Regt. volunteered for South Africa, in Feb., 1900—although still suffering from the effects of service on the West Coast—decided on accompanying it, but died a few weeks later, succumbing to enteric after a short illness.

Bingham.—Lieut. John Anderson Bingham, 23rd Co. I.Y., died at Calvinia on the 11th Feb., 1902, from wounds received at De Hook on the 5th. He was the son of William Bingham, Esq., J.P., Lingdale House, Claughton, was born Oct. 9th, 1874, and educated at Merchiston School, Edinburgh, where he played in the football team. He held the rank of lieut. in the 8th V.B. Liverpool Regt. Lieut. Bingham was present at several engagements in Cape Colony with the columns under Col. Henniker-Major and Lieut.-Col. Doran, Royal Irish Regt.

Birch.—Capt. Charles Francis Grey Birch, 1st Batt. South Lancashire Regt., was killed in action at Spion Kop in the operations on Upper Tugela, Jan. 24th, 1900, while endeavouring to rescue a wounded man. He was the son of the late Col. Birch, of Lympstone Grange, South Devon, late colonel commanding the 4th Batt. of the North Lancashire Regt., was born in Nov., 1866, and educated at Rugby. He entered the South Lancashire Regt. from the 4th Batt. Loyal North Lancashire Regt., in Dec., 1888, and was promoted lieut. May, 1890, and capt. April, 1898. A memorial cross has been erected over his grave near Spion Kop.

Birch.—Lieut. Birch, Canadian M.I., was killed in action at Reit Vlei, July 16th, 1900. This officer resisted and drove back several attacks made by the Boers, and fell while directing and encouraging his men. Sir A. Conan Doyle, in writing of this action, says: " The British loss included two gallant young Canadian officers, Borden and Birch. The enemy tried to assault the position, but were beaten back each time with loss."

Bird.—2nd Lieut. Hubert Bertram Drought Bird, 9th Battery Royal Field Artillery, died of enteric at Winburg Hospital, Orange River Colony, July 28th, 1900. He was the third son of J. D. Bird, Esq., M.B., of 70, Lower Leeson Street, Dublin, who died quite suddenly in South Africa in Dec. 1902. His mother was the daughter of the Rev. J. P. Bertram, Queenstown, Cape Colony, and a niece of Sir Theophilus Shepstone. 2nd Lieut. Bird was born in Rouxville, O.R.C., in Sept., 1879, and educated in Dublin at St. Stephen's Green School (Mr. Strangway's). He passed into the Royal Military Academy, Woolwich, soon after his sixteenth birthday, and entered the Royal Field Artillery, in June, 1898. He accompanied his Battery to South Africa, and was with it in many engagements in the Cape and Orange River Colonies until taken ill. A monument has been erected by his comrades to his memory at Winburg. It bears the inscription: "Greatly loved by officers and men."

Blackburn.—Capt. Leslie Dewing Blackburn, p.s.c., Scottish Rifles, died of wounds received in action at Crocodile's Poort, Oct. 22nd, 1899. He was born on June 29th, 1865, and educated at Clifton. He entered the Scottish Rifles on Aug. 23rd, 1884; was adjutant from Nov. 1891 to Nov. 1895, and promoted capt. April 16th, 1894. When scouting with six of his men on the northern frontier of the Transvaal, in thick bush, he found his small force in the presence of a considerable Boer commando. His party concealed themselves, but Capt. Blackburn's foot was noticed by the enemy, and a sudden volley was fired, wounding him mortally. His companions remained with him and succeeded in driving off the Boers. Capt. Blackburn had sufficient strength left to dictate his report of the action and then leant back and died.

Blackett.—Lieut. Algernon Carey Blackett, South African Constabulary, was killed in the engagement at Syferfontein, about nine miles north of Vaal Station, on Feb. 8th, 1902. He was the youngest son of the late Capt. E. A. Blackett, R.N., of Wylam, Northumberland; was born May, 6th, 1873, and educated at Bedford Grammar School and Wellington College, also at Emmanuel College, Cambridge. Lieut. Blackett was in South Africa when war was declared and joining Bethune's M.I., served with it till March, 1901. He was then transferred to the South African Constabulary, and while with that force, was severely wounded on Oct. 12th, 1901, but on recovering rejoined and served until his death. He was awarded the Queen's medal with six clasps, also the King's medal.

Blackwood.—Capt. Alexander Thomas Blackwood, 1st Batt. South Staffordshire Regt., died on April 20th, 1902, at Moolmaanspruit, near Ficksburg, of wounds received in action the same day at Olivier's Farm. He was the eldest son of Capt. T. Blackwood (late Inniskilling Dragoons), of Ayr, was born in Aug., 1872, and educated at Victoria College, Jersey. He entered the South Staffordshire Regt., in Jan. 1892, was promoted lieut. July, 1894, and capt. June, 1900. Capt. Blackwood, who was with the 2nd battalion of his regiment in India, proceeded to South Africa on being promoted, and joining the 1st battalion, served throughout the remainder of the war up to the time of his death. He was mentioned in despatches, L.G., July 18th, 1902, for his gallantry at Moolmaanspruit on April 20th. (*See Capt. Sir T. Fowler.*)

Blair.—Capt. Hugh Maxwell Blair, Seaforth Highlanders, was killed in action at Koodoosburg, Feb. 7th, 1900. He was the eldest son of the late Alexander Blair, Esq., Advocate-Sheriff of the Lothians and Peebles. He was born in 1872, educated at Edinburgh Academy, also Sedbergh School, and at the latter was in his school football team. He entered the Seaforth Highlanders from the Royal Military College (passing out first), in 1891, being promoted lieut. 1894, and capt. Nov., 1899. Capt. Blair served with the 2nd battalion with the Chitral Relief Expedition of 1895, and was present in the engagement at Mamugai, receiving the medal with clasp. He was employed for a short time with the West African Frontier Force. At Koodoosburg, his carotid artery was cut by a bullet from a shrapnel shell and some of the men of his company took it in turns to press the artery, hoping thus to prevent loss of blood and to save his life, but their efforts, although continued for some hours, proved unavailing.

Blake.—2nd Lieut. Robert Charles Sydney ffrench Blake, 2nd Batt. East Kent Regt. (The Buffs), was killed accidentally May 19th, 1902, at Alkmaar. He was born July, 1880, educated at Eton (Mr. Donaldson's), and entering the Buffs in May, 1901, served in South Africa from the latter part of that year up to the time of his death.

Blanchard.—Lieut. L. Blanchard, Canadian M.I., died at Kroonstad, June 15th, 1900, from wounds received in action at Roodevaal on June 7th.

Bland.—Sub-Lieut. Horatio Skene Bland, of H.M.S. "Beagle," was drowned in the act of landing at Seal Island, Mossel Bay, Cape Colony, Sept. 29th, 1901. He was the eldest son of the late Capt. Horatio Bland, formerly of the King's Own Scottish Borderers, of Caunton Manor,

Newark, Notts; was 21 years of age, and educated at Stubbington School, Fareham, Hants. Passing into the "Britannia," in July, 1894, he was promoted midshipman Nov. 1896, and sub-lieut. May, 1900. He is buried in Mossel Bay cemetery.

Blandy.—Capt. Robert Acton Blandy, Colonial Defence Force (Molteno section), was killed in action near Molteno, Nov. 22nd, 1901. He was the eldest son of the late Adam Fettiplace Blandy, Esq., of the Warren, Abingdon, was born in March, 1870, and educated at Clifton College. Capt. Blandy, who had been articled to Messrs. Foster and Browne, mining engineers, at Cardiff, went to Cape Colony in Dec. 1896, to take charge of collieries at Molteno, where he was very successful. On the outbreak of the war he joined the Frontier Mounted Rifles as lieut., and first served with Major-Gen. Sir W. F. Gatacre's column and afterwards with Major-Gen. Brabant, being present at many engagements in the N.E. of Cape Colony. He was killed while reconnoitring in the Bamboo mountains. Capt. Blandy had dismounted near some rocks where it was believed some Boers were concealed. He rushed forward calling on his men to "come on as they are sure to run." Lieut. King, who was with him, was wounded, and while going to assist him, Capt. Blandy was mortally wounded at about 15 to 20 yards range. Lieut.-Gen. Sir J. D. P. French telegraphed greatly regretting Capt. Blandy's death, and stating "he has done excellent service, we are much indebted to him." Capt. Blandy is buried at Molteno. His grave is in a corner of the cemetery there, near that of Capt. de Montmorency.

Blewitt.—Lieut. Charles Oakes Bates Blewitt, 1st Batt. Rifle Brigade, was killed in action near Blood River Poort, Sept. 17th, 1901. He was born in July, 1875, and educated at Wellington, where he was in the Blucher and a school Prefect. He entered the Rifle Brigade in July, 1896, from the Royal Military College, and was promoted lieut. Dec. 1898. He served in the Ladysmith Relief Operations of the 5th to the 7th Feb., 1900, including the action at Vaal Kranz, when he was severely wounded. Lieut. Blewitt was mentioned by Gen. Lord Kitchener in his despatch of Sept. 17th, 1901, for "his gallant conduct." He is buried at Vryheid.

Blount.—Major Charles Hubert Blount, 20th Battery Royal Field Artillery, died from dysentery, at Wynberg, Feb. 23rd, 1900. He was born in July, 1855, educated at Uppingham from 1868-71, entered the Royal Artillery in Aug., 1875, being promoted capt. Aug., 1884, and major 1892. He served as adjutant of Volunteers from June, 1888, to Sept., 1892.

Blundell-Hollinshead-Blundell.—Lieut. Wilfrid Astley Blundell-Hollinshead-Blundell, Grenadier Guards, died of wounds received in action at Belmont, Nov. 23rd, 1899. He was the eldest son of Canon Blundell Hollinshead-Blundell, of Halsall, was born in May, 1871, and educated at Eton (Mr. Cornish's). He entered the Grenadier Guards in 1892, being promoted lieut. Feb., 1897. The author of "The Great Boer War" writes, that Lieut. Blundell was shot by a wounded Boer "to whom he was offering his water bottle." *The Times* History of the War, however, mentions that whether the wounded Boer fired "from deliberate treachery or in an unreasoning agony of fear and terror, it is impossible to say."

Blunt.—Brevet-Major Robert Bruce Blunt, Lancashire Fusiliers, died Feb. 20th, 1902, of wounds received the day previously at Llangelegen, near Vryheid. The eldest son of George H. Blunt, Esq., Leicester, he was born May 17th, 1873, and educated at Wyggeston School, Leicester, and afterwards at Rugby. He entered the Lancashire Fusiliers in 1892, was promoted lieut. Jan., 1894, capt. Sept., 1899, and brevet-major Nov., 1900. He served in the campaign in the Soudan under Lord (then Sir Herbert) Kitchener, in 1898, as adjutant of the 2nd Batt. Lancashire Fusiliers, was present at the battle of Khartoum, receiving the British medal, and the Khedive's medal with clasp. He also took part in the occupation of Crete in 1898. In the South African War Major Blunt served with the 2nd Batt. Lancashire Fusiliers, with the Ladysmith Relief Force, and was present at Spion Kop and the engagement of Venters Spruit (severely wounded). He was appointed Staff Officer for Intelligence from Oct., 1900, and at the time of his death was Staff Officer, Dundee Sub-district. He was mentioned in despatches, L.G., Sept. 10th, 1901, for his services, and was promoted to a brevet majority. Major Blunt was adjutant of his battalion from March, 1896, to March, 1900. He is buried at Dundee.

Booth.—Brevet-Major Arthur William Calvert Booth, 1st Batt. Northumberland Fusiliers, was killed in action near Bloemfontein Water Works, March 31st, 1900. He was the eldest son of W. Booth, Esq., was born in June, 1867, entered the Northumberland Fusiliers Aug., 1886, being promoted lieut. Feb., 1891, capt. Jan., 1895, and brevet-major July, 1899. He served with the 2nd Batt. Northumberland Fusiliers throughout the Hazara campaign of 1888, receiving the medal with clasp. He took part in the operations on the Niger, 1897-98, when he was mentioned in despatches, and received the brevet of major and the medal with clasp. He was employed with the West African Frontier Force from Dec., 1897, until Feb., 1900, then rejoining his battalion in South

Africa. A few weeks afterwards he was killed while serving with the M.I., and with four men was holding a position at a most critical moment to cover the retreat of the main body. He is stated to have behaved most gallantly. A tablet has been erected in his memory at Catterick.

Borden.—Lieut. H. L. Borden, Canadian M.I. (Major King's Canadian Hussars), was killed in action at Reit Vlei, July 16th, 1900. He was the only son of the Minister of Militia in Canada. He was mentioned in despatches by Gen. Lord Kitchener, L.G., Sept. 10th, 1901, also in the despatch of Sept. 8th, 1901, for "gallantry in action, and for stubborn fighting." (*See Lieut. Birch.*)

Bowen.—Major Robert Scarlett Bowen, 2nd Batt. King's Royal Rifle Corps, was killed in action at Wagon Hill, Ladysmith, Jan. 6th, 1900. He was born in 1862, educated at Cheltenham College, and entered the 28th Foot in 1880, being transferred to the 60th Foot the same year. He was promoted lieut. in 1881, capt. 1890, major April, 1899. At Wagon Hill, Major Bowen calling for volunteers, dashed with eight men across a fire-swept space at a strong position held by the enemy. They were all killed. Major Bowen is buried in a grave with four other officers on a plateau half way up the nek between Wagon Hill and Cæsar's Camp, close to where he fell. The names of the officers are 2nd Lieut. F. H. Raikes, Lieut. N. M. Tod, Major D. Mackworth, Major R. S. Bowen, and 2nd Lieut. W. H. T. Hill. The officers lie in the order given from the left, and a marble cross and pedestal with their names inscribed has been erected. It bears this inscription, "In token of affection and regard by their brother officers." To this memorial five separate crosses have been added by relatives, and a kerb encloses the whole. Major Bowen was mentioned in despatches, L.G., Feb. 8th, 1901, for his gallant services. His name is inscribed on the Eleanor Cross War Memorial at Cheltenham College.

Boyd.—Capt. A. J. Boyd, South African Constabulary, died of enteric at Pretoria, on April 20th, 1902.

Boyle.—Lieut. Cecil D. Boyle, O.R.C. Police, Assistant District Commissioner at Lindley, was taken prisoner by the Boers at Dewetsdorp on Nov. 23rd, 1900, and was shot probably on Jan. 2nd, 1901. This officer's death formed the subject of a trial for murder, which took place in Feb. 1903, at Bloemfontein, the prisoner being acquitted. It appears that Lieut. Boyle when captured by the Boers, was tried by a Krygsraad presided over by General De Wet and was acquitted. Lieut. Boyle was however, afterwards taken to a lonely spot and told that he had been sentenced to death. He then knelt to pray and was shot in the back while doing so. The man Barend Celliers who was acquitted admitted shooting Lieut. Boyle, but stated in his defence that it was done by order of Gen. Philip Botha.

Boyle.—Capt. Cecil W. Boyle, Oxfordshire Yeomanry Cavalry, killed in action near Boshof, April 5th, 1900, was the first officer of the I.Y. who fell in the war. He was educated at Clifton, where he was head of Brown's House. He went to South Africa in Dec., 1899, taking with him thirty of his own horses for active service. He was an enthusiastic officer, a keen sportsman, and well known with the Warwickshire Hounds. His death was much regretted in the Midlands. The loss of Capt. Boyle is referred to with regret by Lieut.-Gen. Lord Methuen in his despatch of April 6th, 1900, L.G., Feb. 8th, 1901.

Brabant.—Lieut. Arthur Edward Brabant, Imperial Light Horse, died at Ladysmith Nov. 5th, 1899, of wounds received in action two days previously. He was the son of Major-Gen. Sir E. Y. Brabant, K.C.B., C.M.G., M.L.A., of Cape Town, and now Commandant General of the Colonial Defence Force. His mother, Mary Burnet, is a daughter of the late Rev. Canon James Craigie Robertson, formerly of Canterbury, and the author of "The History of the Christian Church." Lieut. Brabant was born Nov. 12th, 1865, and educated in South Africa. He had been engaged as a Mining Engineer for some years in Johannesburg, but on the outbreak of war, at once volunteered for active service and joined the Imperial Light Horse. At Elandslaagte his bravery is stated to have been most conspicuous; at this battle he greatly assisted in rallying some men at a critical moment in the charge against the Boer counter attack. Lieut. Brabant was mentioned in despatches for his services. He is buried in Ladysmith cemetery, in grave No. 6, next to Capt. Knapp, and next but one to Lieut. Egerton, of H.M.S. " Powerful." Lieut. Brabant had previously served in the Matabele War. (*See Major Taunton.*)

Bradburn.—Lieut. H. H. Bradburn, New Zealand M.I., died of wounds received in action at Crocodile Drift Aug. 19th, 1900.

Bradbury.—Lieut. Lewis Balfour Bradbury, 2nd Batt. Gordon Highlanders, died on Oct. 22nd, 1899, of wounds received in action at the battle of Elandslaagte on the previous day. He was the only son of the late J. L. Bradbury, Esq., Bengal Civil Service, and Mrs. Bradbury, of 7, West Maitland Street, Edinburgh. Lieut. Bradbury was born in Nov., 1877, educated at Edinburgh Academy, and entered the Gordon Highlanders from the Royal Military College, from which he passed with honours, in Feb., 1897, being promoted lieut. April, 1899. He was a well-known athlete, a first-rate football player, and a good runner, both at one hundred yards and the quarter mile. At school he was first at these distances for three years in succession, and at Sandhurst and the Army Athletic Meeting he was a well-known successful competitor. After serving in India for about one year, he went with his battalion to South Africa, in Sept., 1899, and proceeded to Ladysmith. At Elandslaagte he was mortally wounded while rushing forward and leading some men of his company to attack the Boer position.

Bradshaw.—Capt. William Edmond John Bradshaw, York and Lancaster Regt., was killed in action at the engagement at Zoutspan Drift, O.R.C., on Dec. 13th, 1899. He was born in 1868, joined the York and Lancaster Regt., 1888, was promoted lieut. 1890, and capt. June, 1899. He served in the Soudan campaign under Lord (then Sir Herbert) Kitchener in 1898, and was present at the battles of Atbara and Khartoum, mentioned in despatches, and received the Fourth Class of the Order of the Medjidie, British medal and Khedive's medal with two clasps. Col. Miles reports concerning Capt. Bradshaw, that "he was an energetic and valuable officer, and I deeply regret his loss."

Brancker.—2nd Lieut. Grafton Lloyd Dulany Brancker, South Staffordshire Regt., killed in action at Ficksburg, June 25th, 1900, was born Dec. 23rd, 1876. He joined the first battalion of his regiment from the Militia Dec., 1899, and accompanied it to South Africa in March, 1900.

Brasier-Creagh.—Capt. George Percy Brasier-Creagh, 9th Bengal Lancers, commanding Roberts' Horse, was severely wounded near Karreefontein on April 23rd, 1900, and died four days later at Eirstelaagte. Born in 1864, he entered the East Surrey Regt. from the 9th Batt. King's Royal Rifle Corps, May, 1884, and joined the Indian Staff Corps, May, 1886, being promoted capt. May, 1895. From 1889 to 1894, he was A.D.C. to the Viceroy of India. Capt. Brasier-Creagh acted as the late Sir William Lockhart's orderly officer in the second Miranzai Expedition (mentioned in despatches). He also took part in the Isazai Expedition of 1892, and the Chitral Expedition of 1895 with the relief force, being awarded the medal with clasp. In the operations on the North-West Frontier in 1897, he served with the Malakand Field Force, and with the Tirah Expeditionary Force, being mentioned in despatches, L. G., June 7th, 1898. At the time of his death Capt. Brasier-Creagh was in command of Roberts' Horse, which corps greatly distinguished itself.

Brass.—Capt. Ernest Henry Brass, East Yorkshire Regt., was drowned whilst attempting to swim the Wilge River, on Nov. 10th, 1901. He was the son of the Rev. H. Brass, formerly rector of St. Matthew's, Red Hill, was born in 1869, and educated at Uppingham, 1883-88, and Clare College, Cambridge (Johnson Exhibitioner). Capt. Brass entered the East Yorkshire Regt., in May, 1891, being promoted lieut. Oct., 1894, and capt. Oct., 1899. He was selected for special service in South Africa in Nov. 1899, and had acted for some time at the base at Cape Town as an Embarking Staff Officer, graded as D.A.A.G.

Brassey.—2nd Lieut. Percy Frederick Brassey, 9th Lancers, was killed in the engagement near Kimberley, between Feb. 14th-16th, 1900. He was the second son of Albert Brassey, Esq., M.P., of Heythrop, by his marriage with the Hon. Matilda Maria Helena, second daughter of the late Baron Clanmorris. 2nd Lieut. Brassey was born Dec. 1876, educated at Eton (Mr. Mitchell's), and entered the 9th Lancers May, 1899, with which he had served from the commencement of the war.

Brenes.—Lieut. Francis George Dominic Brenes, 5th Batt. Royal Fusiliers, attached to 5th M.I., was killed in action at Amajuba, on March 29th, 1902. He was educated at Dulwich College, and entered his regiment in Dec., 1900, being promoted lieut. May, 1901. He had the local rank of lieut. in the army, and when killed was in command of a small detachment at Amajuba, about five miles off the Standerton-Ermelo road. He and another officer with their handful of men planned an attack on a neighbouring Kraal, wherein they had heard some Boers were concealed. In the fighting which ensued Lieut. Brenes, while leading his men, was shot through the heart. His name is inscribed on a tablet on the outside of the New Memorial Library erected at Dulwich College in remembrance of Alleynians who fell in the war.

Bright.—Lieut. Ashley Rowland Bright, 1st Batt. Oxfordshire Light Infantry, was killed in action near Paardeberg, Feb. 18th, 1900. He was the son of G. Bright, Esq., 25, Victoria Square, Clifton, was born Nov., 1872, educated at Winchester, and entered the Oxfordshire Light Infantry from the Militia, Dec., 1894, being promoted lieut. Nov., 1897. Lieut. Bright first served in Natal with the Ladysmith Relief Force, and was afterwards present with his battalion at the action at Klip Drift and the relief of Kimberley. At the time of his death, he was entitled to the medal with five clasps, including one for the relief of Ladysmith. His death is mentioned in the despatch of F.-M. Earl Roberts from Paardeberg, of Feb. 28th, 1900.

Brindley.—Capt. George Frederick Wallace Brindley,

2nd Batt. Manchester Regt., died of wounds received in action at Holland, Dec. 19th, 1901. He was born July, 1874, entered the Manchester Regt. from the 4th Batt. Lancashire Fusiliers, Dec., 1896, being promoted lieut. Nov., 1897, and capt. Oct., 1900. He was seconded from his regiment for service with the M.I.

Brine.—Lieut. Robert Walter Maxwell Brine, Northumberland Fusiliers, was killed in action at Belmont, Nov. 23rd. 1899. He was the son of Col. Bruce Brine, Royal Engineers, and most of his ancestors had served in the navy and army. His grandfather and two of his great-uncles were admirals, and he had three uncles who rose to high military rank, one of them being a major-gen. Lieut. Brine was born on June 23rd, 1875, educated at Marlborough, where he was in the Cadet Volunteer Corps, and entered the Northumberland Fusiliers from the Hertford Militia, in Dec., 1895, being promoted lieut. Dec., 1897. He served in the Nile Expedition of 1898, and was present at the battle of Khartoum, receiving the medal with clasp. His name is inscribed on a tablet placed in Marlborough College Chapel in memory of all Marlburians who fell in the war.

Broadbent.—Lieut. John W. Broadbent, 8th Batt. I.Y., killed in action at Gelegenfontein, O.R.C., on Nov. 24th, 1901, was educated at Rugby, and entered the I.Y. March, 1901, with the rank of lieut. in the army.

Broadley.—Capt. Thomas Stephen Charles William Broadley, 1st Batt. Royal Scots, died of enteric at Sterkstroom, Feb. 18th, 1900. He was born in Jan. 1868, educated at Eton (Mr. Dalton's), and entered the Royal Scots from the 4th Batt. Middlesex Regt., Jan., 1890, being promoted lieut. April, 1893, and capt. Feb., 1897. He accompanied his battalion to South Africa in Oct., 1899, and served with it in the north of Cape Colony.

Brodie.—Capt. Alastair William Mathew Brodie, Seaforth Highlanders, was killed in action at Magersfontein Dec. 11th, 1899. He was the second son of the late Hugh Brodie, Esq., of Brodie Castle, Forres, N.B., and of Lady Eleanor, daughter of Henry, second Earl of Ducie, was born in April, 1871, and educated at Winchester. Passing out with honours from the Royal Military College, he joined the Seaforth Highlanders in 1890, was promoted lieut. in 1892 and capt. 1898. He served in the Hazara Expedition in 1891, with the second batt. receiving the medal with clasp. He also saw service with the Chitral Relief Force under Sir Robert Low, in 1895, was present at the engagement at Mamagai, and received the medal with clasp. He was specially employed in West Africa in 1897-98, in the Royal Niger Constabulary against the Slave Raider, Prince Arku, and distinguished himself in the attack on Kiffi, where his horse was shot under him, and in storming the town, he was reported as the first man to scale a wall eight feet high. In South Africa Capt. Brodie was adjutant of his battalion and served with it up to the action in which he fell. He was killed close to the Boer trenches. His body was brought back to the Modder River and buried there.

Bromfield.—Capt. Charles Gwyn Trivet Bromfield, 87th Co. 22nd Batt. I.Y., died of wounds received in action near Boshof, Feb. 16th, 1902. He was educated at Malvern College, and joined the I.Y. as a lieut. March, 1901, from the ranks of the 20th Middlesex V.R. Corps, being promoted capt. in July, with the rank of capt. in the army. He served in South Africa from early in 1901 up to his death.

Brooke.—Lieut. Edward Vanreenen Ingham Brooke, 2nd Batt. Yorkshire Light Infantry, was killed in action near Brakenlaagte (20 miles north west of Bethel), Oct. 31st, 1901. He was the youngest son of Archdeacon Brooke, Vicar of Halifax, was born in Sept., 1877, and educated at Charterhouse and Magdalen College, Oxford, where he took his B.A. degree and honours in 1898. He entered the Yorkshire Light Infantry from the 3rd Batt. West Riding Regt., in May, 1899, being promoted lieut. Feb., 1900. Lieut. Brooke was a fine athlete, and the possessor of eleven silver cups, prizes for running and jumping. He was present at the battles of Belmont, Graspan, Modder River, and Magersfontein, and afterwards took part in the operations round Lindley and Bethlehem, being present at the surrender of Prinsloo. From Jan. to April, 1901, he served in the column under Maj.-Gen. Smith-Dorrien. When he fell he was with the 3rd Co. M.I., which suffered severely. The attack of the enemy was made in mist and heavy rain, and in overwhelming numbers by the Commandoes of Grobler, Oppermann, and Louis Botha. His name is inscribed on the tablet in the War Memorial Cloister erected at Charterhouse.

Brooks.—Lieut. S. F. Brooks, Volunteer Company East Surrey Regt., died of enteric at Newcastle, June 9th, 1900. He was educated at Harrow. He was promoted lieut. in the 3rd Volunteer Batt. East Surrey Regt., March, 1897, and appointed to the Volunteer Company in March, 1900, with the rank of lieut. in the army.

Brown.—Capt. Arthur Wale Brown, 1st Batt. Suffolk Regt., died at Pretoria, from wounds received in action on Jan. 6th, 1900, at Rensburg. The son of J. Brown, Esq., Coombe Villa, Teignmouth, he was born in 1867, and educated at Allhallows School, Honiton. He joined the Suffolk Regt. in 1889, was promoted lieut. 1893, capt. 1898, and accompanied his battalion to South Africa in Nov., 1899. (*See Lieut.-Col. Watson.*)

Brown.—Lieut. A. Wylde Brown, Natal Carabiniers, died of enteric, at Pietermaritzburg, on May 28th, 1900.

Browne.—Major Henry Montague Browne, 1st. Batt. East Lancashire Regt., died of enteric at Bloemfontein, May 23rd, 1900. He was the eldest son of the Rev. H. G. Cavendish Browne, Rector of Bredon, and grandson of the late Hon. Henry Montague Browne, Dean of Lismore. Major Browne was born Nov., 1857, and entered the 30th Foot from the Militia in Sept., 1878, being promoted lieut. Feb., 1881, capt. 1887, and major Nov., 1899. He served with the Chitral Relief Force, under Sir Robert Low, in 1895, with the 1st Batt., receiving the medal with clasp. He accompanied it to South Africa in Jan., 1900, and was present at the battle of Paardeberg and in the advance on Bloemfontein.

Browne.—Lieut. James Cavendish Browne, I.Y., died at Vrede, Oct. 23rd, 1900.

Bryan.—Lieut. Harold William Bryan, 28th Co. I.Y., was killed in action at Hardeville, near Harrismith, Oct. 22nd, 1901.

Bryant.— Civil Surgeon H. Bryant, attached Royal Army Medical Corps, died of enteric while on service in South Africa.

Buchanan.—Lieut. Daniell Buchanan, Kitchener's Horse, was killed in action near Paardeberg, Feb. 18th, 1900. Born in 1863, he was the second son of James Buchanan, Esq., late of Briar Hill, Campden, Gloucestershire, and Sackville, Tralee, Ireland (now of Scarborough). When the war broke out Lieut. Buchanan was acting as Mining Engineer at Aguas Calientes, Mexico, where he had been since 1889, and in that country was noted for his fine physique and as a daring rider and splendid shot. He responded promptly to the call of his country, and resigning his important post went to South Africa and joined Kitchener's Horse as a trooper, but within a week was given a commission. He took part in the advance on Jacobsdal, and was present at the action of Klip Drift and Klip Kraal and the capture of Cronje. In the action in which he fell he was at first severely wounded, but in spite of this again stood up and fired, and as he refused to surrender was shot down. He was one of four brothers who served throughout the war; another brother is Vicar of St. Thomas's, Leeds.

Buchanan-Riddell.—Major Henry Edward Buchanan-Riddell, p.s.c., 2nd Batt. King's Royal Rifle Corps, died of enteric, at the Base Hospital, Natal, March 16th, 1900. He was a son of the Rev. J. C. Buchanan-Riddell, was born in Jan., 1860, and educated at Haileybury. He entered the 60th Foot in Aug., 1879, being promoted lieut. July, 1881, capt. Oct., 1888, and major Sept., 1895. He married in Nov., 1888, Mildred, the daughter of the Rev. C. Phelips, of Buckworth. He served with the 3rd Batt. 60th Rifles in the South African war of 1881. With the same battalion he took part in the Egyptian War of 1882, was present at the reconnaissance from Alexandria, on Aug. 5th, the engagement at Tel-el-Mahuta, the action at Kassassin on Sept. 9th, and at the battle of Tel-el-Kebir, receiving the medal, with clasp, and Khedive's star. He served in the Soudan Expedition in 1884, and was present at the engagements at El Teb and Tamai (two clasps). He also took part in the Soudan Campaign in 1885 (clasp). In South Africa he was wounded at the battle of Elandslaagte, and was afterwards appointed D.A.A.G. in Ladysmith, which post he held till taken ill. He was mentioned in despatches by Lieut.-Gen. Sir G. White, Dec. 2nd, 1899, and again in the despatch of March 23rd, 1900, L.G., Feb. 8th, 1901.

Buchanan-Riddell. — Lieut. - Col. Robert George Buchanan-Riddell, commanding the 3rd Batt. King's Royal Rifle Corps, was killed in action near Spion Kop, Jan. 24th, 1900. A son of the Rev. J. C. Buchanan-Riddell, he was born in 1854, entered the 60th Foot from the West Kent Militia, 1875, was promoted lieut. 1878, capt. 1884, major 1892, and lieut.-col. 1898. He served in the South African war of 1881. He was adjutant of volunteers 1890-95, and in 1896 married Agnes, daughter of Sir W. H. Houldsworth, Bart., M.P. for North-West Manchester. Lieut.-Col. Buchanan-Riddell fell while leading and cheering on his regiment to endeavour to ease the pressure to our troops on Spion Kop. A bullet pierced his brain as he was reading an order which had been sent to him by Maj.-Gen. Lyttelton. He was mentioned in despatches L.G., Feb. 8th, 1901, by Gen. Sir R. Buller, who referred to the great loss the country had sustained by the death of Lieut.-Col. Buchanan-Riddell.

Bull.—Lieut. Arthur Bull, 3rd Batt. Royal Inniskilling Fusiliers (Fermanagh Militia), died of wounds received in action at Rooival April 11th, 1902. He was on special service with the M.I. attached to the 21st battalion at the time of his death, and held the rank of lieut. in the army, being graded as a staff-lieut. He entered the 3rd Batt. Royal Inniskilling Fusiliers May, 1900, and saw much service during the war.

Bull.—Capt. George Parker Bull, 4th Batt. North Staffordshire Regt. (3rd King's Own Stafford Militia), died from empyema at Beaufort West, Cape Colony, June 11th, 1902. He was the only son of the late Col. J. J. Bull, 56th Regt., of Falmouth, and grandson of the late Sir George Parker, Bart., 74th Bengal Infantry, was 32 years of age, and educated at Cheltenham. He had commanded a Company in the Stafford Militia since 1893, and in 1900 accompanied his battalion to South Africa, serving with it throughout a large part of the campaign, until appointed railway staff officer at Beaufort West, with the local rank of capt. in the army. His name is inscribed in the Eleanor Cross War Memorial at Cheltenham College.

Burch.—Lieut. J. E. Burch, Canadian M.I., was killed in action at Reit Vlei, July 16th, 1900. He formerly served in the 2nd Dragoons.

Burton.—2nd Lieut. Arthur Collingwood Burton, Coldstream Guards, died while *en route* to Cape Town in a hospital train from the front, on Nov. 26th, 1899, of wounds received in the head in action at Belmont three days previously. He was the eldest son of Alfred H. Burton, Esq., of Mansion Place, Queen's Gate, was born April 4th, 1878, educated at Winchester, and entered the Coldstream Guards in May, 1898. 2nd Lieut. Burton was the first officer of that regiment to lose his life in the campaign. He is buried at Wynberg.

Busuttil.—Lieut. Michael Albert Busuttil, 24th Batt. I.Y., died of enteric at Bloemfontein May 13th, 1902. He joined the I.Y. as a second lieut. March, 1901, and was appointed to the 24th Batt. (Metropolitan Mounted Rifles) in Aug., 1901, with the rank of lieut. in the army. He formerly held a commission as 2nd lieut. in the 4th Leicestershire Regt., and was afterwards a capt. in the 4th Batt. (now the 6th Batt.) Manchester Regt.

OFFICERS WHO FELL IN SOUTH AFRICA. 47

Butler.—Lieut. Stanley J. H. Butler, Cornwall and Devon Miners Royal Garrison Artillery (Militia), died of enteric at Standerton June 6th, 1902. He was attached to the 53rd Battery Royal Field Artillery, and also served with the I.Y. with the local rank of lieut. in the army from June 25th, 1901.

Butters.—Captain A. Butters, Commander-in-Chief's Bodyguard, died of wounds received in action, Jan. 6th, 1901.

Buxton.—Lieut. Roland Henry Buxton, 2nd Batt. Norfolk Regt. (M.I.), was killed near Sterkfontein Dec. 13th, 1901. He was born in Nov., 1874, educated at Harrow, entered the Norfolk Regt. June, 1896, and was promoted lieut. Dec., 1897. He served in West Africa in the operations on the Niger, 1897-98, being mentioned in despatches May 23rd, 1899, and was employed with the West African Frontier Force from Feb., 1898, to Feb., 1900. He then proceeded to South Africa and saw service there during 1900-01.

Byrne.—Lieut. Alfonso Byrne, 3rd Batt. Bedfordshire Regt., died of enteric at Bloemfontein June 11th, 1900. He was educated at Wellington, where he was in the Beresford, and entered the 3rd Batt. Bedfordshire Regt. in Feb., 1896, being promoted lieut. Sept., 1897. He was seconded for service in South Africa, and attached to No. 1 Depôt Remount Department.

Caird.—Lieut. Charles Douglas Caird, I.Y., who was killed in action at Kleinfontein, Oct. 24th, 1901, was born in 1867, and educated at Cheltenham. He was formerly a capt. in the 4th Batt. Devonshire Regt., and had been serving in South Africa since March, 1901, with the 5th Batt. I.Y., composed of Northumberland, Shropshire and

Worcestershire Companies. He held the rank of lieut. in the army. His name is inscribed on the Eleanor Cross War Memorial erected at Cheltenham College.

Calvert.—Lieut. Noël Leonard Calvert, 6th Dragoon Guards (Carabiniers), was killed in action Oct. 19th, 1900, near Bethel, during the march of Lieut.-Gen. Sir J. D. P. French's column to Heidelberg. He was born in Dec., 1877, entered the 6th Dragoon Guards from the West Kent Militia Nov., 1899, and was promoted lieut. Oct. 3rd, 1900. Lieut. Calvert joined his regiment in South Africa, and served in O.R.C. and the Transvaal.

Cameron.—Lieut. Allan Cameron, D.S.O., 1st Batt. Gordon Highlanders, was killed in action at Graspan near Reitz, on June 6th, 1901. He was born on Nov. 4th, 1878, educated at Allhallows School, Honiton, and entered the Gordon Highlanders from the 5th Batt. Connaught Rangers (Roscommon Militia), in Oct., 1899, being promoted lieut. May, 1900. He saw much service during the war. He was present at the actions at Modder River and Magersfontein, and the surrender of Cronje at Paardeberg. Lieut. Cameron was killed while assisting to defend a post against very superior numbers. At the time of his death he was serving with the Mounted Infantry of his Batt. He was mentioned in despatches, L.G., Sept. 10th, 1901, also in the despatch of Gen. Lord Kitchener of July 28th, 1901, for "most conspicuous gallantry" and for "having been brought to notice on several previous occasions." He was awarded the D.S.O. for his services.

Cameron.—Lieut. Patrick Cameron, Kitchener's Horse, died at Wynberg, O.R.C., on May 6th, 1901.

Campbell.—Lieut. Alfred Corkram Campbell, 6th

Batt. I.Y., was killed in action at Nooitgedacht, Dec. 13th, 1900. He was the son of the late Capt. Hugh Campbell, R.N., formerly Commander of the Royal Yacht "Victoria and Albert," and educated at Eton (Mr. Wintle's). Lieut. Campbell belonged to the Lothians and Berwickshire Yeomanry, and was gazetted to the I.Y., with the rank of lieut. in the army, May, 1900, joining the 6th battalion in Nov. He was killed while leading and rallying his men to support a detached party which had been attacked by the Boers at early dawn. The yeomen had to climb a precipitous hill 1,000 feet high. Sir A. Conan Doyle thus describes what took place. "One by one the yeomen darted over the edge and endeavoured to find some cover in face of an infernal point blank fire. Capt. Mudie of the Staff who went first was shot down. So was Purvis of the Fifes who followed him. The others springing over their bodies rushed for a small trench and tried to restore the fight. Lieut. Campbell, a gallant young fellow, was shot dead as he rallied his men. Of 27 of the Fifeshires upon the hill, 6 were killed and 11 wounded."

Campbell.—Capt. Ernest George Campbell, 4th Batt. Rifle Brigade, died on July 23rd, 1900, of wounds received two days previously in action near Bergendal. He was born in June, 1873, educated at Eton (Mr. Austen Leigh's), and entered the Rifle Brigade Dec., 1892, being promoted lieut. in July, 1895, and capt., April, 1900. He served with the Tochi Field Force in the operations on the North-West Frontier of India, in 1897-98, and was granted the medal with clasp. Capt. Campbell fell while leading his men to storm a strong Boer position at Bergendal. Sir R. Buller in his despatch of Sept. 13th, 1900, much regrets the death of Capt. Campbell who led his company "most gallantly," L.G., Feb. 8th, 1901.

Campbell.—Major George Campbell, 1st Batt. King's (Liverpool Regt.), died of dysentery, at Middelburg, Transvaal, on March 4th, 1902. The eldest son of the late Sir George Campbell, M.P., he was born in Feb., 1861, and educated at Clifton. He entered the 8th King's Regt., Jan., 1880, was promoted lieut. in Feb., 1881, capt. Nov., 1887, and major Nov., 1898. He was well known as a hunter of big game. Major Campbell was adjutant of volunteers from July, 1896, to July, 1901, when he proceeded to South Africa, being appointed commandant at Godwaan.

Campbell.—2nd Lieut. Harry Alexander Campbell, I.Y., was killed in action at Vlakfontein, May 29th, 1901. He was a son of Col. J. A. Campbell, who saw long service in India. 2nd Lieut. Campbell joined the I.Y. in March, 1901, from the Coorg and Mysore Volunteer Rifle Corps. He was with Lumsden's Horse throughout the advance of F.-M. Earl Roberts from Bloemfontein to Pretoria, and was in several severe engagements, having been wounded while crossing the Vaal River.

Campbell.—2nd Lieut. Ian Alastair Campbell, 2nd Batt. Gordon Highlanders, died of wounds received Oct. 21st, 1899, at the battle of Elandslaagte. He was born in Aug., 1876, educated at Cheltenham and entered the Gordon Highlanders from the Militia, in May, 1898. He proceeded with his battalion to Natal in Sept., 1899. His name is inscribed on the Eleanor Cross War Memorial erected at Cheltenham College.

Campbell.—Lieut. J. C. Campbell, Cape Garrison Artillery, was killed in an accident to an armoured train at Daspoort, on May 5th, 1902.

Campbell.—2nd Lieut. James Ronald McOram Campbell, 1st Batt. Gordon Highlanders, died of wounds received in action at Magersfontein, Dec. 11th, 1899. He was born in 1880, educated at Eton (Mr. Vaughan's), joined the Gordon Highlanders from the Militia, May, 1899, and embarked with the 1st battalion for South Africa in Oct. He then served with the Kimberley Relief Force.

Campion.—Lieut. Charles Campion, I.Y., was killed in action at Vlakfontein, May 29th, 1901. He was the fourth son of Col. W. H., and Hon. Mrs. Campion, of Danny, near Hurstpierpoint, Sussex, and nephew of the present Lord Hampden. He was 24 years of age and educated at Eton (Mr. Mitchell's). He went out with the Ceylon M.I., as a trooper, and after a time served with Brig.-Gen. Broadwood's column, afterwards proceeding to Pretoria as Superintendent of the Police, and eventually joined the I.Y. as lieut.

Cantor.—Lieut. Montagu Grant Cantor, 2nd Batt. Prince of Wales's Own (West Yorkshire Regt.), was killed Feb. 6th, 1901, at Bothwell, in the attack made by Botha on Major-Gen. Smith-Dorrien's force. Lieut. Cantor was born Sept., 1877, entered the West Yorkshire Regt. from the 4th Batt. Durham Light Infantry, in Jan., 1899, and was promoted lieut. the following Nov. He was mentioned in Gen. Lord Kitchener's despatch of July 28th, 1901, for having, during the attack on Bothwell, "headed a party sent to reinforce the trenches, and led most gallantly till killed."

Carbutt.—Lieut. Edward Goddard Carbutt, U Battery Royal Horse Artillery, was killed in action at Kimberley, Feb. 14th-16th, 1900. He was born Sept., 1871, educated at Malvern College, and entered the Royal Artillery in July, 1891, being promoted lieut. July, 1894. Lieut.

Carbutt embarked for South Africa in Dec., 1899, with his battery, which then formed part of the force under Lieut.-Gen. Sir J. D. P. French, assembled at Modder River Camp for the relief of Kimberley.

Carey.—Lieut. Seymour James Carey, 1st Batt. Suffolk Regt., was killed in action, near Rensburg, Jan. 6th, 1900. He was a son of A. Carey, Esq., of 21, Rosary Gardens, London was born Jan., 1874, and educated at St. Paul's School. He entered the Suffolk Regt. in Jan., 1895, being promoted lieut. May, 1897. Lieut. Carey served as Chief of Police in the Monofatsi district of Crete, from Nov., 1898, to July, 1899, and was mentioned in despatches for the services he rendered in that capacity. He accompanied his battalion to South Africa in Nov., 1899. (*See Lieut.-Col. Watson.*)

Carruthers.—Lieut. Bruce Carruthers, Canadian Mounted Rifles, was killed in action at Brakspruit, March 3rd, 1901, on which occasion he greatly distinguished himself. He was mentioned in the despatch of April 8th, 1902, by Gen. Lord Kitchener who reported that Lieut. Carruthers being in command of a detachment of the rear-guard, remained in a position of observation in which he eventually found himself isolated and surrounded by a large body of the enemy. Rejecting all idea of surrender, his small patrol of 21 men fought stubbornly on to the end; no less than six of their number, including Lieut. Carruthers, being killed, and twelve wounded. Gen. Lord Kitchener considers there have been "few finer instances of heroism in the whole course of the campaign."

Cary.—2nd Lieut. Henry James Lucius Cary, 2nd Batt. Devonshire Regt., died of enteric at Standerton, Jan. 2nd, 1901. He was the only surviving son of Col.

Cary, late Rifle Brigade, who retired in Sept., 1889, 2nd Lieut. Cary, was born in Jan., 1872, and educated at Wellington. He entered the Devonshire Regt., April, 1900, from the 3rd Batt., which was embodied, and in which he was then serving as a captain.

Caskey.—Lieut. Lachlan J. Caskey, 5th Queensland Bushmen, was killed in action at Mokaridrift, Caledon River, Sept. 27th, 1901. He was mentioned in the despatch of Gen. Lord Kitchener, Oct. 8th, 1901, for great gallantry. It appears that he and Lieut. P. L. Tudor, New Zealand Mounted Rifles, with only twelve men, crossed the Caledon River, and kept touch with 200 Boers for three days. He displayed great bravery the day he fell, holding a position with his small party for three hours against fifty Boers.

Casson.—Capt. Ferdinand George Casson, Northumberland Fusiliers M.I., was killed in action at Reddersburg, April 3rd, 1900. He was the son of the Rev. George Casson, of Olde Court, Torquay, was born in March, 1864, and educated at Marlborough. He was a good rider and polo player. He entered the Northumberland Fusiliers Aug., 1885, being promoted capt. Oct., 1894. His name is inscribed on a tablet placed in Marlborough College Chapel, in memory of all Marlburians who fell in the war.

Cathcart.—Capt. the Hon. Reginald Cathcart, 4th Batt. King's Royal Rifle Corps, was killed in the operations on the Tugela, Feb. 22nd, 1900. He was the fourth son of Earl Cathcart, was born Nov., 1870, and educated at Eton (Mr. Radcliffe's). He entered the King's Royal Rifle Corps from the Royal Military College in Nov., 1891, being promoted lieut. Jan., 1895, and capt. Jan. 25th, 1900. Capt. Cathcart, who was known by Green Jackets as "Reggie"

Cathcart, left many to mourn for him. He was an athlete and sportsman, and fond of all manly games. In 1896, a team of his battalion, trained and led by him, won at Aldershot the shield presented by H.R.H. the Duke of Connaught, for an obstacle race. Fifteen Regimental teams, each of 106 officers and men, armed and accoutred, competed. Capt. Cathcart held the post of Superintendent of Gymnasia, at Malta, from Nov., 1896, to March, 1899, where he was well known. He belonged to the 4th Batt., but volunteered for active service with the 3rd Batt., and proceeded to South Africa in Nov., 1899. He was present at the battle of Colenso, where his old school friend, "Freddy" Roberts, King's Royal Rifle Corps, fell, and he was one of six brother officers who carried him to his grave at Chieveley. Capt. Cathcart was also at the action at Potgieter's Drift. At Spion Kop the 3rd King's Royal Rifle Corps attacked the two peaks on the north of that position, the right half battalion took the Sugarloaf hill and the left half battalion captured the centre hill of the range. Though lame, and suffering from abscess in the foot, Capt. Cathcart, with his company, led the left half battalion up the precipitous hill, and they were the first to gain the summit. An account of this attack will be found in despatches published in the L.G., Feb. 8th, 1901, page 951, where "F Company leading under Capt. Cathcart" is specially referred to. Capt. Cathcart was also present at the various actions round Cingolo Hill. Having crossed the Tugela on the pitch dark night of Feb. 22nd, he was killed by a random shot, which struck him in the forehead, during a charge with fixed swords. The scene of action—Green Hill—is west of Pieters Station, about three miles due north of Colenso. A marble obelisk now marks the position. It bears this inscription: "In memory of officers, non-commissioned officers, and riflemen, 3rd Batt. King's Royal Rifle Corps, who were killed in action at this spot, Feb. 22nd and 23rd,

1900. They formed part of picquets which drove off the enemy's attack and held this ridge all night, in spite of determined efforts to dislodge them." Beneath this inscription appear the names of Capt. the Hon. R. Cathcart, Sergt. J. Flower, and twenty riflemen.

Cathcart.—Lieut. William Harold Cathcart, 3rd Batt. Worcestershire Regt. M.I., died of enteric at Mafeteng, Basutoland, Jan. 7th, 1902. He was the third son of Col. the Hon. A. M. Cathcart, late Grenadier Guards, of Mowbray House, Ripon. His mother was the only daughter of the third Lord Bolton. Lieut. Cathcart was born May, 1880, educated at Eton (Mr. Austen Leigh's), and entered the Worcestershire Regt. from the 3rd Batt. York and Lancaster Regt., in April, 1900, being promoted lieut. the following Sept. He served in South Africa during 1901.

Cavendish.—2nd Lieut. the Hon. Charles William Hugh Cavendish, 17th Lancers, was killed in action at Diamond Hill, near Pretoria, June 11th, 1900. He was the only son of Lord Chesham, commanding the I.Y., was born Sept., 1878, educated at Eton (Mr. Ainger's), and entered the 17th Lancers from the Royal Military College in Aug., 1898. He proceeded to South Africa in Feb., 1900, and served with his regiment in the O.R.C. and Transvaal until killed at Diamond Hill.

Cavendish-Browne.—Lieut. James Cavendish-Browne, 2nd Co. I.Y., was killed in action at Vrede, Oct. 23rd, 1900. The second son of the Rev. H. G. Cavendish-Browne, Rector of Bredon, near Tewkesbury, he was related to Lord Kilmaine and Viscount Frankfort de Montmorency. Lieut. Browne belonged to the Royal Gloucestershire Hussars, and offered his services early in the war. He went out with the Gloucestershire Company as a trooper, but was transferred to the Glamorganshire, as sergeant, and eventually to the Wiltshire Company I.Y., as lieut.

Cawston.—Lieut. Cecil Faulkner Cawston, 18th Hussars, died of wounds received Feb. 2nd, 1901, in action at Roodepoort. He was the son of George Cawston, Esq., one of the founders of the British South Africa Company; was born in April, 1878, educated at Eton (Mr. Vaughan's), and entered the 18th Hussars in April, 1898. He joined his regiment in the spring of 1899 in Natal, and was employed before the war surveying the country round Ladysmith. He was at Dundee when the war broke out, and was present at the battle of Talana Hill and in the retirement to Ladysmith, where he served throughout the siege. Lieut. Cawston was invalided home with dysentery, but, recovering, returned to South Africa in Sept., 1900, and was with his regiment until he was mortally wounded while in front of a patrol which he was leading.

Challenor.—Capt. Robert Richards Challenor, Lancashire Fusiliers, was killed in action at Boschbult Kleinhardts River, on March 31st, 1902. He was born in May, 1871, entered the Connaught Rangers Jan., 1892, was promoted lieut. Dec., 1893, and capt. into the Lancashire Fusiliers, June, 1900, joining the first battalion in Crete. In Dec., 1901, he was seconded for service with M.I. in South Africa and served there until killed. He had been previously slightly wounded.

Chalmers.—Capt. T. W. Chalmers, 2nd Batt. Canadian Mounted Rifles, killed in action near Belfast, Nov. 2nd, 1900; was educated at the Royal Military College, Kingston, Canada, and was a lieut. in the Reserve of Officers. He had previously served in the North-West of Canada in the rebellion of 1885, being granted the

OFFICERS WHO FELL IN SOUTH AFRICA. 57

medal, and was for eight years an Inspector of the North-West Mounted Police. Capt. Chalmers saw much service in the South African War near Bothaville, Nooitgedacht, and Belfast. At the latter battle he was with an advanced guard under Major Saunders, who, during the fight, was wounded. Capt. Chalmers went to his assistance, although Major Saunders implored him not to come to him under such a heavy fire. He, however, did so, and was killed. He was commended by Major-Gen. Smith-Dorrien for his bravery, who "deplored the death of this splendid officer." Capt. Chalmers was mentioned in Gen. Lord Kitchener's despatch of March 8th, 1901, for "his gallantry and stubborn fighting." He is buried at Belfast, Transvaal.

Chaloner.—Lieut. Richard Alexander Chaloner, 1st Batt. Royal Inniskilling Fusiliers, died at Middlebult on April 21st, 1902, of wounds received in the attack on Major-Gen. Kekewich's column at Rooival, ten days previously. He was born June, 1879, educated at Rossall, and entered the Royal Inniskilling Fusiliers from the 4th Batt. (Royal Tyrone Militia) in March, 1900, being promoted lieut. June, 1900. At the time of his death he was attached to the M.I. Company of his battalion. He had served during the war from early in 1901. He is buried at Middlebult and his grave is marked by a marble tombstone erected by his brother officers.

Chamier.—Lieut. Edwin Harold St. Leger Chamier, 9th Ammunition Column, Royal Field Artillery, died of enteric at Bloemfontein, May 7th, 1900. The eldest son of Edwin Francis Chamier, Esq., of Goodrest, Exmouth; he was born in Aug., 1876, educated at Cheltenham, and entered the Royal Artillery from the Royal Military Academy Woolwich, in Nov., 1895, being promoted lieut. Nov., 1898. Lieut. Chamier was present at the battles of

Paardeberg and Driefontein, and took part in the advance to Bloemfontein. His name is inscribed on the Eleanor Cross War Memorial at Cheltenham College.

Chandler.—Lieut. Edward Heath Chandler, Brabant's Horse, was killed in action at Dordrecht Feb. 16th, 1900. On this occasion Brabant's Horse greatly distinguished itself.

Chapman.—Col. Lionel James Archer Chapman, Royal Field Artillery, died of enteric at Pretoria on Dec. 3rd, 1900. He was a son of the late George Chapman, Esq., of Dieppe, was born July 18th, 1848, and educated at Cheltenham. He entered the Royal Artillery Jan., 1869, was promoted capt. Nov., 1879, major April, 1885, lieut.-col. June, 1895, and brevet-col. June, 1899. He went out to South Africa in Jan., 1900, in command of the 13th Brigade Division of the Royal Field Artillery. He served with distinction, and when Commandant of Pienaars River Station he repulsed, on Sept. 27th, 1900, an attack by the Boers. Col. Chapman was mentioned in despatches, L. G., Feb. 8th, 1901, for his services. His name is inscribed on the Eleanor Cross War Memorial at Cheltenham College.

Chapman.—Lieut. W. Chapman, Natal Mounted Rifles, was killed in action at Farquhar's Farm, Oct. 30th, 1899.

Chapman.—Mr. Chapman was killed at Willow Grange, Nov. 23rd, 1899. He was acting as a guide. Major-Gen. Hildyard, in his report of Nov. 24th, 1899, stated that Mr. Chapman's services were of the greatest value, his intimate knowledge of the ground alone made it possible to carry out the operations, and added: "I sincerely trust it may be found possible to bestow on his widow some mark of recognition of his distinguished service."

Charles.—Lieut. Frank P. J. Charles, 2nd V.B. Welsh Regt., died at Netley on July 4th, 1902, of wounds received in action near Germiston, South Africa, on March 11th, 1902. He entered the 2nd V.B. Welsh Regt., in June, 1900, was promoted lieut. Jan., 1901, and held the rank of lieut. in the army from March 20th, 1902.

Charleton.—Capt. Ernest Edward Janvrin Charleton, 1st Batt. Welsh Regt., died at Johannesburg Jan. 1st, 1902, from injuries caused by a fall from his horse. He was born in July, 1867, entered the Welsh Regt. Feb., 1887, was promoted lieut. Feb., 1889, and capt. Jan., 1897. Capt. Charleton served in South Africa from the commencement of the war, and was first employed as a Station Commandant and Intelligence Officer. He afterwards held the appointment of Station Staff Officer, and was awarded the medal with five clasps.

Charley.—Major John Francis William Charley, 1st Batt. Royal Inniskilling Fusiliers, died of wounds received in action at Colenso, on Dec. 15th, 1899. He was the eldest son of the late John Stouppe Charley, Esq., J.P., of Finaghy House, co. Antrim, and Aranmore, co. Donegal; was born in 1857, joined the 27th Foot, now the 1st Batt. Royal Inniskilling Fusiliers, in 1878, being promoted lieut. in Nov. of the same year, capt. 1885, and major 1893. He served in the campaign on the North-West Frontier of India, under the late Sir William Lockhart, in 1897-98, with the 2nd Batt. Royal Inniskilling Fusiliers, with the Tirah Expeditionary Force, including the operations in the Bara Valley, and the occupation of the Khyber Pass, receiving the medal with two clasps. At the time of his death, Major Charley was second in command of his Batt. He is buried between Chieveley and Colenso. His grave is marked by a marble tombstone, erected by his comrades of the 1st battalion.

Chase.—Quartermaster and Hon. Lieut. James Chase, 1st Batt. Scots Guards, died suddenly at Modder River, Feb. 3rd, 1900. He was born July, 1858, was a warrant officer for six years, and obtained his commission in the Scots Guards in May, 1891. He served in the Egyptian Expedition 1882, was present at the action at Mahuta, and the battle of Tel-el-Kebir, receiving the medal with clasp, and bronze star. Lieut. Chase accompanied his battalion to South Africa in Oct., 1899, and served with it up to the time of his death.

Chenevix-Trench.—2nd Lieut. Christopher Chenevix-Trench, 7th Company Royal Engineers, died of enteric, at Heilbron, on April 13th, 1902. He was the son of Col. and Mrs. Chenevix-Trench, of Broomfield, Camberley, and was born in April, 1881. He was educated at Marlborough, where he gained the Modern School Exhibition, tenable for two years at the Royal Military Academy, Woolwich, which he entered direct from Marlborough. At the Royal Military Academy he was senior under officer, and won the Victoria and Pollock medals, and the sword of honour. 2nd Lieut. Chenevix-Trench entered the Royal Engineers Jan., 1900, and went to South Africa in Feb., 1901, where he was employed in the construction of block-houses. On one occasion, near Boshof, in order to get reinforcements, he made a daring ride to give the required information with the most successful results. He was with a column returning to Boshof from Windsorton Road, which had halted at Tweefontein, and he asked permission to accompany a small party which were being sent out to drive off some Boers. This party went about five miles and was nearly surrounded at Hartbeestpan Farm by the enemy, who were found in considerable force. The officer in command then called for someone to return to Tweefontein to get assistance. 2nd Lieut. Chenevix-Trench volunteered

for the duty. To get back involved passing through a gap
in a wire fence and through a wood now partly occupied
by the enemy. He reached the gap safely, the Boers
close behind and firing at him. He then galloped through
the wood, many Boers trying to cut him off and still
firing at him, some within 20 paces distance. He, however, reached the camp safely, reinforcements were sent,
and the party extricated. 2nd Lieut. Trench died on the
eve of his twenty-first birthday. His name is inscribed
on a tablet which has been placed in Marlborough College
Chapel in memory of all Marlburians who fell in the war.

Chichester.—Lieut. Lionel Chichester, 3rd Batt. I.Y.,
was killed in action at Middleport Farm, Calvinia, Feb. 6th,
1902. He was the eldest surviving son of the late Major-
Gen. Hugh Chichester, Royal Artillery; was born on July
3rd, 1873, and educated at Charterhouse. Lieut. Chichester first went out as a trooper with the C.I.V. in July, 1900,
was present at the battle of Belfast, and then returned with
this corps in Oct., 1900, being awarded the medal with
three clasps. Anxious, however, to again serve the Empire,
and as the war continued, he a second time volunteered,
and went out in the I.Y. in Feb., 1901, in which he was given
a lieutenant's commission. He was attached to the 11th
Co. of the 3rd Batt., and served with it till killed. He saw
much service on his return to South Africa, first in the
Warrenton and Hoopstad districts, and afterwards with
Col. Doran's column. When he fell, a position, which
was fiercely attacked by Smut's Commando, had to be
held, and few men were available. Sir A. Conan Doyle
states, " the Yeomen fought like veterans." A ridge was
committed to the charge of Lieutenants Chichester and
Tabor, with eleven men of the I.Y., their instructions
being " to hold it to the death." The order was obeyed
with the utmost heroism, both officers and six men being
killed, and two wounded. Lieut. Chichester's name is

inscribed on the tablet in the War Memorial Cloister at Charterhouse. (*See Lieut. Tabor.*)

Childe.—Capt. and Hon. Major Charles B. Childe, Shropshire Yeomanry, was killed in action at Sugarloaf Hill, near Trichard's Drift, Jan. 20th, 1900. The eldest son of the late Mr. Childe-Pemberton, of Millichope Hall, Shropshire, he was born in Sept., 1853, and educated at Harrow and Christ's Church, Oxford. He was a keen sportsman. Major Childe discontinued using the name of Pemberton on succeeding to the family estate of Kinlet, Shropshire. He had served in the 57th and 60th Foot in 1874, and entered the Royal Horse Guards in Nov., 1875, being promoted capt. Jan., 1885. His first experience of active service was in the Egyptian Expedition of 1882, when he was present at the battle of Tel-el-Kebir, for which he received the medal, with clasp, and bronze star. He retired from the Royal Horse Guards in 1887, and joined the Shropshire Yeomanry Cavalry. At the outbreak of the war, he proceeded to South Africa, and was given command of a squadron of the South African Light Horse. It is stated that of one troop of thirty men enrolled by him, only one survives, so severe was the fighting and so numerous the engagements in which the South African Light Horse took part. Major Childe was killed while leading his men with great gallantry, and was mentioned in despatches, L.G. Feb. 8th, 1901, for having rendered "gallant service in the capture of Sugarloaf Hill." He was also mentioned in the despatch of F.-M. Earl Roberts, of April 2nd, 1901.

Chisholme.—Col. John James Scott Chisholme, of Stirches, Howick, N.B., Imperial Light Horse, was killed in action at the battle of Elandslaagte, Oct. 21st, 1899. He was the only son of the late J. Scott Chisholme, Esq., of that Ilk and of Stirches, by his marriage with Margaret,

OFFICERS WHO FELL IN SOUTH AFRICA. 63

eldest daughter of the late Robert Walker, Esq., of Mumrells, co. Stirling. Col. Scott Chisholme was born in Aug., 1851, at Stirches, and educated at Loretto School, Musselburgh, and Repton. He joined the 9th Lancers in Jan., 1872, was promoted capt. March, 1878, brevet-major March, 1881, and major Dec., 1884. He was transferred to the 5th Lancers in May, 1889, being promoted lieut.-col. Aug., 1894, and brevet-col. Aug., 1898. He served with the 9th Lancers in the Afgan War of 1878-80, and was present at the capture of Ali Musjid, in the affair at Siah Sung (severely wounded), and the operations around Kabul in Dec., 1879 (wounded). He was mentioned in despatches, L.G., May 4th, 1880, receiving the brevet of major, and the medal with two clasps. He held the appointment of Military Secretary to Lord Connemara, when Governor of Madras for nearly three years. On leaving the 5th Lancers in 1899, Col. Chisholme was permitted to raise a regiment of Imperial Light Horse, composed mainly of refugees from the Transvaal. This he brought in a few weeks to a state of great efficiency, and it was while leading them into action at Elandslaagte that Col. Scott Chisholme met his death. At the time he was hit he was cheering and waving his men forward with a coloured sash, and was in the act of assisting a wounded man. He was first wounded in the leg and through the lung, a third shot piercing his brain. His last words were "my fellows are doing very well." He was mentioned in despatches by Gen. Sir George White, Dec. 20th, 1899, L.G., Feb. 8th, 1901. Col. Chisholme was the last in the male line of an ancient border family. A tablet has been erected at Stirches by his brother officers and countrymen in grateful remembrance of his gallantry and devotion. (*See Capt. C. F. MacCartie.*)

Chrisp.—Lieut. John G. Chrisp, 5th Victorian M.I.

was killed in action at Bedrog, near Vryheid, on Nov. 5th, 1901. He is buried at Vryheid.

Church.—Capt. Bernard Elliott Church, Reserve of Officers, 7th Dragoon Guards, died July 19th, 1900. He was born in March, 1870, educated at Eton (Mr. James'), entered the 13th Hussars Sept., 1889, and was transferred to the 16th Lancers the following Nov., being promoted lieut. May, 1891. He volunteered for service from the Reserve of Officers, and was given the temporary rank of capt. in the 7th Dragoon Guards in Feb., 1900. Capt. Church was one of the first reserve officers to lose his life in the war.

Churchill.—2nd Lieut. Charles Waldo Lionel Churchill, 3rd Batt. Hampshire Regt., died on April 2nd, 1902, at Klerksdorp, of wounds received in action on March 31st. The only son of Lieut.-Col. C. M. Churchill, of Holmwood Park, Wimborne, Dorset, he was in his nineteenth year, and entered the 3rd Batt. Hampshire Regt. in June, 1900. He had been employed with M.I. in South Africa from Dec., 1901, with the rank of second lieut. in the army.

Clapham.—Lieut. W. J. Clapham, Natal Mounted Rifles, was killed in action on Oct. 30th, 1899, in the fighting near Ladysmith.

Clark.—Capt. James Rutherford Clark, 2nd Batt. Seaforth Highlanders, was killed in action at Magersfontein, Dec. 11th, 1899. He was born Oct., 1862, joined the Seaforth Highlanders as lieut. Sept., 1882, and was promoted capt. Oct., 1890. He served in the Hazara Expedition of 1888, as acting-adjutant of the left half battalion, 2nd Batt. Seaforth Highlanders, receiving the medal with clasp. He was also in the Hazara Expedition of 1891, as adjutant of his battalion (clasp). Capt. Clark also served with the Chitral Relief Force, under Sir Robert Low, in 1895, and was present in the engagement at Mamagai, receiving the medal with clasp. He accompanied his battalion to South Africa in Oct., 1899, and joined the Kimberley Relief Force shortly before the action at Magersfontein.

Clarke.—Capt. George Vernon Clarke, 87th Battery Royal Field Artillery, was killed at Uitvlacht April 8th, 1902. He was born in Sept., 1873, educated at Charterhouse, and entered the Royal Artillery in March, 1893, being promoted lieut. March, 1896, and capt. May, 1900. He was killed whilst endeavouring to bring in a man who had been separated from his horse.

Clarke.—Capt. William Willoughby Stanley Clarke, 1st Batt. I.Y., was killed in action at Harrismith Aug. 26th, 1900. He was the eldest son of the late Col. Stanley Clarke, 21st Hussars, was born in 1868, and educated at Cheltenham. At the outbreak of the war Capt. Clarke was engaged in tea planting in Ceylon; but volunteered for active service. His services were accepted and he was granted the rank of capt. in the army from March 10th, 1900, when he joined the I.Y. from the 6th Batt. Worcestershire Regt., in which he had served as a capt. from Aug., 1894. His name is inscribed on the Eleanor Cross War Memorial at Cheltenham College.

Clement.—Lieut. J. Clement, Cape Railway Pioneer Regt., died on June 15th, 1900, of wounds received in action the previous day at Zand River, O.R.C.

Clementi-Smith.—Lieut. E. Clementi-Smith, D.S.O., 11th Batt. I.Y., died on Oct. 4th, 1901, of pneumonia and wounds received in action Sept. 11th, 1901, at Georgiana, Harrismith. He was for several years secretary of the

F

Middlesex Rifle Association, and shot for the Queen's Prize at Bisley as a member of the Middlesex Yeomanry Cavalry, in which he was at one time sergeant-instructor of musketry. Before joining the Middlesex Yeomanry Cavalry, Lieut. Clementi-Smith was an officer in the Canadian Artillery. He went to South Africa as a 2nd lieut. with the I.Y. at the beginning of 1901, and was promoted lieut. in July. He was mentioned in the despatch of Gen. Lord Kitchener, Oct. 8th, 1901, for having "advanced alone to occupy a position the Boers were making for, and though wounded through his right shoulder he continued to fire from the left, keeping the enemy off until he was reinforced." He was awarded the D.S.O. for this act of gallantry.

Clifford.—Lieut. Edward Cofmack Clifford, Bethune's M.I., died of heart disease at Paauwpan on Feb. 28th, 1901.

Clowes.—Lieut. Graham Vinicombe Winchester Clowes, 1st Batt. Gordon Highlanders, attached to De Lisle's M.I., was killed in action near Doorn River Jan. 30th, 1901. He was the son of the late Winchester Clowes, Esq., of Hitchin, Hertfordshire, and grandson of the late George Clowes, of Oak Hill, Surbiton. He was born in Oct., 1880, educated at Eton (Mr. Mozley's), and entered the Gordon Highlanders in Oct., 1899, being promoted lieut. Aug. 1st, 1900. When killed he was serving with the M.I. of his Battalion.

Coates.—Capt. Frederick Raymond Coates, 1st Batt. Northumberland Fusiliers, was killed in action at Elandslaagte, near Klerksdorp, Feb. 25th, 1902. He was the youngest son of Victor Coates, Esq., D.L., of Rathmore, Dunmurry, co. Antrim, was born in May, 1876, and educated at Cheltenham College. He entered the Northumberland Fusiliers from the Militia

Battalion Dec., 1896, was promoted lieut. in 1889, and capt. March, 1901. He saw service in the Soudan campaign under Lord (then Sir Herbert) Kitchener, in 1898, with the 1st Batt. Northumberland Fusiliers, and was present at the Battle of Khartoum, receiving the British medal and Khedive's medal with clasp. He also served during the occupation in Crete in 1898. He was mentioned in despatches, July 18th, 1902, for his good service in South Africa. His name is inscribed on the Eleanor Cross War Memorial at Cheltenham College.

Coddington.—2nd Lieut. Astur Bertrand Coddington, 1st Batt. Essex Regt., was killed in action at Driefontein, March 10th, 1900. He was born in Oct., 1877, educated at Trinity College, Glenalmond, and entered the Essex Regt. in Feb., 1898. This officer's death is mentioned in the despatch of F.-M. Earl Roberts from Bloemfontein March 15th, 1900.

Coe.—Lieut, A. D. L. Coe, Rand Rifles, died from fracture of the base of the skull, through a fall from his horse, at Johannesburg.

Coë.—Lieut. Robert Harry Courtauld Coë, 2nd Batt. Royal Lancaster Regt., was killed in action in the operations at Onderbrook Spruit, on the Tugela, Feb. 22nd, 1900. He was the son of R. W. Coë, Esq., of 7, Pembroke Road, Clifton, Bristol, was born in Oct., 1876, and educated at Clifton College. He entered the Royal Lancaster Regt. from the Royal Military College in Feb., 1897, and was promoted lieut. in March, 1898. He was a good football player, and while at the R.M.C. played for Sandhurst *v.* Woolwich. Lieut. Coë was present at the battle of Spion Kop, and the subsequent operations on the Tugela up to the date of his death, and was granted the medal and two clasps. He lies close to where he fell, Colour-Sergeant Whitehead and seven brave men of Lieut. Coë's Company having gone out to bury him at great risk while the fighting still continued. A marble cross has been erected over his grave by his brother officers. A handsome stained glass window has also been placed in the Chapel of the Royal Military College, Sandhurst, in memory of Lieut. Coë and other comrades who died, or were killed, during the war.

Collins.—Capt. Charles Welman Collins, 2nd Batt. Cheshire Regt., died at Elandsfontein Nov. 14th, 1901, of wounds received in the attack on Col. Benson's column at Brakenlaagte, twenty miles north-west of Bethel, on Oct. 30th. He was the son of Major Joseph Collins, formerly of the same regiment, and now of 6, Waterloo Road, Chester. Capt. Collins was born in Oct., 1872, and educated at Rossall, where he was a school monitor and in the Hockey XI. He was a good cricketer and football player. After leaving Rossall he entered Cambridge University, where he rowed No. 3 in his college boat. In June, 1894, he entered the Cheshire Regt. from the University, and was promoted lieut. Jan., 1897, and capt. Dec., 1900. He was signalling officer to the 10th Brigade in South Africa from Feb. to Dec., 1900, and took part in the advance through O.R.C. to Johannesburg. He then served with Col. Benson's column, from its formation to the time of his death, as signalling officer. He was unmarried. Capt. Collins was mentioned in despatches by F.-M. Earl Roberts, L. G., Sept. 10th, 1901, for having rendered "special and meritorious service;" and by Gen. Lord Kitchener, Dec. 8th, 1901, for his "distinguished good service."

Collins.—Lieut. C. W. Collins, Natal Police, died May 21st, 1900.

Coningham.—Lieut. Col. Charles Coningham, 2nd Batt. Worcestershire Regt., was killed Feb. 12th, 1900, in action at Rensburg. He was the youngest son of the late Lieut.-Gen. Henry Coningham, of the Madras Light Cavalry, and was born at Bangalore in 1851. His brothers were all in the army. He joined the 103rd Foot in 1872, being promoted capt. 1882, major 1891, into the Worcestershire Regt., and became lieut.-col. Dec., 1899. In 1892 he married Constance, youngest daughter of the late Admiral Henry R. Foote, who died in 1896. He took part in the operations of the Soudan Frontier Field Force in 1885-86, receiving the medal and the Khedive's star. Lieut.-Col. Coningham went to South Africa in command of his battalion in Dec., 1899, and on arrival was sent to the north of Cape Colony. At Rensburg there was some heavy firing, and he rose to look for the enemy and also to see that his men kept under cover. Some of his officers implored him to lie down, but he was struck shortly afterwards. As he fell he said: "Don't trouble about me, men." The Boer who killed him was shot by one of the men of E Company. Lieut.-Col. Coningham and Brevet-Major Stubbs, with fourteen non-commissioned officers and men, lie buried on the Worcester kopjes, where they fell. (*See Major Stubbs.*)

Connor.—Capt. Frederick Henry Connor, Royal Irish Fusiliers, died of wounds received in action at the battle of Talana Hill, Oct. 20th, 1899. He was the son of Lieut.-Col. Connor, was born May, 1862, and educated at Cheltenham College and Wellington (where he was in the Combermere and Lynedoch). He joined the Devonshire Regt. from the Militia May, 1884, being transferred to the Royal Irish Fusiliers in Oct. of the same year, and was promoted capt. Aug., 1891. He served in the Waziristan Expedition under the late Sir William

Lockhart in Aug., 1895, as Transport Officer. He was adjutant from Sept. 16th, 1899, of his battalion, which landed at Durban on Oct. 12th, 1899. He fell while rushing forward and leading some of his men. They had been lining a wall parallel to the main position on Talana Hill. Sir A. Conan Doyle thus describes it: "The air was so full of bullets that it seemed impossible to live on the other side of this shelter. Out of the huddled line of crouching men an officer sprang, shouting, and a score of soldiers vaulted over the wall, and followed at his heels. It was Capt. Connor, of the Irish Fusiliers, but his personal magnetism carried up with him some of the Rifles, as well as the men of his own command. He and half of his little forlorn hope were struck down, he, alas, to die the same night." Capt. Connor is buried at Dundee, and a cross has been erected to his memory by his brother officers. His name is inscribed on the Eleanor Cross War Memorial at Cheltenham College. (*See Lieut.-Col. Gunning.*)

Conolly.—Lieut. Thomas Conolly, 2nd Dragoons, was killed in action at Kaalboschfontein, July 11th, 1900. He was the eldest son of the late Thomas Conolly, M.P., of Castletown, Ireland, and was born in Sept. 1870. Lieut. Conolly was educated at Harrow and Trinity College, Cambridge, and entered the 2nd Dragoons from the 3rd Batt. Royal Dublin Fusiliers, June, 1893, and was promoted lieut. Dec., 1894. He served in the Nile Expedition in 1898, being present at the battle of Khartoum, receiving the medal and the Egyptian medal, with clasp.

Constable.—Lieut. Constable, British South Africa Police, died of pneumonia, at Port Elizabeth.

Conway.—2nd Lieut. Frank Conway, 2nd Batt. King's Own Yorkshire Light Infantry, died of enteric at Pretoria Jan. 23rd, 1901. He was the third son of Thomas

Conway, Esq., Home View, Wimbledon, was born in 1870, and educated at Haileybury. This officer was formerly a corporal in the I.Y., and served in the war from early in 1900. He was specially recommended by F.-M. Earl Roberts for a commission, which was awarded him in Sept., 1900, in the Yorkshire Light Infantry. He then served with the second battalion and was present at the action of Nooitgedacht with Col. Clements' column.

Coode.—Lieut.-Col. John Henry Collier Coode, 2nd Batt. Black Watch, was killed in action at Magersfontein on Dec. 11th, 1899. He was a son of Gen. J. P. Coode, Madras Army, and was born June, 1856. He joined the 73rd Foot, Sept., 1875, being promoted capt. April, 1882, major Aug., 1890, and lieut.-col. July, 1898. He served as adjutant to the Auxiliary Forces from May, 1884-89. He married in Dec., 1884, Nellie, fourth daughter of Capt. C. J. Harford, formerly of the 12th Lancers and 15th Hussars. Lieut.-Col. Coode went to South Africa in Oct., 1899, in command of his battalion, which then joined the Kimberley Relief Force shortly before the action at Magersfontein. (*See Major-Gen. Wauchope*).

Coode.—Capt. Percival Coode, D.S.O., West Riding Regt., was killed when with Col. Ternan's column at Hartenbosch near Bultfontein, April 8th, 1902. He was the sixth son of the late Edward Coode, Esq., Polapit, Tamar, Launceston, and was born in 1871. He entered the West Riding Regt. Nov., 1892, being promoted lieut. Jan., 1896, and capt. June, 1900. He served during the operations in Rhodesia, 1896, and was wounded. In consideration of his South African experience he was specially sent from Burmah to the Cape in the early days of the South African War, and saw much service on the Staff and with M.I. He was present at the actions of

Poplar Grove, Driefontein, Houtnek, Zand River, and Diamond Hill, afterwards taking part in the fighting at Wittebergen, Witpoort, Bothaville and Caledon River. He was mentioned in despatches by F.-M. Earl Roberts, L.G., Sept. 10th, 1901, and was awarded the D.S.O., and the medal with five clasps.

Cooper.—Major Francis Edward Cooper, p.s.c., Royal Field Artillery, died of enteric at Mooi River Hospital, Natal, May 26th, 1900. He was the eldest son of Lieut.-Col. the Hon. Edward Henry Cooper, Markree Castle, Collooney, co. Sligo, was born May, 1859, and educated at Eton (Mr. Hales'). He entered the Royal Artillery from the Royal Military Academy, Dec., 1878, was promoted capt. Oct., 1886, and major 1896. In 1882 he served with No. 7 Mountain Battery in the Egyptian War, and was present at the battle of Tel-el-Kebir, receiving the medal with clasp and Khedive's bronze star. He passed the Staff College in 1888, was Staff Capt. for Royal Artillery, North-Western District, July, 1889, to June, 1892, and A.D.C. to the General Officer Commanding North-Western District, July, 1892 to March, 1895. He was appointed Staff Capt. (Intelligence) Headquarters of the Army, from Jan., 1897 to Nov., 1897, D.A.A.G. (Intelligence) Headquarters of the Army, Nov., 1897 to Oct., 1899, when he was appointed A.D.C. to Lieut.-Gen. Sir C. F. Clery, commanding the Second Division of the South African Field Force in Natal. Major Cooper was present at the engagements at Colenso, Vaal Kranz, Pieters Hill, and Monte Christo, and entered Ladysmith with the relieving force. He married in 1883, Ella Beatrice, elder daughter of Major-Gen. M. Prendergast.

Cooper.—Capt. L. P. Cooper, 11th Batt. I.Y., was killed in action at Driespruit July 23rd, 1901. He was the

OFFICERS WHO FELL IN SOUTH AFRICA. 73

fourth son of the Rev. N. Cooper, Oxon Vicarage, Shrewsbury, was 27 years of age, and educated at Shrewsbury School. When the I.Y. was raised in 1900, he joined the Staffordshire Company of the 4th Batt. as a trooper, and saw much active service in the 8th Division under Maj.-Gen. Sir Leslie Rundle during the latter's pursuit of De Wet in the summer of 1900. He was then recommended for a commission, and in March, 1901, was gazetted lieut. in the 53rd Company of the 11th Batt., being promoted capt. June, 1901. (*See Capt. Moor.*)

Corlett.—2nd Lieut. Archibald John Corlett, 2nd Batt. East Kent Regt. (The Buffs), was killed in action near Brakenlaagte, 20 miles north-west of Bethel, Oct. 31st, 1901. He was the son of John Corlett, Esq., of Charlton Court, East Sutton, Maidstone, Kent, proprietor of the *Sporting Times.* 2nd Lieut. Corlett was born in Nov., 1875, and educated at Sutton Valence School. He went out to South Africa before the war, joined the Natal Mounted Police, and served throughout the campaign, being promoted from the ranks of the Natal Police to a commission in the Buffs in May, 1900.

Cotton.—Lieut. Francis Gerald Stapleton Cotton, Royal Engineers, was killed by an explosion at Pienaars River Camp Oct. 6th, 1900. He was the only son of F. M. Cotton, Esq., M.I.C.E., of Holyhead, North Wales, was born May 16th, 1878, and educated at Repton, whence he passed into the Royal Military Academy, Woolwich, 2nd on the list. Lieut. Cotton entered the Royal Engineers Sept., 1897, and after serving at Chatham and Gosport, embarked for South Africa in Feb., 1900. He was promoted lieut. a few days before being killed. He served in the Harrismith and Bethlehem districts, and was awarded the medal with three clasps.

Coulson.—Lieut. Gustavus Hamilton Blenkinsopp Coulson, V.C., D.S.O., 1st. Batt. King's Own Scottish Borderers, and Adjutant 7th Batt. M.I., was killed in the rear-guard engagement at Lambrechtfontein May, 18th, 1901. He was the only son of A. W. Coulson, Esq., of Newbrough Hall, Northumberland. He was born in April, 1879, and educated at Winchester. He entered the King's Own Scottish Borderers from the 4th Batt. Princess of Wales's Own (Yorkshire Regt.) July, 1899, being promoted lieut. July, 1900. He was present at the battle of Paardeberg, where he had his horse shot under him in the charge in which Col. Hannay fell. He then remained out, shooting Boers who came to steal the saddles, etc., of the fallen. He afterwards took part in the advance on Pretoria, and was subsequently present at the surrender of Prinsloo, and later at the action near Bothaville, where Lieut.-Col. Le Gallais fell. Lieut. Coulson was granted the D.S.O. for his gallantry in the campaign in 1900, and was awarded the V.C. for his conspicuous bravery in the action when he fell in rescuing Corporal Cranmer, 7th M.I., under heavy fire (L.G., Sept. 8th, 1902). "On many occasions during the war, Lieut. Coulson had displayed great coolness and gallantry under fire." He was again mentioned in despatches, L.G., Sept. 10th, 1901, also in the despatch of Gen. Lord Kitchener, Dec. 8th, 1901, and it was announced in the L.G., Aug. 8th, 1902, that His Majesty the King had been graciously pleased to approve of the decoration of the V.C. being delivered to the representatives of Lieut. Coulson.

Coulter.—Lieut. S. R. Coulter, 5th Victorian M.I., was killed in action near Hlobane, in the Vryheid district, on Aug. 27th, 1901. He is buried at Vryheid.

Courtenay.—Lieut. George Edward Courtenay, Argyll

and Sutherland Highlanders, was killed in action near Paardeberg, Feb. 18th, 1900. He was born in March, 1875, educated at Wellington (where he was in Saunders' House), and entered the Argyll and Sutherland Highlanders from the Royal Military College in Feb., 1895, being promoted lieut. Oct., 1897. He was serving with the M.I. This officer's death is mentioned in the despatch of F.-M. Earl Roberts, from Paardeberg, Feb. 28th, 1900.

Cowan.—2nd Lieut. Arthur Ernest Alphonsus Cowan, 2nd Dragoon Guards, died of enteric at Elandsfontein, April 11th, 1902. He was born Aug., 1880, and educated at Clifton. He entered the Antrim Artillery in April, 1900, being promoted lieut. the following Sept., and while belonging to it, was specially selected for service in South Africa in 1901. He was granted a commission in the 2nd Dragoon Guards in Oct., 1901, and served with it till his death.

Cowan.—Capt. James William Alston Cowan, D.S.O., 1st Batt. Highland Light Infantry, was killed in action at Magersfontein, Dec. 11th, 1899. He was a son of Mr. J. B. Cowan, M.D., LL.D., was born in Sept., 1868, and educated at Clifton College. He joined the Highland Light Infantry in Jan., 1889, being promoted lieut. Feb., 1891, and capt. Jan., 1897. He was appointed adjutant of his battalion in Jan., 1898, and took part in the occupation of Crete in that year, including the affair of Sept. 6th, being mentioned in despatches, and awarded the D.S.O. Lieut.-Gen. Lord Methuen reported that at Magersfontein Capt. Cowan "gallantly led and rallied his men and was killed at close quarters."

Cowie.—2nd Lieut. William Russell Cowie, 2nd Batt. Seaforth Highlanders, was killed in action at Magersfontein, Dec. 11th, 1899. He was born in Feb., 1878, and joined his regiment from the Militia, April, 1898. He embarked with his battalion for South Africa in Oct., 1899.

Cowlard.—Lieut. Edward G. Cowlard, attached 2nd Batt. Duke of Cornwall's Light Infantry, died of enteric at Springfontein, on March 5th, 1901. He was the second son of C. L. Cowlard, Esq., Clerk of the Peace for the County of Cornwall. Lieut. Cowlard was 23 years of age, and educated at Marlborough. He was a lieut. in the 2nd Volunteer Batt., and was granted the rank of lieut. in the Army on proceeding to South Africa, in March, 1900, as one of the officers of the Volunteer Company attached to the Duke of Cornwall's Light Infantry. His name is inscribed on a tablet placed in the Marlborough College Chapel in memory of all Marlburians who fell in the War.

Cox.—2nd Lieut. Clement Henry Cox, Lancashire Militia Artillery, died of enteric at Newcastle, Natal, June 5th, 1901. He was the youngest son of Alfred Cox, Esq., 28, Park Crescent, W., and was 26 years of age. He obtained his commission in the Lancashire Militia Artillery, Aug., 1900, and was employed with the Remount Department from Jan., 1901. Lieut. Cox went to New Orleans in February, and afterwards to Durban, and on arrival was attached to the 10th Company Eastern Division Royal Garrison Artillery, with which he served till taken ill. He is buried at Newcastle.

Cox.—Lieut. Ernest Cox, 1st Batt. Seaforth Highlanders, was killed in action at Magersfontein, Dec. 11th, 1899. He was the son of Mrs. Cox of Sloane Gardens, S.W., was born in March, 1868, educated at Harrow, and joined his regiment Nov., 1891, being promoted lieut. Sept., 1894. He served in the Soudan campaign, 1898, under Lord (then Sir Herbert) Kitchener, as extra A.D.C.

to Major-Gen. Gatacre, commanding the British Division, and was present at the battle of Khartoum, being mentioned in despatches, L.G., Sept. 30th, 1898. He received the British medal and Khedive's medal with clasp, and the Order of the Fourth Class of the Medjidie. At Magersfontein, Lieut. Cox, rushing forward and leading a few men, endeavoured to climb up the hillside at the south-eastern corner; they got up part of the way but in the end were all killed.

Craigie - Halkett. — 2nd Lieut. Charles Patrick Marjoribanks Craigie-Halkett, 1st Batt. Highland Light Infantry, was killed in action during the fighting on the Modder River, on Feb. 15th, 1900. He was the eldest son of Col. C. Craigie-Halkett, and grandson of Charles Craigie Halkett Inglis, Esq., of Cramond, Midlothian. He belonged to a family that had served in the army, from father to son without a break since Ramillies, where one of his ancestors was killed. Lieut. Craigie-Halkett was born Aug. 25th, 1876, entered the Highland Light Infantry Feb., 1897, and embarked for South Africa in Oct., 1899.

Crallan.—Capt. Ernest C. H. Crallan, Brabant's Horse, was killed at Bird's River, near Dordrecht, Feb. 16th, 1900. He was the second son of the late Rev. J. E. Crallan, Hayward's Heath, Sussex, and Emsworth, Hants. Capt. Crallan was born in 1853. He was a first-rate rider and shot, and had served for some years in the Natal Police, having previously fought against the Boers and Zulus. He had formerly lived in Johannesburg, and soon after the Jameson Raid he moved to Alice in Cape Colony.

Crawford.—Major Frank Fairburn Crawford, Army Veterinary Department, died in the Base Hospital at

Pietermaritzburg, of dysentery, Jan. 16th, 1900, after three days illness. He was the son of Andrew Crawford, Esq., was born in 1861, educated at the Grammar School, Maidstone, and was an excellent cricketer, playing for his county while at school. He was well known in cricket circles in South Africa and India. He joined the Veterinary Department in 1873, being promoted veterinary-surgeon (first class), 1883, and vet.-major 1893. Major Crawford served with the Bechuanaland Expedition, under Sir Charles Warren, 1884-85, also in the operations in Zululand, 1888. He accompanied the Indian Contingent to South Africa, and landed at Durban, Oct. 7th, 1899. He married in 1882 Frances, daughter of Benjamin Hill, Esq., Resident Magistrate, of Longford.

Crawley.—Capt. Henry H. S. Crawley, 53rd East Kent Company of the 11th Batt. I.Y., died Dec. 26th, 1901, of wounds received at Tweefontein in De Wet's attack on Christmas morning. He was the younger son of the late Capt. R. S. Crawley, 11th Hussars, was born in July, 1872, and educated at Bradfield College, where he was in the cricket and football teams. Capt. H. H. S. Crawley entered the I.Y. in Feb., 1901, and was promoted capt. July, 1901, with the rank of captain in the army. He served in the war during 1901, and had been severely wounded. He is buried at Tweefontein, and his name is inscribed on an obelisk, which has been erected there in memory of all who fell in this action.

Creagh.—Surgeon-Lieut.-Col. James Creagh, 9th Batt. King's Royal Rifle Corps, died of enteric, July 6th, 1900, between Viljoen's Drift and Kroonstad. His battalion was embodied in Dec., 1899, and having volunteered for active service, Surgeon-Lieut.-Col. Creagh proceeded with it to South Africa in Feb., 1900. He then served in Cape and Orange River Colonies until his death.

Creak.—Lieut. William Heywood Creak, 2nd Batt. Loyal North Lancashire Regt., was killed in action at Hartebeestfontein, Feb. 16th, 1901. He was the son of Col. Henry Charles Creak, Bengal Cavalry, was born in June, 1875, and educated at the Merchant Taylors' School. He entered the Loyal North Lancashire Regt. Sept. 1895, and was promoted lieut. June, 1898. He served with the 1st Batt. during the South African War, took part in the operations in the O.R.C., and in the Transvaal, and was also employed as the Signalling Officer of the 1st Division.

Crealock.—Capt. Stradling Louis Vaughan Crealock, Somersetshire Light Infantry, was killed in action in the operations on the Tugela, Feb. 21st, 1900. He was born in July, 1860, and joined the Somersetshire Light Infantry as lieut. Sept. 1884, having previously served five years in the ranks of the Leicestershire Regt., and was promoted capt. June, 1890. He served in the Burmese Expedition of 1886-87, with the 2nd Batt. Somersetshire Light Infantry, receiving the medal, with clasp. He is buried close to where he fell under Fort Wyllie, and near the village of Colenso.

Crewe.—Capt. F. Crewe, Rhodesia Regt., died whilst a prisoner in the hands of the Boers.

Crichton.—Capt. John Ernest Theodore Crichton, M.I. Company, Manchester Regt., died at Belfast Feb. 14th, 1901, of wounds received in action the previous day at Schwartz Kopje. He was born Oct., 1876, educated at Cheltenham, and entered the Manchester Regt. Sept., 1896, being promoted lieut. Oct., 1897, and capt. Sept., 1900. Capt. Crichton served throughout the siege of Ladysmith, and afterwards in the Transvaal, and was mentioned in despatches, L.G., Sept. 10th, 1901. His name is inscribed on the Eleanor Cross War Memorial erected at Cheltenham College.

Crofton.—Major Henry William George Crofton, 3rd Batt. East Surrey Regt., was killed in action in Feb., 1902, in the attack on a convoy thirty miles from Fraserburg. He was transferred as a capt. from the 3rd Batt. East Surrey Regt. to the 3rd Royal West Surrey in Feb., 1900, and, volunteering for active service, proceeded to South Africa. In May, 1901, he was promoted major in his old corps, the 3rd East Surrey, which had also been embodied, and was then in South Africa. In the Boer onslaught in which he was killed, the convoy, which was proceeding from Beaufort West, was attacked by Malan's Commando. The escort was overwhelmed, after a brave defence, and Major Crofton was killed. He had held the post of Station Commandant (graded as a Staff Capt.), and had been awarded the medal and two clasps.

Croker.—2nd Lieut. William Charles Robert Croker, 1st Batt. Royal Munster Fusiliers, was killed in action at Boshof Feb. 23rd, 1902. He came of a race of soldiers, and was the only son of the late Major W. Croker, 27th Inniskillings (now the Royal Inniskilling Fusiliers). He was born at Trough Castle, Limerick, June, 1882, and entered the Royal Munster Fusiliers from the Royal Military College in May, 1900. On the day he was killed 2nd Lieut. Croker was on convoy duty, and with a small party of sixteen men got separated from the main body, and being largely outnumbered and their ammunition expended, were called on to surrender. 2nd Lieut. Croker's answer was "never," and he was then shot dead at close quarters. Corporal Cahill, the next senior, on refusing to surrender, was also killed. 2nd Lieut. Croker and Corporal Cahill are buried at Boshof, and a memorial has been erected at Kimberley to their memory, and that of five soldiers of their company, who fell in this engagement.

Cropper.—Lieut.-Col. Edward Denman Cropper, of the I.Y., and of the Pembroke Yeomanry Cavalry, died of pneumonia, March 29th, 1901, at 29, Wimpole Street, at the age of 46. He was the only son of the late Edward Cropper, Esq., Swaylands, Kent, and was educated at Eton (Mr. Day's). He served in the Zulu War, 1879, as orderly officer to Sir Evelyn Wood, and was present in the engagement at Ulundi, being mentioned in despatches, L.G., Aug. 21st, 1879. Two years later he took part in the Boer War as orderly officer to Sir Evelyn Wood, when he was again mentioned in despatches. He was awarded the Albert medal of the Second Class and the bronze medal of the Royal Humane Society for attempting to save a man by jumping overboard from the steamship "Idaho" on the bar off San Francisco on Aug. 6th, 1878. He obtained his commission as capt. in the Pembroke Yeomanry, June, 1893, being subsequently granted the rank of hon. major, and since Feb., 1900, had been a capt. in the I.Y., serving with the 9th (Col. Howard's) Batt., with the rank of capt. in the army. He was advanced to the rank of major and hon. lieut.-col. in the Pembroke Yeomanry in Jan., 1901. Lieut.-Col. Cropper was mentioned in despatches, L.G., Sept. 10th, 1901, and was granted the D.S.O.

Crowle.—Lieut. Percival Hugh Santo Crowle, Roberts' Horse, was killed near Bloemfontein, March 31st 1900. He was the son of John Crowle, Esq., 36, Phillimore Gardens, Kensington, was aged 28, and educated at Manor House, Clapham, and afterwards at Downing College, Cambridge. He qualified as a solicitor in 1894. At the outbreak of the war, Lieut. Crowle was at Sydney, but hurried to Capetown, and, offering his services, joined Roberts' Horse as a lieut., was present at the relief of Kimberley, and instrumental in capturing a Boer convoy, including the wagon of Gen. Botha. He afterwards took part in the advance on Bloemfontein, and served in the operations near that town till killed.

Crozier.—Capt. M. K. Crozier, Cape Police, died of disease at Daniel's Kuil during the war.

Cuming.—2nd Lieut. Harry Wilfrid Cuming, 1st Batt. Devonshire Regt., was killed in action at Kruger's Post Oct. 1st, 1900. He was born Dec., 1876, and entered the Devonshire Regt. as a University candidate in Jan., 1900. He had previously served in the 3rd London Volunteer Rifle Corps.

Cumming-Bruce.—Capt. the Hon. James Frederick Thurlow Cumming-Bruce, p.s.c., 2nd Batt. Royal Highlanders, died of wounds received in action at Magersfontein, Dec. 11th, 1899. He was the eldest son of Lord and Lady Thurlow, and, on his mother's side, grandson of the late Earl of Elgin. He was born in 1867, educated at Eton (Dr. Warre's), whence he passed direct into the Royal Military College, Sandhurst, and joined the Royal Highlanders, Sept., 1885, being promoted capt. Feb., 1893. He embarked for South Africa in Oct., 1899, with his battalion which, on arrival, joined the Kimberley Relief Force. After he was wounded at Magersfontein he was removed to the hospital at Wynberg, where he died a few days after the battle in which his battalion suffered so severely. Capt. Cumming-Bruce married in 1891, Cecily, daughter of the late T. H. Clifton, Esq., Lytham Hall, Lancashire.

Cummings.—2nd Lieut. Basil Eric Cummings, 15th Company Western Division Royal Garrison Artillery, died of enteric at Deelfontein May 9th, 1900. He was born in March, 1880, educated at Marlborough, and entered the Royal Artillery, June, 1899. His name is inscribed on a tablet placed in Marlborough College Chapel in memory of all Marlburians who fell in the war.

Cunningham.—Lieut. Alexander Crossley Cunningham, 3rd Batt. Argyll and Sutherland Highlanders (attached to 20th Company I.Y.), was killed in action near Smithfield, on Oct. 24th, 1901. He was born on Jan. 22nd, 1877, educated at Loretto School, Musselburgh, and at the Royal Agricultural College, Cirencester. He was fond of games, and at Loretto played in his school teams at cricket and football. He entered the 3rd Batt. Argyll and Sutherland Highlanders, Oct., 1897, and was promoted lieut. Feb., 1900. Lieut. Cunningham volunteered for active service and joined the Fife and Forfarshire Light Horse Company of the 6th Batt. I.Y., May, 1901, with the rank of lieut. in the army. He then served in the Cape and Orange River Colonies until killed.

Cunningham.—Lieut. George Archibald Duncan Forbes Cunningham, 1st Batt. Essex Regt., died of enteric on Jan. 25th, 1902, at Standerton. He was the youngest son of the late James Elliot Cunningham, Esq., 47, St. Aubyns, Hove, Sussex, and was born in Dec., 1876. He joined the Essex Regt. from the 3rd Batt. (Essex Rifles Militia), April, 1900, and was promoted lieut. the following Oct. He served in the war during 1900-01, and was awarded the medal and three clasps.

Curtis.—Capt. Arthur William Curtis, 47th Battery Royal Field Artillery, died of enteric on March 9th, 1900, at Ladysmith. He was a son of the Rev. J. G. Curtis, was born in March, 1870, and educated at Haileybury College. He entered the Royal Artillery, Feb., 1890, was promoted lieut. Feb., 1893, capt. Jan., 1900, and served in the Isazai Expedition, 1892. He married Mary, daughter of Lieut.-Gen. S. F. G. Annesley in Sept., 1898.

Curry.—Capt. William Michael Curry, Imperial Light Horse, died at Rietfontein July 7th, 1900. He was mentioned in despatches, L.G., April 16th, 1901.

Cutbill.—Lieut. Cecil E. Cutbill, Uitenhage Volunteer Rifles, died of enteric at Cradock, Nov. 13th, 1901. He was the second son of Col. Cutbill, p.s.c., recently commanding 4th Batt. Royal Irish Rifles, and formerly commanding the 1st Batt. Lieut. Cutbill was educated at Forest School, Walthamstow. He had previously served in Loch's Horse, was granted a commission in the Uitenhage Rifles as lieut., and served with that corps till his death.

Cuthbert.—2nd Lieut. Sidney William Cuthbert, 3rd Batt. Argyll and Sutherland Highlanders, died Feb. 25th, 1902, from wounds accidentally received at Wynberg near Cape Town. He entered his regiment in July, 1900.

Dalbiac.—Major Henry Shelly Dalbiac, I.Y., was killed in action at Senekal May 24th, 1900. He was born June, 1850, educated at Eton (Miss Drury's), and had formerly been in the Royal Artillery, which he entered Aug., 1871, and retired in 1887. He was a famous athlete and daring steeplechase rider, and had had a brilliant career. When a cadet at the Royal Military Academy, he won the "Bugle," and shortly before proceeding to South Africa, although 49 years of age, he won the race open to all winners of that trophy at the Royal Military Academy sports. Major Dalbiac was a contributor to many sporting papers. He was with Earl (then Sir F.) Roberts in the famous Kandahar march, and was twice mentioned in despatches. He served in the Egyptian War 1882, being severely wounded (having his horse shot under him) at the battle of Tel-el-Kebir, was again mentioned in despatches, and was awarded the medal with clasp and Khedive's star, and also received the Fourth Class of the Order of the Medjidie. He then returned to India, but some time afterwards retired. Major Dalbiac joined the I.Y. as a capt. Feb. 3rd, 1900, and proceeded to South Africa, serving in the Cape and Orange River Colonies. The day he fell he had entered Senekal, regardless of danger, with a small party of Yeomanry in advance of the main body, when he was suddenly fired on by the Boers in the chief street of the town and killed.

Dalrymple-Hay.—Lieut. John Douglas Dalrymple-Hay, 1st Batt. Gordon Highlanders, died in the Langman Hospital, Bloemfontein, of enteric May 26th, 1900. He was the only surviving son of Major and Mrs. Dalrymple-Hay, of Dunlop, and grandson of Admiral Sir John Dalrymple-Hay. He was born Aug., 1874, and educated at Marlborough. Lieut. Dalrymple-Hay joined the Gordon Highlanders from the 3rd Batt. Sept., 1896, and was promoted lieut. Nov., 1898. He served in the campaign on the North-West Frontier of India, 1897-98, under the late Sir William Lockhart, with the Tirah Expeditionary Force, being present at the engagement at Dargai Oct. 18th, at the assault of the Dargai Heights on the 20th, the capture of the Sampagha and Arhanga Passes, and in the subsequent operations in the Maidan, Waran, and Bara Valleys, for which services he was awarded the medal and two clasps. He served in the Kimberley Relief Force under Lieut.-Gen. Lord Methuen, and was present at the battle of Magersfontein, also taking part in the battles of Paardeberg, Driefontein, and the advance on Bloemfontein. The name of Lieut. Dalrymple-Hay is inscribed on a tablet erected in Marlborough College Chapel in memory of all Marlburians who fell in the war.

Daly.—2nd Lieut. Cornelius Joseph Daly, Royal Irish

Fusiliers, was killed in action at Pieters Hill, Feb. 27th, 1900. He was born Feb., 1878, and entered the 2nd Batt. Royal Irish Fusiliers from the 4th Batt., in Jan., 1899. 2nd Lieut. Daly went to South Africa with the 2nd Batt. of his regiment, Oct., 1899, and served with the Ladysmith Relief Force. He was present at the battle of Colenso, and the fighting on the Tugela, in which his battalion took part up to his death at Pieters Hill.

Dalyell.—Lieut. Charles William Parry Dalyell, Royal Garrison Artillery, died of enteric at Pretoria, Dec. 7th, 1900. He was born in 1877, and educated at Trinity College, Glenalmond. He was fond of games and was in the College team for football and cricket. He entered the Royal Artillery Sept., 1897, being promoted lieut. in 1900. One of his Commanding Officers writing of him says " the service has lost a most promising officer."

Dalzel.—Lieut. Augustus Frederick Dalzel, Devonshire Regt., was killed in Ladysmith by a Boer shell, Dec. 27th, 1899. He was the only son of the late William Frederick Blygh Dalzel, M.D., Surgeon-Major Bengal Army, was born Sept., 1870, educated at Haileybury, and joined the Devonshire Regt., Jan., 1892, being promoted lieut. May, 1895. He served with the first battalion of his regiment in the campaign on the North-West Frontier of India, 1897-98, under the late Sir William Lockhart, with the Tirah Expeditionary Force, being present at the capture of the Sampagha and Arhanga Passes, receiving the medal with two clasps. Lieut. Dalzel was serving with his battalion in Natal, when war broke out, was in the fighting round Ladysmith, and served in the town during the siege until killed.

Danks.—Lieut. Cyril German Danks, 1st Batt. Manchester Regt., died May 31st, 1900, at the Cambridge

Hospital, Aldershot, from the effects of a wound received at the battle of Elandslaagte. He was the only son of the Rev. G. W. Danks, Vicar of Morton, Gainsborough, was born Sept., 1875, and educated at Haileybury. He entered the Manchester Regt. from the 4th Batt. South Staffordshire Regt., May, 1897, being promoted lieut. April, 1898. He was serving with his battalion in Natal when war was declared, and was wounded in his first battle, while leading his men. Lieut. Danks was then removed to Pietermaritzburg, operated upon by Sir F. Treves and his wound healed. He was soon after invalided, and was subsequently found fit for duty at home, and rejoined April 17th, 1900. He was, however, again taken ill and died. He was buried at Morton, June 4th, 1900, with full military honours, the local volunteers attending, and furnishing a firing party.

Darter.—Lieut. C. T. Darter, Namaqualand Border Scouts, was killed in action at Garies, on March 18th, 1902.

Davidson.—Lieut. Francis Coventry Dudfield Davidson, Royal Lancaster Regt., died of wounds, Feb. 23rd, 1900, received in the operations on the Tugela. He was the second son of Lieut.-Col. C. M. Davidson, 14, Victoria Park, Dover, of His Majesty's Body Guard, and formerly of the 4th King's Own Regt. and Royal Munster Fusiliers. Lieut. Davidson was born Aug., 1874, educated at Westminster School, and entered the Royal Lancaster Regt. in March, 1895, being promoted lieut. Jan., 1897. He was mentioned in despatches, L.G., Feb. 8th, 1901, for " gallant and meritorious service."

Davies.—Civil Surgeon Herbert Davies, Welsh Military Hospital, died at Springfontein of dysentery, June 15th, 1900. He was the son of Henry Davies, Esq., J.P.,

Carns Lodge, near Lancaster, and was 26 years of age. Educated at Shrewsbury School, and Owen's College, Manchester, he took the M.B., and Ch.B. Degrees at Victoria University in 1898. He had been House Physician at the Brompton Hospital for Consumption, and was House Surgeon to the Royal Infirmary, Manchester. At the commencement of the war, he volunteered for active service, and proceeded soon afterwards to South Africa. (*See Captain Moor.*)

Davenport.—Lieut. George Holt Davenport, 3rd Batt. King's Royal Rifle Corps, died of enteric at Standerton, June 23rd, 1901. He was a son of Capt. and Mrs. Davenport, Bembridge, Isle of Wight, was born Dec., 1877, educated at Charterhouse, and entered the King's Royal Rifle Corps from the 3rd Batt. Royal Sussex Regt., May, 1898, being promoted lieut. Oct., 1899. He served from the commencement of the war with his battalion in the Natal Field Force, and was present at all the actions which led up to the relief of Ladysmith and also took part in the subsequent advance into the Transvaal. His name is inscribed on the tablet in the War Memorial Cloister at Charterhouse.

Davies.—Lieut. Byam Henry Ernest Davies, M.I., 3rd Batt. Wiltshire Regt., was killed in action Feb. 4th, 1902, at Winbult, near Lindley. He was the eldest son of Byam Martin Davies, Esq., of Corsley House, Warminster, Wilts, and Waltham Place, Maidenhead. Lieut. Davies was 23 years of age, and educated at Eton (Mr. Austen Leigh's). He joined his regiment March, 1900, being promoted lieut. in the following July.

Dawson-Scott.—Lieut. Geoffrey Nicholl Dawson-Scott, Royal Garrison Artillery, died Dec. 31st, 1900, from atrophy of the liver. He was born Oct., 1874, and educated at Wellington (Combermere, 1888-91). He entered the Royal Artillery from the R.M.A., June, 1895, being promoted lieut. in June, 1898, and proceeded to South Africa in Jan., 1900.

Day.—Major Charles Russell Day, Oxfordshire Light Infantry, died from wounds received in action near Paardeberg, on Feb. 18th, 1900, during the pursuit of Cronje. He was the only son of the Rev. Russell Day, rector of Horstead, Norwich, was born April, 1860, and educated at Eton (Mr. Carter's). He entered the Oxfordshire Light Infantry from the 3rd Royal Lancashire Militia, Jan., 1882, promoted capt. July, 1889, and major Oct. 1899. Major Day was a fellow of the Society of Antiquaries, and was well known in the musical world. In 1890 he was employed in connection with the musical department of the Royal Military Exhibition at South Kensington, and in 1892 served as a member of the English Committee of the Vienna International Musical Exhibition; he also served in a similar capacity for the Paris Musical Exhibition of 1900. He was the author of "Music and Musical Instruments of Southern India and The Deccan." Major Day accompanied his battalion to South Africa in Dec., 1899, and was present at the fighting at Klip Kraal, where his field glasses were broken to pieces by a bullet. He also took part in the Relief of Kimberley; and at Paardeberg was struck down when going to the assistance of Corporal Knowles, who was wounded, and whose life he saved. After he had been wounded, and while being attended to, Major Day's first thought was for the Corporal, adding "never mind me." He is buried at Paardeberg; his funeral was most pathetic. Among many others attending were some thirty men of his battalion who had been wounded—a sad picture. One who was present adds "not many of us returned with dry eyes."

de Freville.—Major Edward Henry de Freville, 15th Batt. I.Y., late 8th and 11th Hussars, resigned his commission as capt. in the I.Y., Sept. 25th, 1901, and died shortly afterwards at Scarborough. He was the eldest son of the late Rev. Charles Greene, formerly Chaplain to the forces at Chatham, and changed his name on succeeding to the de Freville family estates at Hinxton, Saffron Walden, and Shelford, Cambridgeshire. Major de Freville was educated at Eton (Mr. Stevens'), went out to South Africa, March, 1900, with the I.Y.; and after much service was invalided home, but never recovered from the illness which he had contracted during the war. He was mentioned in despatches, L.G., Sept. 10th, 1901.

de Guerin.—Lieut. S. C. W. de Guerin, 33rd East Kent Company I.Y., died of enteric at Norval's Pont, Feb. 11th, 1902. He joined the I.Y. as a 2nd lieut. March, 1901, and was promoted lieut. in May. He had previously served as a trooper in the Cape Mounted Rifles.

de Kock.—Lieut. Christian G. de Kock, Clanwilliam Convoy Guard (late Western Province M.I.), was killed in action in the Clanwilliam District on Oct. 31st, 1901.

de Montmorency.—Capt. the Hon. Raymond Harvey Lodge Joseph de Montmorency, V.C., 21st Empress of India's Lancers, and commanding de Montmorency's Scouts in South Africa, was killed in action, near Stormberg, Feb. 23rd, 1900. He was the eldest son of the late Viscount Frankfort de Montmorency, K.C.B., and Rachel, his wife, daughter of F.-M. Sir John Michel, K.C.B. Capt. de Montmorency was born Feb. 1867, and educated at Marlborough. He joined the Lincolnshire Regt. from the Royal Military College, Sept., 1887, being promoted to a lieutenantcy in the 21st Lancers, Nov., 1889, and becoming capt. Aug., 1899. When a lieut., he served in the Soudan campaign, 1898, and was present at the battle of Khartoum, being mentioned in despatches, L.G., Sept. 30th, 1898, was awarded the V.C. and the British medal and Khedive's medal with clasp. It is written of him "his early death cut short the career of one who possessed every quality of a partisan leader." He had raised a corps of scouts, over whom he had a remarkable influence. He knew no fear. His death is mentioned in the despatch from Paardeberg, Feb. 28th, 1900, by F.-M. Earl Roberts, where Capt. de Montmorency is stated to have been "a very promising officer." Capt. de Montmorency is buried in Molteno cemetery. His name is inscribed on a tablet placed in Marlborough College Chapel in memory of all Marlburians who fell in the war.

Denne.—Major Henry William Denne Denne, p.s.c., 2nd Batt. Gordon Highlanders, was killed in action at the battle of Elandslaagte, Oct. 21st, 1899. He was born in 1860, educated at Harrow, and joined the 75th Foot, Jan., 1880, being promoted lieut. March, 1881, capt. July, 1887, and major Oct., 1897. He saw service in the Egyptian War of 1882, with the 1st Batt. Gordon Highlanders, and was present at the battle of Tel-el-Kebir (medal with clasp and Khedive's star). He also served in the Soudan Expedition, 1884, as Transport Officer, with the 1st Batt. Gordon Highlanders, and was present in the engagements at El Teb and Tamai (two clasps); also in the Nile Expedition, 1884-85, with the River Column under Major-Gen. Earle (clasp). He held the appointment of A.D.C. in Egypt, April, 1886, to Sept., 1887, and at Malta, Jan., 1888, to Jan., 1889. He was afterwards Station Staff Officer (first class) in India, and was appointed D.A.A.G., Bengal, from Nov., 1895, until he rejoined his battalion to proceed with it to South Africa, in Sept., 1899.

Dennis.—2nd Lieut. George Barlow Bartley Dennis, 23rd Field Company Royal Engineers, was killed in action at Wagon Hill, Ladysmith, Jan. 6th, 1900. He was the eldest son of E. R. Bartley Dennis, Esq., of Harrow, Barrister, Middle Temple. 2nd Lieut. Dennis was born Nov., 1878, and educated at Harrow, which he entered as a mathematical scholar. He joined the Royal Engineers, March, 1898, and in Sept., 1899, was sent to the 23rd Field Company at Ladysmith, and served with it during the siege until his death. In the early morning of Jan. 6th he was with the detachment of Royal Engineers on Wagon Hill, under Lieut. Digby Jones, and when the latter officer was seen to fall, it was thought that he was only wounded. 2nd Lieut. Dennis, then helping to carry a stretcher, went forward from rock to rock to assist Lieut. Jones, and was stooping over him when he fell—shot through the brain—"across the body of his friend and comrade." He was mentioned in despatches, L.G., Feb. 8th, 1901. (*See Lieut. Jones.*)

Dennis.—2nd Lieut. John Tracton Dennis, 2nd Batt. Royal Dublin Fusiliers, died in hospital, at Aliwal North, from enteric, May 2nd, 1900. He was educated at Cheltenham, and entered the Royal Dublin Fusiliers from the Gloucestershire Royal Engineer Volunteers, Nov. 4th, 1899. He served with his battalion, in Natal, with the Natal Field Force, and had been wounded. His name is inscribed on the Eleanor Cross War Memorial at Cheltenham College.

Denny.—Capt. Peter Robert Denny, 1st Dragoon Guards (attached 14th Hussars), was killed in action at Roodekop, near Dewetsdorp, April 25th, 1900. He was a son of the late William Denny, Esq., and his wife, Lelia Mathilda Serina, now Lady Samuelson, of 56, Princes Gate, S.W. Capt. Denny was born at Dumbarton in Jan., 1875, and educated at Winchester. After leaving school he intended entering the engineering works of Messrs. Denny, of Dumbarton, but his love of sport and adventure made him join the army. He entered the 1st Dragoon Guards in Dec., 1895, from the 3rd Batt. Queen's Royal West Surrey Regt., being promoted lieut. July, 1896, and capt. Dec., 1899. Soon after joining his regiment he accompanied a brother officer, Major Quicke (also killed during the war), on a shooting expedition to Somaliland. Capt. Denny volunteered for active service, and proceeded to South Africa with the 14th Hussars, Dec., 1899, and served with the Natal Field Force till the Relief of Ladysmith, when he was transferred to Bloemfontein. He was then sent with the column—in command of a squadron—which was detached to relieve Dewetsdorp, and met his death in the fighting near the town. He is buried close to where he fell and a memorial cross has been erected over his grave. A tablet to his memory has also been placed in Bloemfontein Cathedral.

Dent.—2nd Lieut. Francis Noel Dent, 6th Inniskilling Dragoons, was drowned at Norval's Pont, Orange River, March 15th, 1900. He was the youngest son of the late Stanley Dent, Esq., and of Mrs. Dent, 115A, Sloane Street, S.W. He was born Dec., 1877, and educated at Eastbourne College and at Col. Fox's, Farnham. 2nd Lieut. Dent entered the 6th Dragoons from the 5th Batt. Royal Inniskilling Fusiliers (Donegal Militia) Oct., 1899, and proceeded to South Africa, Jan., 1900, to join his regiment, arriving Feb. 5th. He, with three other officers, being anxious to be the first of the British forces to cross the Orange River at Norval's Pont, procured a raft, and succeeded in getting safely to the north bank. Returning, however, 2nd Lieut. Dent was drowned, although he was an expert swimmer. One of his companions was nearly drowned also, being saved by a brother officer; but many attempts made to save 2nd Lieut. Dent were unfortunately unsuccessful.

de Rougemont.—Capt. Harold Wake de Rougemont, South African Light Horse, died at Chieveley Jan. 24th, 1900, of wounds received in action the previous day, while assisting a party of Bethune's M.I., in making a reconnaissance from Chieveley Camp. He was son of the late Commander Frank de Rougemont, R.N., of Bradwell, Oxon, was born July, 1877, and educated at Sherborne and University College, Oxford. Capt. de Rougemont was for two years in the Forest Department, Capetown, but on the war breaking out, offered his services and was given a commission in the S.A.L.H. He was promoted lieut. before the regiment left Rosebank Camp, Lieut.-Gen. French having there specially noticed his troop. At the battle of Colenso his bravery was so conspicuous that he was promoted to the command of his squadron, with the rank of captain.

de Villiers.—Lieut.-Col. A. P. de Villiers, commanding the Cape Garrison Artillery, died at Durban Road, on June 12th, 1901.

Dewar.—Capt. Edward John Dewar, King's Royal Rifle Corps, died on Feb. 20th, 1900, of wounds received in action at Paardeberg two days previously. He was born Feb., 1863, educated at Eton (Mr. Cole's), and entered the King's Royal Rifle Corps from the Militia in 1883, being promoted capt. July, 1891. He served in the expedition to Manipur, 1891. Capt. Dewar belonged to the 4th Batt. King's Royal Rifle Corps, but volunteering for active service at the commencement of the war he was seconded for service with the M.I. from Oct. 22nd. His death is mentioned in the despatch of F.-M. Earl Roberts, from Paardeberg, Feb. 28th, 1900.

OFFICERS WHO FELL IN SOUTH AFRICA. 95

Dick.—Capt. and Brevet-Major Colin Eccles Dick, Royal Irish Fusiliers, died Sept. 29th, 1901, of wounds received in action at Vryheid. He was born Dec., 1864, and after a little over seven years in the ranks, was given a commission in the Royal Irish Fusiliers, Feb., 1893, being promoted lieut. April, 1897, and capt. Feb., 1900. He served with the Natal Field Force for the relief of Ladysmith, being mentioned in despatches, L.G., Feb. 8th, 1901, and received the brevet of major from Nov. 29, 1900, in the Gazette of Aug. 27th, 1901. He was also mentioned in the despatch of Gen. Lord Kitchener, Oct. 8th, 1901, for "consistent gallantry and good leading, especially on Aug. 28th," the day he was mortally wounded. Major Dick is buried at Vryheid.

Dick-Cunyngham.—Lieut.-Col. William Henry Dick-Cunyngham, V.C., commanding 2nd Batt. Gordon Highlanders, died Jan. 7th, 1900, from wounds received in action at Ladysmith on the previous day. He was mortally wounded by a stray bullet at 3,000 yards from the enemy. He was the fifth and youngest son of the late Sir William Hanmer Dick-Cunyngham, eighth baronet, of Prestonfield and Lambrughtoun, co. Ayr. Lieut.-Col. Dick-Cunyngham was born June, 1851, and educated at Trinity College, Glenalmond. He entered the 92nd Highlanders in 1872, was promoted lieut. 1873, capt. 1881, major 1891, and lieut.-col. 1897. He served in the Afghan War, 1878-80, and was present on transport duty in the advance on Kandahar and Khelat-i-Gilzai under Sir Donald Stewart; with the Thul Chotiali Force under Major-Gen. Biddulph (mentioned in despatches); under Earl (then Sir Frederick) Roberts in the Koorum Valley Field Force in the 92nd Gordon Highlanders, including the engagement at Ali Kheyl; he also took part in the operations round Kabul, Dec., 1879, including the attack on the Sherpur Pass, being mentioned in despatches and awarded the V.C. He was with the Maidan Expedition in 1880 as acting adjutant of a wing of the 92nd Gordon Highlanders, including the engagement at Charasiah, April 25th (mentioned in despatches); accompanied Earl Roberts in the famous march to Kandahar, and was present at the reconnaissance of Aug. 31st, and at the battle of Kandahar (mentioned in despatches, and received the medal with two clasps and bronze star). He was awarded the V.C. "for the conspicuous gallantry and coolness displayed by him on Dec. 13th, 1879, at the attack on the Sherpur Pass in Afghanistan, in having exposed himself to the full fire of the enemy, and by his example and encouragement rallied the men, who, having been beaten back, were at the moment wavering at the top of the hill." He served in the Boer War, 1881, as adjutant of the 92nd Gordon Highlanders, and was subsequently D.A.A.G. in Bengal. He went to Natal from India in command of the 2nd Batt. Gordon Highlanders, and led them into action at Elandslaagte. He fell early in the charge, wounded by a bullet in the leg. A sergeant of his battalion writes concerning him that on this occasion "he lay and cheered on the men; he tried to be up at the end of the charge, but could not manage it." He completely recovered from this wound, and returned to duty only to be again struck down, Jan. 6th, this time mortally. He was uncle to Sir William Dick-Cunyngham, the present baronet, and married in 1883, Helen, daughter of Mr. Samuel Wauchope, C.B. Lieut.-Col. Dick-Cunyngham is buried in the Town cemetery at Ladysmith. The Gordon Highlanders have erected a cairn to his memory on the spot where he fell.

Dickinson.—Lieut. Harold Lissaman Dickinson, 7th New Zealand M.I., was killed in action at Langverwacht near Klip River, Feb. 24th, 1902. The only son of Mrs.

OFFICERS WHO FELL IN SOUTH AFRICA. 97

Dickinson, 5, Cranmer Square, Christchurch, New Zealand, he was born in Manchester, England, Oct., 1875. Having been taken to New Zealand when only three years old, he was educated there at Christ Church College, where he served in the College Volunteer Corps. He was an excellent shot and a good horseman. Lieut. Dickinson accompanied the 1st New Zealand Contingent to South Africa as a trooper and served under Lieut.-Gen. French. He was present at the action of Slingersfontein, Jan. 15th, 1900, where the New Zealanders behaved with such gallantry, Capt. Madocks the officer in command killing the Boer leader. The charge with fixed bayonets ordered by Capt. Madocks, in which Lieut. Dickinson took part swept the Boers from the hills, and is mentioned in the despatch of Lieut. Gen. French, Feb. 2nd, 1900. Lieut. Dickinson was also present at the relief of Kimberley, the battles of Paardeberg, Driefontein and Sanna's Post, the advance on Pretoria and the action at Diamond Hill. In Feb., 1901, he returned to New Zealand, but being given a commission as lieut. he was back again in South Africa in April and saw much fighting. In the action in which he was killed, the 7th New Zealand Contingent to which he belonged made a most gallant resistance to an overwhelming attack by the Boers under Manie Botha. Seven out of eight officers were struck down, and of the men 20 were killed and 40 wounded. It is stated that only ten men came out of the fight untouched. Lieut. Dickinson's voice was heard above the noise and firing rallying and cheering his men until he fell shot through the head. Two medals, one with five clasps the other with two, were awarded him for his services.

Dillon.—Lieut. Charles Henry Dillon, Rifle Brigade, died of wounds received in action at Standerton June 8th, 1901. Born in August, 1877, educated at Eton (Mr.

Cornish's), he entered the Rifle Brigade, Feb., 1898, being promoted lieut. Jan., 1900. Lieut. Dillon had been on special service in South Africa with the Rhodesian Field Force from March, 1900, and was mentioned in the despatch of Gen. Lord Kitchener of July 28th, 1901, in that he, when "in command of some scouts shewed great skill in extricating his men from a very difficult position," and as A.D.C. to Col. Grey frequently rendered most "plucky and valuable service."

Dillon.—Capt. Edward Walter Cotter Dillon, 9th Batt. King's Royal Rifle Corps, died of sunstroke at Wynberg, Feb. 7th, 1900. He was the only surviving son of Major-Gen. Edward Sangford Dillon, formerly commanding the 1st Batt. Royal Irish Regt., and grandson of Lieut.-Col. F. E. Dillon, also of the same regiment. Capt. Dillon was born Aug., 1873, joined his battalion in 1893, and was promoted capt. May, 1897. He embarked with it for South Africa, Jan., 1900, and was taken ill soon after landing.

Dimsdale.—Capt. Wilfred Philip Dimsdale, 2nd Batt. Royal Irish Rifles, died April 9th, 1900, of wounds received in action April 3rd and 4th, near Reddersberg. He was the youngest son of the late Baron Dimsdale of Essendon, Herts, was born April, 1870, and educated at Eton (Mr. Rawlins'). He entered the Royal Irish Rifles Nov., 1889, was promoted lieut. July, 1893, and capt. April, 1898. From May, 1897, to March, 1898, he was A.D.C. to the late Lieut.-Gen. Sir Charles Nairne during the latter's tenure of the Bombay Command. While holding this appointment Capt. Dimsdale took part in the operations on the North-West Frontier of India as Extra Orderly Officer to the General Officer Commanding the 1st Division of the Tirah Expeditionary Force, receiving the medal with two clasps. He embarked for South Africa in Oct., 1899, and served with the M.I.

OFFICERS WHO FELL IN SOUTH AFRICA. 99

Dobbie.—Lieut. Wallace Houston Dobbie, O.R.C. Police (late 1st Batt. I.Y.), was dangerously wounded near Ladybrand, and died on Nov. 30th, 1900.

Dodd.—Major Thomas R. Dodd, 2nd Railway Pioneer Regt., died of dysentery at Germiston Feb. 4th, 1901. He was secretary of the Transvaal branch of the South African League, and one of the principle leaders of the second reform movement in Johannesburg. Together with Mr. Clem Webb he was arrested by the Transvaal authorities for presenting a petition to the British Vice-Consul after the murder of Edgar. During the subsequent period before the outbreak of the war he played a prominent part in organising and keeping united the Uitlander community. Major Dodd was a Fellow of the Royal Colonial Institute, and his name is inscribed on a memorial tablet in the hall of the building in Northumberland Avenue, W.C.

Dorman.—Lieut. George Lockwood Dorman, 3rd Batt. the Princess of Wales's Own Yorkshire Regt. (5th West York Militia), died of enteric at Kroonstad March 30th, 1901. He was educated at Eton (Mr. Hare's), and entered his regiment Jan., 1900, being promoted lieut. the following Dec. His battalion proceeded to South Africa Feb., 1900, and Lieut. Dorman served with it in the Cape and Orange River Colonies.

Douglas.—Lieut.-Col. Arthur Baird Douglas, 3rd Batt. Cameron Highlanders, was killed in action at Roodeval, June 7th, 1900. He was the senior major of the 3rd Batt. Cameron Highlanders, in which he was seconded for service with the 4th Batt. Derbyshire Regt. He received his first commission 1872, and was in the reserve of officers. The day he fell, the 4th Batt. Derbyshire Regt., of which he was in command, was guarding the railway, and was fiercely attacked in the early morning by overwhelming numbers of the enemy, under De Wet. They were called on to surrender, and on Lieut.-Col. Douglas scornfully refusing, fire was opened on them from every side. Lieut.-Col. Douglas fell early in the fight, vowing he would shoot the first man who raised the white flag. He and those who were killed are buried near Rhenoster Kopje, Rhenoster River. A cross marks their graves. At the time of his death, Lieut.-Col. Douglas held the position of Secretary to the Junior United Service Club.

Doveton.—Major David Edwin Doveton, Imperial Light Horse, died at Ladysmith, Feb. 14th, 1900, of wounds received in the attack on Wagon Hill, Jan. 6th, 1900. He was mentioned in despatches for his services, by Gen. Sir G. White, March 23rd, 1900 (L.G., Feb. 8th, 1900), and again in the despatch of F.-M. Earl Roberts, L.G., April 16th, 1901.

Dow.—Lieut. John Dow, 2nd Scottish Horse, was killed in action at Hake Banagher, on Dec. 20th, 1901.

Dowie.—Capt. Ronald Mackenzie Dowie, 3rd Batt. Suffolk Regt., died at Kroonstad, Dec. 20th, 1901 from a gunshot wound in the abdomen, received in action near Vredefort three days previously. He was seconded in his battalion for service with the 1st Batt. of his regiment, and formerly held a commission as lieut. in the 4th Batt., being gazetted to a company in the 3rd Batt. in Jan., 1900.

Downman.—Lieut.-Col. George Thomas Frederick Downman, 1st Batt. Gordon Highlanders, died of wounds received in action, Dec. 11th, 1899, at Magersfontein.

He was born in 1855, and came of a Devonshire family. He joined the Gordon Highlanders in 1876, was promoted capt. 1883, major 1891, and lieut.-col. 1899. Lieut.-Col. Downman first saw service with the expedition to the Soudan in 1884 with the 1st Batt. Gordon Highlanders, and was present in the engagements at El Teb and Tamai, receiving the medal with clasp, and Khedive's star. He also served in the Nile Expedition 1884-85, and with the River Column, under Major-Gen. Earle (clasp). He was present with the Chitral Relief Force, under Sir Robert Low, 1895, including the storming of the Malakand Pass, was mentioned in despatches, and received the medal with clasp. He took part in the campaign on the North-West Frontier of India under the late Sir William Lockhart, 1897-98, with the Tirah Expeditionary Force and was present in the engagement at Dargai, Oct. 18th. He was also present at the assault of the Dargai Heights, Oct. 20th (mentioned in despatches), at the capture of the Sampagha and Arhanga Passes, and the subsequent operations in the Maidan, Waran and Bara Valleys, being again mentioned in despatches and receiving the brevet of lieut.-col., and two clasps. Lieut.-Col. Downman succeeded to the command of his battalion in July, 1899, accompanied it to South Africa the following Oct., and joined the Kimberley Relief Force under Gen. Lord Methuen. In the action at Magersfontein, Lieut.-Col. Downman fell mortally wounded within 200 yards of the Boer trenches. The "Retire" had apparently been sounded without authority and Lieut.-Col. Downman jumped up, calling out "Who sounded the 'Retire'?" when he was immediately struck down. Capt. Towse, who endeavoured to carry him to a place of safety, was granted the V.C. for his gallantry and devotion, being ably assisted by Colour-Sergeant Nelson and Lance-Corporal Hodgson. Lieut.-Col. Downman is buried at Magersfontein.

Dowse.—Capt. Henry Esmonde Dowse, Royal Army Medical Corps, died of enteric, at Bloemfontein, May 5th, 1900. He was the second son of the late Henry James Dowse, Esq., was born Jan., 1868, and entered the Royal Army Medical Corps as capt. Jan., 1891. He served with the Chitral Relief Force, under Sir Robert Low, in 1895, receiving the medal with clasp.

Drage.—Lieut. Drage, New South Wales M.I., was killed at Diamond Hill, near Pretoria, on June 11th, 1900.

Drew.—Lieut. Percy James Vaughan Drew, Kimberley Corps, died at Potchestroom on July 28th, 1900.

Drysdale.—Lieut. Robert Drysdale, 1st Batt. Royal Scots. This officer was first reported missing at Slabbert's Nek Aug. 31st, 1901. A Court of Enquiry assembled, and on investigating the circumstances came to the conclusion that Lieut. Drysdale had been killed on the date mentioned. He was born Oct., 1876, entered the Royal Scots Feb., 1897, being promoted lieut. April, 1899. He had served from Nov. 1899, with his battalion, first in the north of Cape Colony afterwards in the O.R.C. and Transvaal.

Du Buisson.—2nd Lieut. Claude Seaton Du Buisson, 2nd Batt. The Queen's Royal West Surrey Regt., died at the Base Hospital, Pietermaritzburg, April 2nd, 1900, of wounds received on the preceding Jan. 20th, in action on the Upper Tugela. He was a son of the late James Du Buisson, Esq., of Tanfield, West Clandon, Surrey, was born Feb., 1876, and educated at Mr. Bartholomew's, Reading; and at Marlborough and Trinity College, Oxford. He entered the Royal West Surrey Regt. July, 1898, and accompanied his battalion to South Africa in Oct., 1899. 2nd Lieut. Du Buisson was present at Willow Grange,

OFFICERS WHO FELL IN SOUTH AFRICA. 103

the battle of Colenso, and the fighting on the Tugela, till wounded. He is buried at Pietermaritzburg. His name is inscribed on a tablet placed in Marlborough College Chapel, in memory of all Marlburians who fell in the war; also on a memorial erected at Guildford by his comrades of the Queen's Royal West Surrey Regt.

Dudgeon.— Lieut. Patrick Wellwood Dudgeon, 1st Batt. King's Own Scottish Borderers, died of enteric, at Krugersdorp, Dec. 30th, 1901. He was born June, 1878, educated at Uppingham, and entered the 3rd Batt. (Scottish Borderers Militia) in Feb., 1899. In Feb., 1900, he was attached for duty to the 1st Batt. South Lancashire Regt. in South Africa, and in March was granted a commission in the 2nd Batt. King's Own Scottish Borderers. In June, 1900, he was transferred to the 1st battalion, was promoted lieut. May, 1901, and served with it up to the time of his death.

Duffield.— Quartermaster and Hon. Capt. Samuel Duffield, Royal Army Medical Corps, died of dysentery, at Pretoria, Jan. 17th, 1901. He served in the ranks for nearly eighteen years, and was employed at the War Office for over four years, being promoted quartermaster in the Royal Army Medical Corps Dec. 1899. He served with the Egyptian Expedition 1882, receiving the medal with bronze star. He was mentioned in despatches, L.G., Sept. 10th, 1901, for his services in South Africa, and was granted the honorary rank of capt. from Nov. 29th, 1900.

Du Moulin.—Lieut. Col. Louis Eugene du Moulin, 2nd-in-command of the 1st Batt. Royal Sussex Regt. was killed in action at Abraham's Kraal, near Koffyfontein, Jan. 28th, 1902. He was born Oct., 1859, entered the 107th Foot, now the 2nd Batt. Royal Sussex Regt.,

Jan., 1880, being promoted lieut. in the following June, capt. April, 1885, major Jan. 1896, and for his services during the South African war, brevet-lieut.-col. in Nov. 1900. He served in the Hazara Campaign 1885, with the 2nd battalion, being mentioned in despatches, and receiving the medal with clasp, with the Chin-Lushai Expeditionary Force 1889-90, on transport duty (mentioned in despatches, clasp), and with the Manipur Expeditionary Force 1891, as Brigade Transport Officer to the Silchar column (clasp). He next saw service with the 2nd battalion in the campaign on the North-West Frontier of India, under the late Sir William Lockhart, 1897-98, in the Tirah Expeditionary Force, including the operations in the Bazar Valley, receiving the medal with two clasps. At the beginning of the South African war Lieut.-Col. du Moulin was second-in-command of the 1st battalion, which was then stationed in Malta. In Feb., 1900, it proceeded to South Africa and then took part in the march from Bloemfontein to Pretoria, including the engagements at Welkom Farm, Zand River and Doorn Kop, the occupations of Johannesburg and Pretoria, and the engagement at Diamond Hill. Lieut.-Col. du Moulin was also present at the engagements round Bethlehem and in the Caledon Valley, and at Retief's Nek and the surrender of the Boer forces at Golden Gate Aug. 1st, 1900. He also took part in the operations round Thaba N'chu, Winburg, and Lindley, and in the engagements at Bothaville and Ventersburg. At one period of the war he was in command of a column and was mentioned in despatches, L.G., July 9th, and Sept. 10th, 1901, was promoted lieut-col. and granted the medal with four clasps for his good services.

Dunn.—Lieut. Joseph Smith Dunn, 2nd Regt. Scottish Horse, died of abscess of the liver and fever, at Pretoria, Jan. 13th, 1902. At the time of his death he was senior lieut. of his regt., and served in the war during 1901. He acted as war correspondent for the *Central News*, London.

Eagar.—Capt. Edward Boaz Eagar, 1st Batt. Northumberland Fusiliers, was killed in action at Belmont, Nov. 23rd, 1899. He was a son of Col. E. H. Eagar, was born April 7th, 1860, and educated at Wellington, where he was in the Blucher. Capt. Eager entered the 41st Foot from the Royal Military College, Aug., 1880, and was transferred to the 5th Foot in Oct. of the same year, being promoted lieut. July, 1881, and capt. Jan., 1890. He was adjutant to the 3rd V.B. Northumberland Fusiliers, June, 1891, to June, 1896. He served in the Nile Expedition 1898, and was present at the battle of Khartoum, receiving the medal, also the Egyptian medal, with clasp. It is stated that he was killed by a wounded Boer who was holding up a white flag. Capt. Eagar was married to a daughter of Col. Thoyts, and left a widow and four children.

Eagar.—Lieut. Col. Henry Averell Eagar, commanding the 2nd Batt. Royal Irish Rifles, died at Burghersdorp Feb. 13th, 1900, from wounds received in action at Stormberg Dec. 10th, 1899. Born in April, 1853, he joined the 83rd Foot from the Royal South Down Light Infantry Militia Dec. 1874, being promoted capt. Jan., 1882, major Dec. 1889, and lieut.-col. Nov. 1896. Lieut.-Col. Eagar fell while leading a small party of men up a precipitous slope, where the attack had come to a stand-still. The author of "*The Times* History of the War" states that had Col. Eagar succeeded in his noble efforts and reached the crest, he "would have commanded the Boer Laager, and perhaps won the day."

Eales.—Major Lionel George Nuttall Eales, 2nd Batt.

East Kent Regt. (The Buffs), died May 2nd, 1902, at Lorenço Marques, on board the transport Avoca, from acute inflammation. Born in July, 1864, he entered the East Kent Regt. Aug., 1884, being promoted capt April, 1893, and major May, 1901. He served with the Manipur Expedition, 1891, as Signalling Officer, being mentioned in despatches, and receiving the medal with clasp. From Nov., 1897, to July, 1901, Major Eales held the appointment of adjutant of the 1st V.B. of his regiment at Dover. He then proceeded to South Africa and was appointed commandant at Eerste Fabreiken and afterwards at Alkmaar.

Earle.—Capt. Sydney Earle, p.s.c., Coldstream Guards, was killed in action at the battle of Modder River, Nov. 28th, 1899. He was born Jan., 1865, educated at Marlborough, and entered the King's (Liverpool) Regt. May 9th, 1885, was transferred to the Coldstream Guards as lieut. May 20th, 1885, being promoted capt. July 27th, 1896. He was appointed D.A.A.G. for instruction, Home District, Sept. 10th, 1898, and in Oct., 1899, proceeded to South Africa as a Special Service Officer. It is stated that Capt. Earle was shot dead by a wounded Boer to whom he was offering his water bottle. His name is inscribed on a tablet which has been placed in Marlborough College Chapel in memory of all Marlburians who fell in the war.

Eaton.—Lieut. Charles Edward Eaton, Roberts' Horse, died of enteric, at Kroonstad, June 4th, 1900. He was the son of the late Robert Eaton, Esq., of Bryn-y-môr, Swansea, and Helen, his wife, The Grange, Bradford-on-Avon. Lieut. Eaton was born Jan., 1869, and educated at Beckenham. He joined Roberts' Horse in Jan., 1900, and was present at the Relief of Kimberley and the battles of Paardeberg and Driefontein, and the advance on Bloemfontein. He also took part in the actions at Sanna's Post, Winburg, and the advance on Kroonstad, and was awarded the medal with three clasps.

Ebsworth.—2nd Lieut. A. Ebsworth, 1st Australian Horse, was killed in action near Bronkhorstspruit, on July 23rd, 1900.

Eddy.—Major Eddy, Victoria Mounted Rifles, was killed in action, near Rensburg, Feb. 12th, 1900. In the action in which Major Eddy was killed, Sir A. Conan Doyle states: "about 100 Australians made a gallant attack on the Boers, who had surrounded a kopje, on which was a party of the 2nd Wiltshire Regt. They relieved the pressure, but at a loss of six officers out of seven, with a large proportion of men. Major Eddy was among the officers who fell." He was mentioned in despatches by F.-M. Earl Roberts, L.G., April 16th, 1901.

Edmonds.—Lieut. Nicholas Gifford Edmonds, 2nd Batt. Royal Highlanders, was killed in action at Magersfontein, Dec. 11th, 1899. He was the son of W. Edmonds, Esq., of Wiscome Park, Colyton, was born Dec., 1872, and educated at Wellington, where he was in Saunders' House, 1887-90. He joined the Royal Highlanders, from the Royal Military College, Oct., 1893, being promoted lieut. May, 1898. He embarked for South Africa with his battalion in Oct., 1899.

Egerton.—Lieut. Frederick Greville Egerton, R.N., H.M.S. "Powerful," died Nov. 2nd, 1899, from wounds received the same day at Ladysmith. He was the son of the late Admiral the Hon. Francis Egerton, of Weybridge, M.P. for East Derbyshire, 1866-68, and was a nephew of the Duke of Devonshire, and of the first Earl of Ellesmere; was 31 years of age, a good sportsman and excellent cricketer. He was promoted lieut. 1891, and in 1897, was appointed Gunnery Officer to H.M.S. "Powerful." The day he was mortally wounded the first 4·7 naval gun had been mounted on Junction Hill, and early in the morning fired her first shot at Long Tom on Pepworth, some 6,500 yards off. The fire of the latter was terribly accurate. A flash was seen and all who could be spared were ordered under cover, Lieut. Egerton and two or three of the gun's crew remaining inside the sandbag parapet. The shell crashed through the embrasure and struck him in the legs. All that was possible was done for him by the medical officer, and then the bluejackets tenderly picked him up. "This will put a stop to my cricket, I'm afraid," was his only remark, and on the way to hospital he stopped his bearers to get a light for his cigarette. His wounds necessitated both legs being amputated, and at first it was hoped that he would have survived; but he died the same evening. He was advanced to the rank of commander for his services, but did not live to hear of his promotion. Lieut. Egerton is buried in the cemetery at Ladysmith. (*See Lieut. Brabant.*)

Elkington.—Lieut. George Edward Elkington, 1st Division Telegraph Batt. Royal Engineers, died of enteric in South Africa, Jan. 12th, 1901. He was the fourth son of the late Lieut.-Gen. Elkington, C.B., and Mrs. Elkington, of Sonning, Berks. Lieut. Elkington was born in January, 1871, and educated at Elizabeth College, Guernsey. He entered the Royal Engineers Feburary, 1890, and was promoted lieut. February, 1893. He served with the Dongola Expeditionary Force, under Lord (then Sir Herbert) Kitchener, in 1896, including the engagement at Firket, and the operations at Hafir, being mentioned in despatches, L.G., Nov. 3rd, 1896, and was awarded the Fourth Class of the Order of the Medjidie, the medal, and the Egyptian medal with clasp. He embarked for South Africa in June, 1900, and served there up to the time of his death.

Elliott.—Civil-Surgeon Albert Ernest Elliott, M.A., died of enteric at Middelburg, Dec. 1st, 1900. He was the youngest son of T. Elliott, Esq., of Bassett Mount, Southampton, was 31 years of age, and educated at Cheltenham, and St. John's College, Cambridge. He got his "blue" for Rugby football in 1891, and his International cap for England in 1894. After leaving Cambridge, he pursued his studies at St. Thomas's Hospital, taking the diplomas of M.R.C.S. and L.R.C.P., in 1898, and was for some time Resident Medical Officer at Queen Charlotte's Lying-in-Hospital. At the outbreak of the war, he was one of the first to offer his services, and at the end of 1899 was sent to Natal, where he was attached to No. 4 Field Hospital. He moved with the hospital to Spearman's Farm, and was there during the battles of Spion Kop and Vaal Kranz, then back to Chieveley, and afterwards on to Ladysmith. Sir F. Treves wrote concerning him: "He was an admirable surgeon, and if I saw a figure going round the tents at unusual hours of the night, I knew it was Elliott. The soldiers were much attached to him, and he to them." He was in medical charge of the 21st, 42nd, and 53rd Batteries at the time of his death. On Nov. 13th, he went out for a five days march, although he had been ill and in hospital for the previous fortnight. He insisted however that he was perfectly well, and went with the column, only to get a relapse, from which he died on Dec. 1st. He was mentioned in despatches for his services. Surgeon Elliott, who was unmarried, is buried in Middelburg cemetery, and a cross is erected over his grave. His name is inscribed on the Eleanor Cross War Memorial at Cheltenham College.

Elliott.—Captain Herbert W. Drummond Elliott, South African Irregular Forces, was killed near Ugie Nov. 21st, 1901, whilst leading an attack on the Boers under Bezuidenhout at Gatberg Nek. He was the son of Major Sir Henry George Elliott, Chief Magistrate of Tembuland, an old Crimean officer.

Ellis.—Lieut. Thomas Flower Ellis, Thorneycroft's M.I., was at first reported missing Jan. 24th, 1900, but it was afterwards discovered that he had been killed in action on that date at Spion Kop. He was 31 years of age, and was educated at Sherborne. At Spion Kop he was close to Capt. Saunders-Knox-Gore, who also fell in this action. As nearly all their men had been either killed or wounded, these two officers, standing amidst the bodies of their comrades, were firing with the rifles of the men who had been struck down. Several times the Boers advanced but had been driven back, and at last Lieut. Ellis fell. It is thought that he had no identification card with him, hence the delay which at first took place in reporting his death.

Ellison.—Capt. George Paget Ellison, 9th Lancers, died of enteric at Kroonstad April 7th, 1900. He was the second son of Col. R. G. Ellison, of Boultham Hall, Lincolnshire, and younger brother of Capt. R. T. Ellison, 2nd Life Guards. Capt. G. P. Ellison was born in Dec., 1868, and educated at Marlborough. He entered the 9th Lancers Aug., 1888, being promoted lieut. Jan. 1890, and capt. Dec., 1895. He served as A.D.C. to Major-Gen. Hon. Sir R. A. J. Talbot at Aldershot from May, 1896, and went in the same capacity to Egypt Jan., 1899, but gave up his appointment at the commencement of the war in order to go on active service. His name is inscribed on a tablet which has been erected in Marlborough College Chapel in memory of all Marlburians who fell in the war.

Elsworth.—Lieut. A. Elsworth, New South Wales M.I., was killed in action during the war.

Elton.—Capt. Erle Godfrey Elton, 2nd Batt. Royal Highlanders, was killed in action at Magersfontein Dec. 11th, 1899. He was a son of Col. F. C. Elton, R.A. Capt. Elton was born June, 1869, and educated at Wellington, where he was in the "Hill" 1882-86. He entered the R.M.C., Sandhurst, in the latter year, and joined his regiment in Aug., 1888, was promoted lieut. Aug., 1890, and capt. July, 1898. He embarked with his battalion for South Africa in Oct., 1899.

Elworthy.—Capt. Charles Kershaw Elworthy, 6th Dragoon Guards (Carabiniers), was killed in action at Zand River May 10th, 1900. He was the elder son of Charles James Elworthy, Esq., of Wellington, Somerset, was born Sept., 1865, and educated at Clifton College. He entered the Carabiniers Jan., 1889, being promoted capt. Sept., 1895, and at the time of his death was the senior of his rank in his regiment. In the engagement at Zand River he was with a detached party of cavalry which was suddenly attacked by a strong force of the enemy, and in the severe fighting which ensued Capt. Elworthy was killed.

Ely.—Lieut. Thomas Butler Ely, 2nd Batt. Royal Dublin Fusiliers, died of enteric on board the S.S. "Orcana," at sea, April 15th, 1900. He was the only son of Major-Gen. Ely, and was born Sept., 1875, educated at Brighton, entered the Royal Dublin Fusiliers Dec., 1897, and was promoted lieut. Oct., 1899. He was present at the battle of Talana Hill, where he took command of his company, as his captain was killed. He then took part in the retirement on Ladysmith, and went south with his battalion before the investment of that town was complete. He was then present at all the battles and actions on the Tugela, in which his battalion took part, and entered Ladysmith with the relieving force. He afterwards contracted enteric, was invalided, and died as stated.

Engelbach.—Civil Surgeon Engelbach was killed in action in 1900, during the first part of the war. He was mentioned in despatches by F.-M. Earl Roberts, L.G., Sept. 10th, 1901, for his services.

Englebach. — Capt. Francis Joyce Englebach, 1st Batt. East Kent Regt. (The Buffs), was killed in action near Bothaville, Nov. 6th, 1900. He was born Oct., 1867, and served in the ranks for nearly eight years, gaining his commission in The Buffs June, 1894, being promoted lieut. May, 1897, and capt. April, 1900. He served throughout the operations of the Chitral Relief Force, under Sir Robert Low, 1895, with the 1st Batt. The Buffs, receiving the medal with clasp. He also saw service in the operations on the Niger in 1897-98, including the expedition to Siam, and received the medal with clasp. He was mentioned in despatches, L.G., Sept. 10th, 1901, for his services in South Africa.

England.—Capt. Alick Thornber England, p.s.c., 1st Batt. Derbyshire Regt. (Sherwood Foresters), died at Sterkstroom of enteric, Feb. 24th, 1900. He was born on March 9th, 1869, educated at Bedford Grammar School, and entered the Derbyshire Regt. Aug. 23rd,

1888, being promoted lieut. July, 1890, and capt. July, 1895. He graduated at the Staff College in Dec., 1899, and proceeding immediately after to South Africa, served in the north of Cape Colony.

Erskine.—Capt. W. C. C. Erskine, Field Intelligence Department (attached to 16th Brigade Staff, late Bethune's M.I.), was killed in action near Fouriesberg Oct. 7th, 1901. He was a Fellow of the Royal Colonial Institute, and his name is inscribed on a memorial tablet in the Hall of the building in Northumberland Avenue, W.C.

Erskine-Flower.—Lieut. Henry Noel Clare Erskine-Flower, Scottish Horse, died at Rustenburg Military Hospital Nov. 22nd, 1901, of wounds received in action at Moedwill (seven miles east of Magota Nek), Rustenburg, Sept. 30th. He was the only son of the Rev. H. H. Flower, rector of St. Columba's Episcopal Church, Edinburgh, and grandson of the late Col. H. Knight-Erskine, of Pittodrie, Aberdeenshire. Lieut. Erskine-Flower, who was 20 years of age, enlisted in Jan., 1900, as a trooper in Lord Lovat's Corps of Highland Scouts, and proceeded with them to South Africa. He was first wounded in July of that year, and after being four months in hospital at Deelfontein was invalided home. On recovering, he received a commission in the Duke of Edinburgh's Own (Edinburgh Artillery Militia), and in June, 1901, again proceeded to South Africa, being attached to the Scottish Horse, with which he served until again wounded. He is buried at Rustenburg.

Ethelston.—Commander Alfred Peel Ethelston, R.N., H.M.S. "Powerful," was killed in action at Graspan, Nov. 25th, 1899, in the splendid advance made by the Naval Brigade. He was the son of R. P. Ethelston, Esq., of

Hinton, Salop. Commander Ethelston entered the Royal Navy as a cadet in July, 1875, was promoted sub-lieut. Dec., 1882, lieut. Feb., 1885, and commander Jan., 1897. As a sub-lieut. of H.M.S. "Helicon," he had served during the Naval and Military operations in the Eastern Soudan, at Suakin, in 1884-85, and was awarded the medal and bronze star. At the battle of Graspan Commander Ethelston was in command of the sailors of the Naval Brigade serving with the Kimberley Relief Force. Sir A. Conan Doyle thus describes the action of the Naval Brigade: "the losses in that rapid rush were terrible, yet they swarmed up, their gallant officers, some of them little boy middies, cheering them on." Ethelston, the commander of the "Powerful," was struck down. Plumbe and Senior of the Marines were killed. "Little Huddart, the middy, died a death which is worth many inglorious years." Out of a total of 190 killed and wounded at Graspan, it is stated that no fewer than 105 fell to the Naval Brigade. Commander Ethelston is buried close to Enslin Station, a little east of the siding there, beside Major Plumbe and Capt. Senior. (*See Major Plumbe.*)

Eustace.—Capt. Alexander Rowland Eustace, 2nd Batt. East Kent Regt. (The Buffs), was killed in action at Driefontein, March 16th, 1900. He was born Aug., 1859, educated at Brighton College and Eton (Mr. Vidal's), and joined the Buffs from the 2nd Brigade Scottish Division Royal Artillery July, 1882, being promoted capt. March, 1893. Capt. Eustace embarked with his battalion (which formed part of the 6th Division) for South Africa in Dec., 1899, and was present at the Battle of Paardeberg. His death is mentioned in the despatch of F.-M. Earl Roberts, from Bloemfontein, March 15th, 1900.

Evans.—Lieut. Ernest C. Evans, Jannenville District

Mounted Troops (late 2nd Tasmanian M.I.), died at Klipplaat, during the war.

Evans.—Lieut.-Col. R. W. Evans, Natal Volunteer Composite Regt., was killed in action at Llangelegen, near Vryheid, Feb. 19th, 1902. He served in the Natal Mounted Rifles and was mentioned in despatches, L.G., July 29th, 1902, for his services. Lieut.-Col. Evans is buried at Durban.

Evans-Freke.—Lieut. the Hon. Cecil Montague Evans-Freke, 16th Lancers, died June 15th, 1900, of wounds received on the 2nd *idem* in action near Orange Grove, South Africa. He was the youngest son of the eighth Lord Carbery and Victoria Lady Carbery, of Glaston House, Uppingham, and was an uncle of the present peer. Lieut. Evans-Freke was born in Sept., 1876, and educated at Eton (Mr. Vaughan's). He entered the 16th Lancers from the Royal Military College, April, 1897, being promoted lieut. Oct., 1899. Lieut. Evans-Freke proceeded to South Africa in Feb., 1900, and was present at the relief of Kimberley, the battle of Paardeberg, and the advance on Bloemfontein. A tablet has been erected at Glaston in his memory by his brother officers.

Eykyn.—Capt. Cecil Eykyn, 2nd Batt. Royal Highlanders, died Feb. 8th, 1900, of wounds received in action at Koodoosberg on the previous day. He was a son of the late Thomas Eykyn, Esq., 47, Hyde Park Gate, was born June, 1867, and educated at Harrow. He entered the Royal Highlanders from the 3rd Batt. King's Own Yorkshire Light Infantry July, 1889, being promoted lieut. Jan., 1891, and capt. Nov., 1898. He had served with his battalion in the Kimberley Relief Column, and was present at the battle of Magersfontein.

Eyre.—Lieut. C. G. Eyre, 10th Batt. I.Y., was killed in action near Sterkfontein, Nov. 15th, 1901. He was educated at Winchester, and joined the I.Y. Jan., 1901, with the rank of lieut. in the army. He had previously served in the Royal Scots Fusiliers, and when gazetted to the I.Y. was sergt.-major of the 5th New Zealand Contingent.

Falcon.—Lieut. Guy Falcon, Roberts' Horse, was treacherously shot dead in Cape Colony on Oct. 16th, 1901. He was educated at St. Bee's School.

Fane.—Capt. Ralph Nevile Fane, 4th Batt. North Staffordshire Regt., died of pneumonia at Wynberg, Cape Colony May 27th, 1900. He was the younger son of Col. Francis Fane, of Fulbeck, was 30 years of age, and educated at Wellington where he was in the Blucher 1884-86. He was appointed lieut. 1889, and promoted capt. 1894. His battalion was embodied Jan., 1900, and Capt. Fane volunteering for active service, proceeded with it to South Africa in March, and served with it till his death.

Farmer.—2nd Lieut. J. C. Farmer, Royal Welsh Fusiliers, died of wounds received in action at Buffelshoek Oct. 22nd, 1900. 2nd Lieut. Farmer who had been nominated for a commission by the authorities of universities and colleges, was gazetted to a 2nd lieutenantcy Oct. 26th, four days after his death. He had however been granted seniority in the Royal Welsh Fusiliers from May 23rd, 1900, as he had been serving in South Africa in the I.Y.

Fawssett.—Capt. Rupert Fawssett, R.A.M.C., died of dysentery at Bloemfontein May 6th, 1900. He was the third son of the late Rev. Robert Fawssett, of 36,

Crockerton Road, Upper Tooting, S.W. Capt. Fawssett was born March, 1869, and educated privately, afterwards studying at St. Thomas's Hospital. He entered the Royal Army Medical Corps in July, 1895, being promoted capt. July, 1898. From 1897, Capt. Fawssett had been attached to the 2nd Life Guards, and when the Composite Regt. of Household Cavalry was formed, he accompanied it to South Africa as Medical Officer. He was present at the relief of Kimberley and the battles of Paardeberg and Driefontein, and the capture of Cronje. He then took part in the advance on Bloemfontein where he died. His name is inscribed on a framed tablet placed in the Court House of the Spelthorne Division of Middlesex in memory of those belonging to the Division who fell in the war.

Feilden.—Major Cecil William Montague Feilden, D.S.O., 2nd Dragoons (Royal Scots Greys), died Feb. 19th, 1902, from wounds received in action at Klippan, near Springs the previous day. He was the eldest surviving son of Major-Gen. Randle Joseph Feilden, C.M.G., of Witton Park, Lancashire, and Mrs. Feilden, daughter of James Hozier, Esq., of Mauldslie Castle. Major Feilden was born Jan., 1863, educated at Eton (Mr. Wolley Dod's), and entered the 2nd Dragoons Aug., 1882, being promoted capt. Feb., 1891, and major July, 1901. He had served as A.D.C. to the Lieut.-Gen. and General Governor of Ireland almost uninterruptedly from Feb., 1891 to Oct., 1895, when he was appointed Private Secretary to the Commander-in-Chief, which post he held till Jan., 1897. He then returned to Ireland as extra A.D.C. to the Lieut.-Gen. and General Governor of Ireland, and held this position till he went to South Africa at the outbreak of the war. He saw much service during the campaign, having taken part in the relief of Kimberley and the subsequent advances on Bloemfontein and Pretoria, and was mentioned in despatches, L.G., Sept. 10th, 1901, and was awarded the D.S.O.

Fellowes.—Lieut. Navarino Bulwer Fellowes, 2nd Batt. West India Regt., was killed in the action of Roodepoort, Nov. 17th, 1901. He was a son of Col. C. M. N. Fellowes, of the Croft, Milton Kingsbridge, Devon, born June, 1874, and educated at the United Service's College, Westward Ho. Failing to pass the army examinations he enlisted in the 2nd Life Guards, and served in the ranks for seven years. He went out to South Africa with the Household Cavalry Composite Regt., and in August, 1900, being then a corporal, was nominated for a commission by the Commander-in-Chief. He was appointed 2nd lieut. in the West India Regt., August, 1900, being promoted lieut. Feb., 1901. Lieut. Fellowes was seconded in his regiment for special service. He again sailed for South Africa with the Manchester Militia M.I. (under Capt. Jackson the Arctic Explorer) in Jan., 1901. He saw much fighting during the first phase of the war, and was present at the relief of Kimberley, and the battles of Paardeberg and Diamond Hill. At Roodepoort, his force greatly outnumbered, was called on to surrender, his only reply, till he was mortally wounded, was to go on firing, his servant, Private Tierney, being killed beside him. The warrant and non-commissioned officers of the 2nd Life Guards have erected a tablet in his memory, at the Chapel in Regent's Park Barracks. His name is also inscribed on a memorial tablet at the United Services College, Westward Ho.

Fenner.—Vet.-Lieut. E. A. L. Fenner, 47th Company I.Y., died of pneumonia at Vrede, South Africa, July, 1900. Lieut. Fenner was a member of the Royal College of Veterinary Surgeons, and was appointed to the I.Y. Feb. 21st. 1900, with the rank of Vet.-lieut.

Fergusson.—Lieut. Gilbert Chas. Dalrymple Fergusson, 2nd Batt. Rifle Brigade, was killed in action in a sortie from Ladysmith Dec. 11th, 1899. He was the only surviving son of Col. J. A. Fergusson, p.s.c. (late of the Rifle Brigade), St. Philip's Lodge, Cheltenham, Professor of Tactics, Military Administration, and Law at the Royal Military College, Sandhurst, up to Aug., 1900. Lieut. Fergusson was a nephew of Sir James Fergusson, M.P., was born Aug., 1874, and educated at Marlborough, where he was in the football team, being an excellent half-back. He was also capt. of the Rifle Corps. He joined the Rifle Brigade from the Militia Sept., 1896, being promoted lieut. Dec., 1898. Lieut. Fergusson served in the Soudan campaign under Lord (then Sir Herbert) Kitchener, 1898, with the 2nd Batt. Rifle Brigade, and was present at the battle of Khartoum, receiving the British medal with clasp. He afterwards served in Crete, and was employed as Departmental Commissioner, being mentioned in despatches by Sir H. Chermside. Lieut. Fergusson accompanied his battalion to South Africa in Oct., 1899, from Crete, and served with it in Natal till his death, being present at the battle of Lombard's Kop. He is buried at Ladysmith. His name is inscribed on a tablet which has been placed in Marlborough College Chapel in memory of all Marlburians who fell in the war.

Ferns.—Lieut. R. J. Ferns, Scottish Horse, died of enteric at Durban on March 3rd, 1901.

Field.—Lieut. Henry Norman Field, 1st Batt. Devonshire Regt., was killed in action at Wagon Hill, Ladysmith, Jan. 6th, 1900. He was the third son of Mr. Justice Field, formerly of the Calcutta High Court. Lieut. Field was born in 1873, and educated at Marlborough. He entered the Devonshire Regt., 1893, being promoted lieut. July, 1896, and served in the campaign on the North-West Frontier of India, under the late Sir William Lockhart in 1897-98 with the Mohmand Field Force, as Assistant-Superintendent of Army Signalling, including the engagement at the Badmanai Pass (mentioned in despatches). He also saw service with the Tirah Expeditionary Force, including the capture of the Sampagha and Arhanga Passes, being mentioned in despatches and receiving the medal with two clasps. Lieut. Field commanded one of the companies in the ever-to-be-remembered charge, made by the Devon Regt. at Wagon Hill, which was led by Col. Park. He fell while leading his company. At the end of the fighting the three companies were commanded by colour-sergeants—Capt. Lafone being also killed—and the third officer, who is now in possession of the V.C., was severely wounded. Lieut. Field, who also distinguished himself at Elandslaagte, was mentioned in despatches by Lieut.-Gen. Sir G. White from Ladysmith, dated Dec. 2nd, 1899, also in the despatch of March 23rd, 1900, L.G., Feb. 8th, 1901. His name is inscribed on a tablet placed in Marlborough College Chapel in memory of all Marlburians who fell in the war.

Field.— Capt. Percy Neville Field, Scottish Horse, was killed at Doornlaagte March 2nd, 1902. He was a son of J. B. Field, Esq., of Worthing, and enlisted at the beginning of the South African war as a trooper in the Natal Mounted Rifles, and after fighting at Elandslaagte, was in Ladysmith throughout the siege. He carried off a wounded officer under fire at Lombard's Kop, assisted in the destruction of the Boer Guns on Gun Hill, and was severely wounded in the Wagon Hill engagement. On recovering, he was given a commission, and, entering the Scottish Horse as a subaltern, was afterwards promoted to the rank of capt. After his promotion he was seriously wounded on three occasions. At Moedwill, Sept. 30th, 1901, he was shot through the jaw, and came to England as a convalescent in Dec., but returned the following January with a draft of Lovat's Scouts. He was twice mentioned in despatches for his "good services," L.G., Aug. 20th, and Dec. 3rd, 1901.

Fife.—Lieut. Hugh Wharton Fife, Duke of Cornwall's Light Infantry, was killed in action at Johannesburg May 30th, 1900, when serving with Sir Ian Hamilton's division. He was born Dec., 1870, and educated at Bradfield College, 1886-90, where he was in the cricket and football teams. He afterwards went to Cambridge University, and entered the Royal Military College, Sandhurst, as a University Candidate 1891, passing first on that list, and received his commission as 2nd lieut. April, 1893, being promoted lieut. Aug. 1896. In South Africa he first served with the Kimberley Relief Force and was wounded at Graspan. He was afterwards present at Paardeberg, and the advance on Bloemfontein and Johannesburg.

Finch.—Lieut. Edward Harlee Finch, 2nd Batt. Royal Scots Fusiliers, was killed at Frederickstad Oct. 21st, 1900. He was the third son of Henry Finch, Esq., Ashurstwood, East Grinstead, Sussex, was born May, 1876, and educated at Haileybury. Lieut. Finch was appointed to the Lancashire Fusiliers Sept. 5th, 1896, and transferred to the Royal Scots Fusiliers the same month, being promoted lieut. Dec., 1898. He was assistant-adjutant of his battalion, and had served with the Natal Field Force and in the subsequent advance into the Transvaal. He was working his maxim gun when killed.

Finlay.—2nd Lieut. Francis Henry John Finlay, 1st

Batt. Leinster Regt. (Royal Canadians), died of dysentery, at Vrede, Dec. 11th, 1900. He was born Jan., 1879, educated at Cheltenham, and entered the 5th Batt. Royal Dublin Fusiliers 1897, being promoted capt. in Dec. 1899. This rank, however, he resigned in order to join the regular army and proceed to South Africa. He was then granted a commission in the Leinster Regt. April 4th, 1900, and joined the first battalion, with which he served till his death. His name is inscribed on the Eleanor Cross War Memorial erected at Cheltenham College.

Firth.—Lieut. Francis Spencer Firth, 2nd Batt. East Kent Regt. (The Buffs), died of enteric June 1st, 1900, at Bloemfontein. He was born Sept., 1879, educated at Malvern College, and entered the Buffs Aug. 1899. He embarked with his battalion for South Africa in Dec., 1899, and served with the Division. He was present at Klip Drift, the battle of Paardeberg, and the advance on Bloemfontein.

Fisher.—Capt. Arthur Alexander Fisher (retired pay), late Prince of Wales's Own West Yorkshire Regt., died March 12th, 1902. He was the second son of Herbert W. Fisher, Esq., 19, Second Avenue, Hove; was born Aug., 1866, educated at Winchester, and entered the West Yorkshire Regt. Sept., 1887, was promoted lieut. 1889, capt. in 1895, and retired in Aug., 1901. Capt. Fisher served with the Dongola Expeditionary Force, under Lord (then Sir Herbert) Kitchener, 1896, receiving the Egyptian medal; also in Uganda 1898, receiving the medal with two clasps. From May, 1900, he served as a Special Service Officer with the Rhodesian Field Force in the South African Campaign, and was awarded the medal with two clasps.

Fisher.—Capt. John Francis Fisher, Royal Garrison Artillery, died of wounds received in action near Villiersdorp, Nov. 20th, 1901. He was the eldest son of John Fisher, Esq., of St. Edith's, Wiltshire, was born in June, 1868, and educated at Winchester. He entered the Royal Artillery July, 1887, was promoted lieut. July, 1890, and capt. April, 1898. Capt. Fisher served in the campaign on the North-West Frontier of India, 1897-98, under the late Sir William Lockhart, with the Tirah Expeditionary Force, receiving the medal with two clasps. He had been serving in South Africa on special service from Nov., 1899, and at the time of his death held the local rank of major, whilst commanding the 2nd Batt. Railway Pioneer Regt. His working party of Pioneers was suddenly attacked, and Capt. Fisher was mortally wounded.

Fitzgerald.—Capt. C. H. Fitzgerald, 67th Company I.Y., died Jan. 20th, 1902, of wounds received in action three days previously at Driekuyl, Bezuidenhoutskraal. He had served with the I.Y. throughout the war, and was promoted lieut. from corporal in June, 1900, and capt. Nov., 1901. He was mentioned in despatches, L.G., Sept. 10th, 1901, for his services. His name is engraved on a Latten Brass placed in St. Paul's Cathedral in memory of all ranks belonging to the 18th, 21st, and 23rd Battalions I.Y., who fell in the war.

Fitz-Herbert.—Capt. Henry Fitz-Herbert, Reserve of Officers, late Royal Berkshire Regt., died Jan. 11th, 1901, of wounds received in action at Murraysburg. He was the eldest son of the late John Knight Fitz-Herbert, Esq., of Twynham, Bournemouth. He was born June, 1862, and educated at Wellington, where he was in the Anglesey, 1876-79. He entered the Royal Berkshire Regt. from the Royal Military College May, 1882, and was promoted capt. April, 1891. Capt. Fitz-Herbert served throughout the campaign in the Eastern Soudan of 1885 with the first battalion of his regiment, and was present in the reconnaissance to Hasheen Feb. 1st, in the engagements at Hasheen and Tofrek, and the operations at, and destruction of, Tamai. For these services he was awarded the medal with two clasps and the bronze star. He also served in 1885-86 with the Soudan Frontier Field Force. In South Africa he was present at the battle of Colenso, but was captured by the Boers. On the arrival of F.-M. Earl Roberts in Pretoria Capt. Fitz-Herbert was liberated, and was again in action the very day of his release. He then continued to serve in the war until killed, and was present at many actions.

Fitz-Hugh.—Civil Surgeon R. T. Fitz-Hugh, died at Deelfontein of enteric June 15th, 1900. He was 28 years of age, educated at Shrewsbury School, and when there was in the eleven for both cricket and football. (*See Capt. Moor.*)

Fletcher.—2nd Lieut. Arthur Charles Septimus Fletcher, 1st Batt. Royal Irish Regt., died of enteric at Bloemfontein May 24th, 1900. He was 20 years of age, and entered the Royal Irish Regt. from the Royal Military College Jan., 1900, only four months before his death. He proceeded to South Africa in Feb., and joined the first battalion of his regiment, but contracted enteric a few weeks after arrival.

Fletcher.—Major Edward Walter Fletcher, 1st Batt. Northumberland Fusiliers, was killed in action at Lichtenburg March 3rd, 1901. He was the eldest son of the late Col. H. C. Fletcher, C.M.G., Scots Guards, by his marriage with Lady Harriet Marsham, 2nd daughter of Charles, 3rd Earl of Romney. He was born Jan., 1865,

OFFICERS WHO FELL IN SOUTH AFRICA. 125

educated at Cheltenham, and entered the Essex Regt. from the 3rd Batt. Royal Scots May, 1885, was transferred to the Northumberland Fusiliers as lieut. July, 1885, being promoted capt. Dec., 1892, and major July, 1900. He served with the 2nd Batt. Northumberland Fusiliers throughout the Hazara Campaign 1888, receiving the medal with clasp, and was A.D.C. (extra) to the Viceroy of India Aug. to Sept., 1888. Major Fletcher served in South Africa from the commencement of the war, and was present at the action at Stormberg Dec. 10th, 1899. After Pretoria was entered by F.-M. Earl Roberts, Major Fletcher commanded a post at Vereeniging, and subsequently joined his battalion at Lichtenburg, where he fell in the attack on that place by De La Rey. His name is inscribed in the Eleanor Cross War Memorial erected at Cheltenham College.

Fletcher.—2nd Lieut. Walter John Cumberlege Fletcher, 1st Batt. Loyal North Lancashire Regt., died at Kimberley, Oct. 18th, 1899. He was born Nov. 26th, 1879, educated at Tonbridge School, and entered his regiment from the Militia May, 1899. He then joined the 1st battalion in Capetown, and proceeded to Kimberley in October with the wing of his battalion, which was sent there to assist in holding the town. He was the first officer to die during the war.

Flower.—Lieut. Richard Fordham Flower, 2nd Batt. I.Y., was killed in action at Haman's Kraal, Aug. 20th, 1900. He was educated at Eton (Mr. Luxmoore's). Lieut. Flower, who was a 2nd lieut. in the Warwickshire Yeomanry Cavalry, entered the I.Y. Feb. 7th, 1900, with the rank of lieut. in the army, and proceeded to South Africa with the Warwickshire Company of the second battalion.

Forbes.—Lieut. Archibald Jones Forbes, D.S.O., 2nd Batt. South Wales Borderers, died of dysentery at Pretoria, May 13th, 1901. He was born Jan., 1873, and entered the South Wales Borderers, May, 1893, being promoted lieut. Nov., 1895. He was fond of games and a good cricketer. He served in the operations in the Niger Territories, 1898, including the Benin Hinterland and Siama Expeditions, being mentioned in despatches, and receiving the D.S.O., and medal with clasp. He accompanied his battalion to South Africa in Jan., 1900, and was present with the 7th Division in the advance on Bloemfontein and Pretoria. He was mentioned in despatches, L.G., Sept. 10th, 1901.

Forbes.—Capt. Dudley Henry Forbes, 3rd Batt. Royal Scots, died of enteric at Kroonstad, April 21st, 1901. He was the son of William Forbes, Esq., of Callander, was 28 years of age, and educated at Eton (Mr. James'). He had been promoted capt. in the 3rd Batt. Royal Scots, May, 1897. Capt. Forbes's battalion was embodied in Dec., 1899, and, volunteering for active service, he proceeded with it to South Africa, March, 1900. He then served in the Cape and Orange River Colonies and was appointed commandant at Roodeval Spruit.

Forbes-Leith.—2nd Lieut. Percy Forbes Forbes-Leith, 1st (Royal) Dragoons, died Dec., 31st, 1900, at Newcastle, Natal, from a relapse after enteric. He was the only son of A. J. Forbes-Leith, Esq., Fyvie Castle, Aberdeenshire, N.B. 2nd Lieut. Forbes-Leith was born March, 1881, and educated at Eton (Mr. Rawlins'). He entered the 1st Dragoons Feb., 1900.

Ford.—2nd Lieut. Reginald Ford, Army Service Corps, died of enteric at Ventersdorp, May 27th, 1901. He was elder son of Lieut.-Col. A. E. Ford, formerly of the North Somerset Yeomanry, and grandson of the late James Ford, Esq., of Bristol, was 21 years of age, and educated at the United Services College, Westward Ho. He joined the I.Y. in 1900, and obtained his commission in the Army Service Corps, March, 1901. His name is inscribed on a tablet erected at the United Services College, Westward Ho in memory of the old pupils who fell in the war.

Ford.—Lieut. F. C. M. Ford, D.S.O., Reserve of Officers, was killed in action at Moolmeisjesfontein, Oct. 17th, 1901. He was a major in the South African Constabulary, and had formerly served in the Durham Light Infantry, in which he was promoted lieut. Oct., 1897.

Fordyce-Buchan.—Capt. George Charles Fordyce-Buchan, 65th Battery Royal Field Artillery, died of enteric at Bloemfontein, May 21st, 1900. He was born in Aug., 1867, educated at Eton (Mr. Everard's), and entered the Royal Artillery, Feb., 1887, was promoted lieut. Feb., 1890, and capt. Sept., 1897. He accompanied the 65th Battery to South Africa in Nov., 1899, and served with it in the advance on Bloemfontein.

Forrest.—Lieut. A. A. Forrest, West Australian M.I., was killed at Brakpan, Eastern Transvaal, May 16th, 1901. He was mentioned in the despatch of Gen. Lord Kitchener, July 28th, 1901, for "conspicuous gallantry," and his services were brought to the notice of the Australian Government.

Forrester.—Surgeon-Lieut.-Col. James Stevenson Forrester, Royal Horse Guards, F.R.C.S.Edin., died of enteric on board S.S. "Dunera" between Durban and Capetown on June 18th, 1900. He was born Oct., 1852, educated at the Edinburgh Academy, and joined the

Army Medical Service as surgeon in 1874, being promoted surgeon-lieut.-col. 1894. He served in the Egyptian War 1882, and was present at the actions at Kassassin, receiving the medal with clasp and the Khedive's star. He went to South Africa in Jan., 1900, and was in charge of Princess Christian's Hospital in Natal. Lieut.-Col. Forrester is buried in the military cemetery at Woodstock.

Forrester.—2nd Lieut. Ralph Forrester, 1st Batt. East Lancashire Regt., died of enteric June 6th, 1900, at Bloemfontein. He was born in July, 1877, educated at Harrow, and entered the East Lancashire Regt. from the 4th Batt. East Surrey Regt. Jan., 1899. He proceeded to South Africa in Jan., 1900, and served in the advance on Bloemfontein.

Forster.—Lieut. G. B. Forster, 2nd New South Wales M.I., was killed in action near Bethel Dec. 8th, 1901.

Forster.—Lieut. John Lindsey Forster, 2nd Batt. King's Royal Rifle Corps, was killed in action at Farquhar's Farm, near Ladysmith, Oct. 30th, 1899. He was the eldest son of P. F. Forster, Esq., of Malverley, East Woodhays, Hants, by his marriage with Annie Mary, daughter of J. Lindsey, Esq., late 2nd Life Guards, was born March, 1877, educated at Eton (Mr. Ainger's), and entered the King's Royal Rifle Corps in April, 1897, being promoted lieut. April, 1899. On the outbreak of war, Lieut. Forster was serving with his battalion in Ladysmith, and fell in his first battle.

Forsythe.—Lieut. William George Forsythe, 7th New Zealand M.I., was killed in action at Langverwacht, near Klip River, Feb. 24th, 1902. (*For some particulars regarding this action in which Lieut. Forsythe fell, see Lieut. Dickinson.*)

Fort.—Civil Surgeon Percy Reginald Fort, died of enteric on Feb. 18th, 1902. He was the youngest son of James Fort, Esq., formerly of the 5th Dragoon Guards, was born in 1874, and educated at Merchant Taylors' School. He entered St. Mary's Hospital 1895, and qualified as M.R.C.S. and L.R.C.P. in 1900. He then served as medical officer at York Dispensary, and while holding that position offered his services to the military authorities. He proceeded to South Africa in July, 1901, in the Hospital Ship "Simla," in which he did duty for three voyages. He was then appointed to the 8th M.I., and served with Col. Rawlinson's column; and whilst employed at Ermelo he contracted enteric and died afterwards at Standerton.

Fortescue.—Major the Hon. Lionel Henry Dudley Fortescue, 17th Lancers, was killed in action at Diamond Hill, near Pretoria, June 11th, 1900. He was the third son of the present Earl Fortescue, was born Nov., 1857, and educated at Harrow. He entered the 5th Dragoon Guards Nov., 1876, transferred to the 17th Lancers, Aug., 1877, was promoted lieut. Nov., 1878, capt. Nov., 1886, and major Jan., 1896. He was adjutant of his regiment Dec., 1879 to Feb., 1885, and served with the 17th Lancers in the Zulu War of 1879, was present at the engagement at Ulundi, receiving the medal with clasp. Major Fortescue was A.D.C. to the Major-Gen. commanding the Cavalry Brigade at Aldershot, Feb., 1885, to Dec., 1889, and Commandant School of Instruction, Yeomanry and Volunteer Cavalry, Aldershot, Jan., 1895, to Dec., 1896. He was appointed Assistant Military Secretary, and A.D.C. to Lieut.-Gen. Lord William Seymour, commanding the troops in Canada, June 1898, but resigned his appointment in Nov., 1899, and proceeded to South Africa with his

K

regiment Feb., 1900. He then served in the O.R.C. and in the advance on Pretoria.

Fosbery.—Capt. Francis Langford Fosbery, Royal Irish Regt., was killed in action near Belfast, Jan. 7th, 1901. He was the son of the late Mr. G. L. Fosbery and Mrs. Fosbery, of Bryn Elwy, St. Asaph, was born April, 1870, and educated at Haileybury. He entered the Royal Irish Regt. March, 1891, was promoted lieut. Jan., 1892, capt. Oct., 1899, and served in the operations on the North-West Frontier of India, 1897-98, and on the Samana, receiving the medal with two clasps. Capt. Fosbery fell while in command of a post outside Belfast, consisting of 83 men of his regiment. One of these, Private Barry, was riddled with bullets while heroically destroying a maxim gun with a pick axe. An account of this Boer attack, and Capt. Fosbery's death, is given in Gen. Ben Viljeon's book "My Reminiscences of the Anglo-Boer War." A hand to hand fight took place, and Capt. Fosbery and half his garrison were killed or wounded.

Foskett.—The Rev. C. Foskett, Acting Chaplain, died of enteric at Winburg, O.R.C., during the war.

Foster.—Capt. William Herbert Foster, Army Service Corps, died at Claremont Sanatorium, Feb. 18th, 1900. He was born Nov. 12th, 1868, and educated at Shrewsbury School, where he played in the cricket XI. He entered the Royal Marines Sept. 1st, 1888, was promoted lieut. Sept., 1889, transferred to the Army Service Corps Jan., 1893, being promoted capt. July, 1896. He embarked for South Africa in Oct., 1899, and served in Cape Colony. (*See Capt Moor.*)

Foulerton.—Major Alexander Francis Grant Foulerton, 1st Batt. Leinster Regt., died at Vrede Jan. 5th, 1901. He was born March, 1859, and educated at

Trinity College, Glenalmond. He entered the 109th Foot from the Royal Aberdeenshire Highlanders Militia, Oct., 1880, being promoted lieut. July, 1881, capt. Sept., 1886, and major March, 1896. Major Foulerton served in the Sikkim Expedition, 1888, when he was in charge of the signallers, and received the medal with clasp. He was adjutant of Militia April, 1895, to April, 1900, when he was appointed second-in-command of his battalion, and joined it in South Africa, serving with it up to the time of his death.

Fowler.—Lieut. Robert Nesbitt Fowler, 16th Lancers, died Feb. 26th, 1902, near Calvinia, of wounds received in action the previous day. He was the second son of the late R. D. Fowler, Esq., of Liverpool, and of Mrs. Fowler, Bentley, Hampshire. He was born March, 1875, educated at Leys School, Cambridge, and Brasenose College, Oxford, where he took his B.A. degree in 1897. He entered the 16th Lancers from the 4th Batt. Argyll and Sutherland Highlanders, Jan., 1899, being promoted lieut. the following October. Lieut. Fowler went to South Africa with his regiment in Feb., 1900, and saw much service during the war. He was at one time Transport Officer to a column, and was mentioned in despatches by Lieut.-Gen. Lord Kitchener, March 8th, 1902, for " gallantry in bringing in a dismounted man under heavy and close fire, Dec. 22nd, 1901." A relief bronze and oak tablet has been erected to his memory in Brasenose College, Oxford, by his brother officers.

Fowler.—Capt. Sir Thomas Fowler, 1st Batt. I.Y., was killed in action at Olivier's Farm, Moolman's Spruit, near Ficksburg, April 20th, 1902. He was the son of Sir Robert Fowler, the first baronet, of Gastard, who was Lord Mayor of London 1883-84, and for many years a member of the House of Commons. Sir Thomas Fowler was born in 1868, educated at Harrow, and succeeded his father in 1891. He was a partner in the bank of Messrs. Prescott, Dimsdale & Co., and a lieut. for the County of London. Sir Thomas Fowler, who was a capt. in the Royal Wiltshire I.Y., was appointed lieut. Feb., 1900, and capt. the 1st Batt. I.Y., Jan., 1901, and served throughout the war. The action in which he was killed was one of the last of the campaign. Information had been received that a small party of Boers were in occupation of Olivier's Farm. Some yeomanry and mounted infantry were sent to attack them, but the enemy had apparently been informed, and were in much greater strength than was at first reported. In the attack Sir Thomas Fowler and Capt. Blackwood were killed. Sir T. Fowler was mentioned in despatches, L.G., July 18th, 1902, by Lieut.-Gen. Lord Kitchener, for his gallantry.

Francis.—Capt. Henry F. Francis, Steinaecker's Horse, was killed in action at Opisanes, North Sabie River, near Hassan Ughaz, Aug. 7th, 1901. He was mentioned in despatches, L.G., July 29th, 1902, by Lieut.-Gen. Lord Kitchener.

Fraser.—Capt. Alexander David Fraser, 19th Batt. I.Y., died of enteric at Kimberley, April 28th, 1901. He was the eldest son of Gen. the Hon. Sir David Fraser, K.C.B., of The Grange, Castleconnell, Ireland, and nephew of the seventeenth Lord Saltoun. He was born Oct., 1854, entered the 98th Foot Aug., 1876, being promoted lieut. in the Gordon Highlanders the following Oct., and capt. Dec., 1886. He afterwards joined the Reserve of Officers. He served with the 92nd Highlanders in the Afghan War, 1879-80, and was present in the engagement at Charasiah, Oct. 6th, 1879, and subsequent pursuit, the final occupation of Kabul, expedition to Maidan, the operations between Dec. 10th and 23rd, 1879, and actions of Dec. 23rd, and of Childukhtean. He accompanied Earl (then Sir Frederick) Roberts in the march from Kabul to Kandahar, and was present at the reconnaissance of Aug. 31st, and at the battle of Kandahar, receiving the medal with three clasps and bronze decoration. He also served in the Boer War, 1881, and with the Nile Expedition 1884-85, receiving for the latter the medal with clasp and Khedive's star. In March, 1900, Capt. Fraser was gazetted to the 19th Batt. of the I.Y., and proceeded to South Africa. After serving with the I.Y. he was appointed a Railway Staff Officer in the Kimberley section of the lines of communication, which post he held until his death.

Fraser.—Lieut. Eric Fraser, Lancashire Fusiliers, was killed in action at Spion Kop, in the operations on the Tugela, Jan. 24th, 1900. He was the youngest son of the late James Fraser, Esq., of Newfield, Blackheath Park, S.E. Lieut. Fraser was born Dec., 1878, and educated at Radley and Eton (College), where he gained a King's Scholarship. He entered the Lancashire Fusiliers from the Royal Military College May, 1898, and was promoted lieut. May, 1899. His gallantry at Spion Kop is reported to have been very noticeable, and during the day he is stated to have performed many acts of bravery. He fell shot through the forehead whilst assisting a wounded man of his company. Lieut. Fraser was mentioned in despatches, L.G., Feb. 8th, 1901.

Freislich.—Lieut. Freislich, 1st Grahamstown Volunteers, was killed in action near Poplars Drift, to the east of Osfontein, March 7th, 1900. He was the second son of J. G. Freislich, Esq., formerly Civil Commissioner and Resident Magistrate of George, South Africa, and was 25 years of age. This officer's death is mentioned in the despatch of F.-M. Earl Roberts March 15th, 1900, from Bloemfontein.

French.—Capt. Sampson Gough French, Royal Irish Regt., was killed in action at Gaberones, about eighty miles north of Mafeking, Feb. 12th, 1900. He was born Jan., 1870, educated at Winchester, and entered the Royal Irish Regt. March, 1891, being promoted lieut. Feb., 1892, and capt. Oct., 1899. He had previously served in the operations in South Africa 1896, with the M.I., and was wounded. Capt. French was employed on special service from Sept., 1899, with the Mafeking Relief Force under Col. Plumer.

French-Brewster.—2nd Lieut. Henry Gerald French-Brewster, King's Royal Rifle Corps, was killed in action at Spion Kop, in the operations on the Upper Tugela, Jan. 24th, 1900. He was the second son of the late R. A. French-Brewster, Esq., of Woodbrook and Cloona, Roscommon, and of Clonsilla, co. Dublin, by his marriage with Geraldine, daughter of Henry Ritchie Cooper, Esq., of Ballindallock, Stirlingshire. 2nd Lieut. French-Brewster was born in Sept., 1878, and educated at Eton (Mr. Rawlins'). He entered the King's Royal Rifle Corps from the 3rd Batt. The Queen's, Oct., 1899, and at once joining the 3rd battalion of his regiment, accompanied it to South Africa and was present at the battle of Colenso.

Freshwater.—Quartermaster and Hon. Capt. Arthur Freshwater, Royal Army Medical Corps, of 18, Broadway, West Norwood, died of enteric at Kroonstad Feb. 28th, 1902. He was born Aug., 1855, served in the ranks for nearly fifteen years, was at the War

OFFICERS WHO FELL IN SOUTH AFRICA. 135

Office for over five years, and gained his commission in the Royal Army Medical Corps July, 1894. He served in the Bechuanaland Expedition 1884-85. For his services in South Africa, Capt. Freshwater was mentioned by F.-M. Earl Roberts in his despatch of March 1st, 1902, and was granted the hon. rank of capt.

Fryer.—Lieut. Francis Lyall Fryer, Grenadier Guards, was killed in action at Belmont Nov. 23rd, 1899. He was a son of Sir F. Fryer, Rangoon, was born Aug., 1873, educated at Charterhouse, and entered the King's Own Scottish Borderers Nov., 1892. He was transferred to the Grenadier Guards Jan., 1893, and promoted lieut. March, 1897. Lieut. Fryer was adjutant of the 3rd battalion of his regiment at the time of his death, and fell while leading some of the men of his battalion. Sir H. Colville, in his report, states: "During the assault on Gun Hill, Lieut. and Adjt. Fryer, who was leading the men with extraordinary gallantry, was killed." His name is inscribed on the tablet in the War Memorial Cloister at Charterhouse.

Galbraith.—Lieut. Frederick Alexander Galbraith, 2nd Batt. Middlesex Regt., was killed in action at Spion Kop, Jan. 24th, 1900. He was born July 22nd, 1871, and educated at Marlborough. He entered the Middlesex Regt. from the Militia Dec., 1893, being promoted lieut. May, 1898. He accompanied his battalion to South Africa in Nov., 1899, and served with the Natal Field Force. His name is inscribed on a tablet placed in the Marlborough College Chapel in memory of all Marlburians who fell in the war.

Gale.—Capt. F. G. Gale, Cape Pioneer Railway Regt., was killed in action at Rhenoster June 7th, 1900.

THE "LAST POST":

Gardner.—Lieut. E. W. Gardner, 2nd Brabant's Horse, died of enteric April 5th, 1901, at Graaf Reinet. He was the third son of Major S. H. Gardner, Broomfield, Tiverton, Devon, was born May 15th, 1878, and educated at Blundell's School, Tiverton. Lieut. Gardner joined Brabant's Horse in Dec., 1899, and saw much service during the war, having been present at the actions at Wepener, Dordrecht, Stormberg and Senekal; also at Belfast, Wittebergen and Wepener. He was awarded the medal with four clasps. He is buried in Graaf Reinet cemetery. His commanding officer wrote of him as "a gallant and fearless officer and a true British gentleman."

Garvey.—2nd Lieut. Henry Wiltshire Garvey, Border Regt., was killed in action in the operations on the Upper Tugela Jan. 23rd, 1900. He was the youngest son of Toler R. Garvey, Esq., of Thornvale, King's County, Ireland, was born April, 1876, and entered the Border Regt. in Sept., 1896.

Gates.—Lieut. C. A. Gates, Cape Colony Cyclist Corps, died at Naauwpoort Nov. 22nd, 1901.

Gaussen.—Capt. Charles Louis Gaussen, 91st Company I.Y., was killed in action at Tafelkop, O.R.C., Dec. 20th, 1901. He was the eldest son of David Gaussen, Esq., of Duncote, Towcester, Northamptonshire. Capt. Gaussen was born Sept. 26th 1869, educated at Charterhouse, and entered the 18th Hussars in Oct., 1889. He was transferred to the Indian Staff Corps May, 1892, being promoted capt. in the 3rd Bengal Cavalry Oct., 1900, and joined the Reserve of Officers the following Dec. He went out to South Africa with the 23rd Batt. I.Y. in March 1901, and served with it till his death. Capt. Gaussen was killed while commanding his company which was acting as escort to some guns and which most gallantly sacrificed itself to a man. He was mentioned in despatches, L.G., April 25th, 1902. He is buried at Tafelkop. His name is engraved on a Latten Brass in St. Paul's Cathedral in memory of all ranks of the 18th, 21st and 23rd Batts. I.Y. who fell in the war; also on the tablet in the War Memorial Cloister erected at Charterhouse.

Gawne.—Lieut.-Col. James Moore Gawne, Commanding 2nd Batt. Royal Lancaster Regt., died Dec. 12th, 1900, at Vryheid, of wounds received in action the previous day. He was born July, 1854, educated at Cheltenham, and entered the 4th Foot June, 1874, was promoted lieut. June, 1875, capt. May, 1884, major June, 1893, and lieut.-col. Feb., 1900. He served in the Zulu War 1879, receiving the medal with clasp, and also with the Bechuanaland Expedition under Sir Charles Warren 1884-85. In the action in which Lieut.-Col. Gawne fell, our outposts surrounding Vryheid were suddenly attacked on a dark morning at 2.15 a.m., and a desperate fight ensued. Our troops, however, heroically held their own, and the Boers abandoned the attack towards evening, but Lieut.-Col. Gawne was killed. He is buried in Vryheid cemetery.

Geary.—Lieut. Francis Sandham Geary, Hampshire Regt., was killed in action near Thaba N'chu, April 27th, 1900. He was the second son of Lieut.-Gen. Sir H. Le G. Geary, Governor and Commander-in-Chief at Bermuda. He was born Feb., 1874, educated at the United Services College, Westward Ho, and entered the Hampshire Regt. from the Royal Military College in Oct., 1894, being promoted lieut. Aug., 1897. Before going out to South Africa, Lieut. Geary served as A.D.C. to Sir H. Le G. Geary, who was then commanding the Belfast District. Lieut. Geary was seconded in his regiment from Oct. 22nd, 1899, and served in South Africa with M.I. from the commencement of the war. His name is inscribed on a tablet erected at the United Services College, Westward Ho, in memory of old boys who fell in the war.

Genge.—2nd Lieut. Charles Jarvis Genge, 2nd Batt. Royal Dublin Fusiliers, died of wounds received in action at the battle of Talana Hill, Oct. 20th, 1899. He was the sixth son of the late R. Genge, Esq., Waterston, Dorset, and a brother of Surgeon R. E. Genge, Army Medical Staff, who was killed in 1899 by an avalanche in Kashmir. 2nd Lieut. Genge was born Sept. 22nd, 1877, and educated at Weymouth College, where he was in the school rifle team. He entered the 2nd Batt. Royal Dublin Fusiliers from the 5th Batt. in Jan., 1899, and was serving in Natal on the outbreak of the war. He fell in his first battle, and is buried at Dundee.

Gethin.—Capt. H. Gethin, Marshall's Horse (late Grahamstown Volunteers), was killed in action at Israel's Poort April 25th, 1900.

Gething.—Lieut. James Bagnall Gething, 3rd Batt. South Wales Borderers, died July 3rd, 1901, at Taungs, of injuries received through falling off his horse on the previous day. He was the son of J. E. Gething, Esq., 47, Lancaster Gate, W., was educated at Harrow, and entered his regiment Jan., 1900, being promoted lieut. Jan., 1901. Lieut. Gething volunteered for service in South Africa and proceeded there with his battalion in Feb., 1900, and served continuously up to the time of his death.

Gibson.—2nd Lieut. Lewis Henry Gibson, Highland Light Infantry, died Aug. 14th, 1900, of wounds received in action at Spitz Kop. He was born May, 1881, entered the Highland Light Infantry Feb., 1900, and joined the first battalion in South Africa. He served in the Cape and Orange River Colonies.

Gibson-Craig.—2nd Lieut. Robert James Gibson-Craig, 3rd Batt. Royal Scots, died of dysentery at Naauwpoort April 23rd, 1900. He was 17 years of age, educated at Harrow, and joined his regiment in Oct., 1899. He volunteered for active service and proceeded with his battalion to South Africa in Feb., 1900.

Gibton.—Capt. Lionel William Persse Gibton, 1st Batt. Royal Inniskilling Fusiliers, died of dysentery March 19th, 1900, at Ladysmith. He was the only surviving son of the late Major William Gibton, Kingstown, Ireland, was born Feb., 1865, and educated at Freiburg, in the Black Forest. Capt. Gibton entered the Royal Inniskilling Fusiliers in March, 1887, from the 4th Batt. Royal Irish Regt., being promoted lieut. May, 1889, and capt. Oct. 1896. In Oct., 1899, he accompanied his battalion to South Africa, and was present at the Battle of Colenso, and all the fighting on the Tugela. In the actions of the 23rd and 24th Feb. he was one of four officers of the Inniskillings who were untouched at the end of the two days fighting, and succeeded to the command of the battalion. He then entered Ladysmith with the Irish Brigade. His death made the 25th officer of the 1st Batt. Royal Inniskilling Fusiliers, who was rendered *hors de combat* during the fighting in Natal. Capt. Gibton is buried in the Town cemetery at Ladysmith beside his brother officer, 2nd Lieut. Hutton. A celtic cross of white marble marks the place, and a handsome railing encloses both graves. A marble headstone has also been erected in his memory by his comrades of all ranks.

Giddy.—Lieut. John Giddy, New England Mounted

Rifles (Cape Colonial Irregular Corps), died of enteric at
Dellidilli, Basutoland, on March 28th, 1902.

Gildea.—2nd Lieut. George Frederick Campbell Gildea,
2nd Batt. Royal Scots Fusiliers, died of enteric at Johannesburg April 18th, 1901. He was the only son of the
late Maj.-Gen. Gildea, C.B., formerly of the Royal Scots
Fusiliers, who commanded a battalion in South Africa in
1881. 2nd Lieut. Gildea was born April, 1876, and
educated at Charterhouse. He entered the 1st Lanarkshire Batt. of the Scottish Rifles May, 1896, and was
promoted lieut. May, 1899. In May, 1900, he was
granted a commission in the Royal Scots Fusiliers, and
joined the 2nd battalion in South Africa, and served with it
till his death. His name is inscribed on the tablet in the
War Memorial Cloister erected at Charterhouse.

Giles.—Major George Edward Giles, Reserve of Officers,
formerly Royal Field Artillery, died in a railway train on
his way to Capetown Dec. 19th, 1900. He was born in
1855, and educated at Cheltenham College. He entered
the Royal Artillery 1875, was promoted capt. 1884, and
was serving in South Africa with the Rhodesian Field
Force as hon. major. He served in the Kaffir War 1878
in command of two mountain guns, and was present at
the attack on the Intala Ka Udoda Bush. Major Giles
was appointed afterwards to the command of the Artillery
Troop of the Cape Mounted Riflemen, and served in the
operations against Moirosi, being present at the capture
of his stronghold. He was mentioned in despatches,
L.G., June 11th, 1878, and received the medal with clasp.
He also served in the Basuto War 1880-81. In the South
African War he was employed as a Special Service Officer.
The name of Major Giles is inscribed on the Eleanor
Cross War Memorial at Cheltenham College.

Gilliat.—Lieut. Lionel Howard Gilliat, 16th Lancers, died of enteric, at Barberton, Sept. 23rd, 1900. He was born Oct., 1880, educated at Eton (Mr. Impey's), and entered the 16th Lancers from the 5th Batt. King's Royal Rifle Corps Jan., 1900, being promoted lieut. the following July. He had served in the 5th Batt. King's Royal Rifle Corps from Oct., 1897. A tablet to his memory has been erected by his brother officers in St. Peter's Church, Eaton Square.

Gilpin.—Lieut. A. G. Gilpin, of the 3rd Contingent of Mounted Rifles (Victorian Bushmen), was killed in action at Ottoshoop, on Aug. 20th, 1900.

Girdwood.—Capt. Girdwood, Mafeking Town Guard, was killed Feb. 13th, 1900, during the siege. He was the youngest son of the late James Girdwood, Esq., J.P., of Clonaver, Belfast, and was acting as Chief Assistant to Capt. Ryan, Army Service Corps, and is stated to have rendered valuable service. Capt. Girdwood's death is mentioned in the despatch of Major-Gen. Baden-Powell from Mafeking, May 18th, 1900, L. G., Feb. 8th, 1901.

Girling.—Quartermaster and Hon. Lieut. William Walters Girling, 1st Batt. Coldstream Guards, died at sea on board the transport "Dilwara," May 22nd, 1902. He was born May, 1857, served in the ranks nearly eighteen years, and became quartermaster in the Coldstream Guards May, 1895. He took part in the Soudan Campaign 1885, receiving the medal with clasp and Khedive's star. He had seen much active service in South Africa before he was invalided home, and took part in the advance on Kimberley, including the actions at Belmont, Graspan, Modder River, and Magersfontein. He was also present with his battalion in the operations in the

O.R.C., Feb. to May, 1900, including the actions at Poplar Grove and Driefontein.

Gleeson.—Quartermaster and Hon. Lieut. Patrick John Gleeson, Army Service Corps, died Aug. 14th, 1900, at Naauwpoort. He was born Dec., 1861, and having served in the ranks nearly nineteen years, was promoted quartermaster, with the hon. rank of lieut., in March, 1900. He had served in the Zulu Campaign 1879, and was awarded the medal.

Gloster.—Capt. William Gloster, Royal Irish Regt., was killed in action at Stabbert's Nek, July 23rd, 1900. He was born April, 1863, entered the Royal Irish Regt. from the 4th Brigade South Irish Division, Royal Artillery in May, 1885, being promoted capt. Feb., 1892. He served in the Hazara expedition of 1888 with the 2nd Batt. Royal Irish Regt., including the engagement at Kotkai, being mentioned in despatches and receiving the medal with clasp. He proceeded to South Africa with his battalion in December, 1899, and served throughout the war up to his death.

Godfrey.—Lieut. H. Godfrey, Kitchener's Horse, died in London on April 1st, 1901. He had served in South Africa during the war.

Godfrey-Faussett.—Capt. Fermor Godfrey-Faussett, 2nd Batt. East Kent Regt. (The Buffs), died at Paardeberg Feb. 20th, 1900, from the effects of an accidental gunshot wound. He was born Sept., 1870, was educated at Marlborough, and entered the Buffs from the 4th Batt. Leinster Regt. Sept., 1892, being promoted lieut. July, 1895, and capt. Nov., 1899. Capt. Godfrey-Faussett embarked for South Africa with his battalion in Dec., 1899, and served with the 6th Division in the advance to

Klip Drift and Paardeberg. His name is inscribed on a tablet placed in Marlborough College Chapel in memory of all Marlburians who fell in the war.

Goff.—Lieut.-Col. Gerald Lionel Joseph Goff, Argyll and Sutherland Highlanders, of Hall Park, Hampshire, was killed in action at Magersfontein, Dec. 11th, 1899, He was the eldest surviving son of the late Joseph Goff, Esq., of Burton Grange, Herts, by his marriage with Lady Adela, daughter of the 2nd Earl of Ranfurly. Lieut.-Col. Goff was born March, 1855, and educated at Eton (Mr. Vidal's). He joined the 91st Foot from the Militia in March, 1875, was promoted capt. July, 1884, major Sept., 1892, and lieut.-col. July, 1898. He served with his battalion in the Zulu War of 1879, and was present at the action of Ginginhlovo, receiving the medal with clasp. Lieut.-Col. Goff was adjutant of volunteers from Jan., 1888, to Jan., 1893. He proceeded to South Africa in command of his battalion in Oct., 1899, served with the Kimberley Relief Force, and was present at the battle of Modder River.

Goff.—Capt. William Ernest Davis Goff, 3rd Dragoon Guards, attached Bethune's M.I., was killed in action during a reconnaissance between Blood River and Vryheid May 20th, 1900. He was born June, 1872, and educated at Wellington, where he was in Kempthorne's, 1886-1889. He entered the 3rd Dragoon Guards March, 1892, being promoted lieut. June, 1893, and capt. April, 1899. Capt. Goff was killed while leading his men in an attack on the enemy, and was mentioned in despatches, L.G., Feb. 8th, 1901, for his services.

Going.—Capt. Alexander Charles Going, King's Own Scottish Borderers, was killed in action near Brandfort March 29th, 1900. He was the third son of Alexander

Going, Esq., of Altavilla, Cahir, Ireland, was born Sept., 1866, and educated at Clifton College. Capt. Going entered the King's Own Scottish Borderers from the 4th Batt. Royal Irish Regt., in May, 1880, being promoted lieut. Dec., 1889, and capt. May, 1897. He was present at Paardeberg and in the advance on Bloemfontein. He is buried in Karee cemetery, by the side of his school friend Capt. Marter.

Goldie.—Capt. Adrian Hope Goldie, 14th Battery Royal Field Artillery, was killed in action at Colenso Dec. 15th, 1899. He was born in 1869, educated at Charterhouse, and joined the R.A. in 1889, being promoted lieut. 1892, and capt. 1899. Capt. Goldie accompanied his battery to South Africa Nov., 1899, and joined the Natal Field Force. At the battle of Colenso, what has been described as "a blizzard of lead" from rifles and automatic quick firers, was rained on the batteries, and "every gun had its litter of dead around it." Sir A. Conan Doyle thus continues: "Capt. Goldie dropped dead, so did Lieut. Schrieber. Colonel Hunt fell shot in two places. Officers and men were falling fast." . . . "One gun on the right was still served by four men who refused to leave it. They seemed to bear charmed lives"; first "one gasped and fell against the trail, and his comrade sank beside the wheel with his chin upon his breast. The third threw up his hands and pitched forward upon his face, while the survivor a grim, powder-stained figure, stood to attention looking death in the eyes until he, too, was struck down." The name of Capt. Goldie is inscribed on the tablet in the War Memorial Cloister erected at Charterhouse.

Goodwin.—Lieut. William Harold Goodwin, Royal Dublin Fusiliers (attached to the 38th Company Army Service Corps), died of pneumonia and heart failure at

Pretoria on July 8th, 1902. He was the only son of the Rev. E. H. Goodwin, senior chaplain in the Home District, and honorary chaplain to the King. Lieut Goodwin was born in Feb., 1878, and educated at the High School, Dublin, and at Trinity College. He entered the 4th Batt. Royal Dublin Fusiliers, in March, 1899, was granted a commission in the 1st battalion Feb., 1900, and was promoted lieut. Oct., 1901. He served throughout the war, and at the time of his death was a probationer for the Army Service Corps.

Gore-Booth.—2nd Lieut. Douglas Bloomfield Gore-Booth, 2nd Batt. Dorsetshire Regt., died of enteric at Mooi River, Natal, Jan. 19th, 1900. He was the eldest son of Col. James Gore-Booth, late Royal Engineers, Consulting Engineer to the Secretary for Scotland. 2nd Lieut. Gore-Booth was born Nov. 15th, 1875, and educated at Cheltenham. He entered the Dorsetshire Regt. Dec., 1897, and arrived in South Africa only a few weeks before he died. His name is inscribed on the Eleanor Cross War Memorial erected at Cheltenham College.

Gough.—Col. the Hon. George Hugh Gough, C.B., Assistant Adjutant-General to the Cavalry Division in South Africa, died March 29th, 1900, at Norval's Pont. He was the second son of the second Viscount Gough, and was born in 1852, and educated at Eton (Mr. Durnford's). Col. Gough entered the 14th Hussars Oct., 1871, was promoted capt. July, 1879, brevet-major Nov., 1882, major Dec., 1885, brevet-lieut.-col. June, 1885, and col. Dec., 1889. He served in the Boer War, 1881, first as A.D.C. to the late Sir Thomas Baker, and afterwards as A.D.C. to Sir Evelyn Wood; also in the Egyptian War of 1882 as A.D.C. to Sir Edward Hamley, commanding the Second Division, and was present at the battle of Tel-el-Kebir—where he had his horse killed—

was mentioned in despatches, L.G., Nov. 2nd, 1882, and received the brevet of major, the medal with clasp and Khedive's star, and the Fourth Class of the Order of the Medjidie. He next saw service with the Nile Expedition in 1884-85, in command of mounted infantry, was present at the action at Abu Klea (where he was severely wounded), being again mentioned in despatches, L.G., Aug. 25th, 1885, and awarded the brevet of lieut.-col. and two clasps. Col. Gough was D.A.A.G., Curragh, July 1st, 1887, to Sept. 30th, 1889; Private Secretary to the Commander-in-Chief, January 26th, 1897, to July 12th, 1898; Assistant Military Secretary, Headquarters of the Army, July 13th, 1898, to Oct. 20th, 1898, and Private Secretary to the Commander-in-Chief, Oct. 21st, 1898, to Oct. 8th, 1899, when he was appointed Assistant Adjutant-General to Lieut.-Gen. French, commanding the Cavalry Division in South Africa. Col. Gough is buried at Bloemfontein.

Graham.—Lieut. Charles Noel Andrews Graham, M.I., 3rd Batt. Northumberland Fusiliers, died Oct. 13th, 1901, at Middelburg, Transvaal, of wounds received in action near Koornfontein, Aug. 28th, 1901. He was the only son of the late Major-Gen. F. W. Graham, 12, Ashburn Place, South Kensington, and Mrs. Graham, of Charlecombe, Camberley, Surrey; was born in Sept., 1879, and educated at Cheam, Eton (Mr. Hare's), and Oxford. At Eton he was an enthusiastic volunteer, and a 2nd lieut. in the School Corps. He entered the Northumberland Fusiliers from the 5th Batt. Rifle Brigade March, 1900, being promoted lieut. the following August. Soon after joining the Northumberland Fusiliers he was appointed assistant adjutant to his battalion. In Feb., 1901, a mounted infantry company was formed for service; Lieut. Graham joined it, and proceeding to South Africa, served with it till his death. Whilst being carried from the field wounded and under a heavy fire, he heard a shout "another man hit." In terrible pain and weak, he directed his bearers to leave him and look after the other wounded man; "his one thought," his commanding officer writes, "was always for others."

Grant.—Lieut. Alister Grant, Roberts' Horse, died at Kimberley on Feb. 21st, 1900. He was educated at Harrow.

Grant.—Capt. Edward Chetwood Hamilton Grant, 1st Batt. Argyll and Sutherland Highlanders, died of enteric fever at Kimberley Aug. 25th, 1901. He was born May, 1868, educated at Charterhouse, and entered the Argyll and Sutherland Highlanders Jan., 1888, was promoted lieut. Jan., 1890, and capt. July, 1897. Having served as adjutant of his regiment, June, 1894, to December, 1897, he was then appointed an Instructor on the Staff of the School of Musketry, Hythe, which post he held till Oct., 1899. He was District Inspector of Musketry at Aldershot, Nov. 1899. At the time of his death he was serving as adjutant of the 24th Batt. I.Y., to which he was appointed in April, 1901, having been allowed to give up his staff appointment at Aldershot to enable him to go to South Africa. His name is inscribed on the tablet in the War Memorial Cloister erected at Charterhouse.

Grant.—Lieut. Robert Josceline Grant, 3rd Batt. King's Royal Rifle Corps, was killed in action at Spion Kop Jan. 24th, 1900. He was the son of Lieut.-Gen. Sir Robert and Lady Grant, was born Aug., 1877, and educated at Harrow. He entered the King's Royal Rifle Corps in Jan., 1897, being promoted lieut. in Feb., 1899. Lieut. Grant embarked with his battalion in Oct., 1899, and served with it in Natal, being present at the battle of Colenso.

Gray. — Major Edward Wolfenden Gray, M.B., R.A.M.C., was killed in action at Farquhar's Farm, near Ladysmith, Oct. 30th, 1899. He was born Sept., 1862, and entered the Royal Army Medical Corps Feb., 1887, being promoted major Feb., 1899. He was a B.A. of Dublin University, and took the M.B. and B.Ch. degrees there in 1885, he also received the State Medicine Diploma from the University in 1887, and in 1888 was elected a Fellow of the Royal College of Surgeons in Ireland. Major Gray was also a gold medallist of Jervis Street Hospital, and a member of the British Medical Association. He only arrived in South Africa from Bengal a few weeks before being killed.

Gray.—Capt. the Hon. Lonsdale Richard Douglas Gray, 6th Dragoon Guards, died of enteric at Johannesburg June 10th, 1900. He was the son of the Baroness Gray, was born March, 1870, and educated at Uppingham (where he was in the football XV.); and afterwards at Pembroke College, Cambridge. Capt. Gray entered the 6th Dragoon Guards from the 5th Batt. Rifle Brigade Feb., 1893, being promoted lieut. July, 1895, and capt. May, 1900. He was appointed adjutant of his regiment, Jan., 1899, which post he held till May, 1900, when he was selected as A.D.C. to the officer commanding the 1st Cavalry Brigade. He embarked for South Africa with his regiment in Oct., 1899, and served in the north of Cape Colony, and was present at the relief of Kimberley and the advance on Bloemfontein and Johannesburg.

Green.—Lieut. George Dymoke Green, 59th Company I.Y., of Mackerye End, Harpenden, was killed in action at Modderfontein, Jan. 31st, 1901. He was the eldest son of the late Dymoke Green, Esq., Oaklands, St. Albans, was 29 years of age, and educated at Winchester. He went out as a trooper in the Hertfordshire Yeomanry Jan., 1900, and was granted a commission as lieut. in the following Oct. He is reported to have been killed while bravely attempting to take some provisions to an outpost, which had been surrounded by the Boers.

Greenshields.—Lieut. George Lockhart Greenshields, 13th Company I.Y., died June 9th, 1901, at Grootafdeeling, twenty miles south east of Zeerust, of wounds received in action two days previously. He was the eldest son of Robert Low Greenshields, Esq., of Liverpool, and the Beeches, Malpas, Cheshire. He was born Nov., 1876, and educated at Radley and Oriel College, Oxford, being in the cricket and football teams at both places. He was a keen sportsman and a good rider. Lieut. Greenshields was a partner in the well-known shipping firm of Greenshields, Cowie & Co. Being appointed a 2nd lieut. in the Shropshire Yeomanry March, 1900, he joined the I.Y. in Feb., 1901, with the rank of 2nd lieut. in the army. When lying wounded he continued to cheer his men and urge them on. He is buried at Grootafdeeling.

Greer.—Capt. William Greer, Reserve of Officers attached to 8th Batt. M.I., died of inflammation of the liver, at Johannesburg, May 23rd, 1902. He was born in 1851, and after nearly thirteen years' service in the ranks, was given a commission in the 72nd Foot in 1879, being promoted lieut. 1880, and capt. in the Border Regt. in 1886. His first experience of active service was with the 72nd Highlanders throughout the Afghan War of 1878-80, with the Kuram-Kabul, and Kabul-Kandahar Field Forces. He was present at the attack and capture of the Peiwar

Kotal, the passage of the Chapri defile, and in the engagement at Charasiah, and the operations around Kabul, in Dec., 1879. He accompanied Earl (then Sir Frederick) Roberts in the march to Kandahar, was present at the battle of Kandahar, receiving the medal with four clasps and bronze decoration. For these services he was promoted 2nd lieut. He next served with the 1st Batt. Seaforth Highlanders in the Egyptian War of 1882, was present at the battle of Tel-el-Kebir, and the occupation of Zagazig and Cairo, receiving the medal with clasp and Khedive's star. He had been in South Africa since 1899 as a special service officer for M.I., and acting quartermaster to the 8th battalion.

Gregory.—Lieut.-Col. Arthur Gregory Serocold Gregory, Royal Artillery, Reserve of Officers, died at Durban, Aug. 24th, 1900. Born in May, 1849, he joined the Royal Artillery July, 1870, became capt. Oct., 1880, major July, 1886, lieut.-col. Feb., 1897, retiring in the following April, and joined the Reserve of Officers.

Grenfell.—Lieut. Claude George Grenfell, Thorneycroft's M.I., was killed in action at Spion Kop, Feb. 24th, 1900. He was educated at Harrow. His death is thus described by a non-commissioned officer (Sergt. Just), "Lieut. Grenfell was first wounded in the leg, and a few minutes afterwards in the arm. I was going to bind up his wounds, when he remembered that he had been shot by Boers who were creeping up to the right rear, and he said to me, 'I can get on all right, sergeant; you shoot those men.' I went on shooting, and fired three times when another bullet hit Lieut. Grenfell in the head and killed him."

Grice.—Lieut. George Grice, 2nd Batt. Cameronians (Scottish Rifles), died on Dec. 26th, 1901, of wounds received in action at Tweefontein, in De Wet's attack on Christmas morning. He was holding the temporary rank of capt., whilst acting as adjutant of the 11th (Middlesex and Kent) Batt. I.Y. He was born Jan., 1879, and entered the Scottish Rifles Nov., 1898, was promoted lieut. Oct., 1899, and granted the temporary rank of capt. April, 1901. Capt. Grice accompanied his battalion to South Africa in Oct., 1899, and served from the commencement of the war, being mentioned in despatches L.G., Feb. 8th, 1901. He is buried at Tweefontein, and his name is inscribed on an obelisk which has been erected there, in memory of all those who fell in this action.

Grieve.—Lieut. G. J. Grieve, New South Wales Forces, attached to the Royal Highlanders, was killed in action at Paardeberg, Feb. 16th, 1900. He was mentioned in despatches, L.G., Feb. 8th, 1901, for having rendered valuable service; and again in the despatch of April 2nd, 1901 (L.G., April 16th, 1901).

Grigg.—Civil Surgeon Chapman Grigg, M.D., died of enteric at Wynberg, March 12th, 1900. He was educated at Elizabeth College, Guernsey.

Grogan.—Capt. Edward Bury Grogan, 1st Batt. South Staffordshire Regt., was killed in action at Ficksburg, June 25th, 1900. He was the eldest son of the late Major-Gen. C. E. Grogan, was born Nov., 1864, and educated at Wellington (Griffiths' House), 1878-81. Capt. Grogan entered the South Wales Borderers from the 2nd Brigade Southern Division Royal Artillery, May, 1884, being transferred a fortnight later to the South Staffordshire Regt., and was promoted capt. Feb., 1891. He proceeded to South Africa with his battalion in March, 1900.

Grove.—2nd Lieut. Arthur Langton Grove, 2nd Batt. Norfolk Regt., died of wounds received in action at Buffelsvlei March 12th, 1902. He was the second son of the Rev. W. H. Grove, 15, Rothsay Road, Bedford, late of Cliffe Rectory, Rochester. 2nd Lieut. Grove was born June, 1874, and educated at Winchester. He served in the ranks for three-and-a-half years, proceeded to South Africa at the close of 1899 and was present at the relief of Ladysmith where he was wounded. He was twice mentioned in despatches, L. G., Feb. 8th and Sept. 10th, 1901, was awarded the medal for distinguished conduct in the field, and granted a commission as a 2nd lieut. Sept., 1901, in the Norfolk Regt.

Grover.—Lieut. Percival Charles Grover, 1st Batt. Shropshire Light Infantry, died of wounds received in action at Bloemfontein Water Works March 31st, 1900. He was born March, 1875, educated at Rugby, and entered the Shropshire Light Infantry Feb., 1895, being promoted lieut. March, 1899. He served in the campaign on the North-West Frontier of India under the late Sir William Lockhart, 1897-98, with the Malakand Field Force, including the operations against the Mahmuds, and in Bajour, with the Utman Khel Column, afterwards with the Buner Field Force, including the attack and capture of Tanga Pass, receiving the medal with clasp. Lieut. Grover belonged to the 1st battalion of his regiment in India, but volunteering for active service he was sent to South Africa. His services are mentioned in the despatch of Brigadier-Gen. Broadwood, April 20th, 1900, who reports Lieut. Grover as having shown conspicuous gallantry on the day he was killed, L. G., Feb. 8th, 1901.

Grylls.—Lieut. John Bere Grylls, 66th Battery Royal Field Artillery, died of dysentery July 6th, 1900, at Johannesburg. He was born March, 1876, educated at Rugby and the Royal Military Academy, and entered the Royal Artillery in 1895, being promoted lieut. in Nov., 1898. He was wounded at the Battle of Colenso while endeavouring to rescue a wounded brother officer. On recovering he returned to duty in Jan., 1900, and was present at the relief of Ladysmith, afterwards taking part in the fighting around Warrenton and Fourteen Streams.

Guille.—Major Henry Stevens Le Marchant Guille, Royal Artillery, attached to the Army Ordnance Corps, died at Kimberley May 9th, 1900, of wounds received in action at Warrenton five days previously. He was the youngest son of the late Rev. G. de Carteret Guille of St. George's, Guernsey, and Little Torrington, North Devon. Major Guille was born in Sept., 1862, educated at Cheltenham, and entered the Royal Artillery, Feb., 1882, promoted capt. April, 1890, and major Jan., 1900. Having passed the final examination of the senior class at the Ordnance College, he was Inspector of Warlike Stores at Capetown, 1892-96, and became Ordnance Officer, 4th class, April, 1896. His name is inscribed on the Eleanor Cross War Memorial erected at Cheltenham College.

Guinness.—Lieut.-Col. Eustace Guinness, Royal Artillery, of Kelvin Lodge, Gosforth, Newcastle-on-Tyne, was killed in action near Brakenlaagte on Oct. 31st, 1901. He was the second son of the late Henry Guinness, Esq., Burton Hall, Stillorgan, co. Dublin, was born June, 1860, and educated at Cheltenham. He entered the Royal Artillery from the Royal Military Academy in April, 1879, being promoted capt. Sept., 1887, and major May, 1897. He married Isabel, second daughter of C. L. Bell, Esq., of Woolsington Hall, Newcastle-on-Tyne, and left two sons. Lieut.-Col. Guinness went out to South Africa from Newcastle-on-Tyne with the 84th Battery, Royal Field Artillery, and was mentioned in despatches, L.G., Sept. 10th, 1901, and received a brevet lieut.-colonelcy which was antedated to Nov. 29th, 1900. He had been present at many battles and actions during the war. At Brakenlaagte his conduct was heroic, twenty-nine out of his thirty-two gunners fell around him where they stood. He was mortally wounded while endeavouring with his own hands to fire a round of case shot. Memorials to Lieut.-Col. Guinness have been erected at Newcastle-on-Tyne, and at Stillorgan, and his name is inscribed on the Eleanor Cross War Memorial at Cheltenham College.

Gunning.—Lieut.-Col. Robert Henry Gunning, commanding the 1st Batt. King's Royal Rifle Corps, was killed in action at the Battle of Talana Hill Oct. 20th, 1901. He was the eldest son of Sir George William Gunning, 5th baronet, of Little Horton House, Northampton, was born in 1852, and educated at Eton (Mr. Wayte's). He entered the 68th Foot 1873, was transferred to the 60th Foot 1874, and was promoted capt. 1883, major 1890, and lieut.-col. 1898. He served with the 60th Rifles in the Zulu War, 1879, was present at the action of Ginginhlovo and Relief of Etshowe, and afterwards served as adjutant of the batt. throughout the operations of "Clarke's Column," receiving the medal with clasp. In the Burmese Expedition 1891-92, he was in command of the Baungshè Column during the operations in the Chin Hills, receiving the medal with clasp. At Talana, Lieut.-Col. Gunning fell while leading his batt. in the attack. Sir A. Conan Doyle in writing of this battle states, " It was here between the wall and the summit that Col. Gunning of the Rifles and many other brave men met their end, some by our own bullets and some by those of the enemy," and again "among the killed were many that the army could ill spare. The gallant but optimistic Symons, Gunning of the Rifles, Sherston, Connor, Hambro, and many other brave men died that day." Lieut.-Col. Gunning was mentioned in despatches by Lieut.-Gen. Sir G. White, Dec. 2nd, 1899 (L.G., Feb. 8th, 1901). The gallant colonel of the Rifles is buried in the cemetery just below Talana Hill close to where he fell.

Gurdon-Rebow.—Lieut. Martin Gurdon-Rebow, 3rd Batt. Grenadier Guards, was killed in a patrol engagement near Hanover Road Sept. 16th, 1901. He was the only son of H. J. Gurdon-Rebow, Esq., of Wyvenhoe Park, Essex, was born Feb., 1875, and educated at Eton (Miss Evans'). He entered the Grenadier Guards from the 3rd Batt. Hampshire Regt., being promoted lieut. Dec., 1898. Lieut. Gurdon-Rebow served in the Soudan campaign under Lord (then Sir Herbert) Kitchener in 1898, and was present at the battle of Khartoum, receiving the British medal and Khedive's medal with clasp. He went to South Africa with his regiment from Gibraltar, in Oct., 1899, joining the Kimberley Relief Force, and was present at the action at Belmont, where he was wounded. Recovering however in time, he was present at the Battle of Modder River, and afterwards saw much service during the war. The day he was killed Lieut. Gurdon-Rebow was in charge of a patrol of Grenadier Guards, and Lieut.-Gen. Lord Kitchener in referring to his death says, "I must also make allusion to the very gallant stand made on Sept. 16th by nine men of the 3rd Batt. Grenadier Guards, under Lieut. M. Gurdon-Rebow, who found themselves attacked by some thirty to forty of the enemy near Cyferkuil, ten miles north of Riet Siding." A summons to surrender was refused by Lieut. Gurdon-Rebow, and he and one man were killed and two others dangerously wounded. The sergt. of the patrol was drowned in a gallant attempt to swim the Carolus River in order to get assistance. Lieut. Gurdon-Rebow was mentioned in despatches for special bravery in the action in which he fell. He is buried in De Aar cemetery. A white marble cross has been erected by his brother officers over his grave, which has also been enclosed with a white marble curbing.

Guthrie.—Lieut. David Ernest Guthrie, 39th Company I.Y., died of enteric at Mafeking Feb. 2nd, 1902. He was the son of David Guthrie, Esq., 9, Park Circus Place, Glasgow; was born in Oct., 1870, and educated at Trinity College, Glenalmond (1885-88). He was a good athlete, and when at Glenalmond was in the cricket, football, and shooting teams. Lieut. Guthrie was appointed to the 10th Batt. of the I.Y., May, 1901, and afterwards served with it up to his death.

Guthrie.—Lieut. G. Baillie Guthrie, 35th Company I.Y. (Middlesex), died of enteric, at Naauwpoort, May 16th, 1900. He was the third son of the late James Baillie Guthrie, Esq,, and was 40 years of age. He had attained the rank of captain in the Middlesex Yeomanry, but, volunteering for active service in South Africa, he was granted a commission as lieut. in the I.Y., Feb. 7th, 1900, when he proceeded to South Africa, and served in Cape Colony till his death.

Hall.—Lieut. A. W. Hall, Volunteer Medical Staff, died of enteric at Mooi River, on March 20th, 1900.

Hall.—Lieut. Lewis Duval Hall, 2nd Batt. Rifle Brigade, was killed in action at Wagon Hill, Ladysmith, Jan. 6th, 1900. He was the son of Lewis Duval Hall, Esq., J.P., D.L., of Taverham Hall, Norwich, was born in 1875, and educated at Eton (Mr. Cornish's). He entered the Rifle Brigade from the 3rd Batt. Oxfordshire Light Infantry 1897, being promoted lieut. Oct., 1899. Lieut. Hall took part in Lord (then Sir Herbert) Kitchener's expedition to Omdurman in 1898, and was present at the battle of Khartoum, receiving the medal, also the Egyptian medal with clasp. He also served in Crete. He accompanied his battalion to South Africa in Oct., 1899, and served with it in Ladysmith till killed.

Hall.—2nd Lieut. Rupert Henry Hall, 4th Batt. Sherwood Foresters (Derbyshire Regt.), died June 15th, 1900, of wounds received a week previously in action at Roodeval. He entered the regiment in Nov., 1899, and accompanied his battalion to South Africa in Jan., 1900. (*See Lieut.-Col. Douglas who was also killed in this action.*)

Hall.—Capt. S. E. Hall, 34th (Middlesex) Company of the 11th Batt. I.Y., was killed in action at Tweefontein, in De Wet's attack on Christmas morning, 1901. He entered the I.Y. as a lieut. in Dec., 1900, and was promoted capt. in June, 1901. He is buried at Tweefontein, and his name is inscribed on an obelisk erected there in memory of all who fell in this action.

Hall.—Lieut. W. Hall, South African Light Horse, died of enteric at Heilbron, on Nov. 23rd, 1901.

Halliday.—Surgeon Stratford D. T. Halliday, M.R.C.S., L.R.C.P., R.N., H.M.S. "Redbreast," engaged in blockading duties off Delagoa Bay, was invalided home and died in London, May 5th, 1902. He was educated at Elizabeth College, Guernsey, and was appointed surgeon in the Royal Navy in May, 1898.

Hambro.—2nd Lieut. Norman Joachim Hambro, 1st Batt. King's Royal Rifle Corps, was killed in action at the battle of Talana Hill, Oct. 20th, 1899. He was born in Feb., 1878, and educated at Eton (Mr. Daman's). He entered the King's Royal Rifle Corps Feb., 1899, from the 3rd Batt. Derbyshire Regt. "*The Times* History of the War" states that Lieut. Hambro was killed by our artillery fire. He was twice wounded in the advance and had dragged himself to the summit of the hill as an encouragement to his men, but was killed by our shrapnel. A signaller of the Royal Irish Fusiliers (whose name I have endeavoured to trace, without success), leaped upon a prominent boulder, and standing in the spread of the bullets endeavoured to call up the battery. The shelling was then stopped. Lieut. Hambro is buried at Talana. (*See Col. Gunning.*)

Hamilton.—Capt. H. C. W. Hamilton, Queensland M.I., died of dysentery on July 12th, 1900, at Marandellas.

Hamilton.—Lieut. Henry Rice Hamilton, South African Constabulary (late Rhodesian Regt.), was dangerously wounded June 29th, 1901, and died July 1st at Kromellenboorg. He was educated at the United Services College, Westward Ho (1874-77). Lieut. Hamilton served in Methuen's Horse in 1884-85, and subsequently held a captain's commission in the 4th Batt. Manchester Regt. His name is inscribed on a memorial tablet in his old college at Westward Ho.

Hamilton.—Lieut. the Hon. John David Hamilton, 12th Lancers, died of enteric May 22nd, 1900, at Kroonstad. He was the youngest son of Lord Hamilton, of Dalzell, was born Dec., 1878, and educated at Eton (Mr. Durnford's). He entered the 12th Lancers Nov., 1898, being promoted lieut. Feb. 1900.

OFFICERS WHO FELL IN SOUTH AFRICA.

Hancock.—2nd Lieut. Calverly Trevelyan Hancock, I.Y., was killed in action at Bethlehem, July 13th, 1900. He was the son of the Rev. Prebendary Hancock, The Priory, Dunster, Somerset, and was born in April, 1879. He was educated at Radley, where he was a prefect, and at Christ Church, Oxford. He served in South Africa with the 40th Company of the 10th Batt. I.Y., and saw much fighting near Kroonstad and Lindley. He is buried in the cemetery at Bethlehem.

Hancock.—Lieut. F. E. Hancock, Kitchener's Fighting Scouts, died of enteric at Pietermaritzburg Jan. 15th, 1902.

Hanbury.—2nd Lieut. Edward Mansfield Hanbury, 2nd Batt. East Yorkshire Regt., was killed at Jagersfontein on Oct. 13th, 1900, while in command of the M.I. of the 3rd Batt. South Lancashire Regt. He was the son of the late Mr. Hanbury and Mrs. Hanbury, of Bishopstowe, Torquay, was born in August, 1880, and educated at Lambrook, Bracknell, and at Eton (Mr. Broadbent's). He entered the East Yorkshire Regt., in April, 1900, from the 3rd Batt. South Lancashire Regt. 2nd Lieut. Hanbury fell while on patrol duty; and Lieut.-Gen. Sir T. Kelly-Kenny in announcing his death reported that Lieut. Hanbury was "a young officer of great promise." 2nd Lieut. Hanbury is buried in Trompsburg cemetery; a marble cross has been erected over his grave by his brother officers.

Hankey.—Lieut. Hugh Martin Alers Hankey, 2nd Batt. Royal Warwickshire Regt., was killed in action at Paardeberg, Feb. 18th, 1900. He was born in Nov., 1872, educated at Marlborough and Rugby, and entered his regiment Feb., 1892, being promoted lieut. Jan., 1898. From Dec., 1897 to May, 1898, he was employed in the Egyptian Army, and had passed as an interpreter in Arabic and Turkish. Lieut. Hankey's name is inscribed on a tablet placed in Marlborough College Chapel in memory of all Marlburians who fell in the war.

Hannah.—Lieut. William Maitland Julius Hannah, Leicestershire Regt., was killed at Dundee Oct. 21st, 1899, by a Boer shell from a Creusot gun which fell in the British camp. He was the second son of the Rev. J. J. Hannah, vicar of Brighton, and was born May, 1876, educated at Harrow, and entered the Leicestershire Regt. March, 1896, being promoted lieut. August, 1898. Lieut. Hannah was on leave of absence in England in the summer of 1899, and when war became imminent he asked permission to rejoin his battalion in Natal, which request being granted he arrived in time to proceed with it to Dundee. On the 20th Oct., the day of Talana, the battalion was left in camp to protect it, and on the following day Lieut. Hannah was killed. He is buried at Dundee.

Hannay.—Col. Ormelie Campbell Hannay, late Argyll and Sutherland Highlanders, was killed in the fighting near Paardeberg on Feb. 18th, 1900. He was born Dec., 1848, joined the 93rd Foot Oct., 1867, was promoted lieut. Oct., 1871, capt. in the Argyll and Sutherland Highlanders Nov., 1878, major Jan., 1884, lieut.-col. June, 1893, and brevet-col. June, 1897. Col. Hannay was employed on special service in South Africa during the latter part of the Zulu War in 1879 (medal). He was A.D.C. to the Brigadier-General, Aldershot, April 1st, 1883, to Sept. 30th, 1883, A.D.C. to the Major-General, Bengal, Sept. 27th, 1886, to Dec. 8th, 1886, and A.D.C. to the Lieut.-General, Bombay, Dec. 14th, 1886, to Nov. 20th, 1887. In June, 1899, having commanded his battalion for six years, he was placed on half-pay; in October he was appointed A.A.G. at Portsmouth; and in Dec. he was selected for special service in South Africa. He was killed when leading his mounted infantry against some Boers who held the northern bank of the Modder River. Col. Hannay was twice mentioned in despatches L.G., Feb. 8th, 1901, for having rendered "conspicuously valuable service."

Hannum.— Lieut. C. T. Hannum, Border Scouts, died of acute bronchitis, at Kenhardt, on April 19th, 1901.

Hanwell.—Major Joseph Hanwell, 39th Battery Royal Field Artillery, was killed in action near Ventersburg on Oct. 30th, 1900. He was born in July, 1861, entered the Royal Artillery July, 1881, was promoted capt. April, 1890, and major Oct., 1899. He was a fine horseman and polo player; and had won prizes for pig-sticking. He served with the Burmese Expedition 1886, receiving the medal with clasp, and was A.D.C. to the Major-General commanding Bombay, Feb., 1887, to March, 1891. Major Hanwell had served in the war from its commencement. F.-M. Earl Roberts in his despatch of Nov. 15th, 1900 (L.G., Feb. 8th, 1901) reports with regret the death of Major Hanwell.

Harbord.—2nd Lieut. Horatio Harbord, 3rd Batt. South Wales Borderers, was killed in action at Elandslaagte, near Klerksdorp, Feb. 25th, 1902, during an attack by the Boers on a convoy. He was the second son of the late Hon. Ralph Harbord—a brother of Lord Suffield—by his marriage with Elizabeth Pole, second daughter of E. W. H. Schenley, Esq., Prince's Gate. He was born March, 1875, educated privately, and was fond of all sports, and a good rider. He first served as a trooper in the Leicestershire Yeomanry in 1900, and was granted a commission in the 3rd Batt. South Wales Borderers March, 1901. 2nd Lieut. Harbord served in the operations in Cape Colony, north of the Orange River, also in the operations in Orange River Colony. He is buried at Klerksdorp.

Harding.—2nd Lieut. J. D. Harding, I.Y., died of enteric at Germiston June 3rd, 1901. He joined the I.Y. March, 1901, with the rank of 2nd lieut. in the army. He had previously served as a trooper in the Westmoreland and Cumberland Yeomanry Cavalry.

Harding.—Lieut. L. E. Harding, Commander-in-Chief's Bodyguard, died of wounds received in action at Uitkyk, Feb. 11th, 1901.

Hardman.—Capt. John Wreford Julian Hardman, 1st Royal Dragoons, died at Pinetown Bridge Hospital, Natal, May 30th, 1900. He was born Jan., 1863, educated at Harrow, and entered the 6th Dragoons Aug., 1885, being transferred to the 1st Dragoons Oct., 1885, and was promoted capt. Aug., 1893. Capt. Hardman held the post of adjutant to his regiment Dec., 1894, to Dec., 1898, and was appointed Recruiting Staff Officer (Class II), London Recruiting District, May, 1899, which appointment he held till Oct., when he rejoined his regiment in order to proceed to South Africa. He then served with the Natal Field Force, and was present at the battle of Colenso and the relief of Ladysmith.

Hardwick.—Lieut. Stephen Thomas Hardwick, Royal Field Artillery, was killed in action at Tweefontein, Dec. 25th, 1901, in the attack at dawn by Gen. De Wet. He was the son of the late Phillip C. Hardwick, Esq., 2, Hereford Gardens, and of Mrs. Hardwick (now Mrs. Lascelles), The Rectory, Newton St. Loè, Bristol. He was born April, 1876, educated at Farnboro' and Eton (Mr. Broadbent's), and entered the R.F.A. from the 4th Batt. Middx. Regt. June, 1899, being promoted lieut. Feb., 1901. In 1897-98, Lieut. Hardwick was employed on survey work in Egypt and Sinai, under Capt. Lyons, Royal Engineers. He went to South Africa Feb., 1900, and was given command of a Pom-Pom section, for which he had been specially recommended. Lieut. Hardwick saw much service during the war, and was constantly in action up to the time of his death. At Tweefontein, when the "sweet silence of the Christmas dawn" was broken by De Wet's attack, he rushed to his pom-pom, and working it with his own hands, fired off a few rounds, and then foreseeing that it might possibly fall into the hands of the enemy, he was endeavouring to render it useless when he was shot through the heart. He was mentioned in despatches, and was awarded the medal and four clasps, for Cape Colony, O.R.C., Johannesburg, and Diamond Hill. Major-Gen. Sir Leslie Rundle telegraphed his "own deep regret" at Lieut. Hardwick's death, and added "we have lost a gallant soldier and comrade." Lieut. Hardwick is buried at Tweefontein, and his name appears on an obelisk, erected on the spot where he worked his pom-pom, in memory of all those who fell in this action. His name is also inscribed on tablets in the Church of Bradford-on-Avon, Wilts., in the Chapel at Farnboro' School, and at All Saints', Margaret Street. A window has also been placed to his memory in the Church of Newton St. Loè.

Harland.—Lieut. Edwyn Harland, 2nd Batt. Hampshire Regt., was killed in action at the Relief of Mafeking, May 16th, 1900. He was born July, 1872, and educated at Wellington (Hopetoun, 1886-90), where he was a Prefect, and in the football XV. He entered the Hampshire Regt. from the Royal Military College, July, 1892, and was promoted lieut. June, 1894. Lieut. Harland served in the operations in South Africa, 1896, with the mounted infantry, and was appointed adjutant of his battalion July, 1899, but being selected for special service he proceeded to South Africa, and was employed with the force under Col. Plumer. He was killed whilst successfully saving the life of another old Wellingtonian, Major Bird.

Harper.—Lieut. J. F. Harper, 4th Batt. I.Y., was killed in action at Ladismith, Cape Colony, Sept. 10th, 1901. He first served as a trooper in the I.Y. and was appointed lieut. March 14th, 1901, with the rank of lieut. in the army.

Harris.—Lieut. Eustace Malim Harris, Royal Irish Fusiliers, was killed in action at Machadodorp, Jan. 8th, 1901. He was born Aug., 1874, educated at Bedford Grammar School, and entered the Royal Irish Fusiliers from the 4th Batt. (Cavan Militia) March, 1897, being promoted lieut. April, 1899. He served in the war from its commencement; first with the Natal Field Force, and afterwards in the Transvaal.

Harris.—Capt. Owen Harris, Duke of Wellington's West Riding Regt. and commanding 16th Batt. M.I., died of enteric and pneumonia Oct. 9th, 1901. He was the only son of the late Francis Harris, Esq., M.D., 24, Cavendish Square, London, and the Grange, Lamberhurst, was born Nov., 1863, and educated at Winchester. Capt. Harris entered the West Riding Regt. from the 3rd Batt. Queen's Own Royal West Kent Regt. Jan., 1884, being promoted capt. Feb., 1890. He was adjutant of volunteers Feb., 1892, to Feb., 1898, and held the local rank of major in South Africa from Feb. 22nd, 1901, whilst commanding a battalion of M.I. He served from the commencement of the war, and was wounded in the action at Klip Kraal, and again slightly on Nov. 6th, 1900. He was mentioned in despatches, L.G., Feb. 8th, 1901.

Harrison.—Capt. E. F. Harrison, Canadian M.I., died at Wynberg of enteric June 9th, 1900.

Harrison.—Lieut. John Collison Harrison, 2nd Dragoons (Royal Scots Greys), died Sept. 3rd, 1900, at Pretoria, of wounds received in action, Aug. 26th, 1900, near Belfast. He was born in Aug., 1869, educated at Eton (Miss Evans'), and entered the 2nd Dragoons, June, 1889, being promoted lieut. May, 1891. Lieut. Harrison embarked for South Africa with his regiment in Oct., 1899, and first served in the north of Cape Colony, and afterwards was present at the relief of Kimberley. He then took part in the advance on Bloemfontein and Pretoria.

Harrison.—Lieut. W. Harrison, New South Wales M.I., died at Wynberg May 6th, 1900.

Hartley.—Lieut. G. Hartley, Steinacker's Horse, was killed in action between Tweebosch and Palmietkuil, March 7th, 1902. He was the younger son of R. W. Hartley, Esq., Manager of the National Provincial Bank at Brighton, and was 25 years of age. He went out in the early days of the war with Paget's Horse, and obtained his commission, being appointed Paymaster to Steinacker's Horse, July, 1901.

Harvey.—Lieut. A. V. Harvey, Scott's Railway Guards, died at Devondale during the war.

Harvey.—Major Charles Bateson Harvey, 10th Hussars, was killed in action near Colesberg, Jan. 4th, 1900. He was the younger son of the late Sir Robert Bateson

Harvey, Bart., of Langley Park, Bucks. He was born Jan. 1859, educated at Eton (Mr. James'), and entered the 10th Hussars in 1881, being promoted capt. July, 1889, and major 1897. He served in Egypt in 1884, and was present at the battles of El Teb and Tamai, receiving the medal with clasp and bronze star. He held the post of adjutant of Yeomanry Cavalry from 1894-98. In the action in which Major Harvey was killed, it was found that the Boers had during the night established themselves in rear of the English position. The enemy were, however, driven out, and in their retreat were charged by the 10th Hussars and a squadron of Inniskilling Dragoons. Ninety were killed and twenty-one prisoners taken, while our loss was six killed, among them Major Harvey.

Harvey.—Capt. J. A. Harvey, of the 10th Company of the 4th Contingent New Zealand M.I., was killed in action in the operations at Eland's River, of Major-Gen. Sir F. Carrington's Force, Aug. 16th, 1900.

Harvey.—Capt. Thomas Harvey, Rimington's Guides, died at De Aar, March 1st, 1901, of wounds received in action at Strydenburg, Feb. 24th, 1901.

Hastie.—Lieut. Basil Hepburn Hastie, 2nd Batt. The Queen's Royal West Surrey Regt., killed in action in the operations on the Tugela, Feb., 23rd, 1900, was born May, 1874, and educated at Dulwich College. He entered the Queen's from the Militia, July, 1896, being promoted lieut. March, 1898. He went to South Africa in Oct., 1899, and served with the Natal Field Force. Lieut. Hastie's name is engraved on a tablet erected at Guildford by their comrades in memory of all ranks of the Queen's Royal West Surrey Regt. who fell in the war. His name is also inscribed on a tablet on the outside of the new Memorial Library at Dulwich College.

Hastings.—Lieut. Mark Hastings, 1st Batt. I.Y., was killed in action at Reitz Nov. 10th, 1901. He was the youngest son of W. S. Hastings, Esq., the Grange, Wimbledon. He first served as a trooper in the I.Y., and was granted a commission with the rank of lieut. March 3rd, 1901.

Hawkes.—Capt. Lawrence Harry Hawkes, 2nd Batt. the Welsh Regt., died at Barberton Nov. 13th, 1900. He was born in March, 1864, and educated at Wellington, where he was in Lynedock, 1877-80. He entered the Bedfordshire Regt. Aug., 1883, being transferred to the Welsh Regt. the following month, and was promoted capt. Feb., 1890.

Hawley.—Major Francis Henry Toovey Hawley, 2nd Dragoons (Royal Scots Greys), died after three days illness at Bloemfontein April 27th, 1900. He was the son of the late Gen. Hawley, formerly Assistant Military Secretary, and Deputy-Adjutant-General to the Forces. Major Hawley was born in Aug., 1860, and educated at Eton (Dr. Warre's). He entered the 2nd Dragoons in Aug., 1880, was promoted lieut. June, 1881, capt. Oct., 1887, and major April, 1897, and was adjutant of his regiment from Jan., 1892 to Jan., 1896. He embarked for South Africa in Oct., 1899, served in the Colesberg district, and took part in the relief of Kimberley and the advance on Bloemfontein.

Hay-Coghlan.—Lieut. Percy Hay Hay-Coghlan, Royal Artillery, was killed in action when *en route* from Tarkstaad to East London Sept. 19th, 1901. He was the son of William Mant Hay-Coghlan, Esq., late of the Indian Civil Service, and the grandson of the late Gen. Sir W. W. Coghlan, Royal Artillery, K.C.B. Lieut. Hay-

Coghlan was born in March, 1878, and entered the Royal Artillery Sept., 1897, being promoted lieut. Sept., 1900. He was employed on Special Service in South Africa, and since Jan., 1900, had been on duty with the transport.

Head.—Capt. Leonard Head, 1st Batt. East Lancashire Regt., died May 11th, 1900, of wounds received the previous day in action at Zand River. He was born in June, 1867, and educated at Bedford Grammar School. He entered the East Lancashire Regt. Feb., 1888, promoted lieut. Aug., 1890, and capt. July, 1896. He served with the Chitral Relief Force under Sir Robert Low, 1895, and received the medal with clasp. Capt. Head embarked for South Africa in Jan., 1900, and served in the 7th Division, taking part in the advance on Bloemfontein.

Heath.—Major Edward Kermode Heath, 3rd Batt. South Lancashire Regt., was killed by the derailing and destruction of an armoured train, of which he was in command, near America Siding, May 17th, 1901. He was the only son of the late Edward Heath, Esq., of Manchester and Cheadle, and was 38 years of age, educated at the Rev. J. W. Ripley's Private School, and married in 1887 the youngest daughter of Col. Charles Gooch, of H.M. Bodyguard, who survives him. He was appointed lieut. in June, 1882, placed in the Reserve of Officers March, 1885, and promoted capt. Sept., 1887. At the time of his death he was senior capt. of his battalion with the honorary rank of major. Major Heath embarked for active service with his battalion in Jan., 1900, but was invalided home in July, suffering from enteric. On recovering he again returned to South Africa in the following November, and was given command of No. 6 armoured train, which position he held up to the time of his death.

OFFICERS WHO FELL IN SOUTH AFRICA. 169

Hebden.—Capt. Wilfrid Arthur Hebden, 1st Batt. Essex Regt., died of enteric at De Aar Hospital Jan. 28th, 1900. Born in Feb., 1867, and educated at Harrow, he entered the Essex Regt. Jan., 1886, being promoted capt. July, 1897. Capt. Hebden embarked for South Africa in Nov., 1899, and served in the north of Cape Colony.

Helsham.—Lieut. Somerville Helsham, 11th Batt. I.Y., was killed in action at Bankfontein Nov. 25th, 1901. He had only been appointed to the I.Y. on Oct. 4th, with the rank of lieut. in the army.

Helyar.—Col. Charles Welman Hawker Helyar, 7th Batt. (Staffordshire) I.Y., was first returned as missing, but afterwards was reported as having been murdered by Boers on July 26th, 1900. He was the eldest son of the late C. J. Helyar, Esq., Poundisford Lodge, Pitminster, Somerset, was born Aug., 1844, and educated at Cheltenham. He entered the 29th Foot Feb., 1864, was promoted lieut. Dec., 1865, capt. Oct., 1871, exchanged to the 3rd Hussars July, 1879, became major Oct., 1881, lieut.-col. April, 1891, col. April, 1895, and was placed on half-pay the following Oct. Col. Helyar retired in April, 1899, and was in the Reserve of Officers. He volunteered for service in South Africa, and was appointed commandant of the 7th Batt. I.Y. in Jan., 1900. His name is inscribed on the Eleanor Cross War Memorial erected at Cheltenham College.

Hemmingway.—Lieut. F. L. Hemmingway, Menne's Scouts, was killed in action near Standerton, between May 3rd and 7th, 1901.

Henry.—Lieut. Robert Clive Bolton Henry, 2nd Batt. Royal Dublin Fusiliers, was killed in action at the battle of Colenso, Dec. 15th, 1899. He was born Feb. 1879, educated at Brighton College, and Victoria College, Jersey, and entered the Royal Dublin Fusiliers May, 1898, being promoted lieut. Oct., 1899. He was with his battalion in Natal at the outbreak of the war, and was present at the battle of Talana Hill and in the subsequent retirement on Ladysmith, afterwards accompanying part of his battalion to Colenso and Chieveley before the commencement of the siege. He then served with the Natal Field Force.

Hensley.—Capt. Charles Albert Hensley, 2nd Batt. Royal Dublin Fusiliers, died Jan. 20th, 1900, of wounds received in the operations on the Upper Tugela, near Venter's Spruit. He was the elder son of Albert W. Hensley, Esq., Halifax, Nova Scotia, was born in Prince Edward Island Sept., 1865, and educated at the Collegiate School, Windsor, N.S., and the Royal Military College, Kingston, Canada. Being an enthusiastic and successful sportsman, he was known in his regiment as "the young Shikari." He entered the army Sept., 1885, being promoted capt. July, 1895. Having served in Egypt and India, he proceeded to Natal with his battalion Sept., 1899, and was present at the battle of Talana and in the retirement on Ladysmith. Just before the siege began, he was sent with part of his battalion to garrison Colenso, and was present at the battle of that name and the fighting on the Tugela, being twice wounded. Capt. Hensley, whose family is well known in Canada, married eighteen months before his death the daughter of H. Wylde Brown, Esq., of Pietermaritzburg, who survives him. He was mentioned in despatches, L. G., Feb. 8th, 1901, for his services.

Herron.—Capt. Robert Douglas Herron, 2nd Dragoon Guards (Queen's Bays), was killed in action at Leeuwkop,

April 1st, 1902. He was born Aug., 1867, entered the 2nd Dragoons March, 1888, being promoted lieut. March, 1895, and capt. July, 1897. He had served in South Africa from the end of 1901. (*See Major J. C. A. Walker.*)

Hesketh.—Lieut. Algernon Ernest Hesketh, 16th Lancers, was killed in action in the fighting near Kimberley Feb. 15th, 1900. He was born Nov., 1874, joined the 16th Lancers in Feb., 1895, and was promoted lieut. Jan., 1899. This officer's death is mentioned in the despatch by F.-M. Earl Roberts, from Jacobsdal, dated Feb. 16th, 1900. A tablet has been erected by his brother officers in the Church of the Annunciation, Bryanston Street, W., in memory of Lieut. Hesketh.

Hewett.—Lieut. Arthur Wedderburn Hewett, 1st Batt. Loyal North Lancashire Regt., was killed in action at Hartebeestfontein Feb. 16th, 1901. He was born Dec., 1875, educated at Sutton Valence School, and entered the Loyal North Lancashire Regt. from the Royal Military College Sept., 1896, being promoted lieut. Sept., 1899. He served with the 1st. battalion in South Africa, and took part in the defence of Kimberley, and was also present at the action at Carter's Ridge and the subsequent operations in the O.R.C. Lieut. Hewett saw much service in connection with convoys, and was invalided home Aug., 1900. On recovering, he returned to South Africa in the following Nov., and joined Lieut.-Gen. Lord Methuen's column. He fell while leading his men under a very severe fire from the Boer position.

Hichens.—Capt. Thomas Sikes Hichens, Royal Field Artillery, died of enteric June 11th, 1900, at Bloemfontein. He was born Sept., 1869, educated at Winchester, and entered the Royal Artillery Feb., 1889, being promoted lieut. Feb. 1892, and capt. March, 1899 Capt. Hichens was mentioned in despatches, L. G., Sept. 10th, 1901, for his services.

Hicks.—Capt. Charles Herbert Hicks, Lancashire Fusiliers, was killed in action at Spion Kop Jan. 24th, 1900. He was born in April, 1862, educated at Malvern College, and entered the Lancashire Fusiliers from the Militia Nov. 1884, being promoted capt. Dec. 1892. Capt. Hicks embarked for South Africa Oct. 1899, and served with the Natal Field Force.

Hill.—2nd. Lieut. Arthur Hugh Montgomery Hill, 1st Batt. Royal Irish Fusiliers, was killed in action at the battle of Talana Hill Oct. 20th, 1899. He was born Sept., 1877, educated at Harrow and Trinity College, Cambridge, and entered the 1st battalion from the 4th Batt. (Cavan Militia) May, 1899. 2nd Lieut. Hill accompanied his battalion to Natal from Cairo in Sept., 1899. On arrival the battalion was at once pushed on to Ladysmith and Dundee, and took part in the first battle of the war. 2nd. Lieut. Hill fell close to Capt. Connor in the final assault on Talana Hill while leading his men. He is buried at Dundee, and a tablet has been erected there to his memory by his brother officers.

Hill.—2nd Lieut. Henry Norman Hill, Royal Artillery, was killed in action at Kleinfontein Oct. 24th, 1901. He was born Aug., 1877, educated at Cheltenham, and entered the Royal Artillery in May, 1900. 2nd Lieut. Hill was mentioned in despatches by Lord Kitchener, Dec. 8th, 1901, for "very marked gallantry." His name is inscribed on the Eleanor Cross War Memorial erected at Cheltenham College.

Hill.—Lieut. Hugh Rowley Hill, Royal Field Artillery,

died at Harrismith, July 28th, 1902. He was born Feb. 1880, and entered the Royal Artillery in Nov. 1899, and was promoted lieut. Feb. 1901. He had served in the war during 1901.

Hill.—2nd Lieut. William Henry Tucker Hill, 5th Lancers, was killed in action at Wagon Hill, Ladysmith, Jan. 6th, 1900. He was the son of James Ledger Hill, Esq., Combe Grove, Bath, was born May, 1873, and educated at Charterhouse. He entered the 5th Lancers from the 4th Batt. East Surrey Regt. 1895. At Wagon Hill he came up with a dismounted party to the assistance of the 2nd Batt. King's Royal Rifle Corps, and was struck down while asking his capt., who was wounded, to allow him and his men to join the Devons, who were at that moment about to make their famous charge. When his capt. turned to reply, he found 2nd Lieut. Hill had been killed. The name of 2nd Lieut. Hill is inscribed on the tablet in the War Memorial Cloister erected at Charterhouse. (*See Major Bowen.*)

Hilliard.—Major George Hilliard, M.B., C.M.G., Royal Army Medical Corps, died at the General Hospital, Newcastle, Sept. 7th, from a gun-shot wound received Sept. 5th, 1900, in a reconnaissance at Ingogo. He was born in Oct., 1862, and was educated at the Tipperary Grammar School and Trinity College, Dublin, where he took his degree, and entered the Royal Army Medical Corps as capt. Feb., 1887, being promoted major Feb., 1899. Major Hilliard served in the Ashanti Expedition under Sir Francis Scott in 1895-96, and received the star and also the C.M.G., the latter for "his care and devotion" to the late Prince Henry of Battenberg. He had served throughout the siege of Ladysmith. A handsome memorial, the gift of Her Royal Highness Princess Henry of Battenberg, has been placed over

Major Hilliard's grave. On it is inscribed that it was "erected in grateful remembrance of the devoted care he rendered her husband, by Beatrice Princess Henry of Battenberg."

Hill-Trevor.—Lieut. the Hon. Nevill Windsor Hill-Trevor, Thorneycroft's M.I., was killed in action at Spion Kop Jan. 24th, 1900. He was the third son of Lord Trevor, was born 1869, and educated at Eton (Mr. Redcliffe's). Lieut. Hill Trevor served in the 2nd Life Guards from 1893-97, and on the outbreak of the war he joined Thorneycroft's M.I. as a lieut. At the time of his death he held a commission as 2nd lieut. in the Shropshire Yeomanry. At Spion Kop his section of Thorneycroft's M.I. was exposed to a terrific flank fire, and he and all his men and Lieut. McCorquodale were killed.

Hinks.—Capt. Ernest Hinks, Middelburg District Mounted Troops, was wounded near Middelburg, Cape Colony, May 9th, 1902, and died the following day. He was the fourth son of J. Hinks, Esq., J.P., Chesford Grange, Kenilworth, was born April, 1876, and educated at Leamington College. Capt. Hinks went to South Africa in 1893, and was engaged in farming near Hanover, Cape Colony. At the commencement of the war he volunteered his services as a scout, and his knowledge of the country being soon recognised, he was rapidly promoted, and a commission as capt. granted him, first in French's Scouts, and afterwards in command of the Middelburg District Mounted Troops. He fell whilst leading his men to drive back the enemy who had attacked by night in overwhelming numbers.

Hinton.—Lieut. Claude Harington Hinton, East Surrey Regt., was killed in action in the operations on the Tugela, Feb. 23rd, 1900. He was born in April, 1873, educated at

OFFICERS WHO FELL IN SOUTH AFRICA. 175

Clifton, and entered the East Surrey Regt., Feb., 1893, being promoted lieut. Nov., 1894. He embarked for South Africa in Oct., 1899, and served with the Natal Field Force, and was present at the battle of Colenso.

Hipwell.—Capt. Malcolm George Hipwell, South Australian Bushmen, died of enteric at Kroonstad during the war.

Hirtzel.—Lieut. Guy Dashwood Hirtzel, South African Constabulary, died of abscess of the liver and dysentery at Tafel Kop, April 23rd, 1902. He was the sixth son of George Hirtzel, Esq., of Exeter.

Hobbs.—Lieut. Frank H. Hobbs, 5th Batt. I.Y., died at Lichtenburg of enteric, Feb. 6th, 1902. He entered the 2nd Volunteer Batt. Worcestershire Regt. March, 1900, being promoted lieut. Feb., 1901, and was then seconded in his battalion for service in the I.Y., which he joined in April with the rank of lieut. in the army.

Hobbs.—Major Herbert Thomas de Carteret Hobbs, 1st Batt. West Yorkshire Regt., was killed at Honing Spruit, June 22nd, 1900, in the attack on the railway made by Gen. De Wet. He was the elder son of the late Col. T. F. Hobbs, 6th Regt., of Barnaboy, Frankford, Kings County. His Grandfather, Capt. Thomas Hobbs, when a lieut. in the 92nd Highlanders, was wounded at Quatre Bras. Major Hobbs was born in April, 1857, educated at Wellington where he was in the Orange, 1870-74, and as a Queen's cadet was appointed direct to the 62nd Foot, Feb., 1875, served in India, being promoted capt. Jan., 1882, and was transferred to the West Yorkshire Regt. as major, Feb., 1895. He was in the Army Pay Department from 1885-89, adjutant of his regiment from 1890-93, and adjutant of volunteers from 1893-98. Major Hobbs accompanied his battalion to South Africa as 2nd-in-command, but was taken prisoner in his first engagement at Willow Grange, on Nov. 23rd, 1899. He was mentioned in the despatch of Major-Gen. Hildyard of Nov. 24th as "having led the first line of the assault with judgment and good sense," but having remained to see that some wounded were attended to was unfortunately captured. On Earl Roberts' entry into Pretoria, in June, 1900, Major Hobbs was released and was then appointed 2nd-in-command of a composite battalion, which proceeded to Honing Spruit. He had been with it only a few days, when he was killed, and is buried in the military cemetery of Kroonstad.

Hobson.—Lieut. Richard Leigh Clare Hobson, 4th Batt. King's Royal Rifle Corps, was killed in action at Schippen's Farm June 5th, 1900. He was the second son of Richard Hobson, Esq., St. Marfords, Bromborough, Cheshire, was born April, 1876, educated at Harrow, and entered the King's Royal Rifle Corps in May, 1898, being promoted lieut. Oct., 1899. When he fell he was with a patrol of ten men sent forward from the Vaal River, all of whom were killed or wounded. Lieut. Hobson had sent a runner with a note, asking for assistance, but although reinforcements arrived within an hour, he had meanwhile died from his wounds.

Hodge.—Capt. William Buller Chapell Hodge, 6th Batt. I.Y., died Nov. 1st, 1900, of wounds received the previous day in action at Cypherfontein. He was the only son of the late Chapell Hodge, Esq., Pounds, near Plymouth, was born April, 1865, and educated at Eton (Mr. Marindin's). He entered the 12th Lancers from the 3rd Batt. Devonshire Regt. May, 1887, being promoted lieut. July, 1888, and capt. Dec., 1892, but afterwards retired. He joined the I.Y. Feb., 1900, with the rank of capt. in the army.

Hodgson.—Lieut. Nevil Bursey Hodgson, Army Service Corps, died of enteric at Pretoria, May 27th, 1902. He was the eldest son of Nevil L. Hodgson, Esq., of Woolwich and Blackheath. Lieut. Hodgson served originally in the ranks of the Cape Police. On the recommendation of the Commander-in-Chief in South Africa he was gazetted to a commission in the Army Service Corps, Sept., 1900, being promoted lieut. Dec., 1901.

Hogg.—Lieut. J. Quarrier Hogg, Staff of the Intelligence Dept., died at Jamestown on June 4th, 1901, of wounds received in action. He held a commission in the South African Mounted Irregular Forces.

Holling.—Lieut. A. R. Holling, 1st Imperial Light Horse, was killed at Hartebeestefontein on March 22nd, 1901.

Holt.—Lieut. Holt, Uitenhage Volunteers, died at Port Elizabeth on May 2nd, 1900.

Holt.—Capt. Robert Hughtrede Edward Holt, M.R.C.S., L.R.C.P., L.S.A., died of wounds received in action at Groblers Kloof in the operations on the Tugela, Feb. 21st, 1900. He was the only son of Lieut.-Col. R. W. F. Holt, late R.M.L.I. On his mother's side his great-grandfather, Lieut.-Gen. Sir H. King, fought both in Holland and in the Peninsula with the 5th Fusiliers. Capt. Holt was born in July, 1866, and entered the Royal Army Medical Corps as a surg.-lieut. Jan., 1892, being promoted surg.-capt. 1895. He served in the operations on the North-West Frontier of India, 1897-98, with the Mohmand Field Force, also with the Tirah Expeditionary Force, and was awarded the medal with two clasps. He went to South Africa Nov., 1899, and first did duty in camp at Nottingham Road and Estcourt.

Capt. Holt was afterwards with the 5th Division, and was present at the action of Spion Kop. Just before being killed Feb. 21st, he had gone forward to assist some wounded men, and was kneeling down beside and attending to one when he was shot. Capt. Holt is buried close to where he fell under Fort Wyllie, and an obelisk marks the place where he lies with others of the Somersetshire Light Infantry. The Royal Army Medical Corps have also erected a memorial cross over his grave close to the obelisk. A tablet has been placed in St. Mary's Church, Alverstoke, in his memory. He was mentioned in despatches, L.G., Feb. 8th, 1901, for his services.

Homan.—2nd Lieut. Arthur Charles Fitzgerald Homan, Royal Field Artillery, died of enteric at Naauwpoort, May 11th, 1900. He was the eldest son of the Rev. J. F. Homan, Rector of Chicklade and Pertwood, near Hindon; was born July, 1878, educated at Elizabeth College, Guernsey, and joined the Royal Artillery, Dec., 1897. 2nd Lieut. Homan volunteered at the outbreak of the war, and was accepted for special service, and attached to the Cape Railway Pioneer Regt. He served at Fort Knokke, Orange River, Modder River, and Naauwpoort, and acted as adjutant to several companies, also trained the signallers selected from the regiment, and was afterwards employed repairing the bridges and line at Norval's Pont. He is buried at Naauwpoort; a handsome stone cross and kerb have been erected by the officers and men of No. 2 Company over his grave. In the parish church of Tisbury, Wilts, the officers and men of the Cape Railway Pioneer Regt. have placed a mural tablet to his memory.

Hood.—Capt. Alexander Nelson Hood, 1st Central India Horse, was killed in action at Elandslaagte, near Klerksdorp, Feb. 25th, 1902. He was the eldest son of the Hon. Alexander Frederick Hood, third son of the third Viscount Hood, by his marriage with the daughter of Algernon C. Heber-Percy, Esq. Capt. Hood was born in Oct., 1873; was educated at Radley, and entered the Manchester Regt. from the Royal Military College Oct., 1893, being promoted lieut. July, 1896, and was transferred to the Indian Staff Corps Aug., 1897. He was appointed A.D.C. to the Lieut.-Governor of Bengal Dec., 1899, but resigned this position in order to proceed to South Africa. He joined the I.Y. in Oct., 1901, and then served in the war up to the date of his death.

Hopkins.—Capt. W. F. Hopkins, Medical Staff, Victorian Infantry, died of enteric at Naauwpoort on March 27th, 1900.

Horley.—2nd Lieut. Bernard Joyce Horley, 4th Batt. Derbyshire Regt., was killed in action at Roodeval, June 7th, 1900. He was the son of J. T. Horley, Esq., Roxbro' Park, Harrow, was born in July, 1881, educated at Harrow, gazetted to the 4th Batt. Derbyshire Regt. Dec., 1899, and joined it in South Africa, March, 1900. The day he was killed, 2nd Lieuts. Horley and Lawder, the latter officer being attached to the battalion for duty, were ordered with thirty men to reinforce a party at a railway bridge. To do this they had to cross a piece of embankment on which the Boers were concentrating a heavy fire. At this point 2nd Lieut. Horley was wounded and fell. 2nd Lieut. Lawder picked him up, and carried him to a place of comparative shelter when another bullet, after first wounding his comrade Lawder, struck 2nd Lieut. Horley in the brain killing him instantly. He is buried near Rhenoster Kopje, Rhenoster River, a cross being erected over his grave.

Hoskier.—Lieut.-Col. Commandant F. H. Hoskier,

3rd Middlesex Volunteer Artillery Corps, was killed in action near Schoeman's Farm, Stormberg, Feb. 23rd, 1900. He was educated at Eton (Mr. Daman's), and was a well-known Volunteer officer, having, it is stated, brought the corps which he commanded to a high state of efficiency. He held a certificate for proficiency in several subjects, and had obtained special mention in examinations in tactics, besides being qualified as an interpreter. In civil life Col. Hoskier was a member of the Stock Exchange. At the outbreak of the war he went to South Africa at his own expense, and offered his services to Major-Gen. Sir W. F. Gatacre. Being accepted, he served with Brabant's Horse and Montmorency's Scouts till killed. He fell, shot in five places, the same day as Capt. de Montmorency. H.R.H. The Prince of Wales, the Hon. Col. of the 3rd Middlesex Volunteer Artillery, in addressing the corps on March 4th, 1903, said, " I should like to congratulate you on the numbers which you sent to South Africa, six officers and 1,114 rank and file. Alas! Col. Hoskier was not among those who returned to share with his comrades the welcome home, and we all join in regretting the great loss which the regiment has sustained by the death of that gallant officer."

Howard.—Major A. L. Howard, D.S.O., Canadian Scouts, was killed in action Feb. 17th, 1901, at Evergreen, Eastern Transvaal. He was employed with the machine gun section, and was mentioned in Gen. Lord Kitchener's despatch May 8th, 1901, for having been "repeatedly brought to his notice for acts of gallantry." Major Howard was awarded the D.S.O. for his services.

Howell.—Lieut. Edward Gronow Howell, 2nd Batt. Derbyshire Regt., was killed in action at Blesboklaagte, near Klip River, Feb. 12th, 1902. He was the youngest son of J. H. Howell, Esq., Castle Green, Bristol, was born Feb., 1879, and educated at Rossall. He entered the Derbyshire Regt. from the 4th Batt. South Staffordshire Regt. April, 1900, and was promoted lieut. Feb., 1901. Lieut. Howell first served in his Militia Batt. in South Africa, but being granted a commission in the Line was ordered to Malta. From this station he volunteered for active service, and proceeded with the M.I. to the seat of war, where he was killed as stated. Major Dowell, who was wounded on the same occasion, writes, " Lieut. Howell was close to me when he was shot, and although the Boers were within a hundred yards, he refused to leave me, and stood over me with his revolver until he was himself killed " Lieut. Howell is buried in the embankment close to Klip River Station, with ten others who fell. He was mentioned in despatches by Lieut.-Gen. Lord Kitchener, L.G., April 25th, 1902, for his services; "whilst attending to his commanding officer whom he refused to leave." His last words, as he fell, were " No Surrender."

Hubbe.—Capt. S. G. Hubbe, South Australian Bushmen, was killed in action at Ottoshoop, on Sept. 12th, 1900.

Huddart.—Midshipman Cymbeline Alonso Edric Huddart, of H.M.S. " Doris," was mortally wounded in action at Graspan, Nov. 25th, 1899, and died the same night. He was nearly 19 years of age, and was the son of the late James Huddart, Esq., of Eastbourne. He entered the " Britannia " in 1895, where he was one of the two chief captains of cadets, and passed out with such seniority that he joined the " St. George " on the Cape Station as midshipman June, 1897. On Admiral Rawson's arrival home from the Cape Midshipman Huddart was transferred to the " Doris." At the time of his death he was acting as A.D.C. to Capt. Prothero, commanding the naval brigade with the Kimberley Relief Force. At the battle of Graspan Midshipman Huddart is stated to have " behaved magnificently and still advanced after he had been twice wounded, until he was finally struck down mortally wounded." He is mentioned in the dispatch of Lieut.-Gen. Lord Methuen, Nov. 26th, 1899. Midshipman Huddart is buried close to the hospital at Enslin. (*See Commander Ethelston and Major Plumbe*).

Hudson.—Major Anthony Thomas Philip Hudson, p.s.c., 1st Batt. Manchester Regt., died Dec. 20th, 1901, of wounds received in action at Elandspruit the previous day. Born Feb., 1858, he entered the 63rd Foot Jan., 1878, being promoted lieut. 1879, capt. 1887, and major Jan., 1898. He was D.A.A.G., Mauritius, from March, 1895, to June, 1900. He then served in South Africa, and was commandant at Witklip. Major Hudson was mentioned in despatches by Gen. Lord Kitchener, March 8th, 1902, L.G., April 25th, 1892, for " gallant conduct in the repulse of the Boer attack " on the day he was mortally wounded.

Hudson.—Lieut. John Stanley Hudson, West Kent I.Y., was killed in action at Tweefontein on Christmas morning, 1901. He was the eldest son of the late John Hudson, Esq., of Japan, who died in 1893, and of Mrs. Hudson, late of Hensill, Hawkhurst. Lieut. Hudson was born at Yokohama in Oct., 1874, and was educated at Highgate Grammar School and Eastbourne College. From 1892-99 he was travelling in North America, but on his return volunteered as a trooper, was accepted, and sailed for South Africa in Feb., 1900. He served in the engagements at Senekal, Thaba N'chu, Ficksburg, Harrismith, Bethlehem and Standerton, and rendered such good service that he was given a commission as lieut. It is reported that his cool courage was frequently noticed during the war. The Christmas morning he was killed, the Boers under De Wet had crept up a precipice in overwhelming numbers to attack the British camp. Lieut. Hudson was in temporary command of his squadron, and had just given the order to fix bayonets when he fell mortally wounded. He is buried at Tweefontein, and his name is inscribed on an obelisk which has been erected there in memory of all who fell in this action.

Hughes.—Lieut. Albert Lionel Westropp Hughes, 2nd Batt. Royal Irish Fusiliers, died of enteric at Pretoria Feb. 18th, 1901. He was the son of J. H. Hughes, Esq., was born July, 1872, and educated at Haileybury, entered the Royal Irish Fusiliers from the 4th Batt. East Surrey Regt., June, 1894, and was promoted lieut. June, 1897. Lieut. Hughes accompanied his battalion to South Africa in November, 1899, and served with the Natal Field Force and in the Transvaal. He was mentioned in despatches L.G., Sept. 10th, 1901, for his services. He is buried at Pretoria beside Lieut. Neill, R.E.

Hughes.—Lieut. Louis Campbell Hughes, 2nd Kitchener's Fighting Scouts, was killed in action at Tweefontein, near Heilbron, November 14th, 1901. He was a son of the late Gen. Sir William Hughes, K.C.B., was 24 years of age, and educated at Marlborough. Lieut. Hughes was mentioned in despatches by Gen. Lord Kitchener, Dec. 8th, 1901, " for conspicuous gallantry in action." His name is inscribed on a tablet placed in Marlborough College Chapel in memory of all Marlburians who fell in the war.

Hughes.—Capt. Matthew Louis Hughes, Royal Army Medical Corps, was killed in action at Colenso, Dec. 15th,

1899. He was a son of Col. Emilius Hughes, C.B., A.S.C., of Guildford, was born in 1867, and educated at King's College, London, the University of Edinburgh, and the Rotunda Hospital, Dublin. He joined the R.A.M.C. in 1890, and was mentioned in despatches L.G., Feb. 8th, 1901.

Hughes.—Professor A. W. Hughes, Welsh Hospital, died during the war. He had rendered valuable service. F.-M. Earl Roberts in his despatch of April 2nd, 1901, L.G., April 16th, 1901, mentions him and states that none but those on the spot can realise how much the Welsh Hospital under Professors Jones and Hughes contributed to the comfort and well-being of the sick and wounded.

Hull.—2nd Lieut. Herbert Dauntesey Hull, 1st Batt. Northumberland Fusiliers, was killed in action at Lichtenburg March 3rd, 1901. Born in March, 1878, and educated at Eton (Mr. Impey's), he joined the first battalion in April, 1900, having previously served since July, 1899, in the 5th Batt. (Northumberland Militia) which had been embodied in Dec., 1899, and was stationed at Malta at the time of his transfer.

Hulse.—Major Charles Westrow Hulse, I.Y., was killed in action at Braklaagte, June 4th, 1901. Educated at Radley and Winchester, he was capt. and hon. major of the Duke of Connaught's Own Hampshire and Isle of Wight Artillery; and joined the I.Y. in Feb., 1901.

Humphreys.—2nd. Lieut. Geoffrey Knowles Humphreys, temporarily attached to Army Service Corps, died of enteric at Bloemfontein April 20th, 1901. He was the son of George Beauchamp Humphreys, Esq., Halifax, Yorks, was born Dec., 1878, educated at Heath, in

Yorkshire, and went out to South Africa as a trooper in the 77th Company I.Y. (Manchester), but shortly after arrival was invalided home with enteric. On recovering he returned to South Africa in Jan., 1901, was given a commission as 2nd lieut., and was attached to the Army Service Corps.

Hunnard.—Capt. Frank Hunnard, D.S.O., Army Service Corps, died of enteric at Newcastle, June 13th, 1900. He was the son of John Francis Hunnard, Esq., Westbourne Mansions, Hyde Park, W., was born Jan., 1873, and educated at Aldenham School, Elstree, where he was in the football team. Capt. Hunnard entered the South Wales Borderers from the Royal Military College Dec., 1892, and was transferred to the Army Service Corps in Oct., 1894, being promoted lieut. Sept., 1895, and capt. Sept., 1899. He served in the Nile Expedition of 1898, and was mentioned in despatches, L.G., Dec. 9th, 1898, receiving the D.S.O. and medal, also the Egyptian medal. He went to South Africa in Oct., 1899, as Supply Officer 2nd Infantry Brigade and was entitled to the medal with two clasps for the Tugela Heights and Relief of Ladysmith. He was also mentioned in despatches, L.G., Feb. 8th, 1901, for his services. Capt. Hunnard is buried in Newcastle cemetery, and a handsome cross has been erected over his grave by his brother officers.

Hunt.—Lieut. O. D. Hunt, 31st Company I.Y., died of Bright's disease at Johannesburg, Dec. 20th, 1901. He had been serving as a trooper in the Yeomanry, and was appointed lieut. 9th battalion in March, 1901.

Hunt.—Capt. Percy Frederick Hunt, Bushveldt Carabiniers, was killed in action at Daivel's Kloof, Northern Transvaal, on Aug. 6th, 1901.

Hunter.—Lieut. J. Hunter, Volunteer Company, Argyll and Sutherland Highlanders, died of enteric at Heilbron, June 30th, 1900. He obtained his lieutenant's commission in the 4th (Stirlingshire) Volunteer Battalion in 1898, and on volunteering for active service in South Africa was gazetted a temporary lieut. in the army, Feb. 24th, 1900.

Hutchinson.—Major F. Hutchinson, Imperial Light Horse, died of dysentery, at Harrismith, April 13th, 1902. He enlisted in the early part of the war in Brabant's Horse, and rose successively to sergt., lieut., capt., and major before he was transferred to the Imperial Light Horse. He was educated at Rugby (1872-75).

Hutton.—2nd Lieut. Stamford Henry Hutton, 1st Batt. Royal Inniskilling Fusiliers, died of enteric at Ladysmith April 15th, 1900. He was the younger son of the late Albert Hutton, Esq., of Rockwood, Swanlinbar, co. Cavan, and a nephew of Lord and Lady Singen, of Wetherby Gardens, S.W. 2nd Lieut. Hutton was born Jan., 1880, and was educated at Haileybury, passing thence into the Royal Military College, Sandhurst. He entered the Royal Inniskilling Fusiliers, Dec., 1899, and embarked immediately to join his battalion. He was present at the operations on the Tugela, and in the fighting on Feb 23rd-24th was one of four officers of the 1st Inniskillings who came out untouched, all the others being either killed or wounded. 2nd Lieut. Hutton then entered Ladysmith with the relieving force. He is buried in the town cemetery there, beside Capt. Gibton of the same regiment. A marble headstone has been erected in his memory by his comrades of all ranks, and a handsome railing encloses both graves.

Hylton-Jolliffe.—Lieut. John C. Hylton-Jolliffe, 3rd

Batt. Norfolk Regt., died from wounds received in action at Paardeberg, Feb. 20th, 1900. Educated at Eton (Mr. James'), he entered his battalion as a lieut. in April, 1899, and on the outbreak of the war volunteered for active service. He was then attached for duty to the 2nd battalion in South Africa, and served with it till killed. Lieut. Hylton-Jolliffe is mentioned in the despatch of F.-M. Earl Roberts, Feb. 28th, 1900, from Paardeberg, L.G., Feb. 8th, 1901.

Ingram.—Lieut. H. C. Ingram, Roberts' Horse (attached to Cape Pioneer Railway Regt.), died of concussion of the brain at Germiston, on Dec. 5th, 1900.

Inglis.—Capt. A. W. Inglis, Scottish Horse, was killed in action, near Brakenlaagte, 20 miles North-West of Bethel, Oct. 31st, 1901. He was 24 years of age, and was previously a 2nd lieut. in the I.Y., to which he had been appointed March 20th, 1901.

Irvine.—Lieut. D. W. Irvine, 23rd Batt. I.Y., died of enteric, at Harrismith, March 19th, 1902. He was the son of Charles Irvine, Esq., of Balham, was 24 years of age, and entered the I.Y. in March, 1901, with the rank of lieut. He is buried in the military cemetery at Harrismith. His name is engraved on a Latten Brass, placed in St. Paul's Cathedral, in memory of all ranks of the 18th, 21st, and 23rd battalions I.Y., who fell in the war.

Irvine.—Lieut. Guy Harle Irvine, Royal Army Medical Corps, was killed in action at Sanna's Post, while attending the wounded, March 31st, 1900. He was the son of Surgeon-Major G. N. Irvine, was born Aug., 1875, and educated at Wellington, where he was in the Murray, and left as a Prefect in 1892. He entered the Royal Army Medical Corps July, 1899, proceeded to South Africa the following Oct., and served there till killed.

Irving.—Lieut. T. J. Irving, Scottish Horse, died on Oct. 1st, 1901, of wounds received the previous day in action at Moedwill, seven miles East of Magota Nek in the Magaliesberg.

Jackson.—Capt. Christopher Goddard Jackson, 7th Dragoon Guards, was killed in action when on patrol duty near Arundel, Cape Colony, Dec. 16th, 1899. He was born Feb., 1872, educated at Cheltenham and entered the 7th Dragoon Guards Oct., 1892, being promoted lieut. April, 1896, and capt. Oct., 1899. Capt. Jackson volunteered for active service, and was sent to South Africa at the commencement of the war, and served in the north of Cape Colony. His name is inscribed on the Eleanor Cross War Memorial at Cheltenham College.

Jackson.—Assistant-Surgeon Jackson, attached to 21st Batt. Royal Field Artillery, died of enteric and dysentery at Pretoria, March 9th, 1900. He went with the Indian Contingent to South Africa in Sept., 1899. At the action at Lombard's Kop, while attending to the wounded, he was captured by the Boers, and was then sent to Pretoria, where he died.

Jameson.—2nd Lieut. George Uniacke Jameson, 1st Batt. Border Regt., was killed in action at Potchefstroom, Oct. 8th, 1901. He was the only son of Lieut.-Col. R. Jameson, I.M.S., of Lodeside House, Kilbirnie, Ayrshire, and of Maythorne, Ealing; was born July, 1879, and entered the Border Regt. from the 4th Batt. Highland Light Infantry, Dec., 1900. The action in which 2nd Lieut. Jameson was killed was his baptism of fire. With only ten mounted men and twenty infantry he had charge of a convoy of 40 wagons. They were suddenly surrounded by a large number of Boers. The country was most difficult, but 2nd Lieut. Jameson set a noble example. Although his horse was shot and he himself wounded, he continued to make a splendid resistance to the last, being ably assisted by Private Dunsmore, who was also killed.

Jansen.—Lieut. John Thomas Jansen, Warren's M.I., was killed in action near Plattdrift, June 15th, 1901.

Jeffcoat.—Capt. Henry Jameson Powell Jeffcoat, D.S.O., Royal Field Artillery, commanding the X Section of Pom-poms, was killed in action at Tafelkop, O.R.C., Dec. 20th, 1901. He was the son of Deputy-Surgeon-General Jeffcoat, of Surbiton, was born Jan., 1872, educated at King's School, Rochester, and entered the Royal Artillery from the Wicklow Militia Artillery Jan., 1892, being promoted lieut. Jan., 1895, and capt. March, 1900. Having volunteered for service in South Africa, he was for a time galloper to Lieut.-Gen. French, and was present at the battle of Paardeberg. At Tafel Kop the enemy, in our uniform and wearing our badges, and firing bogus volleys in the direction of distant Boers to keep up the deception, suddenly dashed at our artillery. Capt. Jeffcoat fell, and the gunners were all killed or wounded, only two, although struck and disabled, being still able to continue serving the gun. To these the dying Capt. Jeffcoat bequeathed the sum of £50 each in a will drawn up on the spot. He was mentioned in despatches, L.G., Sept. 10th, 1901, and was granted the D.S.O., and again in despatches, L.G., April 25th, 1902, for the " gallantry with which he continued to work his gun under a close fire." Capt. Jeffcoat is buried about three miles west of Tafel Kop, about midway between that place and Dundas.

Jelf.—Lieut. Richard John Jelf, Royal Engineers, died June 2nd, 1900, on board the troopship "Dilwara" whilst on his way home invalided from Natal. He was the eldest son of Major-Gen. R. H. Jelf, C.M.G., Governor and Commandant of the Royal Military Academy, Woolwich, and was born in 1872. Educated at Cheam and Eton (Mr. Luxmoore's), he obtained his commission in the Royal Engineers, Feb., 1892. Lieut. Jelf was a good horseman, and when stationed at Gibraltar was well known with the Calpe Hounds. He was selected for service in the Telegraph Batt. when on leave from Gibraltar, and sailed for South Africa Oct. 21st, 1899. After serving at De Aar and up to the Modder River, he was transferred with his section of the Telegraph Batt. to Gen. Sir Redvers Buller's command in Natal, and virtually acted as Director of Telegraphs to that officer throughout all his operations up to the Relief of Ladysmith. Having no proper staff to assist him, Lieut. Jelf had frequently to act as a telegraph operator at the instrument. His health subsequently broke down, and he was invalided home. He was mentioned in despatches, L.G., Feb. 8th, 1901, as indefatigable, and having had to work constantly day and night; "no difficulty was too great for him." Gen. Sir Redvers Buller in his despatch Nov. 9th, 1900, wrote, "I cannot omit a reference to the late Lieut. R. J. Jelf, Royal Engineers. A young officer of singular talent and promise, he lost his life from devotion to his duties." In Sept., 1899, shortly before he left for South Africa, Lieut. Jelf married Violet, daughter of Gen. Sir Richard Harrison, Inspector-General of Fortifications.

Jenkins.—Lieut. Charles Morris Jenkins, Thorneycroft's M.I., was killed in action at the battle of Colenso Dec. 15th, 1899. He was 32 years of age, and was formerly a sergt. in the Glamorgan Infantry Volunteers.

Lieut. Jenkins went to South Africa about 1888, and being a civil engineer was employed in the construction of the Harrismith Railway. From 1896 he was engaged on the Pretoria-Petersburg line, but in Oct., 1899, he was ordered to leave the Transvaal. On reaching Natal he offered his services, and was given a commission as lieut. in Thorneycroft's M.I.

Jenkinson.—Major Henry Law Acland Jenkinson, Royal Field Artillery, died of enteric at Farlington Rectory, Havant, Jan. 23rd, 1902. He was the only son of the late Henry Jenkinson, Esq., of Alverston, Warwick, was born Oct., 1863, and entered the Royal Artillery, July, 1882, being promoted capt. Jan., 1891, and major Jan., 1900. He was adjutant Royal Artillery from May, 1892, to Jan., 1900. Major Jenkinson was invalided home from South Africa, where he served as a capt. with G Battery, Royal Horse Artillery, embarking in Oct., 1899, and was in the advance on Bloemfontein. He was also employed under the Chief Censor.

Jennings-Bramly.—Major Alfred Jennings-Bramly, 19th Hussars, was killed in action at Hake-Banagher, Dec. 20th, 1901. He was the son of the late Capt. R. D. Jennings-Bramly, 12, Sussex Mansions, South Kensington, late of Grove Lodge, Southsea, and was born in Aug., 1864. He served in the ranks for over two years, and obtained a commission in the 19th Hussars in Oct., 1889, being promoted lieut. Aug., 1890, capt. Feb., 1897, brevet-major Nov., 1900, and major July, 1901. Major Jennings-Bramly served during the rising in the North-West Territories of Canada in 1885, receiving the medal. For his services during the South African war he was mentioned in despatches, L.G., Feb. 8th, 1901, Gen. Sir R. Buller describing him as "an excellent officer in every way," and recommending him "strongly for advancement." When the Scottish Horse was formed Major Jennings-Bramly was appointed 2nd in command, and, on the death of Major Murray, succeeded to the command.

Jervis-Edwards.—Major Cecil Bradney Jervis-Edwards, p.s.c., Duke of Cornwall's Light Infantry, was killed in action at Mondewens, near Dundee, July 28th, 1901. He was born in Feb., 1866, entered the Duke of Cornwall's Light Infantry Aug., 1885, being promoted capt. Oct., 1893, and received the brevet rank of major Nov., 1900. He was adjutant of his battalion from 1893-97, was a good linguist, and qualified as an interpreter in French. He served with the Wuntho Expedition, 1891-92, in command of a detachment of the 1st battalion of his regiment, receiving the medal with clasp. He was employed on special service in South Africa from Oct. to Dec., 1899, was then appointed A.D.C. to Major General Coke, commanding the 10th Infantry Brigade, and also served as Brigade Major, being present at the Relief of Ladysmith. In Oct., 1900, he was appointed a Staff Officer for Intelligence, and was mentioned in the despatches of Gen. Sir Redvers Buller, March 30th, June 19th, and Nov. 9th, 1900, L.G., Feb. 8th, 1901, and was promoted to a brevet majority for his services.

Johnson.—Lieut. Wilfrid Moss Johnson, 2nd Lancashire Volunteer Artillery, was killed in action at Hamelfontein, near Colesberg, Dec. 17th, 1900. He was the son of S. J. Johnson, Esq., Stanhope House, Woolton, Liverpool, was born in May, 1888, and educated at Sedbergh School, Yorkshire. He volunteered as a trooper in the I.Y., and joined the 32nd Co., sailing for South Africa, April, 1900. At Hamelfontein Lieut. Johnson, with a small party of yeomanry twenty-eight strong, was almost surrounded by about 250 Boers, who called on them to surrender. This the party refused to do, and they fought from 10.30 a.m. till two hours after dark, when the enemy retreated. Lieut. Johnson was shot about 3.30 p.m., and when struck he begged some of his men, who were endeavouring to assist him, and whose safety he was anxious about, to leave him as he was in no pain whatever. He, however, succumbed to his wounds, dying soon afterwards, and is buried at the Farm of Hamelfontein.

Johnson-Smyth.—Major Thomas Roger Johnson-Smyth, 1st Batt. Durham Light Infantry, was killed in action Feb. 5th, 1900, in the operations on the Upper Tugela. He was born June, 1857, educated at Rossall, and joined the 106th Foot from the Antrim Militia, Sept., 1878, being promoted lieut. April, 1879, capt. Feb., 1885, and major Aug., 1896. He served with the Soudan Frontier Field Force, 1885-86, and was present in the engagement at Giniss, receiving the medal and Khedive's star. Major Johnson-Smyth was adjutant of Militia from May, 1887, to May, 1892, and commandant of the School of Instruction, Militia and Volunteers, Aldershot, in 1899. He embarked for South Africa with his battalion in Oct., 1899, served with the Natal Field Force, and was mentioned in despatches, L.G., Feb. 8th, 1901.

Johnston.—Lieut. Alfred G. Johnston, 5th Victorian Mounted Infantry, was killed near Rhenoster Kop on May 7th, 1901.

Johnstone.—Lieut. Halbert Russell Johnstone, 19th Co., 6th Batt. I.Y., died Jan. 6th, 1902, of wounds received two days previously in action at Onverwacht, Ermelo district. He was the son of the late R. Johnstone, Esq., Yokohama, and Mrs. Johnstone, now of Inglewood, Upper Norwood, was born March, 1874, and educated at Dollar, Scotland. He was a fearless rider, and good at all games. Lieut. Johnstone went out at the outbreak of the war, and first served as a trooper in Strathcona's Horse, and saw much service in Natal and the subsequent advance into the Transvaal, for which he was granted the medal with three clasps. He was afterwards given a commission in the Yeomanry, and served with Gen. Plumer's force. At Onverwacht (which means unexpected) some Boers who were dressed like our troops, were mistaken for some New Zealanders, who had been sent on in advance. When the error was discovered, the Boers were quite close to our men. Lieut. Johnstone, who was in command of his company, led it most gallantly, but fell mortally wounded. He died in the ambulance and is buried at a farm near Balmoral, Transvaal. A tablet has been placed to his memory in the cemetery at Annan, Dumfriesshire.

Johnstone.—Lieut. Norman Marshall Johnstone, attached 1st Royal Dragoons, was killed in action in the operations of the Natal Field Force, at Alleman's Nek, June 11th, 1900. He was the fifth son of D. Johnstone, Esq., Croy, Dumbartonshire, was born Aug. 1872, and educated at St. Salvator's School, St. Andrews, and Harrow. He entered the 11th Hussars March, 1893, was promoted lieut. Jan., 1895, and served in the operations on the North-West Frontier of India, 1897-98, receiving the medal with clasp. At the commencement of the war he volunteered and was attached to the 1st Royal Dragoons, and served with that regiment up to the relief of Ladysmith, having been present at all the fighting on the Tugela, including the battle of Colenso and the actions at Acton Homes, Spion Kop, Vaal Kranz, and Pieter's Hill. Lieut. Johnstone was then appointed adjutant of Gough's Composite Regt. of M.I., and afterwards served with it in the advance from Ladysmith, until he fell. He was awarded the medal with five clasps. He is buried at Hartebeestefontein Farm, near Volksrust. A tablet in his memory and that of two other comrades who fell has been placed in Canterbury Cathedral. Lieut. Johnstone was mentioned in despatches, L.G. Feb. 8th, 1901, for his services.

Jones.—Lieut. George Williams Grey Jones, Royal Army Medical Corps, died of enteric Feb. 20th, 1900, in Ladysmith. He was born in August, 1874, and joined the Royal Army Medical Corps, Jan., 1899. Lieut. Jones was serving in Natal at the commencement of the war, and took part in the defence of Ladysmith.

Jones.—Lieut. Robert James Thomas Digby Jones, Royal Engineers, was killed in action at the engagement at Wagon Hill, Ladysmith, Jan. 6th, 1900. He was born Sept., 1876, educated at Seabank School and Sedbergh, Yorkshire, where he was in the school football team, and won the chief mathematical prize. He entered the Royal Engineers, August, 1896, being promoted lieut. August, 1899; was a good all round athlete, and at one time secretary of the Royal Engineers Football Club, being one of its foremost players. Lieut Jones accompanied the 23rd Field Co. Royal Engineers to Natal, June, 1899, and served there from the commencement of the war. He first distinguished himself Dec. 10th, during a sortie from Ladysmith when a Boer 4·7 inch gun on Surprise Hill was destroyed. The first fuze inserted missed fire but Lieut. Jones went back, inserted another fuze and by the explosion the Howitzer was split into fragments. This, gun had been causing much annoyance to the garrison. For this act he was mentioned in despatches. At Wagon Hill his bravery was most conspicuous; on the night of the 5th he was sent there in charge of a working party of Royal Engineers to build an emplacement, and out of this, the Boers who had crept up bare footed, had succeeded in driving them. Our men led by Lieut. Jones, however, retook the position almost immediately. One report states that he shot three Boers, clubbed a fourth and kept them at bay till help arrived. Later on a determined attack was again made by the Boers, when Lieut. Jones shot Commandant Von Wyk, second in command to De Villiers, but was himself killed immediately afterwards. Sir A. Conan Doyle thus mentions this incident, differing slightly from the above: "In a gun emplacement a strange encounter took place at point blank range between a group of Boers and Britons. De Villiers of the Free State shot Miller-Walnut dead, Ian Hamilton fired at De Villiers with his revolver but missed him. Young Albrecht of the Light Horse shot De Villiers. A Boer named De Jaeger shot Albrecht. Digby Jones of the Sappers shot De Jaeger. Only a few minutes later the gallant lad, who had already won fame enough for a veteran, was himself mortally wounded, and Dennis his comrade in arms and in glory fell by his side." Another report states that by his splendid example Lieut. Jones saved Ladysmith. In most books on the war this officer's bravery and intrepid conduct is referred to. He was twice mentioned in despatches, L.G., Feb. 8th, 1901, and again April 19th, 1901, where it is stated by Lieut.-Gen. Sir G. White that he would have recommended Lieut. Jones for the V.C. had he survived, and mentions with regret that he was killed. It was, however, announced in the L.G., August 8th, 1902, that His Majesty The King was pleased to approve of this decoration being sent to the representatives of Lieut. Jones, for his conspicuous bravery " in leading the force which re-occupied the top of the hill at a critical moment, just as the three foremost attacking Boers reached it, the leader being shot by Lieut. Jones." At the Royal Military Academy, Woolwich, in the west octagon of the library, are the names of about 120

ERRATA.

Jones.— Lieut. Philip Astell Jones, 8th Hussars, was killed in action near Dalmanutha, Oct. 13th, 1900. He was the eldest son of Griffith Jones, Esq., of The Bury, Goldington, near Bedford; was born March, 1875, and educated at Rugby, whence he passed direct into Sandhurst. He entered the 8th Hussars Sept., 1895, being promoted lieut. Nov., 1896, and was appointed adjutant of his regiment March, 1899. Lieut. Jones was selected for special service in Natal, under Lieut.-Gen. Sir G. White, but on arrival in Nov., 1899, Ladysmith was already invested, and he was then attached for duty to the Army Service Corps with the Natal Field Force. He was present at the actions at Chieveley, Monte Christo, Pieters Hill, and the relief of Ladysmith. Maj.-Gen. Barton, C.B., to whom he was acting as galloper, brought his good services to notice on two occasions. On the arrival of the 8th Hussars in South Africa, Lieut. Jones, in April, 1900, rejoined his regiment, again taking up the duties of adjutant. He then took part in the advance on Pretoria, and was present at every engagement with his regiment, including the Battle of Diamond Hill, where his gallantry is stated to have been very conspicuous. He was mentioned in despatches L. G., Feb. 8th, 1901. Lieut. Jones is buried at Dalmanutha; a marble cross erected to his memory by his brother officers marks his grave.

distinguished Royal Engineer Officers; the last name added to the list is that of Lieut. R. J. T. Digby Jones.

Jones.—Professor Thomas Jones, F.R.C.S., died of enteric at Springfontein. He was the chief of the Welsh Military Hospital in South Africa, a professor of Owens College, a leading honorary member of the Manchester Infirmary and Hospital Staff, and a renowned operator. After leaving Guy's Hospital he settled in Manchester. When the Welsh Hospital was formed, Professor Jones was asked to take charge of it, which position he accepted and proceeded to South Africa. In mentioning his services F.-M. Earl Roberts in his despatch, L.G., April 16th, 1901, states: "that none but those on the spot can realise how much the Welsh Hospital, under Professors Jones and Hughes, contributed to the comfort and well-being of the sick and wounded."

Julian.—Lieut. Charles John Julian, O Battery, Royal Horse Artillery, died at Vryheid, Nov. 6th, 1901, from perityphlitis. Born July, 1876, and educated at Charterhouse, he entered the Royal Artillery, Sept., 1896, being promoted lieut. Sept., 1899. He went out to South Africa at the beginning of the war, and was at first attached to an ammunition column, afterwards to the 74th Battery Royal Field Artillery, and finally to O Battery, Royal Horse Artillery. Lieut. Julian is buried at Vryheid, and his name is inscribed on the tablet in the War Memorial Cloister erected at Charterhouse.

Kane.—Lieut. Harold Robert Kane, South Lancashire Regt., was killed in action at Fort Itala, Zululand, Sept. 25th, 1901. Born in June, 1878, and educated at Elizabeth College, Guernsey, he entered the South Lancashire Regt., Sept., 1897, being promoted lieut. Oct., 1899. He served with the Natal Field Force, and was present at

the operations of the 17th to the 24th Jan., the 5th to
the 7th Feb., and the 19th to the 27th Feb., 1900, on the
Tugela, and was wounded Feb. 22nd. He was present at
the actions of Spion Kop and Vaal Kranz, being mentioned
in Gen. Sir Redvers Buller's despatches, March 30th and
Nov. 9th, 1900, L.G., Feb. 8th, 1901. When he fell he
was with a strong outpost of about 80 men in front of
Fort Itala, and this party was attacked at midnight by
several hundreds of the enemy. The defence is stated to
have been a most gallant one, and as Lieut. Kane died,
his last words were " No Surrender ! "

Kay.—Fleet-Paymaster William Hobart Fendall Kay
died of enteric March 26th, 1900, at Ascension, on his
way home from South Africa. He entered the Navy in
March, 1864, was promoted Assistant-Paymaster April,
1869, Paymaster Jan., 1885, Staff-Paymaster Jan., 1891,
and Fleet-Paymaster Jan., 1897. Fleet-Paymaster Kay
had seen much active service, and was an old campaigner.
He was in the "Satellite" in 1867, when some piratical
villages in the Nicobar Islands were destroyed and some
European captives were released. He next saw service in
the Abyssinian Expedition, 1868, being granted the medal ;
also, as Paymaster of the Naval Brigade, landed for service
with the Nile Expedition for the relief of Gen. Gordon,
1884-85, when he was awarded the Egyptian medal with
clasp and bronze star. He had been wrecked in H.M.
ship " Amazon," in 1866, and was secretary of the committee presided over by Admiral Sir A. Hoskins, in 1884,
for awarding certificates of character to seamen. Fleet-
Paymaster Kay was appointed to the " Powerful," which
commissioned at Portsmouth, August, 1897. On the way
home from Hong Kong in 1899, owing to the war in South
Africa, the ship was delayed, and a Naval Brigade sent up
to Ladysmith. Fleet-Paymaster Kay accompanied it as
accountant and commissariat officer, and served through-

out the siege. It is stated that "his powers of organization and forethought" were very noticeable. In the last few weeks of the siege he performed the duties of Field-Paymaster to the Army, but unfortunately contracted enteric and was invalided, dying as stated. He is buried in the little cemetery at Ascension.

Keith.—Capt. Clive Skene Keith, I.Y., was killed in action in the operations between Kroonstad and Lindley May 29th, 1900. He was born in May, 1863, educated at Eton (Mr. Shuckburg's), entered the South Staffordshire Regt. from the 5th Brigade Scottish Division Royal Artillery on May 14th, 1884, and was transferred to the 3rd Dragoon Guards a week later, retiring in 1892, after eight years' service. Capt. Keith joined the I.Y. Feb., 1900, being given a commission as capt.

Keith-Falconer.—Brevet Lieut.-Col. Cecil Edward Keith-Falconer, p.s.c., 1st Batt. Northumberland Fusiliers, was killed in action near Belmont on Nov. 10th, 1899, in the reconnaissance made by Col. Gough, 9th Lancers. He was the eldest son of the late Major the Hon. Charles J. Keith-Falconer, late of the 2nd Life Guards, and a grandson of the seventh Earl of Kintore. Lieut.-Col. Keith-Falconer was born in Oct., 1860, educated at Charterhouse, and joined the Northumberland Fusiliers from the Militia Jan., 1883. He became capt. 1892, and passed through the Staff College in 1895, with honours, and in the competition for entrance was at the head of the list of candidates. He served with the 13th Soudanese Batt. in the Dongola Expeditionary Force in 1896, being mentioned in despatches; and acted as Brigade-Major at the engagements of Abu Hamed, Berber, Atbara, and the battle of Omdurman. In recognition of these services he was three times mentioned in despatches, and promoted to a brevet majority Dec., 1897, and to the rank of brevet-lieut.-col. Nov., 1898. He acted as A.D.C. to Lord Loch, when Governor and Commander-in-Chief of Victoria, 1887-89, and subsequently at the Cape of Good Hope, 1889-90. Lieut.-Col. Keith-Falconer went to South Africa in Oct., 1899. He is buried in the cemetery at Orange River. (*See Lieut. Keith-Falconer.*)

Keith-Falconer.—Lieut. Victor Francis Alexander Keith-Falconer, 2nd Batt. Somersetshire Light Infantry, was killed in action at Hussar Hill, near the Tugela, Feb. 21st, 1900. He was a son of the late Major the Hon. Charles James Keith-Falconer, and a grandson of the seventh Earl of Kintore, was born Oct., 1869, and educated at Charterhouse. He entered the Somersetshire Light Infantry March, 1890, being promoted lieut. Aug., 1893. Lieut. Keith-Falconer served in the campaign on the North-West Frontier of India, under the late Sir William Lockhart, in 1897, with the Mohmand Field Force, as adjutant to his battalion, receiving the medal with clasp. For his services in South Africa he was mentioned in despatches, L.G., Feb. 8th, 1901. He is buried close to where he fell, near Fort Wyllie and the village of Colenso. The names of both the above officers are inscribed in a framed tablet placed in the Court House of the Spelthorne Division of Middlesex, in memory of those belonging to the Division who fell in the war; their names are also engraved on the tablet in the War Memorial Cloister erected at Charterhouse.

Kelly.—Lieut. J. P. Kelly, Scottish Horse, was killed in action near Brakenlaagte (20 miles north-west of Bethel), on Oct. 31st, 1901.

Kelly.—Capt. John Kelly, 5th Victorian M.I., was dangerously wounded at Rhenoster Kop May 7th, 1901, and died two days later.

Kemble.—Capt. Charles Morris Kemble, Army Service Corps, died of enteric at Bloemfontein March 29th, 1900. He was the son of C. A. Kemble, Esq., was born June, 1870, and educated at Haileybury. He entered the Yorkshire Regt. from the Glamorgan Artillery, was promoted lieut. Dec., 1893, and transferred to the Army Service Corps, April, 1894, being made capt. Sept., 1898. Capt. Kemble married Sept., 1896, Freda, daughter of Capt. Webber, 45th Regt. He served in the Nile Expedition of 1898, and was present at the battle of Khartoum, being awarded the Medal and the Egyptian medal with clasp. Capt. Kemble embarked for South Africa Oct., 1899.

Kemmis-Betty.—2nd Lieut. Gerald Ernest Kemmis-Betty, Army Service Corps, died of enteric at Howick, Feb. 24th, 1901. He was born March, 1876, entered the 4th Batt. Lancaster Regt. Jan. 1900 (which was then embodied), and proceeded to South Africa. 2nd Lieut. Kemmis-Betty was employed with the transport in South Africa, being graded as a staff capt. from March 16th, 1900, and was transferred to the Army Service Corps in the following September.

Kensington.—Capt. Lord Kensington, 2nd Life Guards, died June 24th, 1900, at Bloemfontein, from wounds received at Houtnek, April 30th. William Edwardes, fifth Baron Kensington in the peerage of Ireland, and second Baron Kensington in the peerage of the United Kingdom, was born in July, 1868, and educated at Eton (Dr. Warre's and Mr. Donaldson's). He was the eldest son of the fourth baron, and entered the 2nd Life Guards from the 7th Batt. King's Royal Rifle Corps, June, 1892, being promoted lieut. April, 1893, and capt. Feb., 1900. Lord Kensington succeeded his father in 1896, and was succeeded in the title by his brother, the Hon. Hugh Edwardes, D.S.O., who is a lieut. in the 15th Hussars.

He was a J.P. and D.L. for Pembrokeshire and a J.P. for Haverfordwest.

Kent.—Capt. Frederic Sidney Kent, 2nd Batt. East Yorkshire Regt. died of pneumonia in Pretoria July 22nd, 1900. He was born Nov., 1871, educated at Highgate School, and entered the East Yorkshire Regt. June, 1894, being promoted lieut. Jan., 1897, and capt. March, 1900.

Kenyon.—2nd Lieut. William Henry Kenyon, Liverpool Regt., died of enteric at No. 4 Stationary Hospital, Newcastle, July 20th, 1900. He was a son of T. Redman Kenyon, Esq., Beaucoin, West Derby, Liverpool, was born in Oct., 1872, and educated privately. He joined the 2nd V.B. Liverpool Regt., 1895, and volunteered for, and proceeded to, South Africa early in 1900. He rendered such good service that he was almost immediately granted a commission in the regular army and joined the 2nd Batt. of the Liverpool Regt. on May 5th. A tablet has been erected to his memory in Sefton Park Presbyterian Church, Liverpool, by all ranks of the 2nd Volunteer Batt. to which he first belonged.

Kerans.—Lieut. P. L. Kerans, Roberts' Horse, died of enteric at Kroonstad, on June 8th, 1900.

Keswick. — Lieut. David Johnson Keswick, 12th Lancers, was killed in action March 7th, 1900, near Poplar Drift, to the east of Osfontein on the Modder River. He was the younger son of W. Keswick, Esq., M.P., Eastwick Park, Surrey, was born Oct., 1876, and educated at Eton (Mr. Radcliffe's). Lieut. Keswick entered the 12th Lancers, Feb., 1897, and was promoted lieut. May, 1898. This officer's death is mentioned in the

OFFICERS WHO FELL IN SOUTH AFRICA. 203

despatch of F.-M. Earl Roberts, from Bloemfontein, March 15th, 1900.

Key.—Lieut. John Reynard Key, 2nd Batt. East Yorkshire Regt., died at Thaba N'chu April 4th, 1901. He was born in Jan., 1878, and entered his regiment from the 3rd Batt. York and Lancaster Regt. Jan., 1899, being promoted lieut. Jan., 1900. Lieut. Key embarked with his battalion for South Africa in 1900, and was employed with the Mounted Infantry.

Kidd.—Veterinary-Surgeon W. Kidd, attached for duty, died at Wynberg, Oct. 29th, 1901.

Kimber.—Lieut. Charles Dixon Kimber (Duke of Cambridge's Own) I.Y., was killed in action at Wildfontein, near Ventersdorp, July 17th, 1901, while endeavouring to save a dismounted sergt. of his troop. Lieut. Kimber was the second son of Henry Kimber, Esq., M.P., Lansdowne Lodge, Putney, and grandson of the late Lieut.-Gen. Dixon, Royal Engineers. He was born Oct. 24th, 1863, and educated at Epsom, and Merton College, Oxford. He was admitted a solicitor in Jan., 1890, and was a member of the firm of Kimbers and Boatman, Lombard Street, E.C. Lieut. Kimber volunteered for service early in 1900, and joined the Duke of Cambridge's Own as a trooper. He was present in the affair of Lindley, and taken as a prisoner to Nooigedacht, but escaped from there, reaching the British lines Aug. 5th, 1900. He was then attached to the 1st Cavalry Brigade for duty, and was appointed lieut. in the I.Y. Sept., 1900, and afterwards saw much service. The evening before he was killed, his squadron consisting of three officers, Lieut. Kimber and 45 men, was sent from camp at Grasslaagte to Wildfontein, distant about thirty miles, to surprise some Boers. Heavy rain fell during the night march, and just as day was breaking the party reached its destination, and having captured some cattle, was attacked by some of Kemp's Commando. The squadron formed a rear-guard, but the Boers succeeded in getting round the left flank, and the cattle had to be abandoned. The party was then ordered to retire, and while the movement was being carried out, Lieut. Kimber heard a shout for help and, looking round, saw one of his sergeants on foot whose horse had bolted. Riding back to assist him, and while the sergeant was in the act of mounting behind him, a Boer fired at them and Lieut. Kimber fell shot through the heart. The sergeant was uninjured. Lieut. Kimber is buried at Pietfontein, on the road to Ventersdorp. A history of this officer's life has been written by his sister, Mrs. Thomson, Eirene, Putney, S.W., published by Nisbet and Co., the proceeds being devoted to the erection of a Soldiers' Home near Pretoria in memory of Lieut. Kimber.

King.—Capt. John Boyd King, Kitchener's Fighting Scouts, was killed in action at Stellenbosch Vlei, Cape Colony, March 8th, 1901, aged 38. The eldest son of Hamilton King, Esq., late of Ayr, N.B., he was born in Kilmarnock, and educated at Ayr Academy and University College, Glasgow. He went to South Africa in 1894, served in the Matabele Rebellion of 1896, and was awarded the medal. Capt. King was in Rhodesia in 1899 when war broke out, and at once offered his services. He joined the Rhodesian Regt., and was present at the Relief of Mafeking, being severely wounded the day our troops entered the town. He then came home, and recovering (after four months) from his wounds, again proceeded to South Africa and joined Kitchener's Fighting Scouts, and in Nov., 1900, was given command of a squadron. He fell at the head of his men while directing their fire, and just before he was killed he shot the Boer Commandant.

Capt. King is buried where he fell and his grave is railed in to mark its exact position.

King.—2nd Lieut. Walter Buchanan King, 1st Batt. Argyll and Sutherland Highlanders, was killed in action at Magersfontein, Dec. 11th, 1899. He was born in May, 1878, and joined the Argyll and Sutherland Highlanders, May, 1898. This officer was first reported missing, but was afterwards found to have been killed as stated. He embarked for South Africa in Oct., 1899, and joining the Kimberley Relief Force was present at the battle of Modder River.

Kinnear.—2nd Lieut. Robert Hill Kinnear, 5th Dragoon Guards, died of enteric at Ladysmith, March 16th, 1900. He was the only son of Robert Shiell Kinnear, Esq., born Feb., 1879, and educated at Harrow. He entered the 5th Dragoon Guards from the 3rd Batt. Black Watch (Royal Highlanders), in May, 1899. 2nd Lieut. Kinnear was with his regiment in Natal on the outbreak of the war, and served throughout the siege of Ladysmith.

Kirk—Lieut. Kirk, Imperial Light Horse, died at Rietfontein, on July 7th, 1900. He was mentioned in despatches, L.G., April 16th, 1901.

Kirk.—Capt. Maurice Wrottesley Kirk, Royal Lancaster Regt., was killed in action at Spion Kop, in the operations on the Upper Tugela, Jan. 24th, 1900. He was the son of Lieut.-Col. Kirk, and was married to Mabel Eleanor, daughter of J. J. Tufnell, Esq. Born April, 1866, and educated at Haileybury, he entered his regiment from the 3rd Batt. The Buffs, Nov. 1887, and was promoted lieut. Dec., 1889, and capt. Nov., 1897. Capt. Kirk embarked for South Africa, Nov. 1899, with his battalion, which on arrival was sent to Natal, where he served with the Natal Field Force until killed.

Knapp.—Capt. J. C. Knapp, Imperial Light Horse, was killed in action in a reconnaissance from Ladysmith, Nov. 3rd, 1899. He was 43 years of age, and was a managing director of Rhodesia, Limited. He had been present at the battles of Elandslaagte and Lombards Kop, and was an old hand in South African warfare. In 1877-78, Capt. Knapp served with the Cape Mounted Rifles, and afterwards held a commission in the Cape Regular Infantry. As pioneer of Buluwayo, he helped to organise the Rhodesian Horse, and was in the Matabele Campaign, commanding Gifford's Horse, when Col. the Hon. Maurice Gifford was wounded. At the outbreak of the South African War, Capt. Knapp, having volunteered for service, was given command of E squadron of Imperial Light Horse, at the head of which he met his death. It is stated that he was the idol of his squadron. He was mentioned in despatches by Lieut.-Gen. Sir G. White, Dec. 2nd, 1899, L.G., Feb. 8th, 1901. Capt. Knapp was a fellow of the Royal Colonial Institute, his name is inscribed on a memorial tablet in the hall of the building in Northumberland Avenue, S.W. (*See Major Taunton.*)

Knight.—Capt. Oswald Thomas Knight, Herschel Native Police, died of heart failure at Herschel, on April 5th, 1902.

Knowles.—Lieut. Alfred Millington Knowles, 3rd Batt. I.Y., was killed in action at Rietfontein, Aug. 9th, 1900. He was the son of Robert Millington Knowles, Esq., Colston Bassett, Nottinghamshire, was 29 years of age, and educated at Charterhouse. He became a capt. in the Nottinghamshire Yeomanry Cavalry, in March, 1899, and on joining the I.Y. in Feb., 1900, was given the rank of lieut. in the army. His name is inscribed on the tablet in the War Memorial Cloister at Charterhouse.

Knowles.—Lieut. Malcolm Knowles, 1st (Royal) Dragoons, died March 28th, 1902, of wounds received in action at Leeuwbosch, south-west of Klerksdorp, four days previously, while leading the advance in one of the drives against De La Rey. He was the only son of Mrs. Knowles, Thorpe Hall, Wycliffe, Darlington, was born June, 1881, and educated at Eton (Mr. Carter's), where he was in the shooting eight. Lieut. Knowles entered the 1st Dragoons from the Royal Military College in Aug., 1900, and was promoted lieut. April, 1901. He is buried in Klerksdorp cemetery.

Knox.—Capt. Charles Stuart Knox, Gloucestershire Regt., died at Colombo, Ceylon, Nov. 26th, 1901. He was the youngest son of Major James Knox, Governor of Wandsworth Prison, was born in Sept., 1872, entered the Gloucestershire Regt., May, 1892, being promoted lieut. July, 1893, and capt. Feb., 1900. Capt. Knox served in the South African War during 1899-1900, and was present at the actions at Rietfontein and Farquhar's Farm.

Knox.—Lieut.-Col. and Brevet-Col. Eustace Chaloner Knox, commanding the 18th Hussars, died in London of acute pneumonia after a few days illness Feb. 18th, 1902. He was the son of the late Lieut.-Gen. Richard Knox, Hon. Colonel of the 18th Hussars, was born in March, 1860, and served in the ranks for nearly three years and a half. He was promoted lieut. in the 18th Hussars, August, 1882, capt. April, 1886, major May, 1896, lieut.-col. Sept., 1900, and brevet-col. the following Nov. Col. Knox was adjutant of his regiment from 1886 to 1891, adjutant of the cavalry depôt from 1894 to 1897, and was then appointed adjutant of the cavalry brigade which post he held till Sept., 1898. He served throughout the Nile Expedition of 1884-85 with the Light Camel Regt., and took part in the operations of the Desert Column, receiving the medal with clasp and Khedive's star. In the South African War he took part in the action at Talana Hill, and the defence of Ladysmith, being mentioned in despatches by Lieut.-Gen. Sir George White, March 23rd, 1900, and by Gen. Sir Redvers Buller, Nov. 9th, 1900, (L.G., Feb. 8th, 1901), receiving the brevet of colonel. In Dec., 1900, he was appointed to the command of the 2nd Cavalry Brigade in South Africa, which appointment he held till July, 1901. At the time of his death, he was at home on leave through ill health. Col. Knox is buried at Brookwood.

Kortright.—Lieut. Mounteney Kortright, 3rd (King's Own) Hussars, died June 21st, 1900, at Johannesburg, of wounds received in action at Rietfontein, May 30th. He was the son of the late Augustus Kortright, Esq., of Furze Hall, Fryerning, Essex, by his marriage with Mary, daughter of the Rev. I. Mounteney Jephson. Lieut. Kortright was born in June, 1872, educated at Tonbridge School, and entered the 3rd Hussars from the 3rd Essex Regt. Jan., 1893, being promoted lieut. Feb., 1894. A tablet has been erected to his memory at Fryerning by the officers of the 16th (Queen's) Lancers.

Kynoch-Shand.—2nd Lieut. R. McK. Kynoch-Shand, 6th V.B. Gordon Highlanders, was killed in action at Spion Kop, Jan. 24th, 1900. He joined his regiment in June, 1898, and, when killed, was serving with the Imperial Light Infantry.

Labram.—(Mr.) Labram was killed at Kimberley, Feb. 9th, 1900. He was an American and Chief Engineer of the De Beers Company, and served during the siege, rendering the most valuable assistance. He succeeded in constructing in the mining workshops, with the aid of tools specially made, a 28-pounder rifled gun. This gun was called "Long Cecil," and was a rifled breech-loader of 4·1 in. calibre and 10 ft. in length, with a range of about 10,000 yards. In order to reply to "Long Cecil," the Boers mounted an enormous gun on Kamfersdam, about four miles from Kimberley. By an extraordinary chance, Mr. Labram was killed in his bedroom in the Grand Hotel by a 96 lb. shell from this Boer gun. The shell entered the window and, exploding, killed him instantly. A servant who was in the room with him escaped uninjured.

Lace.—2nd Lieut. Francis Edward Lace, 14th Hussars, died of septicœmia at Newcastle Oct. 21st, 1901. He was born in July, 1881, and joined the 14th Hussars from the Royal Military College in Jan., 1900.

Lafone.—Capt. William Bautcher Lafone, 1st Batt. Devonshire Regt. was killed in action at Wagon Hill, near Ladysmith, Jan. 6th, 1900. He was the fourth son of Alfred Lafone, Esq., of Hanworth Park, Middlesex, at the time M.P. for Bermondsey. Capt. Lafone was born in 1860, educated at Dulwich College and Haileybury, and entered the 11th Foot in 1880, was promoted lieut. 1881, and capt. 1888. He served in the operations on the North-West Frontier of India, 1897-98, with the Tirah Expeditionary Force, receiving the medal with two clasps. At Wagon Hill Capt. Lafone was in the ever memorable charge made by the Devon Regt., led by Col. Park. Capt. Lafone was twice wounded, but continued to lead his company until he fell shot through the head. He was mentioned in despatches by Lieut.-Gen. Sir George White, from Ladysmith, Dec. 2nd, 1899, and again in the despatch of March 23rd, 1900 (L.G., Feb. 8th, 1901). The name of Capt. Lafone is inscribed on a framed tablet placed in the Court House of the Spelthorne

Division of Middlesex in memory of those belonging to the division who fell in the war. His name also appears on a tablet on the outside of the New Memorial Library at Dulwich College.

Laing.—Major (local Lieut.-Col.) D. Tyrie Laing, Commander-in-Chief's Bodyguard, was killed in action Jan. 3rd, 1901. He was in command of a force sent to reconnoitre from Lindley to Reitz. They were suddenly attacked, and Lieut.-Col. Laing fell, shot through the heart. He was mentioned by F.-M. Earl Roberts in despatches, L.G., April 16th, 1901, who stated that he deeply deplored his death, and that he had shown himself "an officer of great merit, and I am much indebted to him." Lieut.-Col. Laing was a Fellow of the Royal Colonial Institute, and his name is inscribed upon a memorial tablet in the hall of the building in Northumberland Avenue, S.W.

Laird.—Capt. Gordon Laird, 8th Battery Royal Field Artillery, died Oct. 1st, 1901, of wounds received in action the previous day at Moedwill (seven miles east of Magota Nek). Born in May, 1868, and educated at Charterhouse, he entered the Royal Artillery in July, 1887, being promoted lieut. July, 1890, and capt. Dec. 1897. He served in the South African war from 1899, and was mentioned in the despatch of Gen. Lord Kitchener, Oct. 8th, 1901, for his "gallantry." Capt. Laird's name is inscribed on the tablet in the War Memorial Cloister at Charterhouse.

Lake.—Surgeon-Lieut.-Col. William Wellington Lake, of the Militia Medical Staff Corps, died of Bright's disease at Bloemfontein July 13th, 1900. He was educated at St. Thomas's Hospital, and admitted a Licentiate of the Royal College of Surgeons, England, in

1877. Lieut.-Col. Lake was afterwards obstetric House Physician at St. Thomas's Hospital, and House Physician at the City of London Hospital for diseases of the chest. He had been surgeon-major of the Militia Medical Staff Corps since July, 1898, and, having volunteered for service in South Africa, went out with the Volunteer Co. of the Royal Army Medical Corps, and was promoted a lieut.-col. Feb., 1900. He had seen active service as surgeon in the Ottoman Army, having been awarded the medal and Fourth Class of the Order of the Medjidie for his services during the Russo-Turkish war of 1877-78. He had held many public appointments, and was the author of several valuable papers which were published in the professional journals.

Lamb.—2nd Lieut. Edward A. Lamb, New South Wales Mounted Infantry, was killed in action, with Col. Williams' Column, on May 10th, 1901.

Lambton.—Capt. Alexander Frederick Lambton, 1st Batt. Highland Light Infantry, was killed in action at Magersfontein Dec. 11th, 1899. He was the second son of Lieut.-Col. Francis William Lambton, of Brownslade, Pembrokeshire, late Scots Guards, by his marriage with Lady Victoria Alexandrina Elizabeth, eldest daughter of John Frederick, second Earl of Cawdor. He was also grandson of William Henry Lambton, Esq., of Biddick Hall, Durham, brother of the first Earl of Durham. Capt. Lambton was born in Jan. 1869, and educated at Wellington, where he was in the Orange 1880-85, and during the latter year was a Prefect. He joined the Highland Light Infantry from the Royal Military College Aug., 1888, being promoted lieut. May, 1890, and capt. May, 1896. He took part in the occupation of Crete in 1898, including the affair of Sept. 6th, being mentioned in despatches, L.G., Jan. 24th, 1899.

He embarked for South Africa in Oct. 1899, with his battalion, and joined the Kimberley Relief Force under Lieut.-Gen. Lord Methuen shortly before the battle of Magersfontein.

Lambton.—Lieut. Ronald Robert Lambton, 1st Batt. Durham Light Infantry (brother of the above), died of wounds received Sept. 17th, 1901, while serving near Vryheid with Major Gough's Column. He was the 6th son of Lieut.-Col. Francis William Lambton, of Brownslade, Pembroke, late Scots Guards, by his marriage with Lady Victoria Alexandrina Elizabeth, daughter of the second Earl of Cawdor. Lieut. Lambton was born in March, 1879, and educated at Wellington, where he was in the Orange, entered the Durham Light Infantry from the 3rd Batt. (Duke of Cambridge's Own) Middlesex Regt. May, 1899, and was promoted lieut. Nov. 1900. He went to South Africa with his battalion in Oct., 1899, which formed part of the Natal Field Force, was present at the battle of Colenso, and in the operations on the Tugela Jan. 12th and Feb. 6th, 1900, being severely wounded in the engagement at Vaal Kranz. He also took part in the advance through Northern Natal into the Transvaal. Lieut. Lambton was mentioned in despatches by Gen. Lord Kitchener, Dec. 8th, 1901, for his "most gallant conduct in trying to repulse the Boer attack." He is buried at Vryheid.

Lanham.—Lieut. H. W. Lanham, Bethune's M.I., was killed in action during the reconnaissance between Blood River and Vryheid on May 20th, 1900. He is buried at Scheepers Nek.

Lascelles.—Lieut. Alfred Lascelles, T Batt. Royal Horse Artillery, died on May 16th, 1900, at Bloemfontein of enteric. He was born in Sept., 1873, educated at Marlborough, and entered the Royal Artillery in April,

1893, and was promoted lieut. April, 1896. He embarked for South Africa in Dec., 1899, and took part in the battle of Paardeberg and the advance on Bloemfontein. His name is inscribed on a tablet placed in Marlborough College Chapel in memory of all Marlburians who fell in the war.

Laurie.—Capt. John Haliburton Laurie, 1st Batt. Royal Lancaster Regt., was killed in action near Philippolis April 12th, 1901. He was the eldest son of Lieut.-Gen. J. W. Laurie, M.P., 47, Porchester Terrace, W., was born Aug., 1864, at Halifax, N.S., and educated at the Royal Military College, Kingston, Canada. He entered the Royal Lancaster Regt. Sept., 1885, was promoted capt. July, 1895, and employed with the Colonial Forces in Canada from Oct., 1889, to Oct., 1895. Capt. Laurie was a member of the Polo team which won Prince Henry of Prussia's cups on the China Station 1898 and 1899, was the winner of the Sultan of Johore's cup for the shooting championship of the Straits Settlements in 1899, and also won two silver cups at the Royal Military Tournament for tent pegging and lemon cutting. He went to South Africa with the mounted infantry company of his battalion Jan., 1901, and was killed whilst endeavouring to assist one of his men who had been wounded.

Lawley.—2nd Lieut. William George Hodgson Lawley, 2nd Batt. Middlesex Regt., was killed in action at Spion Kop in the operations on the Upper Tugela, Jan. 24th, 1900. He was born Feb., 1874, educated at Shrewsbury School and at University College, Oxford, and entered the Middlesex Regiment, March, 1897. He accompanied his battalion to South Africa in Nov., 1899, serving in Natal with the Natal Field Force. (*See. Capt Moor.*)

Lawlor.—Lieut. John Lawrence Lawlor, 6th Dragoons,

died of wounds at Waterval Onder on Aug. 30th, 1900. He was born Feb., 1874, entered the 6th Inniskilling Dragoons from the Militia, Dec., 1896, and was promoted lieut. March, 1898. He was adjutant of his regiment from Feb., 1900, and accompanied it to South Africa in Nov., 1899, where he saw much service in the north of Cape Colony, at the relief of Kimberley, and the advance on Bloemfontein.

Lawrence.—Capt. Samuel Lawrence, 2nd Batt. Cameronians (Scottish Rifles), died from dysentery April 18th, 1900, in Ladysmith. He was born March, 1870, served in the ranks for nearly five years, and obtained a commission in the Scottish Rifles as 2nd lieut. Feb., 1895. He was promoted lieut. in July, 1897, capt. Jan., 1900, and proceeded to South Africa, Feb., 1900.

Leask.—Lieut. J. Leask, Queensland M.I., died Aug. 20th, 1900, of wounds received in action on July 21st, near Kosks River, Pretoria.

Leece.—Lieut. G. Leece, 7th New Zealand M.I., was killed in action near Vereeniging on Aug. 24th, 1901.

Le Gallais.—Lieut.-Col. Philip Walter Jules Le Gallais, 8th Hussars, died November 6th, 1900, of wounds received in action near Bothaville. He was born Aug., 1861, educated at Victoria College, Jersey, and entered the 8th Hussars from the 3rd or South Regt. (Royal Jersey Militia), April, 1881, being promoted lieut. July the same year, capt. March, 1888, major April, 1897, and brevet lieut.-col. Nov., 1898. He served in the Nile Expedition of 1897, receiving the medal with clasp; also in the Expedition of 1898, when he took part in the cavalry reconnaissance of April 4th, and the battles of Atbara and Khartoum. He was mentioned in despatches, L.G., May 24th and Sept. 30th, 1898, and received the brevet of lieut.-col., Fourth Class of the Order of the Osmanieh, and two clasps to his Egyptian medal. The day he was killed Lieut.-Col. Le Gallais, ably assisted by Major Lean, had attacked with about 200 men a Boer Laager under De Wet over a thousand strong. Lieut.-Col. Le Gallais' force had got possession of a small shed which was the centre of the Boer fire (one report states that "the bullets were flying like wasps"), and it was here that he was killed. His opponent, Gen. De Wet, eulogises the gallant Le Gallais, as "without doubt one of the bravest English officers he had ever met." Lieut.-Col. Le Gallais, as he expired, said, "Tell my mother that I died happy, as we got the guns." In this action six guns and a pom-pom and 114 prisoners were captured from the Boers. F.-M. Earl Roberts in his despatch of Nov. 15th, 1900 (L.G., Feb. 8th, 1901), reports the death of Lieut.-Col. Le Gallais with deep regret: "a most gallant and capable leader, whose place it will be very difficult to fill." Again in his despatch, L.G., April 16th, 1901, Earl Roberts deeply regrets the death of Lieut.-Col. Le Gallais, and adds that "he rendered brilliant service and gave every promise of rising to the highest rank as a cavalry leader."

Leggatt.—2nd Lieut. Edward Oswell Neville Owen Leggatt, 2nd Batt. Royal Scots Fusiliers, died of enteric at Ladysmith, April 15th, 1900. He was the only surviving son of Gen. O. E. Leggatt, 40, Cheniston Gardens, Kensington, and was born July, 1878. He entered his regiment from the 5th Batt. Lancashire Fusiliers, Nov. 1899, and joined his battalion soon afterwards in Natal, and served in the Natal Field Force.

Legge.—Lieut.-Col. Norton Legge, C.B., D.S.O., 20th Hussars, was killed in action at Nooitgedacht, Dec. 13th,

1900. He was born June, 1860, entered the 20th Hussars from the 3rd Batt. Lancashire Fusiliers, Aug., 1882, was promoted capt. Dec., 1887, and major Oct., 1898. Lieut.-Col. Legge served in the Soudan Campaign in 1885, and was present at the engagement at Hasheen, the attack on the convoy March 24th, and at the destruction of Tamai, receiving the medal with clasp, and Khedive's star. He was also with the Egyptian Frontier Field Force, in 1885-86, was present at the investment of Kosheh, the Relief of Ambigole, the engagement at Giniss, and the subsequent pursuit to Absarat, being mentioned in despatches. His next experience of active service was with the Dongola Expeditionary Force under Lord (then Sir Herbert) Kitchener in 1896, in command of four squadrons of Egyptian Cavalry, including the engagements at Firket (wounded), and Hafir, and the capture of Dongola, when he was again mentioned in despatches, and received the D.S.O., British medal, and Khedive's medal with two clasps. As Brigade-Major of Egyptian Cavalry he also took part in the operations in 1898, including the battle of Khartoum, and subsequent pursuit, was mentioned in despatches, and received two clasps to the Khedive's medal. He served in the South African War from its commencement, and was in command of a corps of M.I.; was mentioned in despatches, L.G., Feb. 8th, 1901, and promoted brevet-lieut.-col. Nov. 29th, 1900, and also awarded the C.B. (*See Lieut. Skene*).

Leicester.—Lieut. Henry Claude Leicester, 1st. Batt. Leinster Regt., died at Vrede March 13th, 1901. He was born May, 1875, entered the Leinster Regt. from the 4th Batt. North Staffordshire Regt., March, 1897, being promoted lieut. March, 1899. He accompanied his battalion to South Africa from Aldershot, April, 1900, and served with it in Cape and Orange River Colonies till his death.

Le Marchant.—Capt. Gaspard de Coligny Le Marchant. 1st Batt. Lancashire Fusiliers, was killed in action at Boschbult, Kleinhardt's River, March 31st, 1902. He was the only son of Mrs. Seymour Le Marchant, and grandson of the late Gen. Sir Gaspard Le Marchant, K.C.B., G.C.M.G., and great grandson of Gen. Le Marchant, who fell at Salamanca. Capt. Le Marchant was born April, 1879, educated at Elizabeth College, Guernsey, and entered the Lancashire Fusiliers May, 1898, being promoted lieut. Jan., 1899, and capt. June, 1901. He went to South Africa from Malta with M.I., Dec., 1901, landing Jan. 14th and was severely wounded at Klip River, Feb. 12th, 1902. He was sent to Elandsfontein Hospital, and at his urgent request was allowed on March 24th to return to duty, and fell as stated seven days after.

Lennox.—Capt. Amyot Maitland Augustus Lennox, 81st Battery Royal Field Artillery, was killed, it is believed, in action at Paardeberg, Feb. 20th, 1900. He was born Oct., 1867, and entered the Royal Artillery, Feb., 1886, being promoted capt. April, 1896. Capt. Lennox, embarked for South Africa in Dec., 1899, with the 81st Battery, which joined the force being assembled for the advance on Bloemfontein. After the battle of Paardeberg, he was at first reported missing, and no date was given regarding his death. A non-commissioned officer of his battery (Bombardier Jefford) however gives some particulars, and writes in the most touching manner concerning the bravery of Capt. Lennox. He states that after a severe day's fighting, when the battery was limbering up, one of the gunners was wounded, and Capt. Lennox went to his assistance, and having attended to him found the gunner was exhausted, he then rode in the dark for a stretcher, to convey the wounded man to hospital. Going to where he saw a light, which he thought was one of our hospitals, but which turned out to be part of the Boer Camp, or a farm-house, Capt. Lennox was treacherously fired upon and killed. After Cronje's surrender the helmet of Capt. Lennox was found in the Boer Camp.

Leslie.—2nd Lieut. Theodore Barrington Norman Leslie, 3rd Batt. Grenadier Guards, died at Wynberg Hospital, Cape Town, Dec. 4th, 1899, from the effect of wounds received at the battle of Belmont. He was the eldest son of R. C. Leslie, Esq., of Ballibay, co. Monaghan, and 22, Cornwall Gardens, S.W., representing the branch of Leslie Earls of Rothes, who settled in Ireland in 1614. 2nd Lieut. Leslie was born Feb., 1878, and educated at Eton (Mr. James'). He entered the Grenadier Guards Jan., 1899, from the 4th Batt. Royal Irish Fusiliers (Monaghan Militia), accompanied his battalion to Gibraltar in Sept., and went on with it to South Africa in Oct. He served with the Kimberley Relief Force under Lieut.-Gen. Lord Methuen, and was severely wounded in the leg at the battle of Belmont Nov. 23rd, but insisted on the others who were struck down being attended to before him. His wound was dressed and he was then transferred to Wynberg Hospital where, on Nov. 29th, it was found necessary to amputate his foot. On Dec. 4th in his sleep he appears to have kicked off a bandage, breaking an artery and died immediately from loss of blood. He is buried in Wynberg cemetery.

Lethbridge.—2nd Lieut. Bertram Escott Lethbridge, 2nd Batt. Rifle Brigade, died at Ladysmith in Nov., 1899, of wounds received in action. He was the son of C. Lethbridge, Esq., of Sherfield Manor, Basingstoke, was born June, 1878, educated at Eton (Mr. Broadbent's), and entered his regiment Nov., 1898. He accompanied his battalion from Crete to South Africa in Sept., 1899, and served with it in Natal till his death.

Lewis.—2nd Lieut. Edward Llewellyn Lewis, 1st Batt.

Welsh Regt., died of dysentery at Rietfontein West, April 4th, 1902. He was the son of Evan Lewis, Esq., of Brynderwen, Llandaffan, was born March, 1879, and joined his regiment in July, 1901.

Lewis.—Brevet-Major Vernon Lewis, 2nd Batt. Royal Scots Fusiliers, was killed in action at Pieters Hill Feb. 27th, 1900. He was the eldest son of Capt. E. Lewis, of the Red House, Guildford, formerly of the Royal Scots Fusiliers and 8th King's Liverpool Regt. Major Lewis was born Sept., 1879, educated at Sherborne School, and entered the Royal Scots Fusiliers Jan., 1892, being promoted lieut. March, 1894, capt. Oct., 9th, 1899, receiving his brevet majority the following day. He was a first-rate sportsman and a well-known big game hunter. Major Lewis served as a signalling officer 1st brigade, in the Chitral Relief Expedition of 1895, under Sir Robert Low, receiving the medal with clasp. From 1897-99 he was employed with the West African Frontier Force, in which he served with distinction, and for the operations on the Niger 1897-98, including the expedition to Lapia, he was mentioned in despatches, L.G., March 7th, 1899, and, in recognition of his services, was awarded his brevet majority. Major Lewis embarked for South Africa in Oct., 1899, and was present at the battle of Colenso and the subsequent fighting on the Tugela. The day he was killed his gallantry was very conspicuous. Major-Gen. Barton, C.B., commanding the Fusilier Brigade in expressing his regret that Major Lewis had fallen wrote : " Major Lewis held the most important post in command of the company, on the extreme right, and on reaching the top of the hill he carried out my orders most admirably in swinging the right of our line round rapidly to the left and thus enveloping and enfilading the Boer position. The capture of this position on Pieter's Hill resulted directly in the relief of Ladysmith." Major

Lewis at the time of his death was the youngest field officer in the army. He was mentioned in despatches, L.G., Feb. 8th, 1901.

Libby.—Lieut. Arthur Treleven Libby, 2nd Batt. Duke of Cornwall's Light Infantry, died of enteric at Johannesburg Nov. 6th, 1901. The younger son of Capt. Libby, R.N., Cambridge Place, Falmouth, he was born Feb., 1878, and educated at Kelly College, Tavistock, from which he passed direct into Sandhurst, 1896, and entered his regiment Feb., 1898, being promoted lieut. Oct., 1899. Lieut. Libby accompanied his battalion to South Africa at the commencement of the war, was first employed at Capetown, and afterwards took part in the advance on Johannesburg and Pretoria, and was present in all the actions in which his battalion took part, after the occupation of Bloemfontein. He contracted enteric early in 1901, but returned to duty after ten weeks' illness, and was afterwards, at Helvetia, employed escorting convoys towards Lydenburg. In Oct., 1901, he contracted malarial fever in the Komati Valley, and was sent into Johannesburg, where he died, being buried in the cemetery there. A Cornish granite cross has been erected over his grave.

Lincoln.—Lieut. Noel Holmes Lincoln, 2nd Batt. Royal Inniskilling Fusiliers, was killed in action at Boschbult, March 31st, 1902. Born in Sept., 1877, and educated at Bedford School, he entered his regiment Feb., 1898, being promoted lieut. Oct., 1899. He accompanied the battalion to South Africa Jan., 1902, from Mean Meer, and was mentioned in despatches, L.G., 18th July, 1902. His name is inscribed on a tablet in Enniskillen erected by his brother officers to his memory and that of Capt. G. W. Morley, of the same battalion.

Lindsay.—Capt. Michael William Howard Lindsay,

2nd Batt. Seaforth Highlanders, was killed in action near Brakenlaagte (20 miles N.W. of Bethel), Oct. 31st, 1901. He was the second son of Mr. William Alexander Lindsay, K.C. (*Windsor Herald*), and of Lady Harriet Lindsay. He was born 1872, educated at Malvern and entered the Seaforth Highlanders from the R.M.C. July, 1893, being promoted lieut. Oct., 1895, and capt. Nov., 1900. In 1895 he served with the Chitral Relief Force under Sir Robert Low with the 2nd Batt. Seaforth Highlanders, and was present in the engagement at Mamagai, receiving the medal with clasp. At the outbreak of the war Capt. Lindsay accompanied his battalion to South Africa, and took part in the operations under Lieut.-Gen. Lord Methuen for the Relief of Kimberley. He was present at the battle of Magersfontein, and was afterwards employed in the post of station staff officer, and as adjutant of the Scottish Horse. He had been severely wounded, and was mentioned in despatches, L.G., March 16th, 1900, for "gallant and conspicuous behaviour at Magersfontein when in charge of Maxim gun."

Lippert.—Lieut. Wilhelm Arthur David Lippert, 2nd Batt. Royal Lancaster Regt., was killed in action at Vryheid, Dec. 11th, 1900. He was the eldest son of W. A. Lippert, Esq., of Eastbourne, was born Oct., 1878, and entered the Royal Lancaster Regt. from the 4th Batt. Somersetshire Light Infantry April, 1900, being promoted lieut. Aug., 1900. Lieut. Lippert was in charge of a party of ten men on outpost duty, who were suddenly attacked on a dark morning about 2.15. His conduct is stated to have been most gallant. There were four outposts, and these were all fiercely attacked by the enemy, but, owing to the splendid resistance made by the outposts, the troops in rear were not seriously pressed. Lieut. Lippert is buried at Vryheid.

Litkie.—Capt. E. M. Litkie died during the siege of Kimberley. He belonged to the Kimberley Rifles.

Livingstone-Learmonth. — Capt. Lennox Christian Livingstone-Learmonth, Royal Field Artillery, 2nd Cavalry Brigade Ammunition Column, died of enteric May 25th, 1900, at Bloemfontein. Born Dec., 1870, and educated at Eton (Mr. Vaughan's); he entered the Royal Artillery, July, 1890, being promoted lieut. July, 1893, and capt. Feb., 1900.

Lloyd.—Lieut.-Col. George Evan Lloyd, D.S.O., commanding the 1st Batt. West Riding Regt., was killed in Major-Gen. Paget's action at Rhenoster Kop, North-East of Bronkhorst Spruit, Nov. 29th, 1900. He was the eldest son of the Rev. Prebendary Lloyd, Troedvrawr Rectory, Cardiganshire. He was born Oct., 1855, and educated at Tonbridge School. He entered the 70th Foot from the Royal East Middlesex Militia, 1876, transferred to the South Yorkshire Regt. as lieut. Dec., 1876, to the Yorkshire Light Infantry as capt. June, 1883, promoted brevet-major June, 1885, major in the South Staffordshire Regt. Nov., 1890, lieut.-col. on half-pay Nov., 1896, and was given the command of 1st Batt. West Riding Regt. in June, 1897. Lieut.-Col. Lloyd served with the 51st Light Infantry in the Jowaki Expedition, 1877, receiving the medal with clasp. He saw service with the same regiment in the Afghan War, 1878-79, and was present at the attack and capture of Ali Musjid, for which he received the medal with clasp. He was in the Nile Expedition, 1884-85 as commandant at Tangur, mentioned in despatches, L.G., Aug. 25th, 1885, and received the brevet of major, the medal with clasp and Khedive's star, and the Fourth Class of the Order of the Medjidie. His next experience of active service was with the Soudan Frontier Field Force, 1885-87, including the engagements at Giniss (mentioned in despatches, L.G., Feb. 9th, 1886), and granted the D.S.O. He was present at the action at Sarras, mentioned in despatches, L.G., June 17th, 1887, and was granted the Third Class of the order of the Medjidie. He took part in the operations near Suakin, Dec., 1888, including the engagement at Gemaizah, mentioned in despatches, L.G., Jan. 11th, 1889 (clasp); and in the operations in 1889, including the engagement at Toski, mentioned in despatches, L.G., Sept. 6th, 1889 (clasp). He served with the Dongola Expeditionary Force under Lord (then Sir Herbert) Kitchener in 1896 in command of a field column, which he had organised from the Suakin and Tokar garrisons, was mentioned in despatches, promoted to be lieut.-col., and granted the medal; and received the Second Class of the Order of the Medjidie for service under the Egyptian Government. He proceeded to South Africa, Dec., 1899, and commanded his battalion throughout the war, including the relief of Kimberley, battle of Paardeberg, and the advance on Bloemfontein and into the Transvaal. There is an interesting account of Lieut.-Col. Lloyd's death in "My Reminiscences of the War," by Gen. Ben Viljoen. This Boer general thus describes it: " A brave officer who had one of his legs smashed, leant on a gun or his sword, and kept on giving his orders and cheering the soldiers and telling them to charge on. While in this position a second bullet struck him, and he fell mortally wounded." There is a picture in this book entitled, "Battle of Rhenoster Kop. How Col. Lloyd died." A few months later Gen. Ben Viljoen's Burghers, when passing this battlefield and Lieut.-Col. Lloyd's grave, laid a wreath of flowers on the spot where he lies with the words "In memory of a brave enemy'" Lieut.-Col. Lloyd was mentioned in despatches, L.G., Feb. 8th, and Sept. 10th, 1901, this latter making the seventh occasion during his career. He was awarded the C.B.

Lloyd.—Midshipman Lionel George Rodney Lloyd, of H.M.S. " Doris," died April 28th, 1900, of enteric, at Kimberley. He was nineteen years of age and joined the Navy, May, 1897, being promoted midshipman the following July.

Lloyd.—Capt. Thomas Henry Eyre Lloyd, 2nd Batt. Coldstream Guards, died of wounds received in action near Brakenlaagte (20 miles N.W. of Bethel) Oct. 31st. 1901. He was the eldest son of Major-Gen. Thomas Francis Lloyd, of Beechmount, Rathkeale, co. Limerick, was born in May, 1871, and educated at Eton (Mr. Marindin's and Mr. Williams'). He entered the Coldstream Guards, Oct., 1890, being promoted lieut. July, 1896, and capt. April, 1899. Capt. Lloyd had been serving since the beginning of the war, having accompanied his battalion to South Africa in Oct., 1899. He was present at the actions of Graspan, Modder River, Magersfontein, and the advance on Pretoria.

Lloyd.—Major William Reade De la Père Lloyd, 1st Batt. Suffolk Regt., was killed in action in Major-Gen. Smith-Dorrien's engagement of Jan. 26th, 1901. He was the only son of the late Capt. Lloyd, 57th Regt., who was killed in action in New Zealand. Born, Sept. 1860, Major Lloyd entered the 12th Foot, Jan. 1880, being promoted lieut. Jan., 1881, capt. May, 1886, and major Feb., 1897. He served in the Hazara Expedition, 1888, with his battalion, receiving the medal with clasp. Major Lloyd who had served in South Africa from 1899, in the north of Cape Colony and in the Transvaal, was mentioned in despatches, L.G., Sept. 10th, 1901.

OFFICERS WHO FELL IN SOUTH AFRICA. 225

Lockwood.—Lieut. Harry Vernon Lockwood, 2nd Batt. Cameronians (Scottish Rifles), died of enteric on board the "Nubia," Feb. 25th, 1900. He was born June, 1875, educated at Marlborough, and entered the Royal Munster Fusiliers, May, 1897, being transferred to the Scottish Rifles, Aug., 1898. He was promoted lieut. Oct., 1899, and accompanied his battalion in that month to South Africa, but was afterwards invalided. Lieut. Lockwood's name is incribed on a tablet placed in Marlborough College chapel in memory of all Marlburians who fell in the war.

Loftus.—Capt. Francis Cochrane Loftus, 1st Batt. Royal Inniskilling Fusiliers, was killed in action at Colenso Dec. 15th, 1899. He was the eldest son of Mrs. Lindsay Coates, Mount Loftus, co. Kilkenny, and Rockheath Park, Norwich, was born in July, 1873, and educated at Stoneyhurst College. He entered the Royal Inniskilling Fusiliers from the Militia 1892, being promoted lieut. 1895, and capt. Oct., 1899. From April, 1898, to March, 1899, he served with the West African Rifles and took part in the operations in Sierra Leone, in which he was dangerously wounded while gallantly saving one of his men who had fallen under a heavy fire. It is stated that for this act he was recommended for the V.C. Capt. Loftus accompanied his battalion to South Africa, and at Colenso received "his death wound in the head whilst leading and cheering his men on in the foremost ranks of the Irish Brigade." Thus wrote his commanding officer, who himself fell two months afterwards on the Tugela Heights. Capt. Loftus is buried beside Major Charley of the same regiment. His grave, between Chieveley and Colenso, is marked by a marble tombstone erected by his comrades of the 1st battalion.

Lomax.—Capt. David Alexander Napier Lomax, Welsh Regt., was killed in action at Driefontein March 10th, 1900. Born Aug., 1868, he entered the regiment from the 3rd Batt. Northumberland Fusiliers, Dec., 1888, being promoted lieut. Nov., 1890, and capt. June, 1899. When killed he was adjutant of his battalion. Capt. Lomax's death is mentioned in the despatch of F.-M. Earl Roberts, March 15th, 1900, from Bloemfontein, and also in despatch No. 5, March 31st, 1900 (L.G., Feb. 8th, 1901), " for having rendered valuable service."

Long.—2nd Lieut. Lionel William Long, 2nd Batt. Yorkshire Light Infantry, was killed in action at the battle of Modder River Nov. 28th, 1899. He was the son of C. B. Long, Esq., of Southsea, was born March, 1879, and educated at Clifton. He was only appointed to his regiment in Aug., 1899. In the action at Modder River, the company on the left of the line of the Yorkshire Light Infantry suffered severely, all its officers being killed or wounded. While in this state, and with its senior non-commissioned officer uncertain what to do, a major of the battalion took command of it, saying, " Come along, my orphans," and the name stuck to it.

Longden.—Major Arthur Edmund Longden, D.S.O., Army Service Corps, died of enteric, at Germiston, April 20th, 1901. He was the third son of the late Major-General Charles S. Longden, R.A., of Oakwood, Crawley, Sussex, and was born March, 1864. He entered the Lincolnshire Regt. Feb., 1885, transferred to the North Staffordshire Regt. as lieut., March, 1887, and to the Army Service Corps Sept., 1890, being promoted capt. April, 1892, and Major April, 1900. In 1883 he received the Royal Humane Society's testimonial on vellum for saving life on the Thames at Sunbury. Major Longden served in Zululand 1888. In the South African War, he was in Natal under Gen. Sir R. Buller in the operations for the relief of Ladysmith. Since Aug., 1900, he had been on the staff as D.A.A.G. He was mentioned in despatches, L.G., Feb. 8th, 1901, and granted the D.S.O. for his services.

Longfield.—Capt. William M. Longfield, 17th Batt. I.Y., was killed in action at Brakenlaagte, O.R.C., June 4th, 1901. He was 47 years of age, and was educated at Cheltenham, and joined the I.Y. March, 1901, with the rank of lieut. He had previously served as a trooper, and been granted a commission. His name is inscribed on the Eleanor Cross War Memorial erected at Cheltenham College.

Loughlin. — Veterinary-Capt. John Loughlin, Army Veterinary Department, died of hepatitis at Wynberg, Nov. 2nd, 1900. He was born Nov., 1863, entered the Army Veterinary Department July, 1890, being promoted capt. July, 1900. He was appointed to the 1st Life Guards May, 1898.

Lovell.—Lieut. C. H. S. Lovell, Roberts' Horse, died of pulmonary phthisis, at Wynberg, Cape Colony, on April 14th, 1901. He was the son of Capt. Lovell, Brent, Devonshire. Lieut. Lovell had been in Cape Colony for some years, and was Sub-Inspector of Native Police. He had served through the Matabeleland campaign of 1893.

Lovett.—Capt. Richard Gordon Beresford Lovett, 1st Batt. Royal Welsh Fusiliers, died of wounds received in action at Callerberg, May 6th, 1900. He was born in April, 1870, and educated at Sherborne School from 1885 to 1889; he entered the Royal Welsh Fusiliers March, 1891, being promoted lieut. Aug., 1893, and capt. July, 1899. From Sept., 1898, to Sept., 1899, he was employed with the Army Pay Department.

Low.—Lieut. Harry Lawrence Low, M.I. Royal Irish Rifles, was killed at Vaal Bosh Pan, about 40 miles from Hoopstad, March 10th, 1902. This officer was first reported as missing, but it was afterwards discovered that he had been killed. He was the younger son of Mrs. G. Hamilton Low, Montrose, Camberley, and the late George Hamilton Low, Esq., Royal Canadian Rifles, and was born June, 1874. Lieut. Low entered the Royal Irish Rifles Jan., 1895, from the Royal Military College, passing out with honours and gaining the prize for Topography; being promoted lieut. April, 1897. On the outbreak of the war, he was serving with the depôt of his regiment, but, volunteering for active service, was sent to South Africa in Feb., 1900, and joined the mounted infantry of his battalion. He took part in the operations in the Ventersberg district and the relief of Wepener, and afterwards served in the Transvaal and Cape Colony. In his letter of Sept. 14th, 1900, describing one of the actions he was in, when some Boers were captured, he says, "Now comes the best news of all, a wire congratulating us on our prompt action from Lord Roberts." A brother officer writes concerning Lieut. Low: " It will be many a long day before the regiment will forget how, on July 1st, 1901, with fifty Irish Riflemen he attacked and signally defeated 250 Boers." Lieut. Low lost his life under very tragic circumstances. Seeing two horsemen advancing towards him dressed in khaki, etc., he mistook them for our men, and on reaching them all three dismounted, the two Boers keeping their rifles in their hands, Lieut. Low leaving his in the bucket of his saddle. The Boers then called on him to surrender, but, thinking they were our men, he replied that he was one of their officers. Quickly realising his mistake, he closed with one of the Boers (a man named Lombard), and the other Boer (named Kempens) then shot Lieut. Low dead. After Peace was declared his body was found, and was buried at Vaal

Bosh Pan; but in Dec., 1902, some of his battalion being at Modder River and being anxious that his remains should rest there, where so many brave officers and men who were killed in action during the war are buried, his body was disinterred and brought to Modder River, about 100 miles. A marble cross has been erected over his grave by his brother officers. Lieut. Low was granted the medal with three clasps.

Lowry.—Lieut. James Taylor Lowry, 1st Batt. Royal Inniskilling Fusiliers, died Sept. 19th, 1900, in London from blood poisoning contracted on service with his battalion in the campaign on the Tugela. He was the only son of Capt. Edward L. B. Lowry, of Rockdale, Tullyhogue, co. Tyrone, late 41st Regt. Lieut. Lowry was born Aug., 1875, educated at Loretto School, Musselburgh and Rossall, and entered the Royal Inniskilling Fusiliers from the 4th Batt. in Dec., 1896, being promoted lieut. June, 1898. He embarked with his battalion for South Africa Nov., 1899, and served with the Natal Field Force. He was present at the battle of Colenso and the operations from Jan. 17th to 24th, 1900, and also in the fighting at Vaal Kranz; was invalided home from Pietermaritzburg, and arrived in England in April, 1900, but was unable to regain his strength and died as stated.

Loy.—Capt. John Loy, 2nd Kitchener's Fighting Scouts, died of dysentery at Heilbron on Jan. 21st, 1902.

Luard.—Capt. Henry Arthur Luard, 2nd Batt. East Yorkshire Regt., died of enteric at Winburg, O.R.C., Feb. 5th, 1901, while serving on the Staff there. He was the only son of the late Capt. H. R. Luard, Royal Engineers, was born Dec., 1865, and educated at Wellington College, where he was in the Blucher, 1877-84. He entered the Northamptonshire Regt. from the Royal Military College in 1886, being promoted capt. in the 2nd Batt. East Yorkshire Regt. in Feb., 1898. Capt. Luard went to South Africa, Aug., 1900, and served in the Cape and Orange River Colonies up to the time of his death.

Lucas.—Capt. Edward Lucas, Natal Carabiniers, of Richmond, Natal, died at Durban Aug. 7th, 1900. He was the second son of Arthur Lucas, Esq., of Darlington, was educated at Clifton, and was 36 years of age.

Luce.—Lieut. Walter Cecil Luce, Volunteer Company Wiltshire Regt., died of enteric at Springfontein, Feb. 11th, 1901. The youngest son of Col. C. R. Luce, of Halcombe, Malmesbury, he was born Nov., 1873, was educated at Clifton College, and entered the 2nd Volunteer Batt. of the Wiltshire Regt. May, 1896, being promoted lieut. 1899. Lieut. Luce went to South Africa, Jan., 1900, with the Volunteer Service Company to join the 2nd Batt. Wiltshire Regt., and saw much fighting in the O.R.C. and afterwards to the north of Pretoria. He received the rank of lieut. in the army in March, 1900.

Luce.—2nd Lieut. William Scott Luce, Royal Field Artillery, was killed in action at Diamond Hill, near Pretoria, June 11th, 1900. He was born in March, 1880, educated at Clifton College, and entered the Royal Artillery, June, 1899. He accompanied the 82nd Battery to South Africa in January, 1900, and was present at the battle of Paardeberg, and in the subsequent advance on Bloemfontein and Pretoria.

Lund.—Major Alfred Lund, 5th Batt. Royal Fusiliers (Royal Westminster Militia), of Huntington, Chertsey, Surrey, died of enteric at Kroonstad, Jan. 23rd, 1902. Born in May, 1863, and educated at St. Edward's School,

Oxford, he entered his regiment Oct. 1882, being promoted capt. 1888, and major May, 1901. Major Lund was a keen fisherman, and was well known at Dee-Side, Aberdeenshire, and in different parts of Ireland. He accompanied his battalion to South Africa in May, 1901, and served in the Cape and Orange River Colonies up to the time of his death. He leaves a widow and one son.

Lygon.—Lieut. the Hon. Edward Hugh Lygon, 3rd Batt. Grenadier Guards, was killed at Karree Siding, near Modder River, north of Bloemfontein, March 23rd, 1900. He was the second son of the sixth Earl Beauchamp and brother of the present earl. His mother was Lady Mary Catherine, daughter of the fifth Earl Stanhope. Lieut. Lygon was born July, 1873, educated at Eton (Mr. Cole's and Mr. Drew's), and entered the Grenadier Guards from the 4th Batt. Worcestershire Regt. June, 1894, being promoted lieut. Nov., 1897; and was appointed adjutant to his battalion Nov., 1899. He went to South Africa in Oct., 1899, and joined the Kimberley Relief Force; was wounded at the battle of Modder River, Nov. 1899. Lieut. Lygon was Deputy-Lieutenant of Worcestershire.

Lynch.—Capt. Nicholas Marcus Lynch, 1st Batt. South Lancashire Regt., died of enteric at Mooi River Nov. 13th, 1900. He was born April, 1868, and entered his regiment Sept., 1887, being promoted lieut. April, 1889, and capt. Aug., 1894. From May, 1892, to Dec., 1893, he was employed with the Gold Coast Constabulary, and with the West African Frontier Police Force from March, 1898, to Nov., 1899, when he proceeded to South Africa. He then served with the 1st battalion of his regiment and took part in the fighting on the Tugela and the relief of Ladysmith.

Lyon.—2nd Lieut. Henry Francis Lyon, 3rd Batt.

East Surrey Regt., was wounded in action at Stormberg Nov. 28th, 1901, and died the same day. He was the son of William Lyon, Esq., Valparaiso, Chili, was twenty years of age, and educated at Harrow. Lieut. Lyon joined in April, 1901, the 3rd Batt. East Surrey Regt. which was embodied in May, and proceeded with it to South Africa in June.

Lysley.—Capt. Gerald Lowther Lysley, Rifle Brigade, was killed in action near Bergendal, Aug. 29th, 1900. He was born Aug., 1872, educated at Eton (Mr. Broadbent's), and entered the Rifle Brigade, Oct., 1892, being promoted lieut. 1895, and capt. Feb., 1900. At the commencement of the war, he belonged to the 3rd Batt., then in India, but volunteering for active service, was attached for duty to the 2nd Batt. in South Africa. Capt. Lysley fell while leading his company to attack a strong Boer position at Bergendal. Sir. R. Buller, in reporting this action in his despatch of Sept., 13th, 1900, states: "The honours of the assault belong to the Rifle Brigade," and he "much regrets the death of Capt. Lysley, who led his company most gallantly." L.G., Feb. 8th, 1901.

Maasdorp.—Lieut. J. W. Maasdorp, Graaf Reinet District Mounted Troops, 1st City (Grahamstown), Volunteers, was killed at Helgaarth Kraal on Sept. 28th, 1901.

MacBean.—Capt. and Brevet-Major John Emmanuel MacBean, D.S.O., p.s.c., Royal Dublin Fusiliers, was killed in action at Nooitgedacht, Dec. 13th, 1900. He was the elder son of the late Hugh MacBean, Esq., J.P., of Glasgow, and of Mrs. MacBean, 7, Rossetti Mansions, Chelsea, S.W. His mother was a daughter of the late Robert Gilson Cochrane Field, Esq., of Miliken Park.

OFFICERS WHO FELL IN SOUTH AFRICA. 233

Major MacBean was born in Glasgow, June, 1865, educated at St. Andrews and at the Glasgow Academy, and afterwards at the Freiburg University. He entered his regiment May, 1887, being promoted lieut. March, 1889, capt. May, 1896, and brevet-major Nov., 1900. Having first served in India, he passed the Staff College in 1896, and went to Egypt, where he was in the Nile Expedition of 1897, and the action of Abu Hamed (having his horse shot under him), and was mentioned in despatches. He then saw service in the Nile Expedition, 1898, being present at the battles of Atbara and Khartoum, and was again mentioned in despatches and granted the D.S.O. and two medals and five clasps. Major MacBean sailed for South Africa, Oct., 1899, and was appointed brigade-major to the Fusilier Brigade. He was present at the battles of Colenso, Pieters Hill, the Relief of Ladysmith, and afterwards at the actions of Rooidam and Fourteen Streams; he also served with Sir I. Hamilton at Lydenburg. In Nov., 1900, he was appointed staff officer to the force at Krugersdorp, under Major-Gen. Clements, and fell at Nooitgedacht in the attack on the British column by Generals De La Rey and Beyers.

Macaulay.—Lieut. Kenneth Zachary Pollock Macaulay, Loyal North Lancashire Regt., died at Middelburg, Transvaal, Jan. 30th, 1901, of wounds received in action three days previously. He was the second son of Col. C. E. Macaulay, 2, Cathedral Square, Glasgow, was born Sept., 1872, and educated at Trinity College, Glenalmond. He was fond of games and in his college football team. Lieut. Macaulay entered his regiment March, 1894, was promoted lieut. May, 1896, was A.D.C. to the G.O.C. Ceylon, June to Dec., 1899, when he proceeded to South Africa and was appointed railway staff officer, January, 1900, and staff capt. in March. He fell in the firing line of the rear guard retreating from

Carolina, while "encouraging his men in the most gallant manner."

MacCartie. — Capt. Charles F. MacCartie, C.I.E., adjutant Kitchener's Horse, was killed in action at Driefontein March 10th, 1900. He was the eldest son of the late Rev. Joseph MacCartie, M.A., Vicar of Cleveland (who died in Jan. 1902), by his marriage with Mary Frances Thompson, daughter of the Archdeacon of Cork. Capt. MacCartie was fifty-two years of age, and was fond of hunting, racing and steeplechasing. He was educated at Cambridge, and belonged to the Indian Civil Service, in which he attained high rank, having served in India for twenty-five years, and was at one time private secretary to Lord Wenlock, Governor of Madras, being granted the C.I.E. He saw service as a volunteer in Burmah, 1894-95, under Gen. Penn-Symons and was twice mentioned in despatches, receiving the medal and clasp. He had retired from the Indian Civil Service on a pension of £1000 per annum, and was in Australia when the war broke out. Capt. MacCartie accompanied one of the colonial contingents to South Africa, and joining Kitchener's Horse at Modder River Camp was killed in his first engagement a fortnight after his arrival. His death is mentioned in the despatch of F.-M. Earl Roberts March 15th, 1900, from Bloemfontein. It is remarkable that three members of Lord Wenlock's staff who lived with him at Ootacamund, Capt. MacCartie, Col. Scott Chisholme and Capt. De Montmorency, were all killed early in the war.

MacCartie.—Capt. Gerald de Courcey MacCartie, E Division, South African Constabulary, died of wounds received in a skirmish while on patrol duty at Neikkuel, near Hoopstad, O.R.C., Feb. 27th, 1902. He was the third son of the late Rev. Joseph MacCartie, M.A., Vicar of Cleveland (who died in Jan., 1902), by his marriage with Mary Frances Thompson, daughter of the Archdeacon of Cork. Capt. MacCartie was thirty-five years of age, and was educated at King William's College, Isle of Man. He had previously served with Methuen's Horse in South Africa 1884-85. In the recent war he was in the fighting at Modder River and present at the Relief of Kimberley. He was seriously wounded in 1900, and invalided home to England, but on recovering returned to South Africa. Referring to Capt. MacCartie's death, General Baden-Powell wrote saying, " how much he deplored his loss as a comrade and an officer. He was the ideal officer of the force, always cheery and ready for work, and particularly plucky and gallant in action." He is buried at Hoopstad—a cross marks his grave. (A brother of the above two officers, Lieut. I. F. MacCartie, Durham Light Infantry, was killed in action in Upper Burmah in 1886.)

Macdonald.—2nd Lieut. the Hon. Archibald Ronald Armadale Macdonald, 9th Lancers, was killed in action at Krugersdorp on April 17th, 1901. He was the son of the sixth Baron Macdonald, was born May, 1880, educated at Radley, and entered the 9th Lancers from the R.M.C. Feb., 1900.

MacDougall.—Lieut. James Taylor MacDougall, 42nd Battery Royal Field Artillery, was killed in action at Farquhar's Farm, near Ladysmith, Oct. 30th, 1899. He was a son of the late Colonel I. W. MacDougall, was born July, 1871, and educated at Clifton College. He entered the Royal Artillery from the Royal Military Academy July, 1891, and was promoted lieut. July, 1894. He was serving in Ladysmith with his battery when war was declared.

MacDougall.—Lieut. John Patrick MacDougall, 20th Battery Royal Field Artillery, was killed in action near Vlakfontein, May 29th, 1901. He was born Feb., 1875, educated at Clifton College, and entered the Royal Artillery Nov., 1895, being promoted lieut. Nov., 1898. From Jan. 14th to June 2nd, 1899, Lieut. MacDougall was employed with the West African Frontier Force. He proceeded to South Africa Jan., 1900, and was mentioned in despatches, L.G., Sept. 10th, 1901, also in the despatch July 28th, 1901, for "good service at Vlakfontein" on the day he fell.

MacFarlan.—Capt. William MacFarlan, adjutant 2nd Batt. Royal Highlanders, was killed in action at the engagement at Magersfontein, Dec. 11th, 1899. He was born Dec., 1867, educated at Loretto School, Musselburgh, where he played in the cricket XI., and entered the Royal Highlanders Feb., 1888, being promoted lieut. May, 1890, and capt. May, 1898. He was adjutant of his battalion from May, 1897. At Magersfontein, Capt. MacFarlan, with a small party of twenty to thirty men, rushed up the south-eastern corner of the hill, but the converging fire of our infantry and artillery forced them back, and he afterwards fell mortally wounded.

Macgregor.—Major Robert Lipton Macgregor, 1st Batt. Royal Scots, died at Nooitgedacht, April 2nd, 1901. He was born April, 1862, and entered his regiment May, 1882, being promoted capt. June, 1890, and major Oct., 1900. He served in the Bechuanaland Expedition under Sir Charles Warren, 1884-85, with the 1st Batt. Royal Scots, also in the operations in Zululand in 1888. Major Macgregor, who had been serving with the 2nd battalion in India, was posted on his promotion in Oct., 1900, to the 1st battalion, and proceeding to South Africa served there up to the time of his death.

OFFICERS WHO FELL IN SOUTH AFRICA. 237

Mackay.—Lieut. James Eric Mackay, Mounted Infantry Royal Lancaster Regiment, died of wounds received in action at Rustmynziel, Sept. 29th, 1901. He was born March, 1879, and entered his regiment from the 4th Batt. (Royal Lancashire Militia) April, 1900, being promoted lieut. Feb., 1901.

Mackellar.—2nd Lieut. Keith Kinnaird Mackellar, 7th Dragoon Guards, was killed in action near Derdepoort, July 11th, 1900. He was born July, 1880, and entered the 7th Dragoon Guards from the New South Wales Local Military Forces May 26th, 1900.

Mackenzie. — Capt. Cortlandt Gordon Mackenzie, Royal Artillery, of Foxton Grange, Market Harborough, died of enteric at De Aar Jan. 24th, 1900. He was born Dec., 1863, educated at Marlborough, whence he passed into Woolwich and joined the Royal Artillery Feb., 1883, being promoted capt. Feb., 1892. He held the post of adjutant Royal Artillery from 1892 to 1894, and was appointed staff capt. in the Remount Establishment July, 1898. He was a well known polo player and recognised authority on all matters connected with the training and breeding of horses. In June, 1899, Capt. Mackenzie was selected for special service and was sent to South Africa to buy horses and mules, in view of the possible outbreak of hostilities. He was present as the battle of Magersfontein, but shortly after contracted enteric. His name is inscribed on a tablet placed in Marlborough College Chapel, in memory of all Marlburians who fell in the war.

Mackenzie.—Major Kenneth Ross Mackenzie, 2nd Batt. Seaforth Highlanders, was killed in action at Magersfontein Dec. 11th, 1899. He was first returned as missing, but it was afterwards reported that he had been killed on the above-mentioned date. He was born May, 1855, educated at Winchester, and entered the 71st Foot Aug., 1873, being promoted lieut. in the Seaforth Highlanders Nov., 1873, capt. March, 1883, and major Sept., 1891. He served in the Afghan war 1879-80, with the Transport Department, and received the medal; also in the Hazara Expeditions of 1888 (medal with clasp) and 1891 (clasp). Major Mackenzie also took part in the operations in Chitral in 1895, with the Relief Force, and was present at the action at Mamagai and awarded the medal with clasp. He held the post of second-in-command of his battalion since Dec., 1897, and embarked for South Africa in Oct., 1899, joining the Kimberley Relief Force shortly before being killed.

Mackenzie.—2nd Lieut. Rupert Henry Mackenzie, attached 20th Company Army Service Corps (late of Lumsden's Horse), was injured by falling from his horse at Edenburg, August 3rd, 1901, and died the following day. He was the third son of the late Henry Dixon Mackenzie, of Hattigor, Assam, and Dalmore, Southport; and of Mrs. Mackenzie of 60, Redcliffe Gardens, South Kensington. He was twenty-one years of age.

Mackworth.—Brevet-Major Digby Mackworth, Queen's Royal West Surrey Regt., was killed in action at the engagement at Wagon Hill, Ladysmith, Jan. 6th, 1900. He was the eldest son of Col. Sir Arthur William Mackworth, C.B., sixth baronet, of Glen Usk, Monmouthshire, was born May, 1868, and educated at Marlborough. He entered his regiment Sept., 1887, being promoted lieut. June, 1890, capt. Nov., 1896, and brevet-major July, 1899. Major Mackworth served in the Burmese Expedition of 1887-88, and the West African Expedition 1897-98, in the northern territories of the Gold Coast, taking part in the operations against the Binduris, was mentioned in despatches and received the brevet of major. In Oct., 1899, he was employed as a special service officer in South Africa, and proceeded to Ladysmith. At Wagon Hill he was attached to the 2nd Batt. King's Royal Rifle Corps, and heading a charge over an open space of about sixty yards, fell mortally wounded close to the Boer position. One report states that he actually reached the Boer position before being killed. Major Mackworth's name is inscribed on a tablet placed in Marlborough College Chapel in memory of all Marlburians who fell in the war, also on a tablet erected at Guildford, by his comrades of the Queen's Royal West Surrey Regt. (*See Major Bowen.*)

Maclachlan.—Capt. Donald Maclachlan, 1st Batt. Royal Inniskilling Fusiliers, died Feb. 1st, 1900, from wounds received Jan. 21st, 1900, in action at Venter's Spruit. He was the son of the late George Maclachlan, Esq., of Maclachlan, Argyllshire, was born 1866, and entered the 1st Dragoon Guards from the 2nd Brigade, Scottish Division, Royal Artillery (Militia), in Nov., 1887. He was transferred to the 21st Hussars the following month, being promoted lieut. April, 1890, and capt. the 5th Dragoon Guards Nov., 1898, from which he exchanged into the Royal Inniskilling Fusiliers in Feb., 1899. He went to South Africa, Oct., 1899, and was present at the battle of Colenso. Capt. Maclachlan is buried at Spearman's Camp. His grave is marked by a marble tombstone erected by his comrades of the 1st. Batt.

Maclean.—Lieut. John Marsham Maclean, Royal Field Artillery, died Nov. 4th, 1901, at Springs, of wounds received in action near Brakenlaagte (20 miles N.W. of Bethel), Oct. 31st. He was born Oct., 1879, educated at Cheltenham, and entered the Royal Artillery, Dec., 1898, being promoted lieut. Feb. 1901. Lieut. Maclean went to South Africa, Dec., 1899, with the 6th Division Ammunition Column, and afterwards joined the 84th Field

Battery, serving throughout the war. He is buried at Springs, and his name is inscribed on the Eleanor Cross War Memorial erected at Cheltenham College.

MacLean.—Lieut. Norman MacLean, Imperial Light Infantry, died of poisoning at Volksrust on June 23rd, 1900.

Macmullen.—Major Francis Richard Macmullen, 2nd Batt. Wiltshire Regt., died of wounds received Feb. 15th, 1900, in action at Rensburg. He was born May, 1855, entered the 62nd Foot from the West Essex Militia, Aug., 1877, and was promoted lieut. July, 1878, capt. 1885, and major Jan. 1898. He served in the Egyptian War, 1882, and took part in the action at Kassassin, and the battle of Tel-el-Kebir, receiving the medal with clasp and the Khedive's star. Major Macmullen was employed with the Army Pay Department, Oct., 1884 to Oct., 1888, he was also adjutant of the 2nd V.B. East Yorkshire Regt., at Beverley, Jan., 1895 to Dec., 1899, when he rejoined his battalion to proceed to South Africa. He served in the Colesberg operations under Lieut.-Gen. French.

Macnaghten.—2nd Lieut. Stewart Maxwell Macnaghten, 3rd Batt. King's Royal Rifle Corps, died June 26th, 1901, at Heidelberg, from gangrene, following the amputation of his right arm, an operation necessitated by the result of an accident. He was the younger son of Alfred Macnaghten, Esq., 9, Palmeira Mansions, Brighton. He was born May, 1880, educated at Eton (Miss Evans'), and entered the 3rd Batt. King's Royal Rifle Corps from the 7th Batt., June, 1900.

Maddocks.—Lieut. Thomas Brassey Maddocks, 2nd Batt. Somersetshire Light Infantry, was shot through the heart during the re-occupation of Potchefstroom,

Sept. 10th, 1900. He was born Sept., 1874, educated at Shrewsbury School, and entered the Somersetshire Light Infantry, Dec., 1895, from the 3rd Batt. Shropshire Light Infantry, being promoted lieut. October, 1898. Lieut. Maddocks accompanied his battalion to South Africa in Oct., 1899, and served with the Natal Field Force. At the time of his death he was acting on the staff of Major-Gen. Hart-Synnot. (*See Capt. Moor.*)

Maguire.—Capt. Charles James Kinahan Maguire, Royal Sussex Regt., was killed in action at Diamond Hill, near Pretoria, June 11th, 1900. He was a son of the Dean of Bangor, co. Down, was born March, 1872, and educated at Rossall. Capt. Maguire entered the Royal Sussex Regt. from the Militia in March, 1892, being promoted lieut. May, 1894, and capt. April, 1899. At the commencement of the war he was serving at the depôt of his regiment at Chichester, and belonged to the 2nd battalion then stationed in India. Volunteering, however, for active service, he joined the 1st battalion in South Africa in April, 1900, and served with it in O.R.C. and the Transvaal until his death.

Maitland.—Capt. Stuart Cairns Maitland, Gordon Highlanders, was killed in action in the operations of Feb. 23rd and 24th, 1900, on the Tugela. He was the eldest son of D. Maitland, Esq., of Dundrennan, was born Oct., 1873, and educated at Eton (Mr. Ainger's). He entered the Gordon Highlanders, May, 1893, and was promoted capt. Oct., 1899. When war broke out Capt. Maitland was in England on leave from India, but on learning that his battalion was ordered to South Africa, he at once applied to join it. He did not, however, arrive in Natal in time, as his battalion formed part of the Ladysmith garrison, and the siege had commenced. Capt. Maitland was then attached for duty to the 2nd

Batt. Royal Dublin Fusiliers, and was present at the battle of Colenso, and all the fighting on the Tugela, in which the Irish Brigade took part. He is buried beside Lieut.-Col. Thackeray, at the foot of the hill where he fell (known as Hart's or Railway or Inniskilling Hill). A marble headstone has been erected to mark his grave.

Majendie.—Capt. Henry Grylls Majendie, Rifle Brigade, died Feb. 13th, 1900, of wounds received in action the previous day at Dekiel's Drift, Riet River. He was the only son of the late Col. Sir Vivian Dering Majendie, K.C.B., was born March, 1865, educated at Winchester, and entered the Rifle Brigade in 1885, was promoted lieut. June, 1891, and capt. April, 1894. He was adjutant of his battalion from June, 1891-95, and served in the Burmese Expedition of 1888-89 with the 4th Batt. Rifle Brigade, receiving the medal with clasp. Capt. Majendie next saw service in the campaign in the Soudan under Lord (then Sir Herbert) Kitchener in 1898, and was present at the battles of Atbara and Khartoum (mentioned in despatches). He was also in the subsequent operations, being again mentioned in despatches, and received the British medal, the Egyptian medal with two clasps, and was granted the Fourth Class of the Order of the Medjidie. He was appointed to the Egyptian Army from Dec., 1897, and in South Africa was employed on special service.

Mallock.—Lieut. James Raymond Mallock, Lancashire Fusiliers, was killed in action at Spion Kop Jan. 24th, 1900. He was the youngest son of Lieut.-Col. Mallock, of Firlands, Camberley, and formerly of the Royal Fusiliers, was born June, 1873, and entered the Lancashire Fusiliers from the 5th Batt. Royal Fusiliers in May, 1895, being promoted lieut. April, 1898. Lieut. Mallock served in the campaign of the Soudan under Lord (then Sir Herbert) Kitchener in 1898 with the 2nd Batt. Lancashire

Fusiliers, and was present at the battle of Khartoum, receiving the British medal and Khedive's medal with clasp. He proceeded to South Africa with his battalion in Nov., 1899, and served with it in Natal until his death.

Mann.—Capt. Horace Mann, Thorneycroft's M.I., was killed in action at Alleman's Nek, June 11th, 1900. The eldest surviving son of the Rev. C. N. Mann, for many years rector of St. Issey, Cornwall, he was born in 1860, and educated at Allhallowes School, Honiton, and at Marlborough. Capt. Mann entered the 1st Batt. Royal West Kent Regt. in July, 1882, was promoted capt. March, 1890, and served in the Nile Campaign of 1884-85, with his regiment, receiving the medal with clasp and Khedive's star. He was adjutant to the 1st V.B. Royal West Kent Regt. 1892 to 1897, after which he retired from the army. On the outbreak of the war he went out to South Africa, and was appointed capt. in Thorneycroft's M.I. Capt. Mann was present at the battle of Colenso, and in all the operations leading up to the relief of Ladysmith, and the subsequent advance to Alleman's Nek. He was mentioned in despatches by Gen. Sir R. Buller, from Laing's Nek, June 19th, 1901, as having performed good service, L.G., Feb. 8th, 1901. His name is inscribed on a tablet erected in Marlborough College Chapel in memory of all Marlburians who fell in the war.

Manners.—Major Fitzalan George John Manners, Scots Guards, sailed for South Africa March 2nd, 1901, for special service in the M.I., and died at sea on board the S.S. "Tagus," off St. Helena, of enteric, March 15th. He was the youngest son of the late Lord George Manners, Royal Horse Guards, and M.P. for Cambridgeshire, who was the third son of the 5th Duke of Rutland. His mother was Mary Adeliza Matilda, daughter of the 13th Duke of Norfolk. Major Manners was born in Feb., 1866, and educated at Hoddesden, Herts, and at Wellington. He entered the Scots Guards in Aug., 1885, from the Royal Military College, and was promoted capt. May, 1897, and major March 1st, 1901, a few days before his death. He was fond of literature and was editor of the Badminton Diary, and author of several books on drill. Major Manners was considered an expert on heraldry.

Markes.—2nd Lieut. Alfred Ernest Markes, 2nd Batt. Royal Scots Fusiliers, died of enteric at Middelburg, Transvaal, July 4th, 1902. He was the younger son of Alfred Markes, Esq., of 25, Norfolk Crescent, W., and was born in Dec., 1880. He entered the army unattached from the Royal Military College in Jan., 1901, being appointed in March to the Royal Scots Fusiliers. 2nd Lieut. Markes then embarked for active service, and joining his battalion in South Africa served with it in the Transvaal up to the time of his death.

Marriott.—Lieut. D. Marriott, 50th Co. I.Y., died of enteric at Deelfontein, March 30th, 1901. He entered the Hampshire Yeomanry (Carabiniers) as a 2nd lieut. in March, 1900, and on joining the I.Y. was appointed to the 17th battalion with the rank of lieut. in the army from Feb., 1900.

Marsden.—Lieut. Hugh Sidney Marsden, 1st Batt. King's Royal Rifle Corps, was killed in action at Farquhar's Farm, near Ladysmith, Oct. 30th, 1899. He was the only son of F. J. Marsden, Esq., Colne House, Earl's Colne, Colchester, was born Dec., 1871, educated at Marlborough, and entered the King's Royal Rifle Corps from the Royal Military College July, 1897, being promoted lieut. in April, 1899. He sailed for South Africa on board the "Tantallon Castle," Sept. 17th, 1899, to join his battalion then quartered in Natal, and was present at the battle of Talana Hill and the retirement on Ladysmith. When killed at Farquhar's Farm, he was assisting a wounded brother officer (Major Myers) under a heavy fire. Lieut. Marsden's name is inscribed on a tablet placed in Marlborough College Chapel, in memory of all Marlburians who fell in the war.

Marsh.—Lieut. Gerald John Marsh, 1st Batt. Border Regt., died in London on March 17th, 1902, from enteric. He was the third son of the late John William Marsh, Esq., D.L., 71, East India Road, London, and of Scarsdale, Lowestoft, was born Dec., 1874, and entered the Border Regt. Sept., 1895, being promoted lieut. Feb., 1898. He served with his regiment in the South African War, with the Natal Field Force, and was present in the engagement at Willow Grange, and the battle of Colenso (severely wounded). He afterwards served in the Transvaal, and was present at the engagement at Boshfontein.

Marsh.—Major Thomas Alfred Perry Marsh, Royal Army Medical Corps, died of enteric, May 22nd, 1900, at Deelfontein. Born in Feb., 1856, he entered the Army July, 1882, being promoted major in the Royal Army Medical Corps in July, 1894. He served in the Burmese Expedition, 1885-87, in medical charge of a battery of mountain artillery, and was present at several engagements near Ningyan and Yemethen. Major Marsh was in the latter place during its investment in Feb. and March, 1886, and received the medal with clasp. He served in South Africa from Nov., 1899.

Marshall.—Capt. Henry Daily Marshall, 5th Batt. Rifle Brigade, died of enteric, at Pietermaritzburg, Dec. 3rd, 1900. He was born June, 1855, and entered his regiment as capt. from the 19th Middlesex Volunteers, in Aug., 1886.

He had been in the Reserve of Officers since Sept., 1888, and at the time of his death was attached to the regular forces for duty.

Marsham.—Capt. the Hon. Douglas Henry Marsham, 4th Batt. Bedfordshire Regt., attached to the Protectorate Regt., was killed in action at Cannon Kopje, in the defence of Mafeking, Oct. 31st, 1899. He was the third son of Earl Romney, was born 1871, and educated at Charterhouse. Before joining the Bedfordshire Regt., he served for some time in the Bechuanaland Border Police. Capt. Marsham is mentioned in the despatch of Major-Gen. Baden-Powell, May 18th, 1900, L.G., Feb. 8th, 1901. He is buried in the cemetery at Mafeking, and his name is inscribed on the tablet in the War Memorial Cloister erected at Charterhouse.

Martelli.—Lieut. Richard Godfrey Holroyd Martelli, Army Service Corps, died at Bournemouth, Jan. 30th, 1902. He was educated at the United Services College, Westward Ho, and entered the 3rd Batt. Prince of Wales's Leinster Regt. (Royal Canadians) in Feb., 1900, being appointed in Sept. as 2nd lieut. to the Army Service Corps, and promoted lieut. in Nov., 1901. Lieut. Martelli served in the South African war first with his embodied Militia battalion and afterwards with the Army Service Corps. His name is inscribed on a memorial tablet at the United Services College, Westward Ho.

Marten.—2nd Lieut. Leonard Humphrey Marten, 2nd Batt. King's Own Yorkshire Light Infantry, was severely wounded in the attack on Col. Benson's column at Brakenlaagte (30 miles N.W. of Bethel), Oct. 30th, 1901, and died of his wounds at Elandsfontein on Nov. 5th. He was born Dec., 1878, and educated at Shrewsbury School, where he was in the rowing eight. He entered the Yorkshire Light Infantry, May, 1900. At Brackenlaagte, 2nd Lieut. Marten had his thigh broken by the the enemy's fire. When lying wounded he is stated to have been cruelly illtreated by the Boers, in order to get his clothing, boots, &c. (*See Capt. Moor.*)

Marter.—Capt. William Maurice Marter, p.s.c., 1st Dragoon Guards, Brigade Major, died April 3rd, 1900, of wounds received in action on March 29th, at Karee Siding, near Brandfort. He was the son of the late Major-General Marter, King's Dragoon Guards, of Walton, Epping, formerly A.D.C. to Her Late Majesty Queen Victoria. Capt. Marter was born Jan., 1868, and educated at Clifton College, whence he passed into the Royal Military College. In 1886 he passed out with honours, and entered the Royal Fusiliers in Feb., 1887, being promoted lieut. Feb., 1891. He was transferred to the 1st Dragoon Guards in April, 1892, and promoted capt. March, 1896. Capt. Marter had served in Egypt and India and passed the higher standard in Hindustani and Persian. He was appointed D.A.A.G., North-Eastern District, March, 1897, which post he held till Dec., 1899, when he proceeded to South Africa as Brigade Major, 14th Brigade. He took part in the advance on Bloemfontein, through Jacobsdal and Paardeberg, afterwards moving along the railway to Karree. He is buried in the cemetery there beside his school friend, Capt. Going. Capt. Marter married 1897, Mary Edith, third daughter of the late Col. Cuming, formerly of the Cameron Highlanders, of Crover, co. Cavan, who survives him. Her late Majesty Queen Victoria, sent a message of condolence on Capt. Marter's death being reported, and asked for his photograph.

Martin.—Lieut. Charles Edward Martin, 1st. Batt. Leinster Regt. (Royal Canadians), died of pneumonia at sea on board the "Dilwara" whilst *en route* to South Africa on May 1st, 1900. Born in Jan., 1876, he entered the Leinster Regt. from the 3rd Batt. Queen's Own Royal West Kent Regt., March, 1897, being promoted lieut. July, 1899.

Mason.—Lieut. William Anthony Mason, Johannesburg Mounted Rifles, died of enteric at Johannesburg on Feb. 3rd, 1902.

Massy.—Major Hampden Hugh Massy, Royal Engineers, was killed in action in the operations on the Upper Tugela Jan. 24th, 1900. He was born in Feb., 1858, and entered the Royal Engineers, Oct. 1877, being promoted capt. April, 1888, and major Aug., 1896. Major Massy was killed in the firing line, while personally superintending the making of entrenchments; and was twice mentioned in despatches, L.G., Feb. 8th, 1901, for his gallant conduct.

Massy.—Major Hugh Ingoldsby Massy, 1st Batt. Essex Regt., died of enteric at Kimberley, March 22nd, 1900. He was born in January, 1853, and entered the Essex Regt. from the militia, Nov. 1875, being promoted capt. Aug., 1882, and major July, 1891. He embarked for South Africa in Nov., 1899, and served in the Colesberg operations and the relief of Kimberley.

Masterman.—Capt. Henry Wright Masterman, 3rd Batt. Welsh Regt., died of malaria and meningitis at Prieska, Nov. 28th, 1900. He was the son of the late T. W. Masterman, Esq., F.R.G.S., the Hall, Rotherfield, Sussex, and of Mrs. Masterman, now of Lonsdale, Tunbridge Wells; was born in July, 1875, and educated at Tonbridge School and Weymouth College. At the latter he was in the cricket and football teams. On leaving Weymouth College, Capt. Masterman went to

St. John's, Cambridge, and afterwards to Christ's College. When at Cambridge he was capt. in the University Royal Volunteer Corps. In Jan., 1899, he entered St. Bartholomew's Hospital, but his battalion being embodied in Dec., he joined and accompanied it to South Africa in Feb., 1900, and when at Prieska was appointed Garrison Adjutant there, which post he held till taken ill. He is buried at Prieska.

Matthews.—Lieut. George Harold Matthews, 2nd Batt. Gloucestershire Regt., died at Prieska on May 30th, 1900, of wounds received in action at Kheis, two days previously. He was the second son of T. G. Matthews, Esq., J.P., of Newport Towers, Berkeley, Gloucestershire, was born May, 1878, and educated at Eton (Dr. Carpenter's and Mr. Carter's). He was a good sportsman, and entered the Gloucestershire Regt. from the 4th battalion in March, 1898, being promoted lieut. in Feb., 1900. At the time of his death he was serving with the M.I., and fell while leading his men, several of whom have written in admiration of his bravery. Lieut. Matthews had been on picket on the night of the 27th (Sunday) about three miles from Staff Kraal, at the edge of a river, overlooking some Boers who were guarding the drift from the opposite side. The picket being reinforced the following morning, the Boers were forced back and the drift crossed. The party then moved westwards to attack the Boer laager some four miles off. The enemy were driven out, but in attacking some high ground beyond, Lieut. Matthews was twice wounded, and died two days later. He is buried beside Capt. Tindal. A cross has been erected over his grave.

Matthews.—Lieut. Harold Laurence Matthews, 1st Batt. Essex Regt., died of dysentery at Elandsfontein, May 24th, 1902. He was the son of J. H. Matthews,

Esq, Harley House, Regent's Park, and Rippledene, Sunbury-on-Thames, was born in July, 1878, and educated at Harrow, where he played in the school cricket and football teams. He entered the Essex Regt. from the Royal Military College in May, 1898, being promoted lieut. March, 1900. Lieut. Matthews was on continuous active service with his battalion for two and a half years, and took part in the operations around Colesberg, Dewetsdorp, Paardekraal, Komati Poort, including the engagement at Belfast; also Frederickstadt and Heidelberg, and the capture of Carolina, including two engagements at Twyfelaar. He was also present at the operations in the Hopetown district, and was awarded the medal with three clasps, also the King's medal. A tablet has been erected to his memory in the church at Elandsfontein, and his name is inscribed on a framed tablet placed in the Court House of the Spelthorne division of Middlesex, in memory of all those belonging to the division who fell in the war.

Maunsell.—Major Lucius Augustus de Vere Maunsell, 9th Batt. King's Royal Rifle Corps, and late of the Leicestershire Regt., died on Jan. 24th, 1900, on board the S.S. "Nile," while going to South Africa with his battalion. Born in August, 1863, he entered the Leicestershire Regt. from the Militia in May, 1885, and was promoted capt. 1894. He retired July 24th, 1895, and on the same day was promoted to a majority in the 9th Batt. King's Royal Rifle Corps. His battalion was embodied in Dec., 1899, and volunteering for active service, Major Maunsell embarked with it in Jan., 1900.

Maxwell. — Lieut.-Col. Cedric Maxwell, Royal Engineers, died at Rouxville May 20th, 1901, from concussion of the brain, received through a fall from his horse. He was a son of Lieut.-Col. C. F. Maxwell, formerly of the 82nd Regt., was born July, 1854, and educated at Henley Grammar School, from which he passed into the Royal Military Academy, Woolwich. He entered the Royal Engineers, April, 1873, being promoted capt. Jan., 1885, major April, 1893, and brevet lieut.-col. Nov., 1900. He served in the Afghan War of 1878-80, and was present in the operations around Kabul, being mentioned in despatches and receiving the medal. He also saw service with the Zhob Valley Expedition of 1884. He arranged the defence of Wepener, and his services are mentioned in the despatch of Lieut.-Col. Dalgety, commanding the Cape Mounted Rifles, April 29th, 1900. Lieut.-Col. Maxwell is stated as having "selected a position and assisted in every way," L. G., Feb. 8th, 1901.

May.—Quartermaster and Hon. Capt. James May, 3rd Batt. Grenadier Guards, was found dead in his bed on the morning of Feb. 4th, 1901, at Houtkraal. He was born Sept., 1857, and served in the ranks for eleven and a half years, was warrant officer over six years, and became lieut. and quartermaster in the Grenadier Guards in April, 1895. He was mentioned in despatches, L.G., Sept. 10th, 1901, for his services, and was promoted to the honorary rank of capt. Nov. 29th, 1900.

McCarthy-O'Leary.—Lieut.-Col. William McCarthy-O'Leary, commanding the 1st Batt. South Lancashire Regt., was killed in action at Pieter's Hill Feb. 27th, 1900. He was the third son of J. McCarthy-O'Leary, Esq., a former High Sheriff of Cork, was born Jan., 1849, and educated at Stoneyhurst. He entered the 82nd foot in April, 1869, being promoted lieut. Feb., 1871, capt. March, 1878, major Aug., 1883, and lieut.-col. Nov., 1896. He was adjutant Auxiliary Forces, 1883-88. He was one of the tallest men in the army, fond of games, and a keen sportsman, and is stated to have shown "the greatest interest in all which concerned the welfare of those under his command." He embarked for South Africa in command of his battalion Nov. 1899, and served with the Natal Field Force. At Pieter's Hill, while leading his battalion to attack the Boer position Col. McCarthy-O'Leary, just before he fell, said : " Remember, men, the eyes of Lancashire are watching you." He was twice mentioned in despatches for his services, L.G., Feb. 8th, 1901, by Gen. Sir R. Buller, who referred to the great loss that the country had sustained by his death.

McClintock-Bunbury.—2nd Lieut. the Hon. William McClintock-Bunbury, 2nd Dragoons (Royal Scots Greys), died of wounds received in the fighting round Kimberley, Feb. 14th to 16th, 1900. He was the eldest son of Lord Rathdonnell, a representative peer of Ireland; was born in 1878, and educated at Eton (Mr. Donaldson's). He entered the Scots Greys from the Militia in Jan., 1899, and served with his regiment in South Africa from the commencement of the war, in the north of Cape Colony, and afterwards in the advance of Lieut.-Gen. French on Kimberley.

McClure.—2nd Lieut. Robert Hamilton McClure, 2nd Batt. Seaforth Highlanders, was killed in action at Paardeberg, Feb. 18th, 1900. Born in March, 1881, he entered the Seaforth Highlanders, Aug., 1899, and embarked for South Africa in October. The late Major-Gen. Sir H. Macdonald, in his report concerning the battle of Paardeberg, states that 2nd Lieut. McClure succeeded in crossing the river, but, " I regret to say, lost his life." 2nd Lieut. McClure's death is also mentioned in the despatch of F.-M. Earl Roberts, Feb. 28th, 1900, from Paardeberg, also in that of March 31st for having "rendered valuable service," L.G., Feb. 8th, 1901.

McCorquodale.—Lieut. Hugh Stewart McCorquodale,

Thorneycroft's M.I., was killed in action at Spion Kop, Jan. 24th, 1900. He was the youngest son of the late George McCorquodale, Esq., of Newton-le-Willows and Gadlys, Menai Bridge, Isle of Anglesey, by his second wife Emily, daughter of the late Rev. T. Sanderson, vicar of Doddington, Lancashire. Lieut. McCorquodale was born Aug., 1875, and educated at Harrow, where he was in the school football team. From Harrow he went to Trinity College, Cambridge, and took his degree in June, 1897. He was fond of all sports, shooting, hunting, fishing, and when at Cambridge, was whip to the drag hounds. He had intended joining his brothers in business, but when the war broke out went to South Africa and joined Thorneycroft's M.I. on Jan. 23rd, 1900. In the battle the next day he and his men were exposed to a terrific flank fire. Mr. Winston Churchill, M.P., states that the night before Spion Kop, when crossing the pontoon bridge over the Tugela, he heard his name called, and recognised the face of a boy he had known at Harrow; this was Lieut. McCorquodale, who said he had just arrived and hoped "to get a job." Next day Mr. Churchill heard that some one who could not be identified had been found leaning forward on his rifle dead. A pair of field glasses, broken by a bullet, bore the name "McCorquodale." Joined in the evening, killed at dawn, "gallant fellow, he had soon got his job; the great sacrifice had been required of the Queen's latest recruit." Lieut. McCorquodale is buried on the field of battle where he fell. (*See Lieut. Hill-Trevor.*)

McCutchan.—2nd Lieut. Philip Andrew McCutchan, 2nd Batt. Wiltshire Regt., died of enteric Oct. 9th, 1900, at Pretoria. He was the son of Lieut.-Col. J. S. McCutchan, retired A.M.S., was born in April, 1878, and educated at Bedford Grammar School and Brighton College. He served in the ranks of the Border Regt. for three years and a half, and, when a lance-sergeant, gained his commission in the Wiltshire Regt. in May, 1900.

McKeich.—Lieut. Robert McKeich, 2nd Brigade New Zealand Contingent, was killed at Nitnengt, near Vereeniging, on June 4th, 1902. He was the last officer killed in the war.

McKenzie.—Lieut. S. M. McKenzie, Driscoll's Scouts, died of tubercle on the lung at Wynberg, on March 28th, 1902.

McLachlan.—Lieut. W. McLachlan, Bethune's M.I., was killed during the reconnaissance between Blood River and Vryheid on May 20th, 1900. He is buried at Scheeper's Nek.

McLaren.—Lieut. J. L. McLaren, 105th Co. 8th Batt. I.Y., died of phthisis, at Deelfontein, on March 12th, 1902. He had been formerly a captain in the 2nd Volunteer Batt. West Yorkshire Regt., and entered the I.Y. in April, 1901, with the rank of lieut.

McLaren.—2nd Lieut. William Victor St. Clair McLaren, 1st Batt. Argyll and Sutherland Highlanders, died of syncope at Pretoria, July 26th, 1900. He was born in May, 1877, educated at Merchiston, Edinburgh, and entered his regiment from the 4th Batt. Cameronians (Militia), June 3rd, 1899. He accompanied the 1st Batt. Argyll and Sutherland Highlanders to South Africa in Oct., 1899, and served with the Kimberley relief force, afterwards taking part in the advance on Bloemfontein and Pretoria.

McLean.—Capt. Douglas Hamilton McLean, 69th Co. I.Y., of Stoberry Park, Wells, Somerset, died of enteric at Johannesburg on Feb. 5th, 1901. He was the son of the late Hon. J. D. McLean, formerly Colonial Treasurer of Queensland, Australia, and was 37 years of age. Capt. McLean was educated at Eton (Mr. Carter's), and was well-known as a University Rowing Coach. He held the rank of capt. in the North Somerset Yeomanry Cavalry, and entered the I.Y. in March, 1900, with the rank of lieut., and was promoted capt. in the following August. Before his death Capt. McLean had been employed under the Military Governor of Pretoria.

McQueen.—Lieut. Malcolm Stewart McQueen, Indian Staff Corps, was killed in action at Benginsel, O.R.C., on March, 3rd, 1902. He was the son of Lieut.-Gen. Sir John McQueen, was born in Nov., 1877, and educated at the United Services College, Westward Ho. In 1897 Lieut. McQueen entered the Somerset Light Infantry, at Peshawur, subsequently joining the 23rd Punjab Pioneers and 4th Gurkhas, and afterwards the 20th Punjab Infantry in April, 1899, with which corps he served throughout the China War. Shortly after his return to India he was selected for service in South Africa with the 16th M.I., and served with that corps till his death. The day he fell he was in command of a small party which was surrounded by the enemy, and refusing to surrender, he was killed whilst encouraging his men. When only 13 years of age he gained the honorary certificate of the Royal Humane Society for saving a boy's life in the river Medway. Lieut. McQueen's name is inscribed on a memorial tablet at the United Services College, Westward Ho.

Meek.—Lieut. Alexander John Grant Meek, 6th Inniskilling Dragoons, died on June 7th, 1900, at Pretoria, of wounds received in action the previous day. He was the eldest son of Alexander Grant Meek, Esq., was born in May, 1880, educated at Harrow, and entered the 6th Dragoon Guards in Jan., 1899, being promoted lieut. the following Oct. He accompanied his regiment to South Africa in Oct., 1899, and served with it in the Colesberg operations, the relief of Kimberley, and the advance on Bloemfontein and Pretoria.

Meeking.—Capt. Bertram Charles Christopher Spencer Meeking, 10th Hussars, died of enteric at Bloemfontein on April 16th, 1900. He was the eldest son of Colonel Meeking, of Richings Park, Colnbrook, Bucks, and 31, Belgrave Square, S.W., by his marriage with Adelaide Caroline, fourth daughter of Christopher Tower, Esq., of Huntsmore Park, Bucks. Capt. Meeking was born in March, 1864, educated at Eton (Mr. Cameron's and Mr. Mozley's), and entered the 10th Hussars in Feb., 1888, being promoted lieut. Sept., 1890, and capt. Jan., 1897. He was present at the relief of Kimberley, and took part in the advance on Bloemfontein.

Meeking.—2nd Lieut. Kenneth Charles Edward Meeking, 2nd Batt. Grenadier Guards, died of enteric at Bethlehem on Feb. 2nd, 1902. He was the youngest son of Col. Meeking, of Richings Park, Colnbrook, Bucks, and 31, Belgrave Square, W., and brother of Capt. Meeking, 10th Hussars, who died April 16th, 1900. 2nd Lieut. Meeking was born in April, 1880, educated at Eton (Mr. Impey's), and entered the Grenadier Guards from the 4th Batt. Bedfordshire Regt. (Hertford Militia) in Jan., 1900. He at first served with the 3rd Batt. Grenadier Guards in South Africa till July, 1901, when he joined the 2nd battalion, afterwards serving with it till his death.

Mellish.—Lieut. Lawrence Oliver Falaise Mellish, 2nd Batt. Wiltshire Regt., died of enteric, at Bloemfontein, June 2nd, 1900. He was born in Jan., 1876, educated at St. Paul's School, and was a good cricketer and all round athlete. He entered the Wiltshire Regt. in May, 1897, being promoted lieut. July, 1898, and accompanied his battalion to South Africa in Dec., 1899, and served with it in the Colesberg operations and the subsequent advance from the north of Cape Colony.

Menzies.—Capt. Angus Menzies, 1st Batt. Manchester Regt., died at Paardeplaats, on Jan. 22nd, 1902, of wounds received in action. He was born May, 1871, and entered his regiment in Nov., 1890, being promoted lieut. July, 1893, and capt. Feb., 1898. He saw service with the 2nd battalion in the Miranzai expedition of 1891. Capt. Menzies had served throughout the South African war with the 1st battalion, with which he was present throughout the siege of Ladysmith, being slightly wounded at Wagon Hill. He was afterwards commandant at Wit Klip, and was mentioned in despatches, L.G., Sept. 10th, 1901.

Menzies.—Midshipman James Menzies, H.M.S. "Doris," died of enteric, at Bloemfontein, on May 18th, 1900. He was the only son of Hugh James Menzies, Esq., of 87, King Henry's Road, N.W., was born in May, 1882, and educated at Waltham College, and on the training ship, "Conway," from which he gained a cadetship into the Royal Navy. He joined H.M.S. "Repulse" in Sept., 1898, and in 1899 was appointed to H.M.S. "Doris." He was present at the battle of Paardeberg and in the advance on Bloemfontein. Commander Grant, in his despatch of Oct. 30th, 1900, reports Midshipman Menzies' death with deep regret, as he was "a young officer of great promise." It is believed that he was the youngest officer who lost his life in the war.

"A boy who fell at England's call;
And what could Nelson's self do more?"

Mettam.—Lieut. Charles Mettam, Mafeking District

Mounted Rifles, died of pericarditis, at Mafeking, during the war.

Meyricke.—Lieut. Robert Evelyn Meyricke, Royal Engineers, died of enteric at the Base Hospital, Pietermaritzburg, on March 8th, 1900. He was born in July, 1874, educated at Cheltenham and entered the Royal Engineers from the Royal Military Academy, Nov., 1894, being promoted lieut. Nov., 1897. Lieut. Meyricke was stationed in South Africa before the commencement of the war, and served in Natal up to the date of his death. His name is inscribed on the Eleanor Cross War Memorial erected at Cheltenham College.

Meyrick.—Capt. St. John Meyrick, Gordon Highlanders, was killed in action at Doornkop on May 30th, 1900, during Lieut.-Gen. Ian Hamilton's operations near Johannesburg. He was the son of Sir Thomas Charlton-Meyrick, of Apley Castle, Shropshire, by his marriage with Mary Rhode, second daughter of Col. Frederick Hill, and niece of Rowland, second Viscount Hill. Capt. Meyrick was born in Aug., 1866, and educated at Cheam School, Eton (Mr. Durnford's), and Trinity College, Cambridge. He entered the Gordon Highlanders from the 3rd. Batt. Cheshire Regt., Dec., 1886, being promoted capt. in 1897. For three years he acted as extra A.D.C., and for two years as A.D.C. to the Lord Lieutenant of Ireland. When war broke out Capt. Meyrick was serving at the depot of his regiment at Aberdeen, but proceeded to South Africa in Feb. 1900. On rejoining his battalion he took part in the advance on Johannesburg, in the brigade under Major-Gen. Smith-Dorrien. The day he was killed at Doornkop, Capt. Meyrick was leading his company to attack the Boer position; and Sir A. Conan Doyle mentions that his "splendid corps, the Gordons, lost nearly a hundred men in their advance over the open."

OFFICERS WHO FELL IN SOUTH AFRICA. 259

Miers.—Lieut. Roland Hill Macdonald Capel Miers, Somersetshire Light Infantry (attached to South African Constabulary), was murdered at Riversdraai Sept. 25th, 1901, by a party of three Boers who approached his outpost carrying a white flag. He was the second son of Lieut.-Col. Capel H. Miers, late of the Queen's Own Cameron Highlanders, of Wingfield House, Stoke, Devonport; was born at Edinburgh, April, 1876, educated at the Oratory School, Edgbaston, and entered the Somersetshire Light Infantry from the 3rd Batt. in Dec., 1896, being promoted lieut. May, 1899. He was a good athlete, and won the Officers' Army Championship middle-weight boxing in 1898 and 1899, and also Sandow's gold medal for physical development. Lieut. Miers was appointed to the South African Constabulary, Dec., 1900; in Jan., 1901, he raised the Utrecht Mounted Police, and was wounded Feb. 5th, but soon recovered. An interesting account of how this officer was murdered appeared in the *Times*, Nov. 9th, 1901. He appears to have ridden out to meet three Boers, who had been signalling with a white flag, conveying the idea that they wished to surrender. Lieut. Miers on approaching them was barbarously shot dead. A non-commissioned officer, who suspected that foul play had taken place, rode out to search for Lieut. Miers, and found him lying dead with his faithful dog beside him. His murderer, a man named Solomon Van Aan, was afterwards tried, found guilty, and shot at Heidelberg in June, 1902. By the irony of fate, the firing party consisted of some of Lieut. Mier's own regiment. When killed, Lieut. Miers was holding the temporary rank of capt. in the South African Constabulary.

Mildmay.— Capt. Alexander Richard Mildmay, 3rd Batt. King's Royal Rifle Corps, was killed in action near Blood River Poort, Sept. 17th, 1901. He was born in

March, 1873, educated at Eton (Mr. Marindin's and Mr. Williams'), and entered the King's Royal Rifle Corps from the 3rd Batt. Hampshire Regt. in Oct., 1893, being promoted lieut. Nov., 1896, and capt. Feb., 1901. He served with the Composite Regt. of Mounted Infantry in South Africa, and was mentioned in despatches, L.G., Feb. 8th, 1901, also in the despatch of Gen. Lord Kitchener, Oct. 8th, 1901, for his plucky, determined, and successful pursuit of Olivier's convoy, Aug. 3rd, 1901, with an inferior force; also for quickness and initiative, Aug. 23rd, when it was chiefly due to him and Capt. S. F. Mott, that the enemy were prevented from escaping. Capt. Mildmay is buried at Vryheid.

Miller.—Lieut. Alexander Rowley Miller, 3rd Batt. Royal Inniskilling Fusiliers, died of dysentery at Kaffir Kop, May, 15th, 1902. He was the son of Major Rowley Miller, of Mill Bank, Omagh. Lieut. Miller was born in May, 1880, educated at the Portora Royal School, Enniskillen, and Barbourne College, Worcester. He was fond of all games and a good rider. He entered his regiment Nov. 1899, and was promoted lieut. Feb., 1900. Soon after being gazetted he volunteered for active service, embarked for South Africa in March, 1901, and, on arrival, was attached for duty to the 1st battalion. Lieut. Miller afterwards served in Cape Colony with Col. Allenby's column in the Magaliesberg; and in the O.R.C. on the Kroonstad-Bethlehem blockhouse line. On one occasion Lieut. Miller was chosen as the bearer of an important despatch to Lord Kitchener, and had to ride through a very dangerous part of the country, and for the good performance of this duty he was awarded a commission. He was then gazetted 2nd lieut. in the 1st Batt., April 23rd, 1902. He is buried at Bethlehem. A cross marks his grave.

Miller.—Capt. D. F. Miller, 3rd Batt. New South Wales M.I., died of enteric at Harrismith, March 29th, 1902. He is buried at Harrismith military cemetery, and a marble cross marks his grave.

Miller-Wallnutt.—Major Claude Charles Miller-Wallnutt, D.S.O., 2nd Batt. Gordon Highlanders, was killed in action at Wagon Hill, Ladysmith, Jan. 6th, 1900. He was the only son of Mrs. Miller-Wallnutt, Edinburgh, was born 1861, educated at Edinburgh Academy, and entered the 75th Foot from the Argyll and Bute Artillery Militia, 1881, being promoted lieut. 1882, capt. 1888, and major 1898. He took part in the Egyptian Expedition, 1882, and was present at the battle of Tel-el-Kebir, receiving the medal with clasp, and the bronze star. He served in the Soudan in 1884, under Sir Gerald Graham, was in the battles of El Teb and Tamai (two clasps), and also took part in the Soudan Expedition up the Nile, in 1885, under Major-Gen. Earle (clasp). His next experience of active service was in the operations in Chitral in 1895, when he accompanied the relief force under Sir Robert Low, and was engaged in the storming of the Malakand Pass, receiving the medal with clasp. He took part in the operations on the North-West Frontier of India, 1897-98, was engaged with the Tirah Expeditionary Force, was present at the action at Dargai, being mentioned in despatches and receiving two clasps and the D.S.O. Major Miller-Wallnutt accompanied his battalion to South Africa in Sept., 1899, and was in Ladysmith when war was declared. At Wagon Hill, he had come up in command of a company of Gordons, to reinforce the defenders at a critical moment. He was with Lieut. Jones, Royal Engineers, and was killed, shot, it is believed, by the Boer General, de Villiers, who had planned, and was leading the attack, but almost at the same moment a sapper shot de Villiers through the head.

(*See Lieut. Jones.*) The author of "The Great Boer War" describes the stalwart Miller-Wallnutt as "a man cast in the mould of a Berserk Viking." He was mentioned in despatches, L.G., Feb. 8th, 1901.

Milligan.—Lieut. F. W. Milligan, Rhodesian Regt., was killed in action at Ramathlabama, near Mafeking, March, 31st, 1900. He was educated at Eton (Mr. Coles'), and was a famous Yorkshire cricketer. He formed one of a relieving force, under Col. Plumer, endeavouring to reach Mafeking, but, being fiercely attacked by the Boers on the date mentioned, they were compelled to retreat. Lieut. Milligan and Capt. Crew Robertson were killed. A brass tablet has been placed in Lowmoor Church, Yorkshire, in memory of Lieut. Milligan.

Mills.—2nd Lieut. George Ernest Mills, Derbyshire Regt., was killed in action at Moedwill (7 miles east of Magota Nek), Sept 30th, 1901. He was born Nov., 1882, and entered the Derbyshire Regt. from the 4th Batt. Bedfordshire Regt. (Hertfordshire Militia), May, 1901. 2nd Lieut. Mills was mentioned in despatches by Gen. Lord Kitchener, Oct. 8th, 1901, for "his example and disregard of danger."

Mills.—Capt. Sidney Mills, 2nd Batt. Rifle Brigade, died Feb. 2nd, 1900, of wounds received in action Jan. 6th at Wagon Hill, Ladysmith. He was born in July, 1867, educated at Harrow, and entered the Rifle Brigade Jan., 1889, being promoted lieut. Nov., 1891, and capt. 1896. He served in the campaign in the Soudan under Lord (then Sir Herbert) Kitchener in 1898, with the 2nd Batt. of his regiment, and was present at the battle of Khartoum, receiving the British medal and Khedive's medal with clasp. He accompanied his battalion to South

Africa in Sept., 1899, and served with it during the siege of Ladysmith until killed.

Milton.—Major Percy William Albert Alfred Milton, 1st Batt. Yorkshire Light Infantry, was killed in action at Magersfontein, Dec. 11th, 1899. He was born May, 1860, and entered the 51st Foot from the R.M.C., May, 1878, being promoted lieut. Dec., 1878, capt. Jan., 1884, brevet-major Sept., 1891, and major in March, 1894. He held the appointment of Station Staff Officer 1st Class, Bombay, from 1892-96, served with his battalion in the Afghan War of 1879-80, and was present in the engagement at Nargashai as orderly officer, being mentioned in despatches and receiving the medal. Major Milton served with the Burmese Expedition, 1886-87, with the 1st Batt. Yorkshire Light Infantry, during the latter part of the time in command of the M.I., being mentioned in despatches and receiving the medal with clasp. He also served with the 2nd Batt. of his regiment in the Zhob Field Force in 1890 under Gen. Sir George White during the Zhob and Kiderzai Expeditions and in the march to Vihowa, was again mentioned in despatches and given the brevet rank of major. In South Africa he was commanding the M.I. with the Kimberley Relief Force and was present at the actions at Belmont (mentioned in despatches), Graspan, and Modder River. Lieut.-Gen. Lord Methuen, in his despatch of Feb. 15th, 1900, concerning the battle of Magersfontein, reported that Major Milton in that action " behaved gallantly, and was shot three times before he died. He was making a successful effort to rally some men of the Highland Brigade." (*See Major Ray.*)

Milward.—Capt. Thomas Walter Milward, 1st Batt. Essex Regt., died of pneumonia May 10th, 1900, at Bloemfontein. He was the son of Col. T. W. Milward, Royal

Artillery, C.B., A.D.C. to Her late Majesty Queen Victoria, was born in April, 1867, and educated at Wellington, where he was in the Hardinge and Combermere, 1880-86. He was a College Prefect and in the football XV. He entered the Essex Regt. from the R.M.C. Feb., 1888, was promoted lieut., Aug., 1890, and capt. Feb., 1898. He held the appointment of adjutant of his battalion from Aug., 1892-96. He was wounded at the battle of Paardeberg, but in spite of his wound continued to keep with his battalion throughout the march to Bloemfontein, and was present at the battle of Driefontein, when the 1st Essex and the 1st Welsh drove the enemy from their entrenchments at the point of the bayonet.

Minniece.—Major James Minniece, M.D., M.Ch., Royal Army Medical Corps, died of enteric at Ladysmith, March 17th, 1900. He was born in May, 1859, entered the Royal Army Medical Corps as capt. Feb., 1887, and was promoted major Feb., 1899. Major Minniece, who had been serving in the Punjab, went to South Africa with the Indian Contingent in Sept., 1899, and was attached to the 5th Dragoon Guards.

Minshull-Ford.—Major Francis Charles Minshull-Ford, D.S.O., South African Constabulary (late Bethune's M.I., and formerly 2nd Batt. Highland Light Infantry), was killed in action at Mooline Tagesfontein, Transvaal, on Oct. 18th, 1901. He was the eldest son of the late Capt. J. R. Minshull-Ford, 8th The King's (now the Liverpool) Regt., of Llwyngwern, Montgomeryshire, and Mrs. Minshull-Ford, of Shorncliffe Road, Folkestone. Major Minshull-Ford was born 1870, and entered the Highland Light Infantry in 1892, was promoted lieut. 1894, and was voluntarily placed on the Reserve of Officers' List in 1897.

OFFICERS WHO FELL IN SOUTH AFRICA. 265

Moberly.—Lieut. Alfred Joseph Moberly, Royal Garrison Artillery, died at Smaldeel, South Africa, July 7th, 1901. He was born in Sept., 1877, educated at Bedford Grammar School, and entered the Royal Artillery, Sept., 1897, being promoted lieut. in Sept., 1900.

Moeller.—Lieut. Bernhardt Adolph William Charles Moeller, 2nd Batt. Middlesex Regt., died at Standerton, December 23rd, 1901, of wounds received in action on December 19th, at Kaffirspruit. He was the son of Felix Moeller, Esq., of 22, Leadenhall Street, E.C., and was born July, 1872. He entered the Middlesex Regt. from the Honourable Artillery Company, May, 1900, being promoted lieut. Feb., 1901. He had for several years held a commission in the infantry battalion of the Honourable Artillery Company. On the enrolment of the C.I.V. he went out as one of the officers of the mounted infantry of that corps, and during its formation acted as adjutant, and is stated to have earned high praise for his work. Lieut. Moeller took part in the fighting at Jacobsdal and Paardeberg, and was sent from the latter place as one of the escort to Cronje's force as far as Modder River. After much hard work during the further advance he was given a commission as 2nd lieut. in the Middlesex Regt. in Natal, but was soon sent back to mounted infantry work, and for some time had command of a company. He was awarded the medal with six clasps and was mentioned in despatches, L.G., April 25th, 1902, by Gen. Lord Kitchener for his "gallantry in action." A marble chancel screen has been erected to Lieut. Moeller's memory in St. Peter's Church, Belsize Park, Hampstead.

Moir.—Lieut. George Gordon Moir, 3rd Batt. King's Own Scottish Borderers, died of enteric May 18th, 1900, at Bloemfontein. He was the eldest son of Capt. J. G. Moir, late 19th Foot, was 28 years of age, and educated at Marlborough. He was temporarily attached to the 1st Batt. King's Own Scottish Borderers from the 3rd battalion from Jan. 4th, 1900. Lieut. Moir's name is inscribed on a tablet placed in Marlborough College Chapel in memory of all Marlburians who fell in the war.

Moir.—Capt. Moir is mentioned by the author of " The Great Boer War " as having been killed in the action at Reitz, O.R.C., June 6th, 1901. Capt. Moir took part in the gallant defence made by Major Sladen's force against very superior numbers of the enemy under Gen. de Wet, who was defeated. The fight is described as having been " a Wagon Hill on a small scale."

Moloney.—The Rev. John Moloney, Chaplain's Department, died of enteric at Springfontein, July 3rd, 1900.

Monro.—Lieut. Charles Gordon Monro, Gordon Highlanders, was killed in action at Elandslaagte, Natal, Oct. 21st, 1899. He was born in Sept., 1872, educated at Harrow, and entered the Gordon Highlanders, June, 1892, being promoted lieut. Aug., 1896. Lieut. Monro accompanied his battalion to Natal from India, Sept., 1899, and served with it in Ladysmith till his death.

Montgomery.—Lieut. F. C. Montgomery, Roberts' Horse, died March 18th, 1901, of wounds received the previous day in action near Lichtenburg.

Monypenny.—2nd Lieut. Douglas Blackwell Monypenny, Seaforth Highlanders, died Feb. 19th, 1900, of wounds received in action near Paardeberg the previous day. He was the youngest son of the late J. R. B. Monypenny, Esq., of Pitmilly, Fife. He was born in May, 1878, and educated at Fettes College, Edinburgh, where he played in the cricket and football teams, and ranked very highly as a three-quarter back. He also obtained his International Cap for Scotland at Rugby football. 2nd Lieut. Monypenny entered the Seaforth Highlanders from the 3rd Batt. Loyal North Lancashire Regt., Oct., 1899. He was present at the actions of Magersfontein and Koodoosdrift. The late Maj.-Gen. Sir H. Macdonald in his report mentions with regret that this officer had lost his life. The death of 2nd Lieut. Monypenny is also mentioned in the despatches of F.-M. Earl Roberts, Feb. 28th, 1900, from Paardeberg, and March 31st, from Bloemfontein, in which 2nd Lieut. Monypenny is referred to as having "rendered valuable service," L.G., Oct. 8th, 1901.

Moody.—Capt. Henry de Clervaulx Moody, South Wales Borderers, was killed in action at Nooitgedacht, Dec. 13th, 1900. He was the son of the late Major-Gen. R. C. Moody, R.E., was born Feb., 1864, and educated at Rugby. He entered the Queen's Royal West Surrey Regt. in Aug., 1883, being promoted capt. March, 1892, and joined the South Wales Borderers Sept., 1894. He served in the Burmese Expedition 1885-87, with the 2nd Batt. The Queen's, under the late Sir W. S. A. Lockhart, and received the medal with clasp. Capt. Moody had seen much service in South Africa and had been A.D.C. to Major-Gen. Clements, commanding the 12th infantry brigade from Dec., 1899. Capt. Moody was mentioned in despatches, L.G., Sept. 10th, 1901.

Moor.—Capt. Hatherly George Moor, Royal Garrison Artillery, was killed in action at Palmietfontein, July 19th, 1900. The younger son of the Rev. Canon Moor, of St. Clement's, Truro, he was born in July, 1871, and educated at Shrewsbury School. He entered the Royal Artillery from the Militia, Nov., 1890, was promoted lieut. Nov., 1893, and capt. Oct., 1899. He was employed with the Colonial Forces in West Australia since July

14th, 1899, commanding the Permanent Garrison, Albany. Capt. Moor had previously served in South Africa in the operations in 1897, and was then specially employed with the British South African Police. He was mentioned in despatches, L.G., Feb. 18th, 1898, and was granted the medal. In June, 1899, he was appointed to command the Permanent Garrison at King George's Sound, West Australia, with the local rank of major, and on the outbreak of the war was given the command of the West Australian contingent. At Slingersfontein, Feb. 9th, he narrowly escaped being killed through assisting a wounded man and giving him his horse. He was mentioned in the despatch of F.-M. Earl Roberts, March 1st, 1902. On the right side of the memorial window placed in the chapel of Shrewsbury School in remembrance of fourteen Salopians who fell in South Africa, is depicted a realistic scene from the Boer War. In this representation Capt. Moor is shown defending a kopje near Colesberg. On the occasion referred to, he, with his West Australians, held his position against great odds, for which service he was afterwards publicly thanked by the general officer commanding his division.

Moore.—Capt. Barrington Shakespear Moore, Army Service Corps (attached to District Mounted Troops), was killed in action near Graaf Reinet, July 14th, 1901. He was born in April, 1874, and entered the Royal West Kent. Regt. from the 3rd Batt. King's (Liverpool Regt.) in Dec., 1893. He was a good athlete and rider, and joined the Army Service Corps as lieut. Sept., 1896, being promoted capt. Nov., 1900. He proceeded to South Africa Oct., 1899, and served from the commencement of the war. He was placed in charge of the issue store at Pretoria (graded as a staff captain) from Aug. 1900.

Moore.—Lieut. Cyril Hartley Moore, 35th Company

Imperial Yeomanry, was killed in action near Harrismith, July 28th, 1901. He was born July, 1876, and was educated at St. John's College, Winnipeg, and Malvern College. He went to South Africa in April, 1900, and saw much service. He was invalided home in December, but, on recovering, returned in April, 1901. The action in which he was killed took place at a farm about 22 miles from Ladysmith, and the Boers succeeded in cutting off the retreat of the small party of ten men he commanded. Three times the enemy called on him to surrender, but on Lieut. Moore refusing to do so, he was shot through the heart. Of his party seven fell killed or wounded. On July 31st, the Boers allowed his body to be sent for, and then expressed their admiration of his bravery and their regret at having to shoot him as he would not surrender. He is buried in Harrismith cemetery. A marble cross has been erected over his grave by the officers and men of his company.

Moore.—2nd Lieut. Charles Roland Moore, Royal Munster Fusiliers, was killed in action at Mooifontein, between Bethel and Standerton, May 25th, 1901. He was the youngest son of Col. Francis Moore, late 8th The King's Regt. and Royal Munster Fusiliers, of 20, Waterloo Crescent, Dover. 2nd Lieut. Moore was born in Jan., 1881, and educated at Elizabeth College, Guernsey. He entered his regiment in August, 1899, and served with his battalion from the commencement of the war, taking part in the actions at Fourteen Streams, Warrenton, and also in Lieut.-Gen. Lord Methuen's march to relieve Col. Spragge near Lindley. He was present at the fighting near Bethlehem, the surrender of Prinsloo, and the defence of Peinaars River Station. He fell while leading his company protecting a convoy. He was granted the medal with three clasps. 2nd Lieut. Moore is buried in Standerton cemetery, and a marble cross has been erected by his brother officers over his grave. A tablet has also been placed to his memory in St. Peter's Church, Guernsey.

Moore.—Major Stephen Blyth Moore, I.Y., died of enteric at Wynberg Hospital, near Cape Town, June 4th, 1901. He was the second son of the late Richard Moore, Esq., of Killashee, Co. Kildare, was in his fifty-first year, and educated at Harrow. He entered the Royal Scots in 1869, being promoted capt. Nov., 1878, and served with that regiment till 1888, when he retired as capt. and joined the Reserve of Officers. Soon after the commencement of the South African War, Major Moore was employed on the staff of the I.Y. in London, with the rank of major from Feb., 1900, and then proceeded to South Africa, where he was second in command of the I.Y. Base Depôt at Cape Town. He had shortly before his death returned to Elandsfontein and had been appointed to command the camp at Greenpoint, Cape Town.

Moore.—Lieut. Walter Moore, Gorringe's Flying Column, died of pneumonia at Burghersdorp Nov. 6th, 1901. He was the third son of the late Robert Lyon Moore, Esq., J.P., D.L., of Molenan, co. Londonderry, and Cliffe, Belleek, co. Fermanagh, was thirty years of age, and educated at Winchester. Lieut. Moore had served in the I.Y., and was with the force captured at Lindley, and after his release promoted to be a lieut. in Gorringe's Column. He is buried in Burghersdorp cemetery.

Morgan.—Lieut. A. A. Morgan, Kitchener's Fighting Scouts, died of enteric at Bloemfontein, Feb. 17th, 1902.

Morley.—Capt. George Wheeler Morley, 1st Batt. Royal Inniskilling Fusiliers, died of enteric at Mooi

River, April, 10th, 1900. He was the son of Lieut.-Col. Morley, who commanded the Army Service Corps in Jersey, and had retired in 1892, but was recalled to duty on the outbreak of the war, and died of enteric in 1902. Thus father and son died during the war. Capt. Morley was born Jan., 1872, and educated at Cranbrook Grammar School. He entered the Royal Inniskilling Fusiliers from the 5th Batt. Royal Fusiliers in Dec., 1893, being promoted lieut. May, 1897, and capt. March 20th, 1900. He served in the campaign on the North-West Frontier of India with the 2nd Batt. of his regiment, in the Tirah Expeditionary Force, under the late Sir William Lockhart in 1897-98, including the operations in the Bara Valley and the occupation of the Khyber Pass, receiving the medal with two clasps. Capt. Morley, who was at home on sick leave from India in 1899, volunteered for active service and was accepted. On arrival in Natal he joined the 1st battalion of his regiment, and was with Gen. Sir R. Buller's Force, being present at the engagements of Spion Kop, Vaal Kranz, and Pieter's Hill, and entered Ladysmith with the relieving force. Capt. Morley is buried at Mooi River, a marble headstone, erected by his comrades, marks his grave. His name is inscribed on a tablet in the Lych Gate of Barnes Parish Church, erected to the memory of all those belonging to the parish who fell in the war. There is also a tablet in his memory in Soberton Parish Church, placed there by the members of the choir which he frequently assisted when at Soberton, and his brother officers have also erected a memorial tablet at Enniskillen, on which his name appears.

Morrell.—Capt. G. Morrell, Prince Alfred's Volunteers, died in Bloemfontein Hospital in June, 1900.

Morris.—Lieut. George Augustus Morris, 6th West

Australian M.I., was killed in action at Rolspruit, Feb.
13th, 1902.

Morris.—Lieut. George Ernest Wood Morris, M.I.,
Queen's Own Royal West Kent Regt., died Jan. 28th,
1902, of wounds received in action two days previously
near Ermelo. He was the only son of Col. W. J. Morris,
of Brynderwen, Usk, Monmouthshire, and was born
March, 1880. He entered the Royal West Kent Regt.
from the 3rd Batt. Dorsetshire Regt., April, 1900, being
promoted lieut. April, 1901, while employed with M.I.
He was present at many actions. His name is inscribed
on a tablet underneath the stained glass window erected
in All Saints' Church, Maidstone, to the memory of all
those belonging to the Queen's Own Royal West Kent
Regt. who fell in the war.

Morris.—Lieut. Thomas Morris, 6th Dragoon Guards,
was killed in action at Springbokfontein, Jan. 26th, 1902,
first reported as missing, it was afterwards discovered that
he had been killed. He was the only son of the late Thomas
Morris, Esq., of Coomb, Carmarthenshire, was born May,
1879, and educated at Cheltenham. He entered the 6th
Dragoon Guards from the 3rd Batt. South Wales Borderers in Oct., 1899, passing second on the Cavalry List,
and was promoted lieut. May, 1900. Lieut. Morris took
part in the advance on Johannesburg and Pretoria, and
the subsequent engagements around Belfast and Mac-
hadadorp and the advance to Barberton. The day he
was killed he had been called on to surrender, and on
scornfully refusing was shot down. Lieut. Morris was
buried by some Boers in a little farmyard at Oshock,
Transvaal. His name is inscribed on the Eleanor Cross
Memorial at Cheltenham College.

Morrison.—Capt. Maskell Mackenzie Downie Morrison,

Royal Garrison Artillery, died of asthma at Bethulie, Oct. 7th, 1901. He was born in June, 1869, entered the Royal Artillery, Feb., 1888, being promoted lieut. Feb., 1891, and capt. Sept., 1898. From April, 1896-1901, he was adjutant of the 2nd Hampshire Volunteer Artillery.

Morritt.—Lieut. Robert Alexander Morritt, 17th Lancers, was killed in action at Modderfontein, near Tarkastad, Sept., 17th, 1901. He was born in May, 1877, and educated at Eton (Mr. Austen Leigh's). He entered the 7th Dragoon Guards, May, 1898, being transferred to the 17th Lancers on the 18th of the same month, and was promoted lieut. March, 1900. Lieut. Morritt, who accompanied his regiment to South Africa in Feb., 1900, had served throughout the war. In the action in which he was killed, Smut's Commando made a most determined attack on a squadron of the 17th Lancers posted to close the Boer egress to the South. The enemy, during a mist, and clothed in khaki, were mistaken for our troops, and got to close quarters, with the advantage of ground, before the error was discovered. The squadron offered a splendid resistance, but suffered severely, three officers, Lieuts. Morritt and Sheridan and 2nd Lieut. Russell with twenty men, being killed. In addition, two officers and thirty men were wounded. One report gives the total losses as thirty-four killed and thirty-six wounded. The three officers mentioned fell whilst leading and encouraging their men. Another squadron, arriving in support, the enemy were compelled to break off the engagement.

Motum.—2nd Lieut. Hill Motum, Donegal Artillery, Southern Division R.A., died suddenly at Lindley, Jan. 14th, 1901. He was born July, 1880, and educated at Trinity College, Glenalmond. He entered the Donegal Artillery in Oct., 1900.

Mourilyan.—Lieut. Hubert Lionel Mourilyan, 1st Batt. Royal Warwickshire Regt., was killed in action at Pieter's Hill, Feb. 27th, 1900. He was born Nov., 1875, entered the West Yorkshire Regt. March, 1895, and was transferred to the Royal Warwickshire Regt., Aug., 1898, having previously accepted employment with the West African Regt., with which he served up to the end of 1899. Lieut. Mourilyan was in the Ashantee Expedition of 1895-96, and was awarded the star. He also served in the operations in Sierra Leone, 1898-99, in the Karene Expedition, and also in the Protectorate Expedition as orderly officer. He was a fellow of the Royal Colonial Institute, and his name is inscribed on a memorial tablet in the hall of that building in Northumberland Avenue, S.W. Lieut. Mourilyan was mentioned in despatches, L.G., Feb. 8th, 1901.

Muller.—Capt. Edward B. Muller, Kaffrarian Rifles, was killed in action at Ramathlabama, March 31st, 1900, in Gen. Plumer's attempt to relieve Mafeking. He was the son of Major Muller, and was educated at Wellington College.

Mulloy.— Lieut. Charles Coote Mulloy, 2nd Batt. Queen's Own Royal West Kent Regt., died of abscess of the liver at Kroonstad, March 14th, 1901. He was the eldest son of Col. Mulloy, late Royal Engineers, of Hughestown, co. Roscommon, and Kelvedon, Reading, was born Nov., 1875, and educated at the United Services College, Westward Ho. He entered the Royal West Kent Regt. from the Royal Military College in March, 1896, and was promoted lieut. in Sept., 1898. One of his old schoolfellows writes, "he was good at games and work, and very popular at Sandhurst and in his regiment." Lieut. Mulloy was present at the fighting at Biddulphsberg and the action at Wittebergen. In a letter written shortly before his death, he thus described the life at Frankfort: "About twice a week we have a stiff little fight, otherwise the monotony of this place is unbroken." His name is inscribed on a memorial tablet in the United Services College at Westward Ho; it is also engraved underneath the stained glass window in All Saints' Church, Maidstone, erected to the memory of all those of the Queen's Own Royal West Kent Regt. who fell in the war.

Munn.—Lieut. Edmund Leonard Munn, Royal Army Medical Corps, died of enteric May 23rd, 1900, at Boshof. He was born Jan., 1875, and joined the Royal Army Medical Corps in July, 1899.

Munn.—Major Frederick Henry Munn, D.S.O., 2nd in command of the 1st Batt. Royal Irish Fusiliers, died of measles and pneumonia at Springfontein, Aug. 31st, 1901. He was born Sept., 1857, educated at Shrewsbury School, and entered the 89th Foot, now the 2nd Batt. Royal Irish Fusiliers, Sept., 1876, being promoted capt. March, 1883, and major July, 1888. He served with the 2nd Batt. of his regiment in the Soudan Expedition in 1884, was present in the engagements at El Teb and Tamai, and received the medal with clasp and Khedive's star. Major Munn accompanied his battalion to South Africa in Sept., 1899, and was present at the battle of Talana Hill, and took part in the retirement on Ladysmith and the action at Lombard's Kop. He subsequently commanded the detachment at Witpoort which was attacked on July 16th, 1900, his orders being to "hold it at all costs." The Boers called on Major Munn to surrender, but, scornfully refusing, he held out from daybreak till 2 p.m., when the enemy retired. F.-M. Earl Roberts telegraphed, "The fight on the 16th was most successful, I heartily congratulate you and all concerned," and in his despatch of Oct. 10th, 1900, L.G., Feb. 8th, 1901, he reported that this detachment "had greatly distinguished itself." The general officer commanding also telegraphed, "Well done, Irish Fusiliers." Major Munn was again mentioned in despatches March 1st, 1902, and awarded the D.S.O. He is buried in the military cemetery at Springfontein, and a tablet has been erected there to his memory by his brother officers. (*See Capt. Moor.*)

Munroe.—Lieut. J. G. S. Munroe, Kitchener's Horse, was killed in action at Houtnek, April 30th, 1900.

Munster, Earl of.—Major the Earl of Munster, D.S.O., 3rd Batt. Royal Scots (Edinburgh Light Infantry Militia), was accidently killed at Lace Mines, Feb. 2nd, 1902. He was better known by the courtesy title of Lord Tewkesbury, which he bore from the time of the death of his elder brother, Viscount FitzClarence, in 1870, until April, 1901, when he succeeded to the Earldom. Geoffry George Gordon, third Earl of Munster, was the third and eldest surviving son of the second Earl by his marriage with Wilhelmina, daughter of the Hon. John Kennedy-Erskine, second son of the twelfth Earl of Cassilis and first Marquis of Ailsa. Major the Earl of Munster was born in July, 1859, entered the 60th Foot from the 1st West York Militia (now the 3rd Batt. King's Own Yorkshire Light Infantry) June, 1879, was promoted lieut. Feb., 1881, capt. June, 1888, and retired in 1895. He served in the Afghan War Dec., 1879, to Oct., 1880, and was present at the engagements at Ahmed Kheyl and Urzoo, near Ghaznee, and accompanied Earl (then Sir Frederick) Roberts in the march to Kandahar, and was present at the battle of Kandahar, receiving the medal with two clasps and bronze decoration. He also saw service with the 3rd Batt. of the K.R.R. Corps in the Boer War of 1881. He joined the 3rd Batt. Royal Scots in March, 1896, and was promoted major June, 1901. When the

OFFICERS WHO FELL IN SOUTH AFRICA. 277

battalion was embodied in Dec., 1899, Lord Tewkesbury, as he then was, joined, and had since that time served with it at home and in South Africa. He was mentioned in despatches and received the D.S.O.

Murch.—Lieut. Denis Jerom Murch, Q Battery Royal Horse Artillery died April 25th, 1900, of wounds received in action at Sanna's Post on March 31st. He was the only son of the late Arthur Murch, Esq., born Dec., 1874, and educated at Charterhouse. He entered the Royal Artillery, June, 1895, being promoted lieut. June, 1898. His name is inscribed on the tablet in the War Memorial Cloister at Charterhouse.

Murdoch.—Lieut. Archibald José Campbell Murdoch, 1st Batt. Cameron Highlanders, was killed in action at Nooitgedacht, Dec. 13th, 1900. He was born June, 1876, and educated at St. Paul's School and Trinity College, Glenalmond. He entered the Cameron Highlanders from the 3rd Batt. West Riding Regt. May, 1897, being promoted lieut. Nov., 1898. He served in the Soudan campaign under Lord (then Sir Herbert) Kitchener, 1898, with the 1st battalion of his regiment, and was present at the battles of Atbara and Khartoum, receiving the British medal and Khedive's medal with two clasps. Lieut. Murdoch had seen much service during the South African War at Heilbron, Vredeport, and other places, and when killed was in charge of a picquet of twenty-five men, of which six were killed and twelve wounded.

Muriel. — Capt. Charles Leslie Muriel, 2nd Batt. Middlesex Regt., was killed in action at Spion Kop in the operations on the Upper Tugela, Jan. 24th, 1900. He was born Feb., 1866, and entered the Middlesex Regt. Feb., 1887, being promoted lieut. May, 1889, and capt. Oct., 1895. He was adjutant of his battalion from Oct., 1895-99. At Spion Kop Capt. Muriel was first shot through the cheek whilst giving a cigarette to a wounded man. He then continued to lead his company, and was shortly afterwards shot through the brain.

Murphy.—Lieut. Arthur Edward Murphy, 5th Victorian M.I., was killed in action between Driefontein and Middelkraal, May 29th, 1901. He was the second son of the late Edward J. Murphy, Esq., Melbourne, Australia, and Mrs. Murphy, of 3, Coleherne Road, S.W. He was born in Toorak, Melbourne, May, 1863, and educated at the Roman Catholic College, Beaumont, Old Windsor. After leaving school he returned to Australia and was engaged in farming. He was a good sportsman, a reckless rider, and fond of adventure. At Colac, Australia, he was chairman of a company, but resigned his position in order to join the 5th Australian Contingent and go to South Africa. He arrived in Durban, March, 1901, and was then sent to Pretoria and afterwards to Middelburg, and served in the latter district until his death. At the end of May there had been continuous fighting for a week near Middelkraal. The day Lieut. Murphy fell his Commanding Officer reports "he was killed well in front of his men, gallantly leading them, and was shot through the heart." He had previously been wounded in the head, and his hat had four bullet holes in it. Colonel Beatson wrote concerning him : " Had he lived I should have recommended him strongly for the D.S.O." Lieut. Murphy is buried at Middelkraal under some blackwood trees close to a Dutch farm. Many Boer women, weeping bitterly, attended his funeral, as he had been very kind to the refugee women and children.

Murray.—Capt. and Brevet-Lieut.-Col. the Hon. Andrew David Murray, Cameron Highlanders, was killed in action near Quaagersfontein (by some called Elandskloof, near Zastron), Sept. 20th, 1901. He was the second son of the late Viscount Stormont, and was brother and heir-presumptive of the Earl of Mansfield. Born Sept., 1863, and educated at Wellington, where he was in the Lynedoch, and well known for his pluck and humour; he entered the Yorkshire Regt., 1884, from the 3rd Batt. of the Black Watch (Royal Highlanders), being promoted lieut. in the Cameron Highlanders the following Dec., capt. March, 1893, brevet-major Nov., 1898, and brevet-lieut.-col. Nov., 1900. Lieut.-Col. Murray had seen much active service. He was in the Soudan Expedition of 1884-85 with the Cameron Highlanders and received the medal with clasp and Khedive's star. He next served throughout the operations of the Soudan Frontier Field Force, 1885-86, with his battalion, and was present at Kosheh during its investment and in the engagement at Giniss. He also served in the campaign in the Soudan under Lord (then Sir Herbert) Kitchener in 1898 with the 1st Batt. Cameron Highlanders, and was present at the battles of Atbara (despatches, L.G., May 24th, 1898) and Khartoum (despatches, L.G., Sept. 30th, 1898). He was also in the subsequent operations Sept. and Oct., being again mentioned in despatches, L.G., Dec., 1898, and received the brevet of major and the British medal and Khedive's medal with two clasps. Shortly after the outbreak of the South African War, Lieut.-Col. Murray, who was serving at the depôt of his regiment at Inverness, was appointed to the command of Lovat's Scouts, and trained and led them in such a manner that he more then once earned the praise of F.-M. Earl Roberts. The services of Lieut.-Col. the Hon. A. D. Murray are mentioned in the despatch of Lieut.-Gen. Sir A. Hunter, Aug. 4th, 1900, from Fouriesberg, L.G., Feb. 8th, 1901. He was awarded the brevet of lieut.-col.

Murray. — 2nd Lieut. Alastair Heneage Murray, Grenadier Guards, died June 3rd, 1900, from wounds received in action at Biddulphberg, May 29th. He was the eldest son of C. J. Murray, Esq., M.P. for Coventry, and of Lady Anne Murray, was born in April, 1878, and educated at Eton (Mr. Broadbent's). He entered the Grenadier Guards from the 3rd Batt. Seaforth Highlanders, Nov., 1899. During the battle at which 2nd Lieut. Murray was mortally wounded, he received a compound fracture of the thigh and was severely burned by the fire on the veldt.

Murray.—Capt. the Hon. Edward Oliphant Murray, Cameron Highlanders, was killed in action at Quaagersfontein (by some called Elandskloof, near Zastron), in the engagement with Kritzinger, Sept. 20th, 1901. He was the second son of Lord Elibank, and brother of the Master of Elibank, and was born in Oct., 1871. He entered the Cameron Highlanders from the Royal Military College, 1891, being promoted lieut. June, 1893, and capt. May, 1898. He was A.D.C. to the Major-General Commanding the Infantry Brigade, Gibraltar, Nov., 1900, to Jan., 1901. In the early part of 1901 Capt. Murray was appointed adjutant of Lovat's Scouts, and after training the new contingent of the corps he proceeded with it to South Africa.

Murray.—Capt. Fergus Murray, Scottish Rifles, was killed in action at Spion Kop, on the Upper Tugela, on Jan. 24th, 1900. He was the younger son of the late Commander John Murray, R.N., of Murraythwaite, Dumfriesshire, born Feb. 1868, and educated at Clifton College. He entered the Scottish Rifles in March, 1889, and was promoted lieut. March, 1892, and capt. Oct., 1897. At Spion Kop he was wounded in five places, but he still continued to command his company, staggering amongst his men till killed. Capt. Murray's name was brought to notice by his commanding officer for having

OFFICERS WHO FELL IN SOUTH AFRICA.

rendered special valuable assistance Jan. 24th, and he is mentioned in the despatch of Lieut.-Gen. Sir Charles Warren, of Feb. 1st, 1900, for initiating an advance in the face of a heavy fire.

Murray.—Major Frederick Dymoke Murray, Black Watch (Royal Highlanders), was killed in action at Brakenlaagte (20 miles N.W. of Bethel), Oct. 31st, 1901. He was the son of Charles Frederick Murray, Esq., was born in April, 1872, and educated at Eton (Mr. Mozley's). He entered the Black Watch in Dec., 1891, being promoted lieut. July, 1896, capt. Nov., 1900, and brevet-major Feb., 1901. He was A.D.C. to Sir W. F. Hely-Hutchinson, Governor of Natal, from Aug., 1898, but on the outbreak of war was permitted to serve in Ladysmith before the siege, and afterwards with the Natal Field Force. He again took up his duties as A.D.C. in Aug., 1900, but in the following March was appointed to the Scottish Horse as major in command of the 2nd Regiment, which he had assisted Lord Tullibardine to raise. Major Murray was mentioned in despatches by Gen. Sir Redvers Buller, June 19th and Nov. 9th, 1900, (L.G., Feb. 8th, 1901). Gen. Sir R. Buller reported Major Murray "had great ability and energy, cool in danger, he possesses enterprise and organising power. I recommend him for advancement." He was promoted to a brevet majority for his services.

Murray.—2nd Lieut. John Gammel Duff Murray, Gordon Highlanders, was killed in action at the battle of Elandslaagte, Oct. 21st, 1899. He was the son of Surg.-Col. John Murray, A.M.S., born Jan, 1878, and educated at Wellington, where he was in the Anglesey. He entered the Gordon Highlanders from the Channel Islands Militia, March, 1899, and had proceeded with his battalion from India to Natal in September.

Murray.—Lieut. R. H. Murray, Graaf Reinet District Mounted Troops, was killed in action at Tweefontein, May 2nd, 1902.

Murrell.—Capt. G. Murrell, Prince Alfred's Volunteer Guard, died of enteric June 6th, 1900, at Bloemfontein.

Myers.—Major William Joseph Myers, 7th Batt. King's Royal Rifle Corps, was killed in action near Ladysmith, Oct. 30th, 1899. He was the son of the late T. B. Myers, Esq., of Porters, Shenley, Herts, born in Aug., 1858, and educated at Eton (Mr. Wolley Dod's). He entered the 16th Foot in May, 1878, being transferred to the 60th Rifles, Feb., 1879, and was promoted lieut. Nov., 1880, and capt. March, 1888. He subsequently joined the Reserve of Officers, and entered the 7th Batt. King's Royal Rifle Corps, was promoted major Feb., 1899, having been given the honorary rank two years previously. He was acting adjutant of the 4th Eton College Volunteer Batt. Oxfordshire Light Infantry. Major Myers served with the 3rd battalion of the 60th Rifles in the Zulu War, April to Sept., 1879 (medal with clasp). He took part in the operations of the Soudan Frontier Field Force, 1885-86, as A.D.C. to Sir Frederick Stephenson, and was present at the engagement at Giniss (medal, Fourth Class of the Order of the Medjidie, and the Khedive's star). He served in the Hazara Expedition, 1891, with the 1st Batt. King's Royal Rifle Corps (medal with clasp); in the Miranzai Expedition in the same year with the same battalion, including the engagements at Sangar and Mastan (clasp), and with the Isazai Expedition in 1892. Major Myers left the regular army in order to satisfy his taste for travel and Eastern art. He had succeeded in obtaining a fine collection of Saracenese lamps and armour. Wherever there were remains of ancient Persian or

Saracenic culture he was a constant visitor and purchaser. His collection is in the South Kensington Museum. (*See Lieut. Marsden.*)

Napier.—Lieut. Basil Napier, 34th Company I.Y., died at Senekal, of wounds received in action, Dec. 28th, 1900. He was the eldest son of the Hon. Mark Napier, and grandson of the late Lord Napier and Ettrick, formerly Ambassador to the Russian and other Courts and Governor of Madras. Lieut. Napier was twenty-one years of age.

Neave.—2nd Lieut. Arthur Cormack Neave, 1st Batt. Princess of Wales's Own Yorkshire Regt., was killed in action near Paardeberg, Feb. 18th, 1900. He was born in June, 1877, and entered his regiment from the New Zealand Local Military Forces Nov., 1899. This officer's death is mentioned in the despatch of F.-M. Earl Roberts from Paardeberg, Feb. 28th, 1900. 2nd Lieut. Neave was also mentioned in despatches, L.G., Sept. 10th, 1900.

Neill.—Lieut. Colin Eric Smith Neill, Royal Engineers, died of enteric at Pretoria, Feb. 17th, 1901. He was born in Aug., 1876, educated at Charterhouse, and entered the Royal Engineers Dec., 1895, being promoted lieut. Dec., 1898. He was present at the battle of Colenso and was in the actions at Spion Kop and Vaal Kranz, and in the engagements on the Tugela before the relief of Ladysmith. Lieut. Neill took part in the subsequent advance into the Transvaal under Gen. Sir Redvers Buller, and in the operations under Lieut.-Gen. Sir F. Clery, near Standerton. Lieut. Neill is buried at Pretoria beside Lieut. Hughes, Royal Irish Fusiliers. His name is inscribed on the tablet in the War Memorial Cloister at Charterhouse.

Nelles.—Lieut. A. H. Nelles, Commander-in-Chief's Bodyguard, died of peritonitis at Bloemfontein, Jan. 29th, 1901.

Nesham.—Lieut. Thomas Peere William Nesham, 38th Battery Royal Field Artillery, was killed in action between Tweebosch and Palmietkuil, March 7th, 1902. He was born in May, 1880, educated at Haileybury, and entered the Royal Artillery Dec., 1898, being promoted lieut. Feb., 1901. At Tweebosch the section of the 38th Battery found itself unprotected, but the detachment continued to serve the guns until every man, except Lieut. Nesham, was killed or wounded. He was then summoned to surrender, and on refusing to do so was shot down. He was mentioned in the despatch of Lieut.-Gen. Lord Methuen from Klerksdorp, March 13th, who reported: "I would also call attention to the gallant manner in which Lieuts. Nesham and Venning, Royal Field Artillery, stuck to their guns." Lieut. Nesham was also mentioned in the despatch of Gen. Lord Kitchener from Pretoria, April 8th, 1902.

Nethercote.—Lieut. G. F. Nethercote, Kitchener's Horse, died of enteric at Florida, South Africa, June 1st, 1900.

Newbury.—Capt. Bertram Archdale Newbury, Duke of Cornwall's Light Infantry, was killed in action near Paardeberg, Feb. 18th, 1900. He was the son of Major T. Newbury, was born in 1865, and educated at Wellington (The Hill) where he was a Prefect and played in the cricket XI., and also represented the college at racquets. He entered the Duke of Cornwall's Light Infantry from the Royal Military College, August, 1884, being promoted capt. July, 1893. He served in the Nile Expedition, 1884-85, with the 2nd battalion of his regiment, and received the medal with clasp and the Khedive's star. This officer's death is mentioned in the despatch of F.-M. Earl Roberts, from Paardeberg, Feb. 28th, 1900.

Newnham.—Lieut. Percival Forbes Newnham, Indian Staff Corps, attached to Thorneycroft's M.I., was killed in action at Spion Kop, Jan. 24th, 1900. He was born in June, 1870, educated at Malvern and Clifton Colleges, and entered the Lancashire Fusiliers Jan., 1892, being transferred to the Indian Staff Corps July, 1895. At Spion Kop he was hit in two places, and was bleeding to death, but he propped himself upon a rock and continued to fire till a third bullet killed him.

Neumeyer.—Lieut. L. Neumeyer, Orange River Colony Police, was, it is believed, killed on Nov. 23rd, 1900, but his body was found the following day, near Aliwal North.

Noble.—Capt. Charles John Herbert Hay Noble, commanding the M.I., 2nd Batt. Manchester Regt., died Nov. 12th, 1901, of wounds received in action at Schalkie Farm, near Bethlehem, the same day. He was the eldest son of Col. C. S. Noble, of Innerwick, Murrayfield, Edinburgh, was born June, 1870, and educated at Haileybury. He served in the ranks for over five years, was given a commission in the Yorkshire Regt. in Sept., 1894, being promoted lieut. Jan., 1897, and capt. in the Manchester Regt. June, 1900. He served with the Isazai Expedition, 1892; and in the campaign on the North West Frontier of India, under the late Sir William Lockhart, 1897-98, with the Tirah Expeditionary Force; as transport officer to the 2nd Batt. Yorkshire Regt. He was present at the capture of the Sampagha and Arhanga Passes, the capture of Bagh, the Dwatoi reconnaissance, the reconnaissance and engagement of the Saran Sar, and engagement Nov. 11th, and took part in the operations in the Bazar Valley, being mentioned in despatches, L.G., April 5th, 1898, and received the medal with two clasps. In September, 1899, Capt. Noble proceeded to South Africa from India on special service, and was through the siege of Ladysmith as transport officer to Lieut.-Gen. Sir Ian Hamilton. He then served at Wynberg and at Senekal, and acted as Intelligence Officer at Bethlehem, and led a successful night attack on a Boer farm in March, 1901. He was afterwards on the Staff of the 17th Brigade, and in Aug., 1901, was given command of the M.I. Company of his battalion. In one engagement he was wounded, and for his services was mentioned in despatches, L.G., May 7th, 1901. He is buried in Harrismith military cemetery.

Noel.—Lieut. B. C. Noel, Imperial Light Horse, died of wounds received in action at Oogvanmarico, July 10th, 1901.

Noel.—Lieut. Edward William Middleton Noel Noel, 2nd Batt. Gloucestershire Regt., died of enteric at Bloemfontein, May 19th, 1900. He was the eldest son of Col. Frederick Noel, late Royal Engineers, and grandson of the late Col. E. Noel, late 31st Regt., and one of His Majesty's Corps of Gentlemen at Arms. Lieut. Noel was born in 1880, and educated at Cheltenham College. He was only gazetted to his regiment from the Royal Military College, Jan. 20th, 1900, being promoted lieut. May 16th, three days before he died. His name is inscribed on the Eleanor Cross Memorial at Cheltenham College.

Noke.—Lieut. W. H. Noke, 7th Batt. I.Y., was killed in action at Vlakfontein May 29th, 1901. He was a son of Major Edward Noke, 1st V.B. Prince Albert's Somersetshire Light Infantry, of East Hayes House, Bath, was born June 21st, 1876, and educated privately. Lieut. Noke went out as a trooper in the 48th Company of I.Y., which acted as special bodyguard to F.-M. Earl Roberts, and subsequently to Gen. Lord Kitchener. He was gazetted to the 7th Batt. I.Y. as lieut. in March, 1901, and was present at many engagements during the war, including the actions at Johannesburg and Diamond Hill.

North.—Capt. Louis Aylmer North, Manchester Regt., died of enteric, at Kroonstad, Dec. 3rd, 1901, after two days illness. He was the second son of North North, Esq., of Thurland Castle, Lancashire, was born April, 1866, and educated at St. Bee's School. He entered the Royal Scots Fusiliers from the 4th Batt. Royal Lancaster Regt., Dec. 14th, 1887, being promoted lieut. Nov. 1st, 1890, and capt. June, 1899. He served in the operations of the North-West Frontier of India, 1897-98, with the Kohat and Kurram Valley Force. At the action of the Uhlan Pass, Aug. 27th, he was severely wounded. He also served with the Tirah Expedition. Capt. North was placed on half-pay in June, 1899, owing to his wound, and on recovering joined the Manchester Regt. Jan., 1901. He served in South Africa with the Manchesters in Cape Colony, Natal, Transvaal and O.R.C., until struck down with enteric. At the time of his death he was in command of the 3rd Shorncliffe M.I. Company, and a tablet has been erected in Shorncliffe Garrison Church to his memory and that of the men of the company who lost their lives during the war.

Northcott.—Major and Brevet-Lieut.-Col. Henry Ponting Northcott, C.B., Leinster Regt. (Royal Canadians) was killed in action at the battle of Modder River, Nov. 28th, 1899. He was the second son of Dr. W. Northcott, Staines, and late of Rochester House, Little Ealing. Lieut.-Col. Northcott was born in Oct., 1856, and was educated privately. He was a good sportsman and fond of all games, being an excellent golf and football player. He entered the 19th Foot, Feb., 1876, being promoted lieut. Feb., 1877, and exchanged to the 2nd West India Regt., Nov., 1878. He became capt. in Feb., 1886, was transferred to the Leinster Regt. the following Sept., promoted major Oct., 1894, and brevet-lieut.-col. July, 1899. His first experience of active service was in the Sherbro Expedition, 1883 with the 2nd West India Regiment, being mentioned in despatches and awarded the medal. He served in the operations in Zululand, 1888, as D.A.A.G. He had held the following Staff appointments : D.A.A.G. for Instruction, South Africa, April, 1888, to June, 1891 ; D.A.A.G., South Africa, June, 1891, to March, 1893 ; Staff Captain (Intelligence) Headquarters of Army, May, 1893, to June, 1895 ; D.A.A.G. (Intelligence) Headquarters of Army, June, 1895, to Oct., 1897. He was on special service in Ashantee, Dec., 1895, to Feb., 1896, and served in the expedition under Sir Francis Scott, being awarded the star. He was appointed Commissioner and Commandant Northern Territories, Gold Coast, in Oct., 1897, and conducted the operations in that region, notably the expedition to Karaga, with much ability. For his services on the Gold Coast he was, in 1899, mentioned in despatches, promoted lieut.-col., and made a C.B. On the formation of the Field Force for South Africa, Lieut.-Col. Northcott was appointed D.A.A.G. on the Staff of the 1st Division, and was present at the actions of Graspan and Belmont. He fell at Modder River while carrying orders for more troops to support the left attack. Lieut.-Gen. Lord Methuen, in his despatch Dec. 1st, 1899, wrote: " The Army has lost one of the ablest officers in the service, and I cannot express the grief his death has caused me." Lieut.-Col. Northcott is buried close to the bank of the Modder River.

Norwood.—Capt. William Blakeney Norwood, Royal Horse Artillery, died in London, Aug. 28th, 1900, from the effects of a sunstroke contracted in South Africa. He was born in July, 1865, educated at Cheltenham College, and entered the Royal Artillery, April, 1885, being promoted capt. in May, 1895. He embarked for South Africa as adjutant Royal Horse Artillery, Brigade Division, Dec., 1899, and served there till March, 1900, when he was invalided home. His name is inscribed on the Eleanor Cross Memorial at Cheltenham College.

O'Brien.—Capt. Walmsley Donat O'Brien, 2nd Batt. Scottish Rifles, was mortally wounded in the operations at Almond's Nek, June 11th, 1900, and died the following day. He was the eldest son of Capt. W. E. F. O'Brien, late 54th Regt., of 23, Cheniston Gardens, Kensington, W., was born Feb., 1872, and educated at Eton (Mr. Cornish's). He entered the Scottish Rifles from the 3rd battalion in March, 1892, being promoted lieut. Oct., 1894, and capt. Feb., 1899. He served with his battalion at the battle of Colenso, supporting the guns of the Naval Brigade, and afterwards with the mounted infantry of the Natal Force up to the Relief of Ladysmith. He then served with the M.I. under Capt. H. P. Gough and Major-Gen. the Earl of Dundonald, and was mortally wounded in the turning movement, which resulted in the capture of Laing's Nek.

O'Brien-Butler.—Lieut. Pierce Edmond O'Brien-Butler, Army Service Corps, died of enteric at Wynberg, Jan. 15th, 1902. He was born in June, 1877, entered the Royal Inniskilling Fusiliers from the 5th Batt. Royal Dublin Fusiliers, April, 1900, and was transferred to the Army Service Corps the following Aug. He was promoted lieut. in the Army Service Corps, Nov., 1901. He embarked for South Africa, Feb., 1900, with the 5th Batt. Royal Dublin Fusiliers; and had served continuously during the war up to the date of his death.

O'Flaherty.—Capt. H. H. O'Flaherty, Commander-in-Chief's Bodyguard, was killed in action near Reitvlei, between July 24th and 28th, 1901. He was formerly in the Imperial Light Horse, and had resided in Johannesburg, where he was well known.

Ogilvy.—Capt. John Herbert Cecil Ogilvy, D.S.O., Gordon Highlanders (att. South African Constabulary), died at Reitfontein West, Dec. 19th, 1901, from a wound received in action at Klipgat two days previously. He was appointed March, 1901, to a company in the Gordon Highlanders, from the Royal Canadian Regt. of Infantry. This unusual mark of distinction to a Colonial officer was earned by brilliant service. He had held the post of adjutant of the 2nd Batt. Royal Canadian Regt., and was afterwards appointed an extra staff officer graded as D.A.A.G. Capt. Ogilvy was mentioned in despatches, L.G., April 16th, 1901, and was awarded the D.S.O.

Ogle.—Lieut. Thomas Frederick Garth Ogle, M.I., 3rd Batt. Royal Fusiliers, was accidentally drowned at Pretoria, Oct. 30th, 1901, while crossing a swollen drift, after a heavy storm. He was the only son of Maj.-Gen. Frederick Amelius Ogle, C.B., late Colonel Commandant of the Royal Marines, and grandson of the late Admiral T. Ogle. He was born July, 1877, educated at Clifton College, and entered the Royal Fusiliers, from the 5th Batt. Rifle Brigade in May, 1898, being promoted lieut. April, 1899.

Oglesby.—Lieut. T. D. Oglesby, Durban Light Infantry, died of dysentery at Estcourt, May 8th, 1900.

O'Hagan.—Lieut. Lord O'Hagan, 3rd Batt. Grenadier Guards, died at Springfontein, Dec. 13th, 1900, of enteric. Thomas Towneley O'Hagan, second Baron

O'Hagan, of Tullahogue, co. Tyrone, in the peerage of the United Kingdom, was the son of the first baron—who was twice Lord Chancellor of Ireland—by his second wife, Alice Mary, daughter of Col. Charles Towneley, of Towneley, Lancashire. He was born in Dec., 1878, educated at the Oratory School, Edgbaston, and entered the Grenadier Guards from the Royal Military College, Feb. 1898, being promoted lieut. Oct., 1899. He succeeded his father in the title in 1885. Lieut. Lord O'Hagan was serving in the 2nd battalion on the outbreak of the war, but he joined the 3rd battalion in Dec., 1899, in order to proceed to South Africa, and served with it up to the time of his death.

Oldfield.—Major Henry Elliott Oldfield, 38th Battery Royal Field Artillery, died at Lindley, July 6th, 1900, of wounds received in action three days previously at Pleisirfontein. He was born in July, 1858, and entered the Royal Artillery, December, 1878, being promoted capt. Jan., 1887, and major Dec. 1896. Major Oldfield proceeded to South Africa in command of his battery in November, 1899, served at Kimberley under Lieut.-Gen. Lord Methuen, and afterwards in the O.R.C., with the force under General Paget. The day Major Oldfield was mortally wounded the guns appear to have come under a severe fire. Sir A. Conan Doyle states: "The escort was inadequate, insufficiently advanced and badly handled . . . and the gallant major, with Lieut. Belcher, was killed in defence of the guns. Capt. Fitzgerald, the only other officer present, was wounded in two places." Major Oldfield was mentioned in despatches, L.G., Sept. 10th, 1901.

Oldnall.—Capt. Henry Cairns Oldnall, Royal Horse Artillery, was killed in action at Tabaksberg, Jan. 29th, 1901. He was born in March, 1868, and entered the

Royal Artillery, Feb., 1886, being promoted capt. May, 1896. He served in the operations on the North-West Frontier of India, 1897-98, with the Malakand Field Force, being present at the action at Landakai and the operations in South Bajaur and in the Mamund Country. Capt. Oldnall was also with the Buner Field Force in the attack and capture of the Tanga Pass, and received the medal with clasp. He served in South Africa from Dec., 1899, and was station staff officer at Rhenoster.

Oliver.—Lieut. Douglas Morison Oliver, 2nd Batt. Norfolk Regt., died at Mylstroom, Aug. 27th, 1900, of wounds received in action two days previously. He was born Sept., 1874, and entered the Norfolk Regt. in April, 1895, from the South-East of Scotland Artillery (Southern Division, Royal Garrison Artillery), being promoted lieut. Sept., 1897. Lieut. Oliver belonged to the 1st battalion in India and was serving at the depôt at Norwich, but volunteering for active service he was sent to South Africa in July, 1900.

Oliver.—2nd Lieut. L. M. Oliver, 6th Dragoons, was killed in action near Heilbron, Nov. 30th, 1901. He was the only son of Mrs. Oliver, of Castle Hill Avenue, Folkestone, was born in 1881, and educated privately. He first entered the 3rd Batt. of the Buffs (East Kent Regiment), Feb., 1900, in which he served in South Africa till Oct., 1901, when he was granted a commission in the 6th Inniskilling Dragoons, a few weeks before he was killed.

Olliver.—Capt. Alwyne Olliver, South African Constabulary (C Division), died of enteric at Pretoria April 28th, 1902.

O'Neil.—Assistant-Surgeon J. T. O'Neil, Indian Medical Service, died at Geluk, Aug. 25th, 1900.

Onraët.—Lieut. Hugh Bernard Onraët, Royal Army Medical Corps, was killed Feb. 27th, 1900, in the attack on Pieter's Hill. He was born in Oct., 1871, and entered the Royal Army Medical Corps, July, 1899. He was mentioned in despatches, L.G., Feb. 8th, 1901.

O'Reilly.—The Rev. Charles Freeman O'Reilly, Chaplain to the Forces, Second Class, died of dysentery, May 10th, 1900, at Bloemfontein. He was born in 1853, became chaplain in the Army Chaplain's Department, Fourth Class, in June, 1882, Third Class, June, 1892, and Second Class, Jan., 1899. Mr. O'Reilly had been stationed in Dublin, and only proceeded to South Africa in April, 1900, and was taken ill soon after his arrival. He is buried at Bloemfontein.

Orlebar.—2nd Lieut. William Aubrey Orlebar, 19th Hussars, died in Ladysmith, Feb. 17th, 1900. He was born March, 1879, educated at Harrow, and entered the 19th Hussars in May, 1898. He proceeded to South Africa with his regiment from India in Sept., 1899, and took part in the defence of Ladysmith up to the time of his death.

Ormond.—Lieut. A. Ormond, Imperial Light Horse, was killed in action at Naauwpoort, Jan. 3rd, 1901.

Orr-Ewing.—Major James Alexander Orr-Ewing, Commanding the Warwickshire Yeomanry, was killed in action at Kleis, May 28th, 1900. He was the younger son of Sir Archibald Orr-Ewing, first baronet, was born 1857, and educated at Harrow and Trinity College, Cambridge, becoming M.A. in 1889. Major Orr-Ewing, who was a very keen and popular sportsman, and a good rider and fisherman, married, in 1898, Lady Margaret Frances Susan, daughter of the late and sister of the present Duke of Roxburghe, and left one daughter,

Millicent Lilian Elizabeth. He joined the 16th Lancers in 1880, was promoted lieut. 1881, capt. 1888, and major 1896. Retiring from the 16th Lancers he joined the Reserve of Officers, and was gazetted a capt. in the Warwickshire Yeomanry, 1898, a Company of which he commanded at the time of his death. He was A.D.C. to Lord Londonderry (Lord-Lieutenant of Ireland) from 1885 to 1890, and A.D.C. to F.-M. Earl Roberts (Commander-in-Chief in Ireland, from 1895 to 1896).

Osborne.—Lieut. John Woodburne Osborne, Scottish Rifles, was killed in action at Spion Kop, in the operations on the Upper Tugela, Jan. 24th, 1900. He was born in June, 1873, and educated at the Collegiate Institute, Brantford; Trinity School, Port Hope; and the Royal Military College, Kingston, Canada. He entered the Scottish Rifles, Nov., 1895, being promoted lieut. Nov., 1897. He was assistant-adjutant to his battalion, and in 1899 was appointed A.D.C. to the Lieutenant-Governor of Bengal, but rejoined his battalion in order to serve in South Africa.

Otter-Barry.—Lieut. Francis Melvil Otter-Barry, U Battery, Royal Horse Artillery, was killed in action at Vlakfontein, O.R.C., Sept. 19th, 1901. He was the son of Robert Melvil Barry Otter-Barry, Esq., of 8, Emperor's Gate, S.W., was born April, 1876, and educated at Marlborough. He entered the Royal Artillery in March, 1896, and was promoted lieut. March, 1899. Lieut. Otter-Barry went to South Africa with U Battery, and took part in the operations at Paardeberg, Feb. 21st to 28th, 1900, and in the subsequent engagements at Poplar Grove, Driefontein, Zand River, and Doorn Kop. He was also present at the occupation of Pretoria and the operations in the O.R.C., which resulted in the surrender of Gen. Prinsloo. At Vlakfontein, where he fell, about fifteen miles south-east of Bloemfontein, Lieut. Otter-Barry, it is stated, behaved most gallantly, and was killed beside his guns. He was mentioned in despatches by Gen. Lord Kitchener, Dec. 8th, 1901, for his "conspicuous good service." His name is inscribed on a tablet placed in Marlborough College Chapel to the memory of all Marlburians who fell in the war.

Owen.—Capt. Hall Owen, Victoria Militia Medical Staff Corps, died of enteric at Chieveley, April 5th, 1900.

Owen-Lewis.—Lieut. Francis Owen-Lewis, 14th Bombay Infantry, was killed in action near Graspan in a reconnaissance with an armoured train, Nov. 24th, 1899. He was the second son of Henry Owen-Lewis, Esq., D.L., of Inniskeen, co. Monaghan, and was born in Aug., 1869. He entered the Durham Light Infantry from the Militia in Feb., 1891, was promoted lieut. March, 1893, and joined the Indian Staff Corps July, 1894. He is stated to have done good work in India, especially in connection with the precautions taken for the suppression of plague at Poona.

Pack - Beresford. — Major Arthur William Pack-Beresford, Royal Artillery, died from enteric at Bloemfontein, March 5th, 1902. He was the second son of the late Dennis W. Pack-Beresford, Esq., of Fenagh House, Bagnalstown, was born April, 1868, and educated at Clifton College. He entered the Royal Artillery Feb., 1887, being promoted lieut. Feb., 1890, capt. Sept., 1897, and brevet-major Nov., 1900. He went out early in the war as a special service officer, serving successively with the South African Light Horse, and in command of Roberts' Horse, and was severely wounded at Sanna's Post, March 31st, 1900, where his gallant conduct is stated to have been very conspicuous. Major

Pack-Beresford was afterwards employed with the South African Constabulary, mentioned in despatches, L.G., Feb. 8th, 1900, and was promoted to a brevet-majority.

Packeman.—Lieut. John Edward Packeman, Imperial Light Horse, was killed in the Boer attack on Wagon Hill, Ladysmith, Jan. 6th, 1900. In this great struggle the Imperial Light Horse rendered splendid service. Ten officers were killed or wounded, and the regiment came out of action commanded by a junior captain.

Paget.—Capt. George Leigh Paget, 1st Batt. Rifle Brigade, died Oct. 9th, 1900, from the severe wound he received in the engagement at Kaapmuiden. He was the eldest son of Sir George Ernest Paget, of Sutton Bonnington, Loughborough, chairman of the Midland Railway Company. Capt. Paget was born in July, 1871, educated at Harrow, and entered the Rifle Brigade Nov., 1891, being promoted lieut. Dec., 1893, and capt. June, 1898. He served with the Natal Field Force from the commencement of the war, and was present at the battle of Colenso and all the subsequent fighting prior to the Relief of Ladysmith, and afterwards took part in the advance into the Transvaal.

Palethorpe. — Lieut. J. Palethorpe, Johannesburg Mounted Rifles, died of enteric at Pinetown, March 23rd, 1901.

Palmer.—Surgeon-Lieut. H. A. Palmer, 5th Victorian M.I., was killed in action near Wilman's Rust, Transvaal, June 12th, 1901.

Paris.—Commander H. G. Paris, Royal Navy, died Sept. 19th, 1900, at Bergen, Norway, from the effect of sunstroke, contracted while serving on transport duties at

Durban. He entered the Navy in 1870, was promoted sub-lieut. 1876, lieut. 1881, and retired as commander 1899. He served as midshipman of the "Niobe" at the bombardment of the fort of Omoa during the civil war in Honduras, 1873, in consequence of an insult offered to the British flag, and was wrecked in the same ship on May 21st, 1874, off the island of Miguelon, near Newfoundland. He was sub-lieut. in the "Achilles" when the fleet went up the Dardanelles during the Russo-Turkish War in 1877, and was lieut. of the "Euryalus" during the Egyptian War, 1882, receiving the Egyptian medal and Khedive's bronze star. He served during the naval and military operations in the Eastern Soudan, 1884 (Suakin clasp), and accompanied Rear-Admiral Sir W. Hewett on a mission to King John of Abyssinia. He was lieut. of the "Agamemnon" ordered from the Mediterranean to take part in the Zanzibar East Coast blockade, 1888, and was employed boat cruising in suppressing the slave trade. He returned from South Africa in July, 1900, and proceeded to Norway and died as stated.

Parker.—Capt. Darwin Harry Parker, 5th Batt. Lancashire Fusiliers, was severely wounded in action at Wonderfontein, Dec. 15th, 1901, and died the same day. He entered the regiment Dec., 1888, was promoted lieut. July, 1890, and capt. Sept., 1900. Capt. Parker served during the war from March, 1900, when he was attached for duty to the 2nd battalion of his regiment with the rank of lieut.

Parker.—Lieut. James Herbert Parker, Kitchener's Horse, was killed in action at Houtnek, May 1st, 1900. He was educated at Harrow.

Parker.—2nd Lieut. Norman James Parker, 2nd Batt. The King's Own Royal Lancaster Regt., was killed in action in the operations on the Tugela, Feb. 22nd, 1900. He was born in April, 1879, educated at Berkhamstead School, and entered his regiment Feb., 1899. He proceeded with his battalion to South Africa Nov., 1899, and served in the Ladysmith Relief Force.

Parker.—Lieut. Percy S. Parker, attached 1st Batt. East Lancashire Regt., died of enteric at Heilbron on Feb. 1st, 1902. He entered the 2nd V.B. East Lancashire Regt., in Jan., 1898, was promoted lieut. March, 1900, and capt. May, 1901. Shortly after the commencement of the war he was attached to the depôt of his regiment at Preston for duty, but volunteering for South Africa, his services were accepted, and he joined the line battalion with the rank of lieut. in March, 1901.

Parr.—2nd Lieut. John Clements Parr, 2nd Batt. Somersetshire Light Infantry, was killed in action in the operations on the Tugela Feb. 21st, 1900. He was the son of the late Gen. William Chase Parr, Indian Staff Corps, of King's Holt, Hants, and nephew of Major-Gen. Hallam Parr, late commanding the 1st Battalion Somersetshire Light Infantry, and now commanding the North Western District. 2nd Lieut. Parr was born in April, 1880, educated at Winchester, entered his regiment Feb., 1899, and accompanied the 2nd battalion to South Africa the following Oct. He is buried close to where he fell, under Fort Wyllie, and near the village of Colenso.

Parsons.—Civil Surgeon C. E. Parsons, died of enteric at Harrismith, Dec., 1900. He was educated at Dover College, and rendered good service during the war.

Parsons.—Lieut. Francis Newton Parsons, V.C., Essex Regt., was killed in action in the engagement at Driefontein, March 10th, 1900. He was the third son of Dr. Charles Parsons, Dover, born March, 1875, and educated at Dover College. He entered the Essex Regt. in Feb., 1896, being promoted lieut. March, 1898. He was present at the battle of Paardeberg, when he was awarded the V.C. (L.G., Nov. 20th, 1900), for gallantry under the following circumstances: "On the south bank of the river Modder, Private Ferguson, 1st Batt. Essex Regt., was wounded and fell in a place devoid of cover. While trying to crawl under cover he was again wounded in the stomach; Lieut. Parsons at once went to his assistance, dressed his wound, under heavy fire, went down twice, still under heavy fire, to the bank of the river to get water for Private Ferguson, and subsequently carried him to a place of safety." At Driefontein Lieut. Parsons "again displayed conspicuous gallantry," and was mentioned in despatches, L.G., Feb. 8th, 1901.

Paton.—Lieut. Harold Percival Paton, No. 1 Troop, Protectorate Regt., was killed in action at Game Tree Hill in a sortie from Mafeking, Dec. 26th, 1899. He was educated at Loretto School, Musselburgh, where he was in the XI. and XV., being a good cricketer and football player. This officer's death is mentioned by Major-Gen. Baden-Powell in his despatch from Mafeking of May 18th, 1900, L.G., Feb 8th, 1901. Lieut. Paton was killed at the very muzzles of the enemy's guns. He is buried in the cemetery at Mafeking.

Patten.—Lieut. E. Patten, Intelligence Department (attached to Rimington's column), died of enteric at Harrismith, Feb. 9th, 1902. He is buried in Harrismith military cemetery.

Paxton.—2nd Lieut. Llewellyn Paxton, 2nd Batt. Bedfordshire Regt., was killed in action at Thaba N'chu, Nov. 16th, 1900. He was born in Oct., 1881, and entered his regiment Jan., 1900.

Pearse.—Capt. C. St. A. Pearse, Canadian Mounted Infantry, died of tuberculosis of the lungs at Pretoria, Oct. 17th, 1900.

Pearson.—Lieut. Reginald William Pearson, 2nd Batt. Rifle Brigade, was killed in action at Ladysmith, Feb. 22nd, 1900. He was the elder son of Rear-Admiral Hugo Lewis Pearson, recently Commander-in-Chief on the Australian station and A.D.C. to Her late Majesty Queen Victoria. Lieut. Pearson was born in May, 1876, and entered the Rifle Brigade from the Devon Artillery Militia in July, 1897, being promoted lieut. Aug., 1899. He served in the campaign in the Soudan under Lord (then Sir Herbert) Kitchener, 1898, with the 2nd Batt. Rifle Brigade, and was present at the battle of Khartoum, receiving the British medal and Khedive's medal with clasp. Lieut. Pearson accompanied his battalion to South Africa, Oct., 1899, and served in Ladysmith during the siege up to the date of his death.

Pechell.—Capt. Charles Augustus Kerr Pechell, 3rd Batt. King's Royal Rifle Corps, was killed in action at Cannon Kopje in the defence of Mafeking, Oct. 31st, 1899. He was the son of Admiral Mark Robert Pechell, and a grand nephew of Sir G. S. Pechell, Bart. He was born July, 1869, educated at Eton (Mr. Everard's), and entered the King's Royal Rifle Corps in Nov., 1890, being promoted lieut. Aug., 1893, and capt. Dec., 1898. He was employed with the Bechuanaland Division British South African Police from Aug., 1898. This officer's death is mentioned in the despatch of Major.-Gen. Baden-Powell, from Mafeking, May 18th, 1900, L.G., Feb. 8th, 1901. Capt. Pechell was the younger brother of Capt. M. H. K. Pechell, who was killed at the battle of Talana Hill.

Pechell.—Capt. Mark Horace Kerr Pechell, 1st Batt. King's Royal Rifle Corps, was killed in action at the battle of Talana Hill, Oct. 20th, 1899. He was the son of Admiral Mark Robert Pechell, and grand-nephew of Sir G. S. Pechell, Bart. He was born in Sept., 1867, educated at Eton (Mr. Tarver's), and entered the Royal Irish Rifles, Feb., 1888. He was transferred to the King's Royal Rifle Corps in the following July, being promoted lieut. May, 1890, and capt. March, 1896. Although only 32 years of age, he had been in five previous campaigns. He served in the Hazara Expedition, 1891, with the 1st battalion of his regiment (medal with clasp); also in the Miranzai Expedition, 1891, with the same battalion, including the engagements at Sangar and Mastan (clasp); and with the Isazai Expedition, 1892. His next experience of active service was with the Chitral Relief Force under Sir Herbert Low, 1895, with the 1st battalion King's Royal Rifle Corps from April 11th to the close of the operations, receiving the medal with clasp. Capt. Pechell took part in 1898, in the Nile Expedition, and was present at the battles of the Atbara and Khartoum, being mentioned in despatches, L.G., Sept. 30th, 1898, and granted the medal, and Egyptian medal with two clasps. In 1897 he was selected for employment in the Egyptian army, but, in Sept., 1899, joined the first battalion of his regiment in Natal. At the battle of Talana, his company was extending behind a wall, and to show above this cover immediately drew the fire of a dozen Boer Mausers. It was here that Capt. Pechell fell while endeavouring to return the Boer fire. He is buried in the cemetery just below Talana Hill.

Peel.—Lieut. Frank Gerald Peel, Loch's Horse, died of enteric, at Springfontein, May 22nd, 1900.

Peel.—Capt. Reginald Arthur Hawarth Peel, 2nd Life

Guards, died of enteric, at Bloemfontein, April 16th, 1900. He was born in April, 1863, and educated at Wellington, where he was in Griffith's, 1876-78. He entered the 2nd Life Guards from the 5th Batt. Royal Irish Rifles in May, 1885, being promoted capt. Nov., 1893. He took part in the relief of Kimberley and the advance on Bloemfontein.

Perceval.—Lieut. Edward Perceval, 4th Batt. King's Royal Rifle Corps, was killed in action at Paardeberg, Feb. 18th, 1900. He was born in Jan., 1877, educated at Winchester, and entered his regiment March, 1898, being promoted lieut. Oct., 1899. He proceeded to South Africa in Oct., 1899, to serve with the M.I.

Perkins.—Lieut. C. N. Perkins joined the Imperial Light Horse in Sept., 1899. He was educated at St. John's School, Leatherhead, where he was in his school cricket and football teams. In South Africa he saw much service under General Sir R. Buller and Lieut.-Gen. Sir J. D. P. French, and was present at all the battles on the Tugela. It is stated that he was one of the first twenty to enter Ladysmith. He afterwards served in the Western Transvaal, and was promoted to a lieutenantcy in the Commander-in-Chief's Body Guard. He returned home in July, 1901, and afterwards was employed in West Africa, where he died of cerebral meningitis.

Petre.—Capt. the Hon. Joseph Lucius Henry Petre Loyal Suffolk Hussars Yeomanry, was killed in action at Spion Kop, Jan. 24th, 1900. He was the youngest son of the late William Bernard, twelfth Lord Petre, was thirty-three years of age, a good sportsman and bold rider. He was educated at a model school at Woburn Park, kept by his elder brother, Monsignor Petre, and afterwards at St. Augustine's, Ramsgate. He was serving with

Thornycroft's M.I. at the time of his death, and was mentioned in despatches, L.G., Feb. 8th, 1901.

Phillips.—Lieut. A. Phillips, 49th Company I.Y., was killed in action at Nonskraal, in the Fauresmith district, Dec. 25th, 1901.

Pickard.—Lieut. H. W. Pickard, Roberts' Horse, died at Bloemfontein, April 18th, 1900.

Pigott.—Lieut. Hugh P. Pigott, Thorneycroft's M.I., died of enteric and pleurisy at Standerton Hospital, Nov. 12th, 1900. He was the only son of Major J. C. M. Pigott, Reserve of Officers, late Royal Berkshire Regt., who was at one time D.A.A. and Q.M.G. Southern District. Lieut. Pigott was twenty-two years of age at the time of his death.

Pile. — Major Lionel Lewis Pile, 1st Batt. East Lancashire Regt., died of enteric at Heilbron, Dec. 4th, 1901. He was born in Nov., 1859, and educated at Clifton. He entered the 59th Foot (now the 2nd Batt. East Lancashire Regt.) in Jan. 1880, being promoted lieut. July, 1881, was attached to the Army Service Corps, August 1889 to August 1894, became capt. Nov. 1890, and major Sept., 1901. Major Pile had served in South Africa from the commencement of the war, and had been employed as brigade-major in 1900.

Pilkington.—Lieut. Frederick Ernest Chomley Pilkington, 18th Hussars, was killed in action at Waterval, near Vryheid, Oct. 6th, 1901. He was born Oct., 1873, entered the 18th Hussars from the 3rd Batt. Royal Irish Fusiliers (Armagh Militia) in Dec., 1899, and was promoted lieut. Feb., 1901. Lieut. Pilkington joined his regiment in South Africa in March, 1901, and served with it in the Transvaal.

Pilkington.—2nd Lieut. Thomas Douglas Pilkington 1st Royal Dragoons, was killed in action at Kaalboshfontein, July 11th, 1900. He was the son of Thomas Pilkington, Esq., J.P. and D.L., of Sandside, Caithness, and St. Helen's, Lancashire. 2nd Lieut. Pilkington was born in June, 1876, educated at Eton (Mr. Durnford's), and entered the Royal Dragoons from the 3rd Batt. South Lancashire Regt. in June, 1897. He was a D.L. for Caithness-shire. He had served in South Africa from the commencement of the war, having embarked with his regiment in Oct. 1899.

Piper.—Quartermaster and Hon. Lieut. Thomas Piper, 2nd Batt. Duke of Cambridge's Own Middlesex Regt., died at Newcastle, Natal, on June 27th, 1902, from inflammation. He was born June, 1858, served in the ranks for over fourteen years, as warrant officer for nearly four years, and was appointed quartermaster to the Essex Regt., in Oct., 1894. Lieut. Piper exchanged to the 2nd Batt. Middlesex Regt. in Aug., 1899, and embarking with it in Nov. he served throughout the war including the operations on the Tugela and the relief of Ladysmith. He was present at the actions at Spion Kop, Vaal Kranz, and Pieter's Hill, and afterwards took part in the operations in Natal, March to May, 1900, and in the advance into the Transvaal, July to Nov., 1900. He was mentioned in despatches, L.G., Sept. 10th, 1901.

Pipe-Wolferstan.—Lieut. Humphrey Francis Pipe-Wolferstan, 2nd Batt. King's Own Scottish Borderers, was killed in action at Spion Kop in the operations on the Upper Tugela, Jan. 24th, 1900. He was born in March, 1874, educated at Rugby, 1888-92, and entered the King's Own Scottish Borderers, March, 1894, being promoted lieut. May, 1897. He served with the Chitral Relief Force under Sir Robert Low in 1895 with the 2nd battalion of his regiment, including the capture of the Malakand Pass, the passage of the Swat River, and the engagement at Panjkora (medal with clasp). Lieut. Pipe-Wolferstan also served with his battalion in the campaign on the North-West Frontier of India under the late Sir William Lockhart, 1897-98, in the Tirah Expeditionary Force, and was present at the engagement at Dargai, Oct. 18th, at the forcing of the Sampagha and Arhanga Passes, in the operations in the Dwatoi country and in the Bara Valley, being mentioned in despatches and receiving two clasps. When killed, Lieut. Pipe-Wolferstan, who had volunteered for active service, was attached to the 2nd Batt. King's Own Lancaster Regt. He was a brother of Lieut.-Col. E. S. Pipe-Wolferstan, 4th Batt. North Staffordshire Regt.

Platt.—2nd Lieut. Cecil Sherman Platt, 5th Dragoon Guards, died of enteric in Ladysmith, Jan. 5th, 1900. He was born in Aug., 1877, educated at Eton (Mr. Everard's and Mr. Lowry's), and entered the 5th Dragoon Guards from the Militia in Nov., 1898. 2nd Lieut. Platt accompanied his regiment from India in Sept., 1899, and served in Natal and in Ladysmith up to the date of his death.

Plomer.—Capt. Alfred Durham Plomer, 1st Batt. King's (Liverpool Regt.), died Aug. 29th, 1900, at Nooitgedacht of wounds received in action at Dalmanutha, Aug. 23rd. He was born in Feb., 1868, educated at Cheltenham College, and entered the Liverpool Regt. in March, 1889, being promoted lieut. Aug., 1890, and capt. July, 1896. Capt. Plomer, who was serving at the depot of his regiment on the outbreak of the war, proceeded to South Africa in Jan., 1900, and served with his battalion in Natal after the relief of Ladysmith, and in the Transvaal. His name is inscribed on the Eleanor Cross Memorial at Cheltenham College.

W

Plumbe.—Major John Hulke Plumbe, Royal Marine Light Infantry, was killed in action at Graspan, Nov. 25th, 1899. The third son of the late Dr. S. A. Plumbe, of Maidenhead, he was born in 1858, and educated at the Oxford Military College. He entered the Royal Marines in 1877, was promoted capt. 1880, and major 1885, and is stated to have been a highly qualified officer, being a specialist in gunnery, fortification, torpedoes, and other subjects. He served in the Royal Marine Batt. in Egypt in 1882, and was present at every action in which it was engaged from the occupation of Alexandria to the actions of Tel-el-Mahuta, Kassassin, Aug. 28th, Kassassin, Sept. 9th, and Tel-el-Kebir, where he was slightly wounded in the hand and hip. He received the medal with clasp and bronze star. In the battle of Graspan Major Plumbe was in command of the Royal Marines belonging to the Naval Brigade. In this action their losses amounted to forty-three per cent., due to the "unflinching and self-sacrificing heroism of the troops that led the assault." Three officers and 72 men of the Royal Marines were killed or wounded out of a total of 5 officers and 190 men. In the Naval Brigade Major Plumbe, Commander Ethelston, Captain Senior, and Midshipman Huddart were killed, and almost all the petty and non-commissioned officers were struck down. Just before he was killed Major Plumbe said, "Rush for the hill, men," and when mortally wounded his last words were, "Forward! never mind me." A pet dog he took into action with him watched by his body for six hours, until the arrival of the ambulance. Major Plumbe was at first buried on the battlefield, but on the morning of Nov. 26th his body was moved, and he now lies close to Enslin Station beside Commander Ethelston and Capt. Senior. Their graves are marked by a large cross. Major Plumbe's servant, Private Doran, died of his wounds. The names of Major Plumbe and his servant are inscribed on the monument erected in the Cambridge enclosure, St. James's Park, by the officers and men of the Royal Marine Artillery and Light Infantry, in memory of their comrades who fell in South Africa and China. (*See Commander Ethelston.*)

Pollard - Lowsley. — Lieut. Inglis de Lisle Pollard-Lowsley, Royal Garrison Artillery, died of enteric at Middelburg, Transvaal, Feb. 26th, 1901. He was the eldest son of Lieut.-Col. Lowsley, late Royal Engineers, was born in Nov., 1875, and educated at Cheltenham. He entered the Royal Artillery from the Militia, July, 1896, being promoted lieut. July, 1899. Lieut. Pollard-Lowsley went to South Africa in March, 1900, for special duty with pom-poms, and commanded a section till the time of his death. His name is inscribed on the Eleanor Cross Memorial at Cheltenham College.

Pollok. — 2nd Lieut. John Frederick Pollok, 9th Lancers, died at Bappisfontein, June 2nd, 1900, of wounds received in action the same day at Orange Grove. He was the 3rd son of the late John Pollok, Esq., J.P., D.L., of Lismany, co. Galway, and of Ronachan, Ayrshire. He was born in Sept., 1876, educated at Charterhouse, and entered the 9th Lancers from the 3rd Batt. South Wales Borderers, Jan., 1899. 2nd Lieut. Pollok served in Cape Colony and with his regiment as part of the Kimberley Relief Force, and afterwards at the relief of that town and the subsequent advance on Bloemfontein. His name is inscribed on the tablet in the War Memorial Cloister at Charterhouse.

Pook.—2nd Lieut. Frederick Albert Betteley Pook, 4th Batt. Cheshire Regt. (2nd Royal Cheshire Militia), died of enteric at Burghersdorp, March 4th, 1901. He obtained his commission as 2nd lieut. in March, 1900, and volunteering for active service joined his battalion, which was embodied, in South Africa, and served with it up to the time of his death.

Poole.—Lieut. W. J. Poole, I.Y., died of dysentery on board the S.S. "Canada," July 28th, 1901, while on passage home from South Africa. He was a 2nd lieut. in the 2nd Tower Hamlets Volunteer Rifle Corps. He entered the I.Y. as a lieut. in April, 1901, and served with the 22nd Batt.

Pooley.—Lieut. A. E. Pooley, 5th Queensland Bushmen, was killed in action at Mokaridrift, Caledon River, Sept. 27, 1901.

Porter.—2nd Lieut. John J. Porter, 2nd Dragoon Guards (Queen's Bays), was killed in action between Carolina and Bethel, Oct. 16th, 1900. He had only just been appointed to the regiment from the 2nd Dragoons (Royal Scots Greys), where he had attained the rank of corporal, and was granted a commission in the 2nd Dragoon Guards.

Porter.—Major Reginald Whitworth Porter, D.S.O., 2nd in command of the 1st Batt. Oxfordshire Light Infantry, died May 10th, 1902, of valvular disease of the heart, on board the transport "Orotava," in which he had been invalided home from South Africa. He was the eldest surviving son of Henry Aylmer Porter, Esq., of Cranbourne Court, Windsor Forest, was born in May, 1856, and educated at Cheltenham. He entered the Oxfordshire Light Infantry in Sept., 1876, being promoted capt. Jan., 1886, and major Nov., 1894. He served in the campaign on the North-West Frontier of India under the late Sir William Lockhart, 1897-98, with the 2nd Batt. of his regiment in the Mohmand Field Force, and with the Peshawur column and the 5th brigade of the Tirah Expeditionary Force, including the operations in the Bara Valley, receiving the medal with two clasps. During the South African war he took part in the march from Modder River to Bloemfontein, and was present in the engagements at Klip Drift, Paardeberg, Poplar Grove, and Driefontein, and the occupation of Bloemfontein. He afterwards served in the O.R.C., and performed the duties of commandant of Reitspruit and Assistant Provost Marshal at Heilbron. He was appointed 2nd-in-command of his battalion from Sept., 1900, and served subsequently as Railway Staff Officer, and was mentioned in despatches, L.G., Sept. 10th, 1901, being awarded the D.S.O. and the South African medal with four clasps and the King's medal with two clasps. Major Porter's name is inscribed on the Eleanor Cross Memorial erected at Cheltenham College to the memory of Cheltonians who fell in the war.

Pott.—Capt. Arthur David Ripley Pott, 3rd Batt. King's Own Scottish Borderers, died from abscess of the liver at Kimberley, Dec. 20th, 1901. He was the eldest son of the late General David Pott, C.B., of Todrig, Selkirkshire, and Borthwickshiels, Roxburghshire, and was born in 1862. He was appointed lieut. in his battalion July, 1886, being promoted capt. March, 1894. Capt. Pott's battalion was embodied in Jan., 1900, and volunteering for active service he proceeded with it to South Africa in Feb. He had held the post of Staff Officer to the Commandant of Schweizer Reneke.

Powell.—Lieut. Charles Folliott Borrodaile Powell, Yorkshire Light Infantry (M.I.), was killed in action at Rietfontein, Transvaal, July 13th, 1901. He was born in Dec., 1879, educated at Rugby, and entered the Yorkshire Light Infantry in August, 1899, being promoted lieut. April, 1900. He was seconded for service with the M.I. in March, 1901, and embarked for South Africa on the 18th of that month. He is buried at Zand River Poort.

Powell.—Lieut. John William Powell, South Australian Contingent, died at Rensberg, Feb. 12th, 1900.

Power.—Major Alfred Richard Power, 2nd Batt. Yorkshire Light Infantry, died of dysentery at St. Michael's Home, Bloemfontein, June 8th, 1900. He was born in Oct., 1857, and entered the 22nd Foot June, 1879, and was transferred to the 51st Foot in the following July. He was promoted capt. Jan., 1886, and major July, 1898. Major Power served in the Afghan war, 1879-80, with the 51st Light Infantry, taking part in the action of Nargashai. He also served in the Burmese Expedition from 1886 to the end of 1887 with the 1st Batt. Yorkshire Light Infantry, receiving the medal with two clasps. He embarked for South Africa in April, 1900, and on arrival proceeded to 'Kimberley. He was then ordered to Kroonstad, and, while on his way was taken ill at Bloemfontein.

Power.—Capt. Sir Elliott Derrick Le Poer Power, 1st Batt. Rifle Brigade, died of enteric at Standerton, Jan. 20th, 1902. He was the fifth Baronet of Kilfane, co. Kilkenny, and succeeded his brother, Sir John Power, a captain in the 5th Batt. Royal Irish Regiment, who died from wounds received in action at Lindley, June 1st, 1900. Sir Elliott Power was born in 1872, and entered the Rifle Brigade from the 4th Batt. The King's Shropshire Light Infantry in June, 1894. He was promoted lieut. June, 1897, and capt. August, 1900. He was employed with the Egyptian Army in 1899, and afterwards served with the 3rd battalion in India. On his promotion to the rank of capt. he was posted to the 1st battalion and served with it during 1901 in South Africa.

Power.—Capt. Sir John Elliott Cecil Power, fourth Baronet of Kilfane, Kilkenny, died June 1st, 1900, . of wounds received three days previously in the opera-

OFFICERS WHO FELL IN SOUTH AFRICA. 311

tions between Kroonstad and Lindley. He was the eldest son of the third baronet, Sir Richard Crampton Power, by his marriage with Florence Anna Maria, only surviving child of the late Robert Elliott, Esq., of Goldingtonbury, Bedfordshire. Sir J. Power was born in Dec., 1870, and succeeded to the title in 1892. He held a commission as capt. in the 5th Batt. Royal Irish Regt. since April, 1896. On the formation of the I.Y., Sir J. Power volunteered for active service, and joined that force in Feb., 1900, as a lieut., and served in South Africa with the Irish Yeomanry up to the time of his death.

Poynder.—Lieut .Geoffrey William Poynder, 2nd Batt. The Queen's Royal West Surrey Regt., died of enteric at Kroonstad, Feb. 18th, 1902. He was born in March, 1874, educated at Charterhouse, and entered the Royal West Surrey Regt. May, 1896, being promoted lieut. Nov., 1897. Lieut. Poynder in 1899 was stationed at the depôt at Guildford, but proceeded to South Africa in March, 1900, and served throughout the war until his death. His name is engraved on a tablet, erected at Guildford by their comrades, in memory of all ranks of The Queen's Royal West Surrey Regt. who fell in the war; also on the tablet in the War Memorial Cloister at Charterhouse.

Pratt.—Capt. James Bonham Tod Pratt, 1st Batt. King's Own Scottish Borderers, died of enteric June 23rd, 1900. He was the eldest son of Col. Henry Hamilton Pratt, late 94th Regt. He was born in Feb., 1862, and educated at Cheltenham College, where he gained a scholarship. He entered the 25th Foot from the Royal Military College Jan., 1881, being promoted lieut. in the following July, and capt. May, 1890. He served with the Chin-Lushai Expeditionary Force in 1889-90, receiving the medal with clasp. Capt. Pratt was adjutant of his battalion, 1894-98. He served in South Africa from Jan., 1900, and was severely wounded at the battle of Paardeberg, Feb. 23rd, but on recovering, rejoined at Glen Station, and entered Johannesburg with the advancing army May 31st. He is buried in the cemetery there. His name is inscribed on the Eleanor Cross Memorial erected at Cheltenham College.

Pratt-Barlow.—Lieut. F. H. Pratt-Barlow, 4th Batt. I.Y., died of enteric at Lindley, Feb. 26th, 1902. He was the only son of Archibald Pratt-Barlow, Esq., of Nottingham, and was nineteen years of age. He was granted a commission in the I.Y. in Oct., 1901, with the rank of lieut.

Preston.—2nd Lieut. John Starkie Preston, 1st Batt. Royal Scots, died of enteric at Dewetsdorp, June 27th, 1900. He was the son of J. Preston, Esq., of Mearbeck House, near Leeds, was born in June, 1879, and educated at Haileybury. He entered the Royal Scots from the 3rd Batt. East Lancashire Regt. in Oct., 1899. 2nd Lieut. Preston served in South Africa with his battalion from the commencement of the war in the north of Cape Colony and afterwards in the O.R.C.

Price.—Capt. Rhys Price, 1st Batt. Welsh Regt., died of blood poisoning at Modder River, March 3rd, 1900. He was born in June, 1865, and educated at Christ's College, Brecon, where he was in the cricket XI. and football XV. He entered the Welsh Regt. from the 3rd South Wales Borderers in Dec., 1888, being promoted lieut. Aug., 1890, and capt. June, 1899. Capt. Price accompanied his battalion to South Africa in Oct., 1899, and served with it in Cape Colony.

Price.—Lieut. Sir Rose Price, Bart., 3rd Batt. King's Royal Rifle Corps, was killed in action, near Villiersdorp,

June 9th, 1901. He was the son of Sir Rose Lambart Price, 3rd baronet, of Trengwainton, Cornwall, by his marriage with Isabella, daughter of the late William Tarleton, Esq. Sir Rose Price was born in July, 1879, and entered the King's Royal Rifle Corps from the 3rd Batt. York and Lancaster Regt., in Oct., 1899, being promoted lieut. Nov. 1900. He proceeded to South Africa in Nov., 1899, and served with the 3rd Batt. King's Royal Rifle Corps with the Ladysmith relief force, and took part in the fighting on the Tugela and the subsequent advance into the Transvaal.

Price-Dent.—Lieut. Phillip Hampton Price-Dent, 1st Batt. Devonshire Regt., died Dec. 31st, 1899, of wounds received in action at Ladysmith four days previously. He was the son of Mrs. Price-Dent, Manor House, Hallerton, Leicestershire. He was born in May, 1870, educated at Cheltenham College, and entered his regiment in May, 1891, being promoted lieut. Feb., 1895. He served with the Chitral Relief Force under Sir Robert Low, 1895, receiving the medal with clasp. He also was with the 1st Batt. Devonshire Regt., in the campaign on the North-West Frontier of India, under the late Sir William Lockhart, 1897-98, and was present at the capture of Sampagha and Arhanga Passes, receiving the medal with two clasps. Lieut. Price-Dent accompanied his battalion to South Africa from India in Sept., 1899, and served in Natal from the commencement of the war. His name is inscribed on the Eleanor Cross Memorial at Cheltenham College.

Prichard.—Lieut. Gordon Fairfax Prichard, 2nd Batt. Lincolnshire Regt., was killed in action at Nitral's Nek, July, 11th, 1900. He was the fourth son of J. C. Collins Prichard, Esq., of Pwllywrack, Cowbridge, Glamorganshire, was born Nov., 1872, and educated at Clifton

College. He entered the Lincolnshire Regt. from the Royal Military College, in March, 1894, being promoted lieut. Feb., 1896. He sailed for South Africa with his battalion in Jan., 1900, and was present at the battle of Paardeberg, and the advance on Bloemfontein and Johannesburg, being awarded the medal with three clasps.

Prickard.—Capt. Harry Seddon Prickard, 2nd Batt. North Staffordshire Regt., died of enteric at Bloemfontein, May 12th, 1900. He was the eldest son of the Rev. W. E. Prickard, of Dderw, Radnorshire, was born April, 1866, and educated at Winchester. He entered the North Staffordshire Regiment in Feb. 1888, being promoted lieut. March, 1890, and capt. Feb., 1896. He served in the operations in Zululand, 1888. Capt. Prickard accompanied his battalion to South Africa in January, 1900, and was present at the battle of Paardeberg and the advance on Bloemfontein.

Prothero.—Capt. Freke Lewis Prothero, 1st Batt. Welsh Regt., died April 24th, 1900, of wounds received in action near Karriefontein, two days previously. He was born in June, 1868, and entered the Welsh Regt. March, 1899, being promoted lieut. Dec., 1890, and capt. July, 1899. He served with the Tirah Expeditionary Force on the North-West Frontier, 1897-98, and was awarded the medal with clasp. Capt. Prothero served with his battalion in South Africa from the commencement of the war, and was present at the battle of Paardeberg and the advance on Bloemfontein.

Quicke.—Capt. and Brevet-Major Francis Churchill Quicke, 1st Dragoon Guards, was killed in action at Riverdale, near Harrismith, Oct. 26th, 1901. He was born in April, 1867, educated at Eton (Mr. Mozley's), and entered the 1st Dragoon Guards from the 4th Batt. Devonshire Regt. in May, 1887, being promoted lieut. April, 1890, capt. Nov. 1895, and brevet-major Aug., 1901. In the early part of the war he was serving with the Kimberley Mounted Corps. Major Quicke was mentioned in the despatch of Gen. Lord Kitchener, Aug. 8th, 1901, for having at Amsterdam, O.R.C., on Aug. 2nd, pursued a convoy for 14 miles, and when he reached the wagons had only seven men with him; with these he rode to the head of the convoy and stopped it, capturing 55 waggons and 16 Cape carts, though a considerable force of the enemy were in the vicinity. For this gallant service he was promoted brevet-major.

Quin.—Lieut. Henry George Quin, 1st Batt. Northumberland Fusiliers, was killed in action at Elandslaagte, near Klerksdorp, Feb. 25th, 1902. He was the eldest surviving son of R. J. Quin, Esq., barrister-at-law of Lincoln's Inn, was born in Dec., 1881, and entered his regiment from the Royal Military College in Aug., 1900, being promoted lieut. Dec., 1901. He had served in South Africa with his battalion from 1900 up to the time of his death.

Raikes.—Lieut. Francis Howard Raikes, 2nd Batt. King's Royal Rifle Corps, was killed in action at Wagon Hill, Ladysmith, Jan. 6th, 1900. He was the only child of Judge F. W. Raikes, of the Leat House, Malton, Yorkshire, was born in July, 1879, and educated at Eton (Mr. Luxmoore's), whence he passed direct into Sandhurst. He entered the King's Royal Rifle Corps from the Royal Military College in July, 1898, being promoted lieut. Dec., 1899. He rejoined his battalion in Natal on war being declared, and was present at the battle of Farquhar's Farm, and afterwards served in Ladysmith. The day he was killed Lieut. Raikes, although he belonged to the 2nd battalion, was in command of a half company of the 1st battalion, and in the early morning of Jan. 6th he had posted his men in two rifle pits which had been constructed on the Nek between Wagon Hill and Cæsar's Camp. At the commencement of the Boer attack he was on the ground between, so that he might better direct the fire of his men. As the enemy continued to approach closer Lieut. Raikes, thinking it would come to hand-to-hand fighting, called out to Sergt. Davies in one of the rifle pits asking if there was room for him. Sergt Davies replied, "Yes; but take care of the heavy fire." Lieut. Raikes replied: "Look out, I am coming," and then ran to the rifle pit but fell dead just as he reached it, shot through the heart. Some reinforcements now arrived, but this young officer and his handful of riflemen had held the enemy in check till 8 a.m. When he fell he was probably the youngest lieut. in the army. He is buried half way up the Nek between Wagon Hill and Cæsar's Camp. The East window of St. Peter's Parish Church, Norton, is dedicated to his memory and that of other comrades who fell Jan. 6th. A bronze memorial tablet has also been erected to Lieut. Raikes in Mold Parish Church, and a brass tablet in the School of Handicrafts at Chertsey, in which Institution he took the greatest interest. (*See Major Bowen.*)

Rait.—2nd Lieut. Walter Garnet Rait, 1st Batt. King's Own Scottish Borderers, died of enteric, at Wynberg, June 22nd, 1900. He was the only son of Lieut.-Col. Rait, C.B., of Anniston, Arbroath, N.B., was born in Nov., 1878, and educated at Rugby. He entered the King's Own Scottish Borderers in Aug., 1898. 2nd Lieut. Rait embarked for South Africa with his battalion Dec., 1899, and served in the Cape and Orange River Colonies. He was present at the battle of Paardeberg and took part in the advance on Bloemfontein.

OFFICERS WHO FELL IN SOUTH AFRICA.

Raitt.—Capt. Arthur Douglas Raitt, 2nd Batt. the Queen's Royal West Surrey Regt., was killed in action on the Upper Tugela, Jan. 1st, 1900. He was born in Jan., 1869, and educated at St. Alban's School, and at the United Services College, Westward Ho. He entered the Royal West Surrey Regt. from the 3rd Batt. King's Own Yorkshire Light Infantry in June, 1890, being promoted lieut. Dec., 1891, and capt. Sept., 1898. Capt. Raitt accompanied his battalion to South Africa in Oct., 1899, and was present at the battle of Colenso. His name is inscribed on a tablet in his old college at Westward Ho; it is also engraved on a tablet at Guildford, erected by his comrades in memory of all ranks of the Queen's Royal West Surrey Regt. who fell in the war.

Ralli.—Major Antonio Stephen Ralli, 12th Lancers, died of enteric at Kroonstad, May 26th, 1900. He was the eldest surviving son of M. Ralli, Esq., who was Prime Minister of Greece during the Græco-Turkish war. Major Ralli was born in May, 1861, and educated at Eton (Mr. James'). He entered the 16th Lancers in Aug., 1880, was transferred to the 12th Lancers the following Dec., being promoted lieut. July, 1881, capt. Jan., 1888, and major Dec., 1896. Major Ralli accompanied his regiment to South Africa in Oct., 1899, and served with the Kimberley Relief Force under Lieut.-Gen. Lord Methuen, also in the relief of Kimberley, the battle of Paardeberg, and the advance on Bloemfontein.

Ralston.—Lieut. James Ralston, 1st Imperial Light Horse, was killed in action at Hartebeestefontein, March 22nd, 1901.

Ramsay.—Lieut. Nigel Neis Ramsay, 2nd Batt. Royal Highlanders, was killed in action at Magersfontein

Dec. 11th, 1899. He was born in 1876, educated at Winchester, and joined the Royal Highlanders in Sept., 1896, being promoted lieut. Aug., 1898. Lieut. Ramsay sailed with his battalion for South Africa in Nov., 1899, and joined the Kimberley Relief Force under Lieut.-Gen. Lord Methuen just before the battle of Magersfontein, in which he fell.

Ramsay.—Major Thomas Burnett Ramsay, M.I. Rifle Brigade, died of dysentery at Elandsfontein, Dec. 20th, 1901. He was the only son of the late Col. William Burnett Ramsay, Rifle Brigade, of Banchory Lodge, Banchory, N.B., a grandson of the first baronet of Balmain. Major Ramsay was born in March, 1862, and educated at Haileybury College. He entered the 5th Lancers in Aug., 1884, was transferred to the Rifle Brigade the following Oct., promoted capt. Nov., 1892, and major Oct., 1901. Major Ramsay served with the Burmese Expedition, 1886-88, receiving the medal with clasp. He was adjutant of his battalion March, 1872 to Dec. 1894, and adjutant of the 5th battalion April, 1897 to April, 1901, when he proceeded to South Africa and was appointed to the M.I.

Raphael.—Lieut. Frederick Melchoir Raphael, 1st Batt. South Lancashire Regt., was killed in action at Spion Kop, Jan. 24th, 1900. He was, the second son of George Charles Raphael, Esq., of 37, Portland Place, W., and Castle Hill, Englefield Green, Surrey. Lieut. Raphael was born in April, 1870, and educated at Wellington (Penny's). He entered the South Lancashire Regt. from the 5th Batt. Rifle Brigade Oct., 1891, being promoted lieut. Feb., 1894. He accompanied his battalion to South Africa in Nov., 1899, and served with the Natal Field Force.

OFFICERS WHO FELL IN SOUTH AFRICA. 319

Rasbotham.—Lieut. Robert Egerton Rasbotham, 1st Batt. Durham Light Infantry, was killed in action at Eden Kop, June 22nd, 1901. The second son of Mrs. Asheton Rasbotham, of Ebnal Grange, Malpas, he was born in August, 1878, and educated at Eton (Mr. Broadbent's). He entered the Durham Light Infantry from the 4th Batt. Royal Welsh Fusiliers in Oct., 1899, and was promoted lieut. March, 1901. He served throughout the Natal campaign, including Colenso, Vaal Kranz, and Pieter's Hill, and was invalided home after enteric in June, 1900, but returned the following September. Lieut. Rasbotham was recommended for the Royal Humane Society's medal for endeavouring to save a drowning soldier at Maritzburg. When killed he was serving with the M.I., and after being mortally wounded he directed his men "not to give in." He was mentioned in despatches, L.G., August 21st, 1901, also in Gen. Lord Kitchener's despatch, July 28th, 1901, for "when in command of a patrol which was suddenly fired on at close quarters and mortally wounded, most gallantly continued to encourage his men till he died." He is buried at Vlakfontein.

Ray.—Major George Lake Sidney Ray, 1st Batt. Northumberland Fusiliers, was killed in action at Magersfontein, Dec. 11th, 1899, while endeavouring to save a wounded comrade. He was a son of Surgeon-Col. Sidney Ray, of Milton-next-Sittingbourne, Kent. He was born May, 1868, and educated at Wellington, where he was in the Hardinge, 1880-85, and in the latter year a Prefect. He was an excellent racquet player, and joined the Northumberland Fusiliers from the Royal Military College in Sept., 1887, being promoted lieut. Oct., 1890, capt. Dec., 1895, and brevet-major Nov., 1898. He had been adjutant of his battalion from 1895. He served in the campaign in the Soudan under Lord (then Sir Herbert)

Kitchener in 1898, and as adjutant to the 1st Batt. Northumberland Fusiliers, was present at the battle of Khartoum, being mentioned in despatches and receiving the brevet of major, the British medal and Khedive's medal with clasp. He also served in the occupation of Crete in 1898. While in South Africa Major Ray acted as assistant correspondent to *The Times* with Lieut.-Gen. Lord Methuen's column. When he fell he was with some M.I. on the right flank endeavouring to prevent a threatening movement of the enemy. This movement, Sir A. Conan Doyle writes, "would have put the Highlanders in an impossible position had it succeeded," and it was in this long and successful struggle to cover the flank of the 3rd Brigade that Major Milton, Major Ray, and many another brave man met his end."

Rayner.—Lieut. George Pritchard Rayner, 49 Co. I.Y., of Trescawen, Anglesey, died of enteric July 1st, 1900, at Bloemfontein. He was 29 years of age, and was educated at Eton (Mr. Merriott's). He was a lieut. in the Montgomeryshire Yeomanry Cavalry, joined the I.Y. in Feb., 1900, and served with it in South Africa up to the time of his death.

Reade.—Lieut. Robert Ernest Reade, D.S.O., 1st Batt. King's Royal Rifle Corps, M.I. Co., died Feb. 4th, 1901, of wounds received in action two days previously at Roodepoort, Boshman's Pan, half way between Middelburg and Ermelo. He was the second son of R. H. Reade, Esq., D.L., of Wilmont, co. Antrim, was born in April, 1879, and educated at Harrow and Trinity College, Cambridge. He was a good rider and Polo player. Lieut. Reade entered the King's Royal Rifle Corps in Aug., 1899, being promoted lieut. May, 1900. Joining the 1st battalion in Natal, Oct., 1899, he was present at the battle of Talana, the retirement to Ladysmith, and was in that town during the investment, being mentioned in despatches, L.G., Feb. 8th, 1901, by Lieut.-Gen. Sir George White, for conspicuous gallantry at the battle of Wagon Hill, where his determination and promptitude greatly contributed to re-occupying a position which had been seized by the enemy. Lieut. Reade had enteric after the relief and was invalided home, but rejoined at Middelburg in Dec., 1900, and was appointed to the M.I., with which he served till his death. On Feb. 2nd he was sent in command of a small party to support a patrol of 18th Hussars under Lieut. Cawston, both officers being mortally wounded, Lieut. Reade being hit in three places. He is buried in a high piece of ground called Boshman's Pan. Lieut. Reade was awarded the D.S.O., L.G., April 19th, 1901.

Rees.—Lieut. James Edward Rees, Western Light Horse (Rhodesia), was injured through a fall from his horse while on service with his regiment at Salisbury, June 2nd, 1902, and died on the 3rd, three days after Peace had been proclaimed. He was a fellow of the Royal Colonial Institute, and his name is inscribed on a memorial tablet in the hall of the building in Northumberland Avenue, S.W.

Reeves.—2nd Lieut. Evelyn Layard Reeves, 4th Batt. Somersetshire Light Infantry, was accidentally drowned while crossing a spruit near Baily, Oct. 29th, 1901. He was the eldest son of E. Gordon Reeves, Esq., of Ceylon, and was in his twentieth year. He was educated at Marlborough, and entered the 4th Batt. Somersetshire Light Infantry in June, 1900, and joined it in South Africa the following December, and served with it up to the time of his death. His name is inscribed on a tablet placed in Marlborough College Chapel in memory of all Marlburians who fell in the war.

Reid.—Civil Surgeon G. F. Reid was killed in action at Tweefontein in De Wet's attack on Christmas morning, 1901. Surgeon Reid was a widower, and previous to the war was practising at Bethlehem; but on Mr. Kruger sending his ultimatum, and war having become inevitable, Surgeon Reid offered his services, which were afterwards accepted. After the advance of F.-M. Earl Roberts into the Transvaal and the capture of Pretoria, Surgeon Reid served with the 3rd Division in the East of the O.R.C. He was later on doing duty at Harrismith, and being anxious to go to Bethlehem, where he possessed some property, Surgeon Reid volunteered to accompany, and proceeded with a column *en route* for that place. He was then employed with the forces protecting the Blockhouse line, and fell in the Boer attack on Tweefontein. He was well known in this district, and was beloved by all, both British and Boer, and the latter expressed the greatest sorrow at his death. He is buried in the military cemetery at Harrismith, a large crowd of civilians and soldiers having been present at his funeral. A cross marks his grave, and his name is inscribed on an obelisk which has been erected at Tweefontein in memory of all those who fell in this action.

Reid.—Lieut. James Cunninghame Corsane Reid, 3rd Batt. Somersetshire Light Infantry, was killed in action at Nooitgedacht, Dec. 13th, 1900. He was the eldest son of the late John James Reid, Esq., Queen's Remembrancer for Scotland, of Mouswald Place, Dumfriesshire, and of Mrs. Reid, of 24, the Avenue, Eastbourne. Lieut. Reid was born in Oct., 1881, and educated at Malvern College. He entered the 3rd Batt. Somersetshire Light Infantry in Nov., 1899, being promoted lieut. Aug., 1900. Soon after the commencement of the war he volunteered for active service, and was attached to the 1st Batt. Argyll and Sutherland Highlanders for duty

with the rank of 2nd lieut. in the army from March 7th
1900. He was subsequently sent to Bloemfontein, after
the occupation of that town. He was then posted to the
M.I. and served in the force under Lieut.-Gen. Sir Ian
Hamilton in the advance to Pretoria. Lieut. Reid saw
much service, and was present at Diamond Hill and
Wittebergen, and was awarded the medal with four
clasps.

Rennie.—Lieut. Coverley James Rennie, 2nd Batt.
Lincolnshire Regt., died at Rietfontein West, August
26th, 1901. He was born in Oct., 1874, entered the
Lincolnshire Regt. Oct., 1894, and was promoted lieut.
Nov., 1897. He served in the campaign in the Soudan
under Lord (then Sir Herbert) Kitchener, 1898, with
the 1st battalion of his regiment, and was present at the
battles of the Atbara (wounded, mentioned in despatches)
and Khartoum, receiving the British medal and Khedive's
medal with two clasps. He served in South Africa with his
battalion from Dec., 1899, and had been severely wounded.

Rennie.—Capt. John Rennie, Colonial Defence Force,
was killed in action at Buffelshoek, Bedford District.

Rhodes.—Lieut. John Fairfax Rhodes, 2nd Dragoons
(Scots Greys), was killed in action at Klippan, near
Springs, Feb. 18th, 1902. The only son of Fairfax
Rhodes, Esq., of Brockhampton Park, Gloucestershire,
and 29, Prince's Gardens, S.W., he was born in Dec., 1877,
and educated at Eton (Miss Evans'). He entered the 2nd
Dragoons in June, 1899, being promoted lieut. Sept., 1900.
He accompanied his regiment to South Africa in Oct.,
1899, and served throughout the war in the operations
in the north of Cape Colony, the relief of Kimberley, and
the advance on Bloemfontein and Pretoria. He subsequently served in the Transvaal. In the action in

which Lieut. Rhodes was killed, his squadron was suddenly attacked by the Boers and lost three officers. The remains of Lieut. Rhodes, accompanied by an escort of a sergeant and eight men of his regiment, were brought home and buried at Charlton Abbott's, near Cheltenham.

Richards.—Lieut. Herbert Samuel Richards, 2nd Batt. North Staffordshire Regt., died of enteric at Johannesburg, Jan. 18th, 1901. He was born April, 1880, educated at Brighton College, and entered the North Staffordshire Regt. in Feb., 1900, being promoted lieut. Dec. 11th, 1900.

Ritchie.—Lieut. Horace William Ritchie, 2nd Batt. North Staffordshire Regt., was first reported as missing at Waterval Drift, Feb. 15th, 1900, but it was afterwards found that he had been killed near Portze, about fifteen miles south of Jacobsdal. He was born in Jan., 1876, educated at Winchester, and entered the North Staffordshire Regt. Feb., 1896, being promoted lieut. Aug., 1898. He accompanied his battalion to South Africa in Jan., 1900.

Roach.—Lieut. J. J. Roach, Damant's Horse, was killed in action at Boshbult, March 31st, 1902.

Robbins.—Lieut. Donald Gorton Robbins, 21st Batt. I.Y. (Sharpshooters), was killed in action near Standerton, Aug. 22nd, 1901. He was the second son of William Edward Robbins, Esq., of Fairlawn, Bexley, Kent. Lieut. Robbins was educated at Berkhampstead School, and joined the I.Y., March 9th, 1901, with the rank of lieut. in the army. The name of Lieut. Robbins is engraved on a Latten Brass, placed in St. Paul's Cathedral, in memory of all ranks belonging to the 18th, 21st and 23rd Batt. I.Y., who fell in the war.

OFFICERS WHO FELL IN SOUTH AFRICA. 325

Robbins.—Lieut. John Henry Robbins, Queenstown Rifle Volunteers, was killed in action at Helpmakaar Farm, near Winburg, O.R.C., Aug. 25th, 1900. He was born in 1875, and educated at Highgate School. He went to South Africa in 1894, and on war being declared joined the Queenstown Corps as a private, and was quickly promoted sergeant, being afterwards granted a commission. The day Lieut. Robbins was killed the Queenstown Rifle Volunteers made a gallant defence. In Helpmakaar Farmhouse they succeeded in keeping off more than a 1,000 Boers, with three guns, under Olivier. When called on to surrender, the volunteers refused with contempt to do so, although 132 rounds from the guns had been fired at the house. Lieut. Robbins and those with him kept their position for two days, when help arrived, and the Boers retired. He is buried in Winburg cemetery. He was mentioned in despatches, L.G., April 16th, 1901.

Roberts.—Lieut. the Hon. Frederick Hugh Sherston Roberts, V.C., King's Royal Rifle Corps, died Dec. 17th, 1899, of wounds received in action two days previously at the battle of Colenso. He was the only surviving son of F.-M. Earl Roberts, Commander-in-Chief, and Nora his wife, was born at Umballa, Punjab, Jan., 1872, and was educated at Eton (Mr. Everard's). He entered the King's Royal Rifle Corps, from the Royal Military College, in June, 1891, being promoted lieut. June, 1894. He served with the Isazai Expedition in 1892, and with the Waziristan Field Force, 1894-95, as A.D.C. to the late Sir William Lockhart, commanding the force, being mentioned in despatches, and receiving the medal with clasp. He served with the Chitral Relief Force under Sir Robert Low, in 1895, with the 1st Batt. King's Royal Rifle Corps, including the capture of the Malakand Pass and the engagement at Khar, receiving the medal

with clasp. He also took part in the campaign in the
Soudan under Lord (then Sir Herbert) Kitchener, in 1898,
as extra A.D.C., and was present at the battle of Khartoum, was mentioned in despatches, appointed to the
Fourth Class of the Order of the Medjidie, and received
the British medal and Khedive's medal with clasp. He
was A.D.C. to the General Officer commanding the Forces
in Ireland from Dec., 1896, to the date of proceeding to
South Africa. At Eton and among all his intimate friends
he was known as "Freddy." Lieut. Roberts was appointed
A.D.C. to Sir Ian Hamilton, commanding an infantry
brigade in Ladysmith, but on arrival in South Africa was
unable to join his new chief owing to the investment of
that town by the Boers. He was present at the battle of
Colenso, where he acted at A.D.C. to Gen. Clery. In
this action he was mortally wounded in a gallant attempt
to save the guns of the 14th and 66th Batteries Royal
Field Artillery, as the detachments serving them had all
either been killed, wounded, or driven from the guns by
infantry fire at close range. The space Lieut. Roberts
had to pass over was swept with shell and rifle fire, and
in the attempt he fell from his horse mortally wounded.
He was then carried by Capt. Congreve and Major
Babtie to a nullah where there was some slight shelter.
For his gallantry Lieut. Roberts was awarded the V.C.,
L.G., Feb. 2nd, 1900. He is buried close to Chieveley
Station, on the Tugela. A memorial to Lieut. Roberts
has been erected in Wellington Barracks, St. James's
Park. (*See Capt. Cathcart.*)

Roberts.—Lieut. James Clarke Roberts, Victorian M.I.,
died at Rensburg, Feb. 12th, 1900.

Robertson.--Lieut. Albert Meyer Robertson, Mossel
Bay District Mounted Troops, died of enteric at Mossel
Bay, May 5th, 1902.

OFFICERS WHO FELL IN SOUTH AFRICA. 327

Robertson.—Civil Surgeon Charles Moir Robertson, died at Brugspruit, Oct. 25th, 1901.

Robertson.—Capt. Claude William Robertson, Royal Marine Light Infantry, serving with the 1st Regt. Australian Bushmen, was killed in action at Selous River, July 22nd, 1900. The third son of Mrs. Robertson, of Meadrow House, Godalming, he was born in Sept., 1868. He was educated at Charterhouse, and entered the Royal Marines in Sept., 1889, being promoted lieut. July, 1890, and capt. Jan., 1898. He served as a lieut. in the Royal Marine battalion landed from the squadron on the West Coast of Africa to punish the King of Benin for the massacre of the Political Expedition in 1897, which ended with the capture of Benin City, Feb. 18th of the same year. For this service he was mentioned in despatches and received the medal with clasp. He afterwards served on the Australian Station, and on the outbreak of war, being at Sydney, volunteered for active service. Being accepted, he proceeded to South Africa in command of B Company of the Australian Bushmen under Col. Airey, and landed at Beira. He was then sent to Buluwayo and served with the force for the relief of Mafeking. He afterwards moved towards Rustenburg, and was killed near Magato Pass as stated. Capt. Robertson is buried at Rustenburg. His name is inscribed on the monument in the Cambridge enclosure, St. James's Park, erected by all ranks of the Royal Marine Artillery and Light Infantry to the memory of their comrades who fell in South Africa and China; also on the tablet in the War Memorial Cloister at Charterhouse.

Robertson.—Capt. Crewe Robertson, Rhodesian Regt., was killed in action at Ramathlabama, near Mafeking, March 31st, 1900. (*See Lieut. Milligan.*)

Robertson.—Capt. Edgar Quartus Robertson, King's

Own Scottish Borderers, was killed in action at Stephanusdrai, July 29th, 1900. He was an Australian by birth, the only son of the late John Robertson, Esq., of Colac, Victoria, and the stepson of L. A. Corbett, Esq., of Waratah, Tiverton, Devon. Capt. Robertson was born in Feb., 1868, and educated at Clifton College. He entered the Scottish Borderers in June, 1889, being promoted lieut. Aug. 1891, Capt. May, 1899, and had served as adjutant at the depôt at Berwick. He went to South Africa with the 1st battalion of his regiment in Jan. 1900, and was placed in command of the M.I. company, and served under Lieut.-Gen. Sir Ian Hamilton. He was in the advance to Bloemfontein and Pretoria, and had been present at twenty-seven engagements before he fell, including Paardeberg and Diamond Hill. He was killed just before Prinsloo surrendered, it is stated by the last shot fired by the enemy. His company had prevented Prinsloo escaping through the Golden Gate, and Capt. Robertson had risen to look at the retreating Boers with his field glasses when a stray bullet struck him.

Robertson.—2nd Lieut. the Hon. Hugh Robertson, 14th Hussars, died from fracture of base of skull, Feb. 1st, 1901, the result of an accident at Johannesburg. He was the younger son of the Right Hon. Lord Robertson, of Porteviot; was born Sept., 1879, and educated at Radley from 1894-96, and afterwards at Eton (Mr. Rawlins'). 2nd Lieut. Robertson first served with the 3rd Batt. Queen's Own Cameron Highlanders from March, 1899, and was promoted lieut. at Aldershot in March, 1900. He volunteered for service in South Africa, and in May, 1900, was employed in the Remount Department. He was afterwards recommended for a commission by F.-M. Earl Roberts, Commander-in-Chief in South Africa; and in Oct., 1900, was appointed to the 14th Hussars as 2nd lieut., and served with that regiment up to the time of his death.

OFFICERS WHO FELL IN SOUTH AFRICA. 329

Robertson.—Capt. Stuart Robertson, 3rd Batt. the Black Watch (Royal Highlanders), attached to the 14th Hussars, died of enteric at Kroonstadt, June 1st, 1900. He was born in Jan., 1865, and joined the 14th Hussars as lieut., Aug. 1885, being promoted capt., Dec., 1889. He retired in 1898, and joined the 3rd Batt. the Black Watch as a capt. in July of the same year. On war being declared, Capt. Robertson volunteered for active service; and was seconded in March, 1900, to join his old corps, the 14th Hussars, in South Africa, and served with that regiment until his death. He is buried at Kroonstadt.

Robertson.—Major M. W. Robertson, Cape Mounted Rifles, served during the war, but was invalided home and died of enteric in England. He was a Fellow of the Royal Colonial Institute, and his name is inscribed on a memorial tablet in the hall of the building in Northumberland Avenue, S.W.

Robinson.—Major Sidney Loftus Robinson, 1st Batt. Argyll and Sutherland Highlanders, died of wounds received in action at Magersfontein, Dec. 11th, 1899. He was born in June, 1860, and entered the 93rd Foot from the Militia, July, 1879, being promoted lieut. in the Argyll and Sutherland Highlanders, July, 1881, capt. Nov., 1888, and major June, 1899. He was adjutant of his regiment from Nov., 1887, to Nov., 1891. Major Robinson served in the campaign on the North-West Frontier of India under the late Sir William Lockhart, 1897-98, with the Tochi Field Force, receiving the medal with clasp. He landed with his battalion in South Africa in Nov., 1899, and was present at the action of Modder River.

x *

Robison.—Lieut. Henry William Stuart Robison, 4th Batt. Manchester Regt., died at Freiberg, Baden, Dec. 23rd, 1901, from the effects of disease contracted on service in the Soudan and South Africa. He was the son of S. G. Robison, Esq., late R.N., and was born in March, 1877, and educated at Allhallowes School, Honiton. He entered the Manchester Regt. in Oct., 1899, having previously served over four and a half years in the ranks, and was promoted lieut. May, 1900. Before receiving his commission he served in the Soudan, being awarded the medal and bronze star, and in the South African Campaign he had held the position of Railway Staff Officer. He took part in the relief of Ladysmith, and was mentioned in despatches, L.G., Feb. 8th, 1901.

Rogers.—Lieut. Henry Paton Rogers, 2nd Batt. Wiltshire Regt., died of enteric at Bloemfontein, May 13th, 1900. He was born in April, 1874, educated at Clifton, and entered the Wiltshire Regt. Oct., 1894, being promoted lieut. July, 1896.

Rolfe.—Lieut. William Rolfe, Cape Mounted Rifles, died at Kimberley on Nov. 13th, 1900, of wounds received in action near Hoopstad, Kimberley, Oct. 23rd.

Rose.—Lieut. Bertram Temple Rose, Thorneycroft's M.I., died of enteric at the Base Hospital, Pietermaritzburg, March 30th, 1900. He was the son of Charles Day Rose, Esq., of Hardwick House, Pangbourne, and 53, Berkeley Square, now M.P. for the Newmarket Division of Cambridgeshire. Lieut. Rose was 25 years of age, and educated at Eton (Mr. Mitchell's). At Spion Kop, on Jan. 24th, 1900, he did splendid service. A messenger to Col. Thorneycroft was shot dead before he could deliver his errand. Lieut. Rose, who apparently knew the message, then crept over and shouted out to Col. Thorneycroft, " Sir Charles Warren has heliographed to say that you are in command, you are a general." Lieut. Rose was then sent with some orders directing the right to be reinforced. He lived through this and much other severe fighting on the Tugela, to die as stated. He was a brother of Capt. C. E. Rose.

Rose.—Capt. Charles Ernest Rose, Royal Horse Guards, was killed in action near Wellow (one report stated Welkom), May 4th, 1900. He was the eldest son of Charles Day Rose, Esq., of Hardwick House, Pangbourne, and 53, Berkeley Square, W., now M.P. for the Newmarket Division of Cambridgeshire. Capt. Rose was born in Dec., 1872, and educated at Eton (Mr. Ainger's.) He entered the Royal Horse Guards in April, 1892, was promoted lieut. April, 1893, and capt. Oct., 1899. He served in the operations on the North-West Frontier of India, 1897-98, with the Tirah Expeditionary Force as extra orderly officer, receiving the medal with two clasps. Capt. Rose also served in the operations in Sierra Leone, 1898-99, in the Protectorate Expedition, and in Nigeria, where he was specially employed from March, 1899, and was slightly wounded. In South Africa Capt. Rose had been on special service since March, 1900, and was employed with mounted infantry.

Rose.—Lieut. F. W. Rose, Cape Police, died at King William's Town, March 24th, 1900.

Ross.—Lieut. Alex Don Ross, 3rd New Zealand Contingent (Rough Riders), died of enteric, at Pretoria, Jan. 10th, 1901.

Ross.—Major Archibald John Joseph Ross, 2nd Batt. Royal Lancaster Regt. (The King's Own), was killed in action at Spion Kop, on the Upper Tugela, Jan 24th,

1900. He was born in Feb., 1859, and educated at Cheltenham. He entered the 4th Foot in May, 1878, and was promoted lieut. March, 1880, capt. March, 1888, and major May, 1894. Major Ross accompanied his battalion to South Africa in Nov., 1899, and served with the Ladysmith Relief Force. On Jan. 23rd he had been left in camp suffering acutely from dysentery, but on the 24th rumours of the terrible fighting going on reached him in his bed in hospital. Unknown to the medical officers, he appears to have left the hospital and to have climbed up to Spion Kop and joined his company in the firing line of his battalion. At dusk his body was found beside some of his men where his company had been fighting all day. His name is inscribed on the Eleanor Cross War Memorial at Cheltenham College.

Rowan. — Lieut. Ernest Courteney Rowan, Army Service Corps, died of enteric at Pretoria, Feb. 25th, 1901. He was born in Feb., 1872, and educated privately and at the High School, Woolwich. In Jan., 1900, he joined the 44th Company I.Y. as a trooper, and quickly rose to the rank of corporal and 2nd lieut. Embarking for South Africa in March, 1900, he saw much service and was awarded the medal with four clasps. At the time of his death he was attached to the Army Service Corps with the rank of lieut.

Royston.—Col.-Commandant William Royston, Natal Volunteer Force, died at Woodstock, Pietermaritzburg, April 6th, 1900. He served throughout the siege of Ladysmith, and was placed in command of one section of the defences. He was several times mentioned in despatches. Sir G. White in his despatch of Dec. 2nd, 1899, stated that "the services which Col. Royston and the forces under his command have rendered to the State and Colony have been of the very highest value";

OFFICERS WHO FELL IN SOUTH AFRICA. 333

and he is described as "a bold and successful leader," and "prompt and ready for any emergency." Col. Royston is again mentioned in the despatch of March 23rd, 1900, in connection with the sortie from Ladysmith of Dec. 7th, 1899, where his gallant behaviour is specially referred to; and finally Sir G. White writes, "I can only repeat the high praise which I had the pleasure to bestow on Col. Royston in my despatch of Dec. 2nd, 1899. He commanded Section D of the defences in an admirable manner," and "continued to the end to perform invaluable service "—" I trust that he may receive some suitable reward." Col. Royston was again mentioned in despatches, L.G., April 16th, 1901. A staff officer writes concerning him that he was "a very gallant soldier and his death was a great loss to the Natal Field Force."

Rudall.—Lieut. Rudall, Imperial Light Infantry, was killed in action at Spion Kop, Jan. 24th, 1900.

Rundle.—Lieut. William John Scott Rundle, D.S.O., 6th Dragoon Guards (Carabiniers), died at Beaufort West, July 30th, 1901, of wounds received in action at Kareebosch, July 19th. He was the eldest son of Dr. George E. Rundle, of Rooty Hill, New South Wales, and was born in March, 1876. He entered the 6th Dragoon Guards from the New South Wales Lancers in Oct., 1899, being promoted lieut. May, 1900. He proceeded to South Africa with his regiment in Oct., 1899, and was present at the operations at Colesberg, the relief of Kimberley, and the occupation of Bloemfontein. He had served in the engagements at Paardeberg, Poplar Grove, Driefontein, and Kroonstad, and took part in the operations under Lieut.-Gen. French at Doornfontein. Lieut. Rundle was appointed A.D.C. to Brigadier-Gen. J. R. P. Gordon, commanding the 3rd Cavalry Brigade, in Sept., 1900, and to Lieut.-Gen. French in Dec., 1900. He also served as adjutant of Brabant's Horse, and the day he was killed he was with the advanced guard of that corps. The Boers had been successfully forced back, when a stray shot struck Lieut. Rundle, severely wounding him in the head. He was mentioned in despatches, L.G., Feb. 8th, 1901, and awarded the D.S.O. He is buried at Beaufort West.

Russell.—Lieut. Cecil Pomeroy Russell, Leicester Regt., died of enteric at Intombi Field Hospital, Ladysmith, Jan. 5th, 1900. He was the eldest son of Col. C. J. Russell, R.E., retired, of Clavinia, Weymouth, was born in Nov., 1875, and educated at Weymouth College, where he was in the rifle team. He was also a good gymnast. He entered the Leicestershire Regt. from the Sligo Artillery Militia in June, 1896, being promoted lieut. April, 1899. He was present at the battle of Talana Hill with his battalion, and the subsequent retirement to Ladysmith, and also at the battle of Lombard's Kop. Several of his direct ancestors served in his regiment (formerly the 17th Foot), one of them at its formation in 1688 to 1729, and the next from 1727 to 1761. Lieut. Russell is buried in the cemetery at Intombi, and a marble cross and pedestal have been erected over the grave to his memory by his brother officers.

Russell.—2nd Lieut. Lionel Phillips Russell, 2nd Batt. West Yorkshire Regt., died Dec. 20th, 1901, of wounds received in action the previous day at Holland. He was the son of Sir W. R. Russell, of Flaxmere, Hastings. He was nominated by the Governor of New Zealand for a commission in the regular army, and was gazetted to his regiment in Jan., 1901, his commission bearing date July 18th, 1900. The day he received his mortal wound the British were suddenly attacked by several hundred Boers who were mistaken for friends, as they were dressed in khaki. 2nd Lieut. Russell fell while leading his men against largely superior numbers.

Russell.—2nd Lieut. Philip Leslie Russell, 17th Lancers, was killed in action at Modderfontein, near Tarkastad, Sept. 17th, 1901. He was born in March, 1878, and entered the 17th Lancers from the 4th Batt. South Staffordshire Regt., March, 1900. He had served with his militia battalion for fifty-one days during its embodiment, and was then granted a commission, and proceeded to South Africa, where he served with the 17th Lancers till his death. (*See Lieut. Morritt.*)

Russell-Brown.—Lieut. Frank Russell-Brown, 1st Batt. Royal Munster Fusiliers, died April 4th, 1900, of wounds received in action near Bloemfontein Waterworks, March 30th. He was the eldest son of the late Col. F. D. M. Brown, V.C., I.S.C., late 101st (now Royal Munster) Fusiliers. Lieut. Russell-Brown was born in March, 1872, and educated at Haileybury. He entered his father's old regiment in Dec., 1892, being promoted lieut. August, 1895. Lieut. Russell-Brown was first employed at Capetown, but in reply to several applications he had made in his great anxiety to join the army of F.-M. Earl Roberts, in active operations (his father had served under Earl Roberts's father), he was sent to Paardeberg. He then joined the M.I., and took part in the advance on Bloemfontein, but fell in his first battle. He married in Aug., 1899, Kathleen, second daughter of D. Colquhoun, Esq., who survives him.

Ryall.—Capt. Charles Ryall, West Yorkshire Regt., was killed in action in the operations on the Upper Tugela, Jan. 21st, 1900. He was born in Jan., 1869, and entered the West Yorkshire Regt. May, 1890, being promoted lieut. Feb., 1892, and capt. Feb., 1899.

Ryan.—Lieut. F. J. Ryan, 6th New Zealand M.I., was killed in action at Paardeplaats June, 16th, 1901.

Sale.—Lieut. A. A. Sale, Tasmanian Mounted Contingent (Bushmen), died April 9th, 1901, of wounds received in action the previous day at Pietersburg.

Salkeld.—Lieut. Philip Salkeld, Cape Mounted Police, was killed during the siege of Kimberley. He was a son of Col. Charles Salkeld, Royal Artillery.

Salmon.—Capt. R. W. Salmon, Victorian M.I., died of enteric at Naauwpoort, March 16th, 1900.

Salt.—Lieut. George Edmund Stevenson Salt, 1st Batt. Royal Welsh Fusiliers, died of enteric April 3rd, 1900, at Modder Spruit, near Ladysmith. He was the third son of Sir Thomas and Lady Salt, of Weeping Cross, Stafford. Lieut. Salt was born in Feb., 1873, and educated at Charterhouse. He entered the Royal Welsh Fusiliers in Dec., 1895, being promoted lieut. March, 1898. He accompanied his battalion to South Africa in Oct., 1899, and served with the Ladysmith Relief Force. He was present at the battle of Colenso and the subsequent fighting on the Tugela. His name is inscribed on the tablet in the War Memorial Cloister at Charterhouse.

Salter.—Capt. Philip Stanley Salter, 7th Batt. I.Y., was killed in action in the attack on Col. Kekewich's column, at Rooival, Transvaal, April 11th, 1902. He was the son of Philip Salter, Esq., of Newlands, Broadclyst, near Exeter. He joined the Devonshire Company of the I.Y. in Feb., 1900, and was promoted lieut. in Feb., 1901, and capt. in July. He served in South Africa from early in the war, and had been wounded at Kranspoort when helping a wounded comrade.

OFFICERS WHO FELL IN SOUTH AFRICA. 337

Sanders.—Major Francis Alexander Sanders, Royal Inniskilling Fusiliers, was killed in action Feb. 24th, 1900, in the operations on the Tugela. He was born in Dec., 1855, and entered the 27th Foot (now the Royal Inniskilling Fusiliers) from the Cavan Militia in Feb., 1878, being promoted lieut. Nov., 1878, capt. Feb., 1885, and major April, 1896. He was adjutant of his battalion from Feb., 1879-86. Major Sanders, who was 2nd-in-command of his battalion, was present at the battle of Colenso and all the fighting on the Tugela up to the time of his death. He is buried at the foot of the hill where he fell, beside Lieut.-Col. Thackeray and Lieut. Stuart. A marble headstone has been erected in their memory by comrades of all ranks of the 1st battalion. Major Sanders' name is also inscribed on an obelisk twenty-seven feet high, erected on the hill (commonly called Harts or Inniskilling or Railway Hill) in memory of all those of the Inniskillings who fell Feb. 23rd and 24th, 1900. He was mentioned in despatches, L.G., Feb. 8th, 1901. (*See Lieut.-Col. Thackeray.*)

Sanders.—Lieut. Lionel Salter Sanders, Imperial Light Horse, was killed in action near Klip Drift, July 31st, 1901.

Sandford.—Capt. Harry Coddington Sandford, Indian Staff Corps, was killed in action at Game Tree in the sortie from Mafeking, Dec. 26th, 1899. He was a member of the Shropshire family of that name residing at Sandford, near Whitechurch, was born in March, 1869, and educated at Allhallowes School, Honiton, and at Clifton. He entered the Royal Artillery, July, 1888, and was transferred to the Indian Staff Corps, March, 1890. He served in Burmah in 1892, receiving the medal and clasp. At Mafeking he was attached to the M.I. Our late beloved Queen showed her sympathy with his family by requesting that his photograph might be sent to her. This officer's death is referred to in the despatch of Major-Gen. Baden-Powell from Mafeking, dated May 18th, 1900, L.G., Feb. 8th, 1901. (*See Capt. Vernon.*)

Sargent.—Lieut. Henry Gresham Forbes Sargent, Indian Staff Corps, died of cholera at Sangor, India, on July 23rd, 1900, on his way to rejoin his regiment after service in South Africa. He was born in Jan., 1871, and was appointed 2nd lieut. in the Lancashire Fusiliers, Nov., 1891, being promoted lieut. Dec., 1892. Joining the Indian Staff Corps in August, 1893, he served in Thorneycroft's M.I., and was present at Spion Kop, where with a party of 29 men it is stated that he rendered splendid service, half of their number being killed.

Saunders-Knox-Gore.—Capt. Cecil Henry Saunders-Knox-Gore, Thorneycroft's M.I., late 6th Inniskilling Dragoons and Queen's Bays, was killed in action at Spion Kop, Jan. 24th, 1900. He was the third son of the late Major-General Saunders-Knox-Gore, R.A., of Belleek Manor, Ballina, co. Mayo, and Ardmore, Torquay, who died in 1902. Capt. Saunders-Knox-Gore was born in Feb., 1862. He entered the army from the R.M.C., passing out with honours, Jan., 1883, and first served in the West India Regt., but exchanged into the Inniskilling Dragoons, Nov., 1885, and afterwards into the Queen's Bays, retiring in 1895. When the war broke out he offered his services which were accepted and he was appointed capt. in Thorneycroft's M.I. He was present at the action at Acton Homes, and when he fell at Spion Kop an officer reports, "he was last seen standing up, pointing with his hand, and encouraging his men, at that moment a Boer bullet passed through his heart." Capt. Saunders-Knox-Gore is buried on Spion Kop, close to where he fell. Col. Thorneycroft wrote

OFFICERS WHO FELL IN SOUTH AFRICA. 339

concerning him, "His memory will ever remain dear to his comrades." Capt. Saunders-Knox-Gore was mentioned in despatches, L.G., Feb. 8th, 1901. (*See Lieut. Ellis.*)

Saunderson.—Capt. Llewellyn Traherne Saunderson, Rifle Brigade, died at Standerton, April 24th, 1902, of wounds received in action two days previously. He was the eldest son of Mr. and Lady Rachel Saunderson, of Dromkeen House, co. Cavan, and of St. Hilary, Glamorganshire. Capt. Saunderson was born in June, 1870, and entered the Rifle Brigade in Oct., 1890, being promoted lieut. June, 1892, and capt. Oct., 1897. When war was declared he was serving with the 4th Batt. of his regiment in Dublin, but volunteering for active service he was sent in March, 1901, to South Africa for duty with the M.I. and served there until his death.

Savory.—Capt. Albert Savory, 4th Hussars, attached to the South African Light Horse, died of wounds received in action South-West of Dalmanutha, Aug. 23rd, 1900. He was the eldest son of the late Albert Savory, Esq., of Sun Rising, Banbury, was born in July, 1878, and educated at Winchester. He entered the 4th Hussars in Oct., 1892, being promoted lieut. March, 1894. He had previously served in the operations on the North-West Frontier of India, 1897-98, with the Tirah Expeditionary Force, and was awarded the medal with clasp. At the time of his death he was serving as a captain in the South African Light Horse.

Schleswig-Holstein, Prince Christian Victor of.—Major His Highness Prince Christian Victor Albert Ludwig Ernst Anton, heir of Norway, Duke of Schleswig-Holstein, Stormarn and the Dithmarscher and of Oldenburg, G.C.B., G.C.V.O, 4th Batt. King's Royal Rifle

Corps, died at Pretoria of enteric Oct. 29th, 1900. He was born at Windsor Castle, April 14th, 1867, and was educated at Wellington and Magdalen College, Oxford. He was an excellent sportsman and cricketer, and at Wellington was in the eleven for three years, during one of which (1885) he was the captain. He was a Master of Arts by diploma of the University of Oxford. Prince Christian Victor entered the King's Royal Rifle Corps from the Royal Military College in Aug., 1888, being promoted lieut. June, 1890, capt. Dec. 3rd, 1896, and brevet-major on the following day. During his military career he had seen much active service, his first experience being in the Hazara Expedition, 1891, was mentioned in despatches, L.G., Oct. 20th, 1891, and received the medal with clasp. He also served in the Miranzai Expedition, 1891 (clasp), and the Isazai Expedition, 1892. He next served in the Ashanti Expedition, 1895-96, being mentioned in despatches, was granted the star and promoted to a brevet-majority. He was also in the Nile Expedition of 1898, mentioned in despatches, L.G., Sept. 30th, 1898, and was granted the 4th Class of the Osmanieh and the medal. During this expedition, on one occasion he had to jump and swim ashore from a sinking gun-boat, with the loss of practically all his belongings. In 1899 Prince Christian Victor had been specially selected for the Staff College, but on the war breaking out he volunteered for active service, and went out to South Africa as assistant staff officer to the 2nd Infantry Brigade. He was present at all the fighting up to the Relief of Ladysmith, including the battle of Colenso, and the actions at Spion Kop, Vaal Kranz, Monte Christo, and Pieter's Hill. At the battle of Colenso a bullet passed through his wallet. He was afterwards present at Alleman's Nek and the advance into the Transvaal. Prince Christian was mentioned in despatches, L.G., Feb. 8th, 1901, also in the despatch of

F.-M. Earl Roberts, L.G., April 16th, 1901, in the following words, "The much to be regretted death of His Highness occurred before I had forwarded the recommendation for reward, which he so well deserved. His sterling qualities as a soldier, his unfailing courtesy and attention to his duties had endeared him to all with whom he came in contact, and his early death is a real loss to the army." A statue to the memory of Prince Christian Victor is being erected at Windsor near the foot of the hundred steps leading to Windsor Castle from Thames Street. The statue, which will be of bronze, will represent the Prince standing bare-headed, with one foot on a boulder and both hands resting on the hilt of his sword. Below will be an inscription, with shields right and left bearing the Prince's coat of arms on one side, and the badge of his regiment on the other.

Schnadhorst.—Lieut. Frank Gladstone Schnadhorst, Kitchener's Fighting Scouts, died Oct. 22nd, 1901, of wounds received in action at Heilbron, O.R.C., on the 4th *idem*. He was the youngest son of the late Francis Schnadhorst, Esq., of Birmingham. Lieut. Schnadhorst was twenty-one years of age, educated at Leys School, Cambridge, and Malvern, and served continuously for eighteen months in South Africa. He had been granted a commission as 2nd lieut. in the Lancashire Fusiliers from June, 1901, for the good service he had rendered, but this advancement was afterwards cancelled, at his own request, as he preferred to serve with the Fighting Scouts. He had also held a commission as lieut. in the Commander-in-Chief's Bodyguard.

Schreiber.—Lieut. Clare Basil Schreiber, 66th Battery, Royal Field Artillery, was killed in action at the battle of Colenso, Dec. 15th, 1899. He was the son of the late Percy Schreiber, Esq., of the Royal Scots. He was born Dec., 1873, and entered the Royal Artillery, from the Lancashire Artillery Militia, July, 1895, being promoted lieut. July, 1898. He proceeded to South Africa with his battery in Oct., 1899, and served with the Natal Field Force. At the battle of Colenso Lieut. Schreiber was instantaneously killed. He was mentioned in despatches, L.G., Feb. 8th, 1901. (*See Capt. Goldie.*)

Schwabe.—Lieut. Horace Foster Schwabe, 2nd Batt. I.Y,, died of typhlitis at Johannesburg, Sept. 25th, 1901. He was the son of the late H. A. Schwabe, Esq., of Lymm, Cheshire, and was twenty-five years of age. Lieut. Schwabe joined the 103rd Company, I.Y., in April, 1901, with the rank of lieut. in the army.

Scobell. — Lieut. John Francis Scobell, 1st Batt. Leicester Regt., died of enteric at Vrede, March 6th, 1901. He was the eldest son of the late Rev. John F. Scobell, was born in June, 1877, and educated at Marlborough. He entered the Leinster Regt. from the 4th Batt. South Staffordshire Regt., Dec., 1897, being promoted lieut. May, 1900. On the outbreak of the war, Lieut. Scobell was serving with his battalion in Halifax, N.S. It was, however, brought home to Aldershot for mobilization, and left for South Africa in April, 1901, Lieut. Scobell accompanying it and serving with it until his death. His name is inscribed on a tablet placed in Marlborough College Chapel in memory of all Marlburians who fell in the war.

Scott.—Capt. Henry Farquhar Scott, 3rd Batt. Royal Berkshire Regt., was killed in action near Hout Kop, June 14th, 1901. He was educated at Eton (Mr. Austen Leigh's), entered his regiment in April, 1897, and was granted the temporary rank of capt. in the army March,

1901, on being employed on special service with M.I. in South Africa.

Scott.—Commandant Scott, when war broke out, was at Vryburg, the capital of British Bechuanaland. The townspeople sympathised with the Boers, but Commandant Scott tried to organise the defence of the town. He then called for volunteers, but got little encouragement, only six men responding. Having no artillery, and getting no sympathy, and being opposed by influential citizens, he was compelled to abandon his charge to the invaders. He then, in great disappointment at his inability to hold Vryburg, rode south with his small detachment of police. He died on his way to reach the British forces.

Seagrim.—Capt. Dudley Gillum Seagrim, p.s.c., Royal Garrison Artillery, died of abscess of the liver at Capetown, May 15th, 1900. He was born July, 1867, educated at Clifton College, and entered the Royal Artillery in July, 1886, being promoted capt. July, 1897. He had qualified as an interpreter in French. He served with the Burmese Expedition, 1885-89, receiving the medal with two clasps; with the Zhob Valley Expedition in 1890; and with the Isazai Field Force, 1892. He also served with the Waziristan Expedition under the late Sir William Lockhart, 1894-95, including the delimitation escort and attack on camp at Wano, for which he received a clasp. He was appointed March 30th, 1899, A.D.C. to the Lieut.-Gen. commanding in the Punjab, but volunteering for active service was selected for special duty in South Africa in Jan., 1900, and served there until his death.

Seale.—Capt. John Whiteaway Seale, Cape Police, died of enteric at Wynberg on March 5th, 1902.

Seeds.—Capt. James Thomson Seeds, 5th Batt. Royal Irish Rifles, died of dysentery and heart failure at Kroonstad, June 1st, 1901. He was the son of the late W. Seeds, Esq., of Ballymott House, near Downpatrick, was born in Oct., 1870, and educated at the High School, Dublin. He was called to the bar in 1895, took his B.A. degree in the same year, M.A. 1898, and LL.D. 1899, at Trinity College, Dublin. He entered the 5th Batt. Royal Irish Rifles, Feb., 1899, was promoted lieut. May, 1900, capt. March, 1901; and volunteering for active service proceeded to South Africa in April, 1901, with his battalion. His name is inscribed on a tablet erected by his comrades in Down Cathedral in memory of all belonging to the 5th Batt. Royal Irish Rifles who fell during the war.

Selous.—Lieut. Harry Dyson Selous, 2nd Batt. Bedfordshire Regt., was killed in action at Paardeberg, Feb. 18th, 1900. He was born in July, 1873, and educated at University College School and Brighton College. He entered the Bedfordshire Regt. in March, 1894, being promoted lieut. Sept., 1896. He was serving at the depôt in 1899, and joined his battalion in South Africa in Jan., 1900.

Senior.—Capt. Guy Senior, Royal Marine Artillery, was killed at Graspan, Nov. 25th, 1899, in the splendid advance made by the Naval Brigade at that action. He was born in Dec., 1875, and was appointed 2nd lieut. Sept., 1893, being promoted lieut. July, 1894, and capt. in June, 1899. He belonged to H.M.S. "Monarch." Capt. Senior was killed instantaneously while leading his men to attack the Boer position. He was first buried near Graspan, close to where he fell, but on Nov. 26th, the day after the battle, his body was moved, and lies near Enslin Station, beside Major Plumbe and Commander Ethelston—a cross marks their graves. The name of Capt. Senior is inscribed on the monument in the Cambridge Enclosure, St. James's Park, erected by their comrades of both corps to the memory of all ranks of the Royal Marine Artillery and Light Infantry who fell in South Africa and China.

Seymour.—Major L. J. Seymour, Cape Pioneer Railway Regt., was killed in action at Zand River, July 14th, 1900. He was an Australian by birth, but was well known in South Africa. At an early age he was consulting engineer of a South American firm, and afterwards served in a similar capacity in the De Beers mines, at Kimberley. Thence he went to Johannesburg where he was employed as chief engineer by Messrs. Eckstein. At the outbreak of the war he raised the Pioneer Railway Company, chiefly composed of mining employés of the Rand, and was appointed major. He was killed while superintending the repair of the railway line to Johannesburg. In the report from Virginia, June 15th, 1900, Lieut.-Col. Capper, describing the action at Zand River, mentions that he "especially deplored the death of Major Seymour, whose loss will not only be felt by us as a regiment, but by the whole of South Africa." He was killed while advancing with the extended line through the bush to clear out the snipers; L.G., Feb. 8th, 1901. Major Seymour was twice mentioned in despatches, L.G., Sept. 10th, 1901.

Shafto.—Lieut. Charles Duncombe Shafto, 1st Batt. Durham Light Infantry, was killed in action in the operations on the Upper Tugela, Feb. 5th, 1900. He was born June, 1878, entered his regiment in Feb., 1898, and was promoted lieut. Jan., 1900. He accompanied his battalion to South Africa in Oct., 1899, and served with the Natal Field Force.

Shand.—Lieut. William Jorie Shand, 1st Batt. Queen's

Own Cameron Highlanders, died Dec. 22nd, 1901, of wounds received in action at Tafelkop, O.R.C., two days previously. He was born March, 1878, educated at Rugby, and entered the Cameron Highlanders from the 3rd Batt. Highland Light Infantry in Jan., 1899, being promoted lieut. the following Dec. He was adjutant of Rimington's Guides, and subsequently attached to Damant's Horse. Lieut. Shand was mentioned in despatches, L.G., April 25th, 1902, for having, with Capt. Webb, " charged forward to a ridge which they held till all but two of their men were killed or wounded, thereby in a great measure saving the guns." Of seven N.C. officers and men, mentioned in despatches for having taken part in this charge, four were killed.

Sharpe.—2nd Lieut. James Minot Sharpe, 4th Batt. North Staffordshire Regt. (3rd King's Own Stafford Militia), died at Carnarvon, Cape Colony, Feb. 23rd, 1902, of wounds received in action near Carnarvon two days previously. He was the eldest son of James Sharpe, Esq., of the War Office, and was twenty years of age. He joined his regiment in Oct., 1901. He had served in the war, 1900-1901, in the Imperial Light Horse.

Shaw.—Lieut. Percy Costello Shaw, 3rd Batt. Royal Munster Fusiliers, died of enteric May 28th, 1900, at Bloemfontein. He entered his regiment Oct., 1899, and proceeded with his battalion to South Africa in April, 1900.

Shaw-Stewart.—Capt. Houston Michael Shaw-Stewart, D.S.O., 17th Lancers, was accidentally drowned July 28th, 1901, while on voyage home from South Africa in S.S. "Canada." He was the son of Sir Michael Robert Shaw-Stewart of Ardgowan, Greenock, by his marriage with Lady Octavia Grosvenor, and therefore a grandson of

Richard, second Marquis of Westminster. He was born in Oct., 1871, and educated at Eton (Mr. Austen Leigh's), where he was second for the Jelf Prize in 1877. He then went to Christ Church, Oxford. Capt. Shaw-Stewart entered the 17th Lancers from the 4th Batt. Argyll and Sutherland Highlanders in Dec., 1894, being promoted lieut. Nov., 1895, and capt. Jan., 1900. He went out to South Africa with his regiment in Feb., 1900, and saw much service during the war. He was mentioned in despatches, L.G., Sept., 10th, 1901, and was awarded the D.S.O. His brother officers have placed a tablet to his memory in St. John's Episcopal Church, Greenock, as a token of their regard and affection.

Shea.—2nd Lieut, Geoffrey Norman Shea, 1st Batt. Royal Munster Fusiliers, was killed at Schotland West, Kroonstad District, April 20th, 1902. He was the son of Mrs. Shea, Village House, Bradfield, was born in Dec., 1880, and educated at Bradfield College, where he played in the football team and was lieut. in the College Rifle Corps. He passed direct from Bradfield into Sandhurst, and passed out first on the list from the Royal Military College in Dec., 1900, gaining the Sword of Honour and the Victoria Medal. 2nd Lieut. Shea entered the army Jan., 1901, was appointed to the Royal Munster Fusiliers March, 1901, and served with them in South Africa up to the time of his death.

Shepherd.—Capt. Charles Shepherd, South African Light Horse, died of enteric at Springfontein, on July 22nd, 1901.

Shepherd.—Lieut. Richard Edmund Shepherd, Yorkshire Light Infantry, was killed in action near Brakenlaagte (20 miles north-west of Bethel), on Oct. 31st, 1901. He was the only son of Col. C. H. Shepherd, D.S.O., lately commanding the 9th Regimental District, Norwich, was born in May, 1875, and educated at Wellington College, where he was for two years in the cricket eleven. He obtained his first commission in the 4th Batt. Essex Regt., April, 1894, in which he was gazetted capt. in May, 1897. He had served in the British South African Police from June, 1898, and was granted a commision as 2nd lieut., Aug. 30th, 1899, in the Yorkshire Light Infantry, being promoted lieut. Aug., 1900. He served with the M.I. from the commencement of the war and was present at the actions of Belmont, Graspan, Magersfontein, relief of Kimberley, and the battles of Paardeberg, Driefontein and Diamond Hill. Lieut. Shepherd was mentioned in despatches and granted the medal with seven clasps.

Sheridan.—Lieut. Richard Brinsley Sheridan, 17th Lancers, was killed in action at Modderfontein, near Tarkastad, on Sept. 17th, 1901. He was born in May, 1874, and educated at Harrow. He entered the 17th Lancers from the 3rd Batt. Royal Scots (Lothian Regt.), in June, 1896, being promoted lieut. April, 1898. Lieut. Sheridan accompanied his regiment to South Africa in Feb., 1900, and served throughout the war up to his death. (*See Lieut. Morritt.*)

Sherrard.—Major John Meade Sherrard, Army Pay Department, died of erysipelas on Nov. 6th, 1900, at Bloemfontein. He was born March, 1848, and was appointed paymaster in the Army Pay Department, May, 1881, and became hon. major in May, 1886, and staff paymaster Oct., 1895. Before entering the Army Pay Department Major Sherrard served regimentally for nearly fourteen years.

Sherston.—Lieut.-Col. John Sherston, D.S.O., p.s.c.,

Rifle Brigade, was killed in action at the battle of Talana Hill, Oct. 20th, 1899. He was the son of Capt. Sherston, formerly of the 6th Dragoon Guards, of Evercreech House, Bath. Lieut.-Col. Sherston was born in July, 1857, and educated at Marlborough. He entered the 75th Foot Feb., 1876, and was transferred to the Rifle Brigade, Feb., 1877, being promoted lieut. Feb., 1878, capt. August, 1884, major Nov., 1894, and lieut.-col. Feb., 1899. He served in the Afghan War, 1878-80, as A.D.C. to his uncle, F.-M. Earl (then Sir Frederick) Roberts, and was present in the engagement at Charasiah, Oct. 6th, 1879, and subsequent pursuit of the enemy (mentioned in despatches), and the operations around Kabul in Dec., 1879, including the investment of Sherpur (mentioned in despatches). He accompanied F.-M. Earl Roberts in the march from Kabul to Kandahar, and was present at the battle of Sept. 1st (mentioned in despatches, medal with three clasps, and bronze decoration). He served with the 4th Batt. Rifle Brigade in the Mahsood Wuzeeree Expedition, 1881, and with the Burmese Expedition in 1886-87, as brigade-major (mentioned in despatches, D.S.O., and medal with clasp). He was brigade-major in Bengal, Feb., 1887, to Sept., 1888, district staff officer, 2nd class, and D.A.A.G., Bengal, Oct., 1888, to March, 1891, D.A.A.G. in India, March, 1893, to Oct., 1898 (additional A.A.G. Head Quarters, India, April, 1895, to August, 1897). From Oct., 1898, till his departure for South Africa, he was A.A.G. in India. In Natal he was serving on the staff of Sir W. P. Symons, and fell while close to him at the edge of the wood in the first battle of the war. Lieut.-Col. Sherston is buried at Talana, and his name is inscribed on a tablet placed in Marlborough College Chapel in memory of all Marlburians who fell in the war.

Showers.—Lieut.-Col. Eden Currie Showers, 2nd-in-command of Lumsden's Horse and late Commandant

Surma Valley Light Horse Volunteers, was killed in action near Thaba N'chu, April 30th, 1900. He was the son of the late Major-Gen. St. George Daniel Showers, of Fort William, Calcutta, and late of Cheltenham. Lieut.-Col. Showers was educated at Edinburgh Academy, and at Wellington, where he was in the Blucher from 1859-62, and played for the school in both the cricket and football teams. He served for some time in the Bengal Constabulary, and had been a tea planter in Assam. A monument, raised by public subscription, has been erected to his memory at Silchar.

Sidney.—Quartermaster and Hon. Lieut. Thomas Alfred Winsmore Sidney, Army Ordnance Department, died of enteric on Jan. 10th, 1901, at East London. He was born in June, 1864, and served in the ranks for nearly twelve years, was a warrant-officer for three and a half years, being promoted assistant-commissary of ordnance April 19th, 1899. He went to South Africa in Oct., 1899, and served there continuously up to his death.

Simpson.—2nd Lieut. Francis James Thomas Uniacke Simpson, Royal Scots Fusiliers, was killed in action at Pieter's Hill on Feb. 27th, 1900. He was born in Nov., 1879, educated at Cheltenham, and entered the Royal Scots Fusiliers from the 5th Batt. Royal Inniskilling Fusiliers in Oct., 1899. 2nd Lieut. Simpson had served through the campaign with the Natal Field Force up to the time of his death. His name is inscribed on the Eleanor Cross War Memorial at Cheltenham College.

Simpson.—Lieut. Tom Thorp Simpson, 1st Batt. Shropshire Light Infantry, died of dysentery at Schhoeman's Kloof on April 30th, 1901. He was a son of Dr. W. S. Simpson, was born in May, 1877, and educated at

Lancing College. He entered the Shropshire Light Infantry from the 4th Batt. in May, 1899, being promoted lieut. Aug., 1900. Lieut. Simpson had served with the 2nd battalion of his regiment in South Africa from the commencement of the war.

Siordet.—Lieut. Frederick John Siordet, West Riding Regt., was killed in action at Paardeberg, Feb. 18th, 1900. He was born in Dec. 1871, educated at Blundell's School, Tiverton, and entered the West Riding Regt. in May, 1891, being promoted lieut. Jan., 1895. This officer's death is mentioned in the despatch of F.-M. Earl Roberts from Paardeberg, Feb. 28th, 1900.

Sitwell.—Major and Brevet-Lieut.-Col. Claude George Henry Sitwell, D.S.O., Royal Dublin Fusiliers, was killed in action in the operations on the Upper Tugela of Feb. 23rd and 24th, 1900. He was the son of Capt. G. T. Sitwell, formerly of the 3rd Dragoons, was born in Oct., 1858, and educated at Haileybury. He entered the 85th Foot from the Huntingdon Militia in Sept., 1878, was promoted lieut. July, 1881, capt. Sept., 1886, transferred to the Manchester Regt. Feb., 1889, being promoted major in the 2nd Batt. Royal Dublin Fusiliers Oct., 1898, and brevet-lieut.-col. Oct., 1899. He served in the Afghan War, 1879-80, with the Kuram Division, Yarmusht Expedition (medal). He also served in the Egyptian War of 1882 with the 1st Batt. Shropshire Light Infantry, took part in the defence of Alexandria, and the occupation of Kafr Dowar and surrender of Damietta, receiving the medal and Khedive's star. Lieut.-Col. Sitwell was in East Africa from 1895-98, and was in command of Expeditions against Kitosh, Kabras, and Kikelwa tribes. He was also in the Nandi Expedition in 1895, when he was mentioned in despatches. He served in Uganda 1897-98 when he commanded the Expedition against Mwanga, and was present at the action near Katonga River and other engagements, being mentioned in despatches, and receiving the brevet of lieut.-col. and D.S.O. Lieut.-Col. Sitwell served with the 2nd battalion of his regiment with the Natal Field Force, and was present at the fighting on the Tugela, being mentioned in despatches, L.G., Feb. 8th, 1901. He married in 1887, Amy, daughter of R. B. Cooke, Esq. (*See Lieut.-Col. Thackeray.*)

Skene.—Lieut. William Skene, Kitchener's Horse, was killed in action at Nooitgedacht, Dec. 13th, 1900. He was the son of T. Skene, Esq., member of the Commonwealth Parliament of Australia, whose father was a member of the Legislative Council of Victoria. Lieut. Skene's mother was the second daughter of Dr. Anderson, who, as private medical officer, accompanied the ninth Baron Napier to China in 1830. Lieut. Skene was born Dec., 1875, at Basset, Branxholme, in the Western District of Victoria, and was educated at the Western District College, Hamilton, and at the Church of England Grammar School, Geelong, where he was a lieut. in the Volunteer Cadet Corps. Subsequently he held a lieut.'s commission in the William's Town Garrison Artillery with a view to adopting the regular army as his profession. Some change in the age regulation, however, prevented his competing, and he then worked on his father's property at Marmoo in the North-West District of Victoria. In Dec., 1899, being anxious to serve the Empire, he, with great difficulty, procured a passage for himself and his horse to Capetown, and on arrival was given a commission as lieut. in Roberts' Horse, and assisted to drill recruits at Rosebank Camp. He was subsequently offered a 2nd lieutenancy in the Royal Field Artillery, for which he had been recommended by the acting Governor of Victoria (Sir John

Madden), but through some mistake the order to join his new corps to which he was gazetted with seniority from May 23rd, 1900, did not reach him, although he was at the time at Rosebank. Lieut. Skene then proceeded to Vereeniging, May 26th, 1900, and was present at the entry into Johannesburg and Pretoria and the battle of Diamond Hill. At Vredefort he was thanked for his services by Col. Ridley. He was also at Elands River where the Australians so distinguished themselves, and in the fighting at Rustenburg and the Magaliesberg, being again in Pretoria in Aug., 1900. Here his appointment to the Royal Artillery reached him, but preferring to remain with his old corps he resigned his commission in the Royal Field Artillery. Lieut. Skene then served with Clements' Column, in which he acted as squadron leader, and afterwards in the O.R.C. in the fighting near Bethlehem and the operations against Gen. De Wet. On Dec. 13th, at the first break of dawn, the camp was attacked, and Lieut. Skene in a half-clad state rushed out to reinforce a picket of M.I. The Boers on a ridge met the advancing men with a terrific fire. Col. Legge was one of the first to fall, shot through the head, and Lieut. Skene was mortally wounded. He, however, until exhausted, continued to call to his men " go on and fight it out," and to his sergeant-major (McNaughton), " Fight on, Mac," when he fell forward on his face dead. Col. Cookson, writing of him, said he was "leading his squadron most gallantly to reinforce the pickets, and this prompt action saved the situation."

Skirving.—Lieut. G. McB. Skirving, 101st Co. 5th Batt. I.Y., died on Sept. 8th, 1901, of wounds received in action at Rhenosterfontein three days previously. He was mentioned in the despatch of Gen. Lord Kitchener, Oct. 8th, 1901, for his "gallantry at Rhenosterfontein" the day he was wounded. Lieut. Skirving had served as a sergeant in Lord Strathcona's Corps, and was appointed to the I.Y. with rank of lieut. in April, 1901.

Slater.—Lieut. Sydney Arthur Slater, D.S.O., 57th Co. 15th Batt., I.Y., died of enteric at Kroonstad, O.R.C., Jan. 29th, 1901. He was the son of the late E. Slater, Esq., of Ashville, Farsley, and Slingsby Hall, Yorkshire; was born in Dec., 1872, and educated at Giggleswick School, near Settle, and at Exeter College, Oxford. He held a commission as a 2nd lieut. in the 3rd V.B. West Yorkshire Regt., but early in 1900 volunteered for active service with the I.Y. In March he was appointed lieut. in the 57th Company, and, proceeding to South Africa, served in the Cape and Orange River Colonies. With ten men, Lieut. Slater is stated to have made a clever capture of Boers in Bultfontein, and, in Sept., when attacked, he made an able defence of the place, and held the enemy at bay until relief arrived. He was mentioned in despatches, L.G., Sept. 10th, 1891, being granted the D.S.O., and received a letter of congratulation from F.-M. Earl Roberts. A tablet has been erected to Lieut. Slater's memory in Giggleswick School.

Smith.—Civil Surgeon E. Smith, attached for duty to the Royal Army Medical Corps, died during the war.

Smith.—Lieut. W. Dixon Smith, Border Mounted Rifles, died in Ladysmith, on Jan. 13th, 1901.

Southey.—Lieut. Arthur Melville Southey, 2nd Batt. Scots Guards, was killed in action at Tiger's Kloof on Nov. 23rd, 1900. He was born Oct., 1872, educated at Eton (Mr. Warre Cornish), and entered the Scots Guards in April, 1892, being promoted lieut. in April, 1897. Lieut. Southey belonged to the 3rd battalion, but volunteering for active service was transferred to the 2nd battalion and proceeded to South Africa in May, 1900.

Sowerby.—Lieut. Francis Hubert Airey Sowerby, 3rd Batt. Durham Light Infantry, died of dysentery at Kroonstad, O.R.C., on April 21st, 1901. He was educated at Wellington (Kempthornes from 1888-90), and entered the 3rd Batt. Durham Light Infantry in Sept., 1898, being promoted lieut. Dec., 1900. He volunteered for active service, and accompanied his battalion to South Africa in Feb., 1900, and is reported to have served with distinction.

Spandow.—Capt. H. J. A. Spandow, Midland Mounted Rifles, was killed in action at Water Kloof, near Craddock, on June 20th, 1901.

Spence.—Col. William Alexander Spence, V.D., late Middlesex Regt., was killed in action near Douglas, May 30th, 1900. He was the son of the late Capt. S. Spence, 28th Gloucestershire Regt., and was educated at Wellington, where he was in the Anglesea from 1859-62, and a Prefect. He entered the 77th Middlesex Regt., from the Royal Military College, Sandhurst, in 1863, and served with it until 1875, when he retired and settled for a time in New Zealand, where he was adjutant of the Volunteer force. He resided at Capetown for many years, where he was adjutant of the Duke of Edinburgh's Own Volunteer Corps, and had commanded it since Dec., 1890. He was always a keen soldier, and popular with all ranks. In 1897 Col. Spence served in the Bechuanaland Expedition. The day he was killed he had brought up 400 of his battalion in admirably extended order to attack the Boers. Although under a heavy fire their losses were slight, three killed and four wounded, but one of the former was Col. Spence. He exposed himself for a moment to give some orders and was immediately struck down. Two of his sons had served in the corps with him, one was granted a commission in his father's old regiment (the Middlesex) in March, 1900, and the other was in the action at which his father lost his life. Col. Spence was mentioned in despatches, L.G., Feb. 8th, 1901, by Sir Charles Warren for his excellent services in the following words: "I regret very much the loss of Col. Spence, commanding Duke of Edinburgh's Own Volunteer Rifles, a most gallant and efficient commanding officer."

Spencer.—2nd Lieut. A. Spencer, Cape Volunteer Medical Staff Corps, died at Krugersdorp on Sept. 26th, 1900.

Spicer.—Lieut. Arthur Reginald William Spicer, 3rd Batt. King's Royal Rifle Corps, died of enteric at Germiston on May 8th, 1901. He was the youngest son of the late Richard Spicer, Esq., born in June, 1878, and educated at Eton (Mr. Everard's and Mr. Benson's). He entered the King's Royal Rifle Corps from the 7th battalion in May, 1899, being promoted lieut. April, 1900. Lieut. Spicer embarked for South Africa in Oct., 1899, and served throughout the war with his battalion.

Spratt.—Lieut. H. Devereux Spratt, 23rd Co. I.Y., died at Mortimer on June 3rd, 1902, of wounds received the previous day at Waterval. He received his death wound, therefore, two days after the treaty of peace was signed. He was the second son of the late Richard Spratt, Esq., of Pencil Hall, Mallow. His mother was a daughter of the late H. Baldwin Foott, Esq., of Carrigacunna Castle, co. Cork. Lieut. Spratt was 35 years of age, a graduate of Trinity College, Dublin, an ardent sportsman, a good rider, and was well-known with the Duhallow Hounds. He was a barrister and gave up a good appointment soon after the war broke out in order to go on active service. In 1900 he was wounded, and also suffered from fever, and was therefore ordered to England in Dec., but having recovered he again went out in the I.Y., and served from March, 1901. Lieut. Spratt saw much service during the war, and latterly was in the columns commanded by Col. Henniker-Major and Lieut.-Col. Doran. The day he was killed Lieut. Spratt was with a party of 20 men, but the Boer commandant, not being aware that peace had been declared, opened fire, and Lieut. Spratt and two men were mortally wounded.

Spreckley. — Lieut.-Col. J. A. Spreckley, C.M.G., Rhodesian Protectorate Regt., was killed in action at Klip Drift, Aug. 20th, 1900. He was the son of Mr. and Mrs. Spreckley of Bournemouth, was born in March, 1865, and educated at Derby School. When seventeen years of age he went to South Africa, and had served in the operations of 1896, being awarded the C.M.G. At the outbreak of the South African War, he joined Maj.-Gen. Plumer's force for the relief of Mafeking. The day he fell his party were surrounded by some Boers, who, being dressed in khaki, were first taken for friends. When the mistake was discovered and Lieut.-Col. Spreckley and his party were called upon to surrender, he replied, " Never, give it to them, lads," and was immediately killed. By his death, Rhodesia lost one of its best known and most popular men. He saw much service during the war, the gallant Rhodesian Regt. to which he belonged having been in many battles and actions. Lieut.-Col. Spreckley was mentioned in despatches, L.G., April 16th, 1901.

Sprenger.—Major C. F. Sprenger, Cape Mounted Rifles, was killed in the fighting round Wepener, April 9th, 1900. He had been a major in the corps since July, 1896. His first war service was in the operations against Langalibalele in 1873. He also took part in the Galeka and Gaika Campaigns, 1877-78, and in the operations against Moirosi in 1879. At the capture of Moirosi's stronghold, he led the storming party, and was promoted capt. for distinguished service. He subsequently served in the operations in Basutoland in 1880-81. At the commencement of the South African War, Major Sprenger was sent with 250 men and the artillery company of the Cape Mounted Rifles to Queenstown, and thence to Sterkstroom and Pen Hoek. He was present at the engagements at Birds River, Dordrecht, and the fighting near Aliwal North, in all of which his gallantry and resource are stated to have been very noticeable. The death of Major Sprenger is referred to in the report of Lieut.-Col. Dalgety of April 29th, 1900, from Jammersberg Bridge, L.G., Feb. 8th, 1901. Major Sprenger was also mentioned in despatches, L.G., April 16th, 1901.

Spring.—Lieut. H. G. Spring, I.Y., was killed in action at Vlakfontein, May 29th, 1901. He was the second son of the Rev. H. C. Spring, of Tiverton, Devon, a retired army chaplain, and now Vicar of Alphington, Devon. Lieut. Spring was educated at Blundell's School, Tiverton, was very fond of games, and, when at school, was captain of both his cricket and football teams. He had served in South Africa during 1900 as a trooper, but he again volunteered and was gazetted in March, 1901, as a lieut. in the I.Y., and attached to the 7th Batt. He is reported to have been killed when lying wounded.

Stabb.—Lieut. Edward Stabb, Royal Naval Reserve, died of fever in Ladysmith, Jan. 15th, 1900. He was serving with the Natal Police and rendered good service during the siege. He was mentioned in the despatch of Lieut.-Gen. Sir George White of March 23rd, 1900, L.G., Feb. 8th, 1901, also in the despatch of Capt. H. Lambton, of June 11th, 1900, who stated that "Lieut.

Stabb volunteered his services which I gladly accepted, and I found him very useful."

Stanley.—Capt. Herbert Foster Wentworth Stanley, 9th Lancers, died April 28th, 1900, of wounds received in action near Dewetsdorp. He was the third son of the late Sidney Stanley, Esq., of Longstone Hall, Cambridgeshire, was born July, 1863, and educated at Eton (Mr. Durnford's). He entered the 9th Lancers in Feb., 1887, being promoted lieut. Nov., 1888, and capt. Sept., 1894. Capt. Stanley accompanied his regiment to South Africa from India in 1899, and served in Natal and the North of Cape Colony, and subsequently at the relief of Kimberley and the advance on Bloemfontein. He afterwards served in the operations near Dewetsdorp.

Stanley.—Lieut. Henry Thomas Stanley, 7th Batt. Imperial Yeomanry, was killed in action at Hekpoort, Sept. 16th, 1900. He was educated at Eton (Mr. Marindin's and Mr. Impey's), and joined the I.Y. in Feb., 1900. He was a well-known cricketer and sportsman. Before joining the I.Y. he had held the rank of lieut. in the West Somerset Yeomanry Cavalry from June, 1898.

Stanton.—Lieut. A. A. Stanton, Commander-in-Chief's Bodyguard, died of peritonitis, at Utrecht, on March 9th, 1901. He was a fellow of the Royal Colonial Institute, and his name is inscribed on a memorial tablet placed in the hall of the building in Northumberland Avenue, S.W.

Stanton.—Lieut. Harold John Stanton Stanton, 2nd Batt. Northumberland Fusiliers, died at Pretoria, Dec. 30th, 1900, of wounds received in action at Nooitgedacht, near the Magaliesberg, on Dec. 13th. He was the elder son of the late Capt. F. R. Stanton, Royal Scots, and of Mrs. Stanton, of 58, Elm Park Gardens, S.W., was born in Dec., 1878, and educated at Radley. He entered the Northumberland Fusiliers from the 3rd Batt. Sherwood Foresters (Derbyshire Regt.) in Oct., 1899, being promoted lieut. Feb., 1900. He accompanied his battalion to South Africa in Oct., 1899, and served with it during the war, with the exception of a short period when he was ill at East London with enteric. He was granted the medal with three clasps. Lieut. Stanton is buried at Pretoria; a handsome memorial cross has been erected over his grave.

Stapleton-Bretherton. — 2nd Lieut. Robert Charles Lucius Stapleton-Bretherton, M.I. Company Royal Fusiliers, was killed in action at Ronderan, Frankfort District, Jan. 30th, 1902. He was the second son of F. A. Stapleton-Bretherton, Esq., of The Hall, Rainhill, Lancashire, and Heathfield House, Fareham, and the Hon. Mrs. Stapleton-Bretherton, a daughter of the twelfth and a sister of the present Lord Petre. 2nd Lieut. Stapleton-Bretherton was born in Aug., 1875, and educated at the Jesuit College, Beaumont, Windsor. He was a keen sportsman and a good rider. He joined the 3rd Batt. Hampshire Regt. in 1894, being promoted capt. 1899, and had served on the West Coast of Africa and held the post of Assistant-Inspector of the Gold Coast Constabulary, in the northern territories till April, 1900. In the following June he was given his commission as 2nd lieut. in the Royal Fusiliers, and joined the 1st battalion in Bombay. He was sent to South Africa in Dec., 1901, to the 20th M.I., under Col. Dawkins, which was operating in the Frankfort district in the operations against De Wet. Some fighting took place on Jan. 28th, and on the following evening the whole column started to attack a large force of Boers about twenty-five miles off.

The Boers were surprised, but made a determined stand. With about ten men, 2nd Lieut. Stapleton-Bretherton rushed forward to attack and, if possible, capture some of the enemy, and was shot through the heart. He is buried on a hill side at Kaffirstad, on the Harrismith-Frankfort road, about twenty miles from the former place. A marble cross and iron fence mark his grave. In the R.C. church of St. Bartholomew's, Rainhill, a handsome cross has also been erected in memory of 2nd Lieut. Stapleton-Bretherton.

Stapleton-Cotton. — Lieut. Wellington Robert Paul Stapleton-Cotton, 19th Hussars, died of enteric in Ladysmith, Jan. 29th, 1900. He was the eldest son of Col. the Hon. Richard Stapleton-Cotton, of Somerford Hall, Brewood, Staffordshire, second son of the 2nd Viscount Combermere. His mother was the Hon. Jane Charlotte, daughter of the 2nd Baron Methuen; Lieut. Stapleton-Cotton was therefore a nephew of Lieut.-Gen. Lord Methuen. He was born in Aug., 1872, educated at Wellington, and entered the 18th Hussars from the Royal Military College in March, 1892, being transferred to the 19th Hussars on the 30th of the same month, and was promoted lieut. Feb., 1894. Lieut. Stapleton-Cotton served in Natal with his regiment, which was sent to South Africa in Sept., 1899, with the Indian contingent, and took part in the defence of Ladysmith until struck down with fever.

Stapylton-Bree.—Lieut. Reginald Robert Stapylton-Bree, Victorian M.I., died of enteric, May 26th, 1900, at Bloemfontein. He was the eldest son of Robert Stapylton-Bree, Esq., of Hamilton, Australia, and grandson of the Hon. S. G. Henty, one of the best-known of the early pioneers of the Colony. Lieut. Stapylton-Bree was nineteen years of age at the time of his death.

Stark.—Dr. Arthur Cowell Stark, M.B., died from injuries received by a Boer shell while standing in the doorway of the Royal Hotel, Ladysmith. The shell took off one leg and injured the other, and Dr. Stark succumbed in an hour. He was the eldest son of the late J. Cowell Stark, Esq., of Torquay, and was educated at Blundell's School, Tiverton, and Clifton College. He afterwards matriculated at Edinburgh University, and was an accomplished naturalist, a great traveller, and one of the first ornithologists of the day. In Sept., 1899, he was in Durban, and war being declared he offered his services, which were accepted. He left Durban for Ladysmith with the last batch of officers who succeeded in entering that town, and rendered good service during the siege.

Stayner.—Capt. F. S. Stayner, 1st Batt. Gloucestershire Regt., died in Ceylon from enteric Oct. 8th, 1900. He had previously served in the South African war from its commencement, and was present at the actions of Farquhar's Farm and Nicholson's Nek, where he was severely wounded and afterwards invalided. He was born in March, 1866, and educated at Marlborough, where he was considered a good athlete and in the football XI. He was the winner of many cups and prizes. He entered the Gloucestershire Regt. from the Militia in May, 1888, being promoted lieut. March, 1890, and capt. Jan., 1898. He served in Malta, Egypt and India, previous to going to South Africa. On recovering from his wound he rejoined his battalion, which was afterwards sent to Ceylon. His name is inscribed on a tablet placed in Marlborough College Chapel in memory of all Marlburians who fell during the war.

Stebbing.—Lieut. Frederic Anderson Stebbing, Royal Welsh Fusiliers, was killed in action, Feb. 24th, 1900, in the operations on the Tugela. He was the younger son of

Lieut.-Col. Frederic Anderson Stebbing, of Ealing, late 8th, King's Regt., was born in June, 1876, and educated at Harrow. He entered the Royal Welsh Fusiliers in Sept., 1896, being promoted lieut. Oct., 1898. Having served with the 2nd battalion of his regiment at Malta, the occupation of Crete, and at Hong Kong, he volunteered for active service at the outbreak of the war, and embarked with the 1st battalion for South Africa in Oct., 1899, and served with the Natal Field Force until killed. He was present at the battle of Colenso and the fighting on the Tugela, and was awarded the medal with two clasps.

Stephenson.—Lieut. W. H. Stephenson, Canadian Scouts, died of enteric at Bloemfontein on Feb. 13th, 1902.

Stevens.—Acting Chaplain the Rev. S. P. Stevens, died of inflammation of the stomach at Winburg, O.R.C., on May 17th, 1902.

Stewart.—Capt. Archibald Dundonald Stewart, 1st Batt. Rifle Brigade, was killed in the railway engagement at Kaap River, near Vlakfontein, on Oct. 9th, 1900. He was born in Feb., 1864, and entered the Rifle Brigade August, 1884, being promoted capt. Nov., 1892. He served with the Burmese Expedition of 1886-88, receiving the medal with clasp. Capt. Stewart also served with the Natal Field Force, and took part in the operations on the Tugela of Feb. 15th to 18th, 1900, and was wounded. On recovering he rejoined his battalion and served with it in the advance into the Transvaal.

Stewart.—Capt. Gilbert Macdonald Stewart, Lancashire Fusiliers, was killed in action at Spion Kop in the operations on the Upper Tugela on Jan. 24th, 1900. He was a son of Mrs. Stewart, of Longton Grove, Sydenham. Capt. Stewart was born in Feb., 1873, educated at Dulwich College, and entered the Lancashire Fusiliers in Feb., 1893, being promoted lieut. Jan., 1896, and capt. Oct., 1899. He served in the campaign in the Soudan under Lord (then Sir Herbert) Kitchener in 1898 with the 2nd battalion of his regiment, and was present at the battle of Khartoum, receiving the British medal and the Khedive's medal with clasp. He was also present during the occupation of Crete in 1898. Previous to proceeding to South Africa he held the post of garrison adjutant at Chatham. Capt. Stewart embarked with the 2nd battalion in Nov., 1899, and served with the Natal Field Force. His name is inscribed on a tablet on the outside of the New Memorial Library erected at Dulwich College, in remembrance of old Alleynians who fell in the war.

Stirling.—Lieut. John Gordon Stirling, D.S.O., 9th Lancers, died at Sialkote, India, from the effects of an accident, May 22nd, 1902. He was born in May, 1874, and entered the 9th Lancers from the 7th Batt. King's Royal Rifle Corps, July, 1895, being promoted lieut. July, 1896. In the South African War he served with the Kimberley Relief Force, and took part in the actions at Belmont and Enslin (severely wounded), also in the operations in the O.R.C., May to Nov., 1900, including the action at Caledon River. In July, 1901, he acted as capt. in the 2nd Batt. I.Y., but at the time of his death was adjutant of the 9th Lancers. Lieut. Stirling was mentioned in despatches by F.-M. Earl Roberts, for having rendered meritorious service, L.G., Aug. 20th, 1901, and was awarded the D.S.O. He was also mentioned in the despatch of Lord Kitchener of May 28th, 1901, for his gallant conduct at Twyfelfontein, O.R.C., on May 27th, 1901, in "returning to fetch a dismounted man," and for "his coolness in action." During his service in South Africa, Lieut. Stirling had lost one arm and been wounded in the other.

Stokes.—Surgeon Sir William Stokes, K.C.B., died at the Base Hospital, Pietermaritzburg, of pleurisy, Aug. 18th, 1900. He was one of those distinguished surgeons who, at the end of 1899, responded to the call of his Sovereign and country and came forward to assist the Empire. He was then appointed a consulting surgeon to the army in South Africa. He was born in March, 1839, and educated at the Royal School, Armagh, and Trinity College, Dublin, where he graduated as B.A. in 1859. He became a Licentiate of the Royal College of Surgeons, Ireland, in 1862, and took his degree in medicine and surgery in the University of Dublin, 1863. After two years further study in Berlin, Paris, Vienna, and London, he commenced practice in Dublin. In June, 1886, he was made a K.C.B., and in 1892 became Surgeon-in-Ordinary in Ireland to her late Majesty Queen Victoria. He was an excellent writer, having written much on clinical and operative surgery; and his favourite recreations were music and travelling. Many of those who were wounded in the Natal campaign, and had the happiness and good fortune to come under his care, look back with gratitude to his skill and gentleness in dealing with their cases. In Natal he was chiefly in the hospitals of Mooi River, Pietermaritzburg, and in Ladysmith after the siege was raised. Believing the war would be over in July, 1900, he had arranged if his services were not further required to return home. Some time previously Sir W. Stokes had been ill from the effects of overwork, and went to Durban for a change. Writing under date June 28th, he said, "I am getting quite well again," and expressed a hope to soon get back to Maritzburg and Newcastle, "as there are cases waiting for me." He returned to work early in July, and having visited the hospitals at Volksrust and Charlestown, he was again taken ill at Maritzburg on Aug. 15th, and died after three days illness. He is buried in the cemetery at Fort Napier, and was interred with military honours, his appointment carrying the rank of a general officer. He was mentioned by F.-M. Earl Roberts in his despatch of April 2nd, 1901, who wrote that the services rendered by Sir W. Stokes "were of incalculable value."

Stoneman.—Lieut.-Col. James Stoneman, Army Service Corps, who died of enteric at Pietermaritzburg, on Dec. 10th, 1900, was born in March, 1855. After departmental service, lasting nearly fourteen years, he was gazetted major in the Army Service Corps in June, 1889, and was promoted lieut.-col. in 1894. He took part in the Egyptian War of 1882, receiving the medal and Khedive's star. In the South African campaign he had served from the commencement of the war, and was employed as a D.A.A.G. on the lines of communication from Sept., 1899. Lieut.-Col. Stoneman, was in Ladysmith throughout the siege. He was mentioned in the despatch of Sir G. White of March 23rd, 1900, who stated that "excellent service has been rendered by Lieut.-Col. Stoneman, Army Service Corps, D.A.A.G." Sir A. Conan Doyle also, in writing of the siege of Ladysmith, mentions that the besieged were fortunate in the presence of a first class organiser, Col. Ward, who "with the assistance of Col. Stoneman, systematised the collection and issue of all food," and adds that, above all, Sir G. White was fortunate "in his commissariat officers, as it was in the offices of Cols. Ward and Stoneman as much as in the trenches and sangars of Cæsar's Camp that the siege was won."

Stopford.—Lieut.-Col. Horace Robert Stopford, Coldstream Guards, was killed at the battle of Modder River Nov. 28th, 1899. He was born in Oct., 1855, and educated at Eton (Mr. Waytes). He entered the 46th Foot in June, 1874, was transferred to the Coldstream Guards as lieut. Aug., 1875, was promoted capt. Oct., 1885, major Nov., 1893, and lieut.-col., to command the 2nd Batt., Feb., 1899. From 1881-85 he was A.D.C. to the General Officer Commanding the Forces in Ireland, and from 1887-89 was Commandant of the School of Instruction for Auxiliary Forces at Wellington Barracks. His battalion, on arrival in South Africa, joined the Kimberley Relief Force, under Lieut.-Gen. Lord Methuen, and took part in the battles of Belmont and Graspan. While leading his battalion at Modder River, Lieut.-Col. Stopford was killed by one of the first shells fired by the Boers in this action. He is mentioned in the report of Major-Gen. Sir H. Colville, concerning the battle of Belmont—" the advance of his battalion was distinctly well performed."

Streak.—Lieut. Streak, Dennison's Scouts, was killed in action at Schweitzerrenneke on Dec. 29th, 1900.

Streatfield.—Capt. Eric Streatfield, D.S.O., 2nd Batt. Gordon Highlanders, died at Fulbrook, Elstead, Surrey, March 26th, 1902. He was the fifth son of the late Lieut.-Col. Henry Dorrien Streatfield, of Chiddingstone, Edenbridge, Kent, Lord of the Manors of Chiddingstone, etc., by his marriage with Marion, daughter of Oswald A. Smith, Esq. Capt. Streatfield was a brother of Lieut.-Col. Henry Streatfield, private secretary to F.-M. Earl Roberts. He was born in Feb., 1864, educated at Radley, where he was in the school rowing and football teams, and entered the Gordon Highlanders from the 4th Batt. Black Watch (Royal Highlanders) in April, 1886, being promoted capt. Sept., 1896. He was A.D.C. to Major-

General Ivor Herbert, commanding the militia of the Dominion of Canada, in May and June, 1890, and again from Dec., 1890, till Aug., 1895, and was adjutant of the 2nd battalion of his regiment from Nov., 1897, to Feb., 1901. Capt. Streatfield was serving in South Africa at the outbreak of the war, having accompanied his battalion from India to Natal in Sept., 1899. He took part in the defence of Ladysmith, being mentioned in the despatches of Sir George White, Dec. 2nd, 1899, and March 23rd, 1900, L.G., Feb. 8th and Sept. 10th, 1901, and was awarded the D.S.O. He retired from the army on account of ill-health March, 14th, 1902, and died as stated on the 26th of the same month.

Strong.—Lieut. Charles Powlett Strong, D.S.O., 2nd Batt. Bedfordshire Regt., was killed in action at Graspan, near Reitz, June 6th, 1901. He was the second son of Lieut.-Col. Strong, Chairman of Peterborough Quarter Sessions, was born in Jan., 1875, and educated at Harrow. He entered the Bedfordshire Regt. from the Royal Military College in March, 1895, and was promoted lieut. July, 1897. He was mentioned in despatches, L.G., Sept. 10th, 1901, also in the despatch of Gen. Lord Kitchener of July 28th, 1901, for having "when in command of a rear guard by his determined resistance to a superior force, enabled the baggage to get across a bad drift without a shot being fired at it," and for having "done consistent good work on many occasions." Lieut. Strong was awarded the D.S.O.

Strong.—Major Sydney Philip Strong, second in command, 2nd Batt. Scottish Rifles, died of wounds received in action at Spion Kop, in the operations on the Upper Tugela, on Jan. 24th, 1900. He was born in Feb., 1858, educated at Winchester, and entered the 90th Foot Jan., 1878, being promoted lieut. August, 1878, capt. Sept.,

1883, and major Oct., 1892. He saw active service with the 90th Light Infantry in the South African War, 1877-78, in the Kaffir Campaign, and the operations against the Galekas. He also served throughout the Zulu War of 1879, and was present at the engagements at Zungen Nek, Kambula, and Ulundi, and was mentioned in despatches, L.G., May 7th, 1879, and received the medal with clasp. Major Strong was adjutant of volunteers from Nov. 1887-92. His death is mentioned in the despatch of Lieut.-Gen. Sir C. Warren of Feb. 1st, 1900.

Stuart.—Lieut. Charles McKay Stuart, South African Town Guards, died of epilepsy at Mossel Bay on Dec. 12th, 1901.

Stuart.—Major Sidney Offord Stuart, F.R.C.S. Edinburgh, Royal Army Medical Corps, died of dysentery at Winburg, O.R.C., on April 18th, 1902. He was born in Nov. 1860, and joined the R.A.M.C. as surgeon, July, 1882, and was promoted major July, 1894. Major Stuart proceeded to South Africa in Nov. 1901, and served in the Cape and Orange River Colonies.

Stuart.—Lieut. Walter Ochiltree Stuart, 1st Batt. Royal Inniskilling Fusiliers, was killed in action in the operations on the Upper Tugela, Feb. 23rd, 1900. He was the son of Major Burleigh Stuart, of Dergmony, Omagh, co. Tyrone, was born in Nov., 1877, and educated at Cheltenham College. He entered the 1st Batt. Royal Inniskilling Fusiliers from the 5th Batt. in Dec., 1897, being promoted lieut. Dec., 1898. He accompanied his battalion to South Africa in Nov., 1899, and was present at the battle of Colenso and all the subsequent fighting on the Tugela up to Feb. 23rd, when he fell shot through the head while leading his men. Lieut. Stuart is buried at the foot of the hill where he was killed (known as Railway or Inniskilling, or Harts Hill), beside Lieut.-Col. Thackeray and Major Sanders. A marble headstone erected by their comrades of all ranks marks the graves. Lieut. Stuart's name is inscribed on an obelisk twenty-seven feet high, erected on this hill, in memory of all belonging to the 1st Batt. Inniskillings who fell on Feb. 23rd and 24th, 1900. His name is also inscribed on the Eleanor Cross War Memorial at Cheltenham College. (*See Lieut.-Col. Thackeray.*)

Stubbs.—Capt. and Brevet-Major Arthur Kennedy Stubbs, Worcestershire Regt., was killed in action at Rensburg, Feb. 12th, 1900. He was the eldest son of Major-General F. W. Stubbs, late Royal Artillery, of 2, Clarence Terrace, St. Luke's, Cork. Major Stubbs was born in Dec., 1867, at Meerut, and educated at Mr. Tottenham's School at St. Leonards, and afterwards at the Oxford Military College, whence he passed into Sandhurst. He entered the Worcestershire Regt. in March, 1889, being promoted lieut. Dec., 1890, capt. May, 1899, and brevet-major on July 1st of the same year. He served in the operations in the Niger Territories in 1898, including the Benin Hinterland and Siama Expedition (wounded), being mentioned in despatches, and receiving the brevet of major and the medal with clasp. Major Stubbs accompanied the 2nd battalion of his regiment to South Africa in Dec., 1899, and on arrival was then sent with it to the North of Cape Colony. At Rensburg the key of the position was a group of three kopjes held by three companies of the Worcestershire Regt., and here the Boers made a fierce attack "in the cold misty light of dawn" on Feb. 12th and got possession of some sangars. They could not,

OFFICERS WHO FELL IN SOUTH AFRICA. 371

however, advance any further owing to the accurate fire of the Worcesters, and a desperate fight then ensued. The right kopje, with a front of about three-quarters of a mile, was held by Major Stubbs and his company, and he was killed while leading and cheering his men on in a forward rush to drive the Boers out of the north-east edge of this kopje. Lieut.-Col. Coningham, who had come up to the point of danger in the first alarm, was killed close to Major Stubbs. Capt. Thomas, who had been sent with his company as a reinforcement, was also severely wounded, and died eight days afterwards. The action lasted the whole day and with darkness the Boers retreated. A cairn has been erected over the graves of Lieut.-Col. Coningham, Major Stubbs, and those of the Worcesters who fell in this action. (*See Lieut.-Col. Coningham.*)

Sutherland.—2nd Lieut. Eric Macnaught Sutherland, 2nd Batt. Seaforth Highlanders, was killed in action near Frederickstad on May 29th, 1902, two days before the treaty of peace was signed. He was the eldest son of Sir Thomas Sutherland, Chairman of the Peninsular and Oriental Steamship Company, who represented Greenock in the House of Commons for sixteen years. Lieut. Sutherland was born in Sept., 1882, and educated at Eton (Mr. Williams'). He passed out of Sandhurst in Dec., 1901, being gazetted to the Seaforth Highlanders, Jan., 1902, and joined the 2nd Batt. in South Africa a few weeks later. The day he was killed he was pursuing some Boers with a handful of horsemen, when they were ambushed by the enemy and 2nd Lieut. Sutherland got separated from his horse. Scorning to surrender, he fought his way on foot for over a mile, and was then shot down by one of the enemy who had got round him. The Boer Commander stated he had seen no finer example of British courage during the war.

Sutton.—Capt. Francis Hubert Clifford Sutton, Royal Canadian Dragoons, died at sea whilst returning from South Africa to Halifax, N.S. He was the only surviving son of the late Rev. Walter Henry Sutton, of South Cerney, Gloucestershire, and was thirty-five years of age.

Swanston.—Lieut. Arthur William Swanston, 6th Inniskilling Dragoons, was killed in action near Ermelo Oct. 16th, 1900. He was the son of J. C. Swanston, Esq., of Bourne End, Bucks, was born in Feb. 1875, and educated at St. Paul's School, and Loretto (Musselburgh), and also at Cambridge. He was fond of games and was in the Loretto XV., and also rowed in the Cambridge eight in 1898. He entered the 6th Dragoons from the Northumberland Artillery Militia, in Nov., 1899, being promoted lieut. Oct. 3rd, 1900. He joined his regiment in South Africa early in 1900, and served with it till killed. His commanding officer in writing concerning Lieut. Swanston's death, states " he fell while trying to bring in wounded troopers, and was shot dead on the second occasion when he was so gallantly trying to save others."

Sykes.—Capt. Herbert Schofield Sykes, Royal Scots Fusiliers, was killed in action at Pieter's Hill, in the operations on the Upper Tugela, Feb. 27th, 1900. He was born at the Manor Adel, near Leeds, in June, 1863, and was educated at Harrow. He entered the Royal Scots Fusiliers, May, 1885, being promoted capt. Aug., 1894. From 1894-99 he was adjutant of the 1st Volunteer battalion at Kilmarnock. He proceeded to South Africa and joined the 2nd battalion of his regiment in Dec., 1899. At Pieter's Hill the Royal Scots Fusiliers were on the British extreme right and rendered splendid service by enveloping the Boer left, thus compelling the enemy to withdraw from their position.

OFFICERS WHO FELL IN SOUTH AFRICA. 373

Symons.—Major-Gen. (local Lieut.-Gen.) Sir William Penn Symons, K.C.B., was mortally wounded Oct. 20th, 1899, at the battle of Talana Hill, and died three days later. He was the eldest son of the late William Symons, Esq., of Hatt, Cornwall, was born in July, 1843, and educated privately. Sir W. Penn Symons married Caroline, only daughter of T. P. Hawkins, Esq., of Edgbaston, Warwickshire. He was a good sportsman and fond of hunting, shooting and fishing. He entered the 24th Foot in March, 1863, being promoted lieut. Oct., 1866, capt. Feb., 1878, major July, 1881, brevet.-lieut.-col. May, 1886, brevet.-col. July, 1887. He had his first experience of active service in South Africa, when, as a capt. of the 24th Foot, he took part in the operations against the Galekas in 1877-78, and in the Zulu war during the following year, being awarded the medal and clasp. He next served with the Burmese Expedition in 1885-89 as D.A.A. and Q.M.G., when he organised and commanded the M.I.; also as brigadier.-general in command of the Chin Field Force (several times mentioned in despatches, brevets of lieut.-col. and colonel, medal with two clasps). He also took part in the Chin-lushai Expedition of 1889-90, in command of the Burmah column (received the thanks of the Government of India, C.B., and clasp). In 1894-95 he commanded a brigade of the Waziristan Field Force, and was mentioned in despatches and granted a clasp. He then served in the campaign on the North-West Frontier of India under the late Sir William Lockhart, 1897-98, in command of the 2nd brigade Tochi Field Force, and afterwards commanded the 1st division of the Tirah Expeditionary Force (twice mentioned in despatches, K.C.B., and medal with two clasps.) He was appointed brigadier-general in Natal, May 15th, 1889, and major-general just before the commencement of the war. At the battle of Talana Hill, about 9 a.m., Sir Penn Symons, accompanied by Col.

Dartnell and Majors Hammersley and Murray, D.A.A.G.s, galloped forward and jumped into a wood, in front of which was the Boer position. Leaving their horses in a donga, they then hurried on, and having arrived at the edge nearest the enemy Major Hammersley was severely wounded. A moment later, at 9.15, Sir P. Symons, as he was stepping through a gap, was struck down, and turning to Major Murray, he said, "I am mortally wounded." He was then assisted and carried back into camp, and as he was being taken away and afterwards when in hospital, his only question was "have they got the hill?" He died on Oct. 23rd, a few hours after the Boers entered Dundee. He was mentioned in the despatch of Lieut.-Gen. Sir George White, from Ladysmith, Dec. 2nd, 1899, for his "energy and courage." Sir G. White considered the country had lost "an officer of high ability and a leader of exceptional valour," L.G., Feb. 8th, 1901. The men of the Durban Light Infantry have erected a memorial over the grave of Sir Penn Symons at Dundee, and an Institute in his memory has been built at Umballa, where he was commanding until summoned to Natal in 1899 to take command of the troops there. (*See Lieut.-Col. Gunning*).

Tabor.—Lieut. J. B. Tabor, 11th Co., 3rd Batt., I.Y., was killed in action at Middleport Farm, Calvinia, Feb. 6th, 1902. He joined the I.Y. in Oct., 1901, with the rank of lieut. in the army. The late Lieut. Spratt, I.Y., describing in a private letter the action in which Lieut. Tabor fell, wrote: "Meanwhile the kopje where Chichester and the 11th I.Y. were, was rushed by the Boers. Tabor lay there, the top of his head shot away and Chichester with his helmet crushed down over his face, streaming with blood. Six men lay dead beside them. They had fought gallantly." Sergt. Ward was also killed, but as he fell he shot his opponent through the head with his revolver. (*See Lieut. Chichester.*)

OFFICERS WHO FELL IN SOUTH AFRICA. 375

Tait.—Lieut. Frederick Guthrie Tait, Black Watch, 2nd Batt. Royal Highlanders, was killed in action at Koodoosberg, Feb. 7th, 1900. He was the son of F. G. Tait, Esq., M.A., Edinburgh University, was born in Jan., 1870, and educated at Edinburgh Academy, and Sedbergh School, Yorkshire, where he was in the football team. On one occasion, at Sedbergh, he saved a schoolfellow from drowning. He was a famous amateur golfer; he held the Amateur Championship for the years 1896 and 1898, and was the runner-up in 1899. Lieut. Tait entered the Leinster Regt. (Royal Canadians), in Oct., 1890, being promoted lieut. April, 1893, and was transferred to the Royal Highlanders June, 1894. He was Superintendent of Gymnasia, Eastern District, from July to Sept., 1898, and held a similar position in the Scottish District from Oct., 1898, to Oct., 1899, when he rejoined his battalion for active service, and accompanied it to South Africa. He served with the Kimberley Relief Force and was present at the battle of Magersfontein, where he was wounded. His wound had scarcely healed when he was again struck down at Koodoosberg; as he was hit his last words were, "they have got me this time." A fund was raised to erect a suitable memorial to Lieut. Tait, and as a result a bed has been endowed in the Scottish South African Hospital. A ward is also to be built and named after him at the Cottage Hospital, St. Andrews.

Taplin.—Lieut. H. E. B. Taplin, Cape Mounted Rifles, was killed in action at Wepener, in the fighting from April 9th to 18th, 1900.

Tarbutt. — Lieut. Charles A. Percy Tarbutt, South African Light Horse, died of typhoid fever at Pretoria, Feb. 13th, 1900. He was the eldest son of Percy Tarbutt, Esq., of the Consolidated Gold Fields of South

Africa. Lieut. Tarbutt was twenty-six years of age, and was educated at University College School (where he was in the football XV.), and at the Bedford Grammar School. When Lieut. Tarbutt landed in South Africa he was given a commission as lieut. in the South African Light Horse. After the battle of Colenso he was reported missing, but it was subsequently discovered that he had been wounded and captured.

Taunton.—Major Charles Edmund Taunton, Natal Carabiniers, was killed in action on Nov. 3rd, 1899, in a reconnaissance from Ladysmith along the Colenso road. The enemy was in considerable force and the officer in command, finding their numbers increasing, determined on withdrawing. Concerning this reconnaissance, Sir A. Conan Doyle writes, "the death of Major Taunton, Capt. Knapp, and young Brabant, the son of the general who did such good service at a later stage of the war, was a heavy price to pay for the knowledge that the Boers were in considerable strength to the south." Major Taunton, who was the only son of Mrs. Taunton, was a keen man of business, well known in South African finance, and a director of many of the older gold mining companies. He was a Fellow of the Royal Colonial Institute, and his name is inscribed on a memorial tablet in the hall of the building in Northumberland Avenue, S.W.

Taylor.—Capt. Herbert Wodehouse Taylor, M Battery, Royal Horse Artillery, was killed in action at Geluk, between Machadodorp and Heidelberg, Oct. 13th, 1900. He was born in June, 1868, and educated at Clifton and Wellington, where he was in the Hopetoun and a Prefect. He entered the Royal Artillery from the Royal Military Academy, Woolwich, in Feb., 1887, was promoted lieut. Feb., 1890, capt. Oct., 1897, and proceeded to South Africa in Jan., 1900.

Taylor.—Lieut. John Taylor, King's Royal Rifle Corps, was killed in action at the Battle of Talana Hill, Natal, Oct. 20th, 1899. He was born in April, 1873, educated at Winchester, and entered the King's Royal Rifle Corps in March, 1895, being promoted lieut. in May, 1898. At Talana his company was extended behind a wall, and to show above this cover was to brave the storm of a dozen Boer rifles. It was here that Lieut. Taylor met his death, while endeavouring to return the enemy's fire. He is buried at Talana.

Thackeray. — Lieut. - Col. Thomas Martin Gerard Thackeray, commanding the 1st Batt. Royal Inniskilling Fusiliers, was killed in action in the operations on the Upper Tugela, Feb. 23rd-24th, 1900. He was born in June, 1849, entered the 16th Foot Nov., 1868, being promoted lieut. in Oct., 1871. He exchanged into the 1st Batt. West India Regt. in Jan., 1876, subsequently obtaining his captaincy in the Royal Inniskilling Fusiliers, March, 1881, being promoted major Dec., 1889, and lieut.-col. to command the 1st battalion of his regiment, Nov., 1897. During 1880 and part of 1881, he served as fort adjutant at Sierra Leone. Lieut.-Col. Thackeray proceeded to South Africa in command of his battalion in Nov., 1899, and being sent on to Natal, joined the Ladysmith Relief Force, under Gen. Sir R. Buller. Lieut.-Col. Thackeray was present at the battle of Colenso and the subsequent fighting on the Tugela up to his death. Mr. Bennett Burleigh relates how at the battle of Colenso Lieut.-Col. Thackeray found himself in command of a mixed party of Inniskillings, Dublins, Connaughts, and Borderers, and saved his party from capture by his wit and fortitude. He was under cover with these men where they had been left, and the order to retire had not reached them. About 1 p.m., an ambulance approached and the red cross was raised. An informal truce was then inaugurated, the

Boer firing ceased and some of them advanced, while
Lieut.-Col. Thackeray was moving off with his men.
The Boer leader called on the party to surrender and lay
down their arms. "No," said Col. Thackeray, "you
advanced under the red cross, and we allowed you to do
so, let us go back and begin the fight again," and continued to argue the point. The Boer then said, "Perhaps
you are right, I'll turn my back and won't see you," and
the commander of the Inniskillings then retired with his
party. Lieut.-Col. Thackeray was killed the same day
as Lieut.-Col. Sitwell of the Dublins, and Thorold of the
Welsh Fusiliers. Sir A. Conan Doyle writes, "Thorold,
Thackeray, and Sitwell in one evening, who can say that
British colonels have not given their men a lead?"
Lieut.-Col. Thackeray was mentioned in despatches,
L.G., Feb. 8th, 1901, by Gen. Sir R. Buller, who referred
to the great loss the country had sustained by his death.
Lieut.-Col. Thackeray, Major Sanders and Lieut. W. O.
Stuart, Royal Inniskilling Fusiliers, all lie beside each
other in one large grave at the foot of the hill where they
fell (known as Harts or Railway or Inniskilling Hill). A
marble headstone has been erected by their brother officers.
An obelisk, 27 feet high, has also been erected by their
comrades on this hill in memory of all ranks of the 1st
Batt. Inniskillings, who fell there. It bears the following inscription, "Near this spot were killed or mortally
wounded on Feb. 23rd-24th, 1900, Lieut.-Col. T. M. G.
Thackeray, commanding, Major F. A. Sanders, 2nd-in-
command, Lieut. W. O. Stuart, and 65 N.C.O. and
men of the 27th Inniskillings whilst advancing to the
relief of Ladysmith."

Theobald.—Lieut. Stanley Reay Theobald, 9th Lancers,
died at Wolvevlei, Cape Colony, on Aug. 12th, 1901, of
wounds received in action three days previously. He
was the son of Col. Percy Theobald, of Cheltenham,

was born in Sept., 1877, and educated at Cheltenham College. He entered the 9th Lancers in Sept., 1897, being promoted lieut. in Oct., 1900. He accompanied his regiment from India to South Africa in Sept., 1899 and served with the Kimberley Relief Force, taking part in the engagements at Belmont, Enslin, Modder River, and Magersfontein, and had been slightly wounded. Lieut. Theobald subsequently served in the advance on Bloemfontein, being present at Paardeberg and Driefontein. On April 28th, 1900, he was reported to have been killed near Thaba N'chu. It was eventually ascertained, however, that he was a prisoner at Pretoria. On the advance of F.-M. Earl Roberts he was released, and then saw much fighting, but having suffered from an attack of enteric had been advised to return home. Lieut. Theobald, however, preferred to remain in South Africa, hoping to see the end of the war. He was mentioned in despatches by Gen. Lord Kitchener on Dec. 8th, 1901, for "exceedingly gallant conduct on several occasions." His name is inscribed on the Eleanor Cross War Memorial at Cheltenham College.

Thomas.—Lieut. A. H. Thomas, Ceylon M.I., died of enteric, at Bultfontein, on Oct. 6th, 1900. He was educated at Harrow, and did good service in the war, for which he was mentioned in despatches, L.G., April 16th, 1901. He was a Fellow of the Royal Colonial Institute, and his name is inscribed on a memorial tablet in the hall of the building in Northumberland Avenue, S.W.

Thomas.—Capt. Berkeley Hardinge Thomas, 2nd Batt. Worcester Regt., died on Feb. 20th, 1900, of wounds received at Rensburg, in the fighting eight days previously. He was born in Jan., 1865, and educated at the United Services College, Westward Ho. He entered the Worcestershire Regt. in Nov., 1887, being promoted lieut. Nov., 1889, and capt. Dec., 1896. At Rensburg, he received a wound in his right side, the bullet passing out close to the spine. Paralysis supervened, and he died in the Portland Hospital, at Rondebosch. His name is inscribed on a memorial tablet in his old college at Westward Ho. (*See Major Stubbs.*)

Thomas.—Lieut. Charles Latimer Thomas, 2nd Batt. West India Regt., died on Jan. 9th, 1901, of enteric, at Kroonstad. He was born Sept., 1875, and entered the Queen's Royal West Surrey Regt. from the 4th Batt. King's Liverpool Regt., in Dec., 1896, exchanged to the West India Regt., Nov., 1898, and was promoted lieut. Oct., 1899. He served in the operations on the North-West Frontier of India in 1897-98, with the Malakand Field, Mohmand Field, and Tirah Expeditionary Forces, receiving the medal with two clasps. He was a probationer for the Army Service Corps, and at the outbreak of the South African war was selected for special service.

Thompson-Pegge.—2nd Lieut. John Francis Thompson-Pegge, 10th Company, Eastern Division, Royal Garrison Artillery, was killed by lightning at Dundee on Dec. 11th, 1900. He was born in April, 1878, and entered the Royal Artillery, Dec., 1897. He is buried in Dundee.

Thomson.—Capt. William Gordon Thomson, 1st Batt. Suffolk Regt., died suddenly at Pretoria on June 9th, 1900. He was born Oct., 1865, entered the Connaught Rangers May, 1885, being transferred to the Suffolk Regt. in the same month, and was promoted capt. Nov., 1894. Capt. Thomson had been adjutant of his battalion from Aug., 1895, to Aug., 1899. He accompanied the 1st battalion of his regiment to South Africa in Nov., 1899, and served with it in the north of Cape Colony, and afterwards in the O.R.C. and Transvaal.

Thornton.—Lieut. Archer Henry Thornton, Brabant's Horse, was killed in action at Wepener, April 12th, 1900. He was the son of Mrs. Thornton, of Park Avenue, East London; was born in Manchester in 1865, and educated at Sandbach Grammar School, Cheshire. He went to South Africa in 1883, served in Rhodesia, and assisted in subduing the Matabele rebellion in 1893. He joined Brabant's Horse in Dec., 1899, as a trooper, but, rising quickly, soon became lieut. Her late Majesty Queen Victoria directed that one of Lieut. Thornton's photographs should be sent to her to be placed in Her Majesty's album of fallen officers.

Thornton.—Capt. Edward Evelyn Danvers Thornton, Army Service Corps, died of enteric at Wynberg, March 10th, 1900. He was born in July, 1867, and educated at Marlborough. He entered the Dorsetshire Regt. Feb., 1888, being transferred to the Royal Munster Fusiliers in the same month, and to the Army Service Corps in Dec., 1889. He was promoted lieut. Dec., 1890, and capt. July, 1893. He served with the Ashantee Expedition under Sir Francis Scott in 1895-96, and was awarded the star. He proceeded to South Africa in Oct., 1899, and served there until his death. Capt. Thornton's name is inscribed on a tablet placed in Marlborough College Chapel in memory of all Marlburians who fell in the war.

Thorold.—Lieut.-Col. Charles Cecil Hayford Thorold, commanding 1st Batt. Royal Welsh Fusiliers, **was** killed in action on Feb. 24th, 1900, in the operations on the Upper Tugela. He was born in Dec., 1852, and educated at Eton (Mr. Durnford's). He entered the 23rd Foot from the 5th Batt. Royal Lancaster Militia in June, 1874, being promoted capt. Oct., 1882, major July, 1890, and lieut.-col. March, 1896. He was adjutant of his battalion from Oct., 1882, to Sept., 1887, and was afterwards adjutant of volunteers from Sept., 1887, to Sept., 1892. Lieut.-Col. Thorold went to South Africa in command of his battalion in Oct., 1899, and was present at the battle of Colenso and the fighting on the Tugela. He was mentioned in despatches, L.G., Feb. 8th, 1901, by Gen. Sir R. Buller, who referred to the great loss the country had sustained by the death of Lieut.-Col. Thorold. (*See Lieut.-Col. Thackeray.*)

Thorold.—Capt. Frederick Temple Thorold, Yorkshire Light Infantry, 3rd M.I. Company, was killed in action at Brakenlaagte (20 miles north-west of Bethel), Oct. 31st, 1901. He was born in March, 1873, and entered the Yorkshire Light Infantry Oct., 1893, was promoted lieut. Dec., 1895, and capt. April, 1900. He served with the 2nd battalion of his regiment in the operations on the North-West Frontier of India under the late Sir William Lockhart with the 4th brigade of the Tirah Expeditionary Force, and took part in the engagement at Shin Kamar, receiving the medal with two clasps. He accompanied his battalion to South Africa in Oct., 1899, and was present at many battles and actions during the war. He took part in the engagements at Belmont, Graspan, Modder River, and Magersfontein, and in the subsequent operations around Lindley in June, 1900, the capture of Bethlehem and Slabbert's Nek, and the surrender of Prinsloo.

Thorold.—Capt. Henry Cecil Thorold, Leicestershire Regt., attached to the 3rd Railway Pioneer Regt., was killed in action near Rietfontein, Feb. 18th, 1902. He was the second son of Sir John Henry Thorold, of Syston Park, Grantham, by his marriage with the Hon. Henrietta Willoughby, eldest daughter of the late and sister of the present Lord Middleton. Capt. Thorold was born in Nov., 1871, educated at Eton (Mr. Mozley's), and entered the Leicestershire Regt. from the Royal Military College in Jan., 1893, being promoted lieut. Dec., 1895, and capt. Oct., 1901. He saw much service during the South African campaign. At the commencement of the war he volunteered for active service, and in Oct., 1899, was posted to the 2nd Batt. Northamptonshire Regt. Capt. Thorold served with the Kimberley Relief Force, and was present at the actions of Belmont, Graspan, and Modder River. He afterwards joined the 3rd Railway Pioneer Regt. as adjutant, and was serving with it when killed.

Thresher.—Lieut. Edward Burnaby Thresher, 1st Batt. Durham Light Infantry, died of enteric at Standerton, April 9th, 1901. He was the son of the Rev. J. H. Thresher, was born in April, 1876, and educated at Wellington, where he was in the Blucher, 1889-93. He entered the Durham Light Infantry from the 3rd Batt. in May, 1897, being promoted lieut. in Oct., 1899. He accompanied his battalion to South Africa in Oct., 1899, and served with the Ladysmith Relief Force and subsequently in Northern Natal and the Transvaal. At the time of his death he was adjutant of his battalion, to which post he had been appointed in May, 1900.

Thurburn.—Capt. Walter Levinge Thurburn, 2nd Batt. Royal Fusiliers, was killed in action in the operations on the Tugela, near Colenso, Feb. 19th, 1900. He was the youngest son of the late Charles Thurburn, Esq., formerly of Alexandria, Egypt, and of Mrs. Thurburn, of Hales Hall, Market Drayton. Capt. Thurburn was born in June, 1870, and educated at Clifton College. He entered the Royal Fusiliers, from the 3rd Batt. Northumberland Fusiliers, in Sept., 1891, being promoted lieut. March, 1893, and capt. Jan., 1899. He was fond of hunting and shooting, and was a member of the Heythorp

Hunt. He went to South Africa with his battalion in Oct., 1899, and was present at the battle of Colenso and all the fighting up to Llangwane Hill, where he fell leading his men against the Boer position. After he received his mortal wound, "his life slowly ebbing away," he continued to direct his men until he fell back exhausted from loss of blood. Capt. Thurburn is buried on Bloys Farm, on the western slope of Llangwane, close to where he died. A carved oak reredos has been erected to his memory in Kiddington Church, near Woodstock, and a stained glass window in the Episcopal Church at Keith, N.B.

Thursby.—Major and Hon. Lieut.-Col. Arthur Edmund Thursby, 5th Batt. Royal Warwickshire Regt. (1st Warwick Militia), of Hardwick Hill, Byfield, Warwickshire, died of enteric at Sutherland, Cape Colony, on March 6th, 1902. He was the eldest son of Arthur Harvey Thursby, Esq., of Culverlands, Berkshire, by his marriage with Mary, daughter of E. N. Kershaw, Esq., of Heskin Hall, Lancashire. Lieut.-Col. Thursby was born Jan., 1861, and educated at Wellington and Trinity Hall, Cambridge. He entered the Lancashire Militia in March, 1880, and in the following year was transferred to the Warwickshire Militia. His battalion was first embodied during the South African war from Jan. to Oct., 1900, and for the second time in Dec., 1901, and at once volunteering for active service, he proceeded with it to South Africa. Lieut.-Col. Thursby, who was a J.P. for Warwickshire, married, in 1889, Maud, daughter of the late Col. Henry Cartwright, of Eydon Hall, Hampshire, by whom he left three children.

Till.—Lieut. Francis Edward Till, 6th Dragoon Guards (Carabiniers), was killed in action at Basfontein, August 14th, 1901. He was the second son of

Edward Till, Esq., J.P., of Weybridge, Surrey, was born in July, 1875, and educated at Wellington, where he was in Brougham's House, 1889-93, and a Prefect. He entered the 6th Dragoon Guards from the Militia in July, 1897, and was promoted lieut. July, 1899. At the outbreak of the war in Oct., 1899, he proceeded with his regiment to South Africa, and served in Cape Colony in the operations round Colesberg. He afterwards took part in the relief of Kimberley and the subsequent advance on Bloemfontein and Pretoria. He was present at the engagements round Belfast and Machadodorp, and the occupation of Barberton.

Timm.—Lieut. A. B. Timm, Nesbitt's Horse, died at Steynsburg on August 20th, 1901.

Tindal-Atkinson. — Navigating Lieut. Paul Weston Tindal-Atkinson, R.N., of H.M.S. "Partridge," died of dysentery at Addington Hospital, Durban, on July 11th, 1900. He was the second son of the Rev. W. R. Tindal-Atkinson, of St. Andrew's, Burgess Hill, Sussex, was born in 1877, and educated at Brighton College and Honiton. He joined the "Britannia" in 1891, and passed out with full marks in signalling and seamanship. He was appointed naval cadet in July, 1891, and midshipman 1893, being promoted sub-lieut. 1897, and lieut. 1899, and was appointed navigating lieut. of H.M.S. "Partridge" at the Cape, where he was instrumental in boarding several foreign ships suspected of carrying contraband. Lieut. Tindal-Atkinson had served as press censor to Gen. Plumer's force for the relief of Mafeking.

Tindal.—Capt. Arthur Henry Uhthoff Tindal, Welsh Regt., died of wounds received in action at Kheis on May 29th, 1900. He was born March, 1858, educated at Malvern College, and entered the 1st Foot in Jan., 1878. He was transferred to the 69th Foot in the following June, was promoted lieut. in the Welsh Regt. Feb., 1881, and capt. Oct., 1887. He was a good rider and shot. Capt. Tindal served in the operations in Sierra Leone from 1898-99, with the Protectorate Expedition as staff officer with the Bandajuma column, and held the temporary rank of major from April, 1899. He was adjutant of the Welsh Regt. from Feb., 1888, to Feb., 1892, and adjutant of Militia from June, 1892, to Nov., 1897. He embarked for South Africa in Feb., 1900, and at the time of his death was on special service. Capt. Tindal is buried at Prieska. (*See Lieut. G. H. Matthews.*)

Tinslin.—Veterinary-Lieut. Robert Tinslin, Johannesburg Mounted Rifles, died of dysentery at Standerton on Jan. 7th, 1902.

Tod.—Lieut. Noel Moir Tod, 1st Batt. the Cameronians (Scottish Rifles), was killed in action at Wagon Hill, Ladysmith, Jan. 6th, 1900. He was the youngest son of John Henry Tod, Esq., was born in Dec., 1875, and educated at Uppingham. He entered the Scottish Rifles from the Royal Military College, passing out with honours in Feb., 1896, being promoted lieut. March, 1898. Lieut. Tod, whose battalion of the Cameronians was serving in India, volunteered for active service, and was attached for duty to the 2nd Batt. King's Royal Rifle Corps, and served in Natal from the commencement of the war. At the battle of Lombard's Kop on Oct. 30th, 1899, his bravery was very conspicuous. He alone worked a Maxim gun, and when he saw that it would have to be abandoned he rendered it useless. On this occasion a bullet passed through his trousers, and another through his coat, and a third through the flesh of his arm. At

Wagon Hill, at a critical moment, Lieut. Tod called on a sergeant and a dozen men to follow him to attack the Boers. This involved crossing about sixty yards swept with rifle fire to get at the enemy. He and his handful of riflemen made a gallant charge, but before they got half the distance Lieut. Tod and seven of his party were killed and one wounded. Lieut. Tod was mentioned in despatches by Lieut.-Gen. Sir George White, from Ladysmith, Dec. 2nd, 1899, and again in the despatch of March 23rd, 1900, L.G., Feb. 8th, 1901. A tablet has been erected in Uppingham School Chapel to his memory and that of his brother, Lieut. J. E. Tod, 2nd Punjab Cavalry, who died in 1892. (*See Major Bowen.*)

Toll.—Surgeon-Capt. J. T. Toll, 1st South Australian Contingent, died of enteric at sea. He had served during the South African War but had been invalided. He was a fellow of the Royal Colonial Institute, and his name is inscribed on a memorial tablet in the hall of the building in Northumberland Avenue, S.W.

Treatt.—Lieut. Graham Boeller Dalhousie Treatt, New South Wales M.I., died of enteric at Capetown on May 14th, 1901. He was the son of F. Burford Treatt, Esq., Resident Magistrate at Singleton, New South Wales, and was twenty-four years of age. Lieut. Treatt obtained his commission in the New South Wales M.I. early in 1901, and was noted as a very daring and expert rider.

Tredennick.—Lieut. Ernest Davey Tredennick, South African Constabulary (A Division), was dangerously wounded in the head at Buffelsdoom on May 30th, 1900, and died the following day at Potchefstroom. He was the son of Dr. Tredennick, of Penlu House, Craven

Arms, Salop. He went to South Africa with the first squadron of Shropshire I.Y., and afterwards served with the Constabulary, having been nominated for a commission by Gen. Lord Kitchener.

Tremearne.—2nd Lieut. Richard Hastings Tremearne, 5th Batt. Royal Warwickshire Regt., died of enteric at Carnarvon, Cape Colony, on April 14th, 1902. He came of an old Cornish family, an ancestor, John Tremearne, having been vicar of Paul, Cornwall, during the time of the Spanish Armada. 2nd Lieut. Tremearne was the son of Shirley Tremearne, Esq., of Calcutta, and Tudor House, Blackheath Park, was born in India, in July, 1879, and educated at Leamington College and Rugby. He first joined the Honourable Artillery Company as a driver, and volunteering for active service, was sent out in July, 1900, to the battery attached to the C.I.V. He was then sent to Pretoria, and afterwards served in the columns under Generals Paget and Plumer. He returned from South Africa in Nov., 1900, and was awarded the medal and three clasps, which was presented to him by His Majesty the King in June, 1901. In Nov., 1901, he was appointed to a commission in the 5th Batt. Royal Warwickshire Regt., and joined it in Cape Colony. 2nd Lieut. Tremearne then served at Sutherland, where he had charge of a line of blockhouses, and Beaufort West, and afterwards at Carnarvon. He is buried at the latter place—a cross has been erected over his grave.

Trow.—Capt. William H. Trow, Volunteer Co., Shropshire Light Infantry, died of enteric at Kroonstad, May 26th, 1900. He came of a Worcestershire hunting family, his father, grandfather, and great-grandfather having kept packs of harriers in that county. Capt. Trow was 35 years of age, a keen sportsman, and by profession a lawyer. He had held a captain's commission in the 1st battalion since June, 1890, and passed the examination in tactics. He volunteered for active service and went to South Africa in Feb., 1900, with the temporary rank of capt. in the army.

Tryon.—2nd Lieut. Guy Thomas Lewes Tryon, 2nd Batt. Grenadier Guards, died of enteric at Harrismith, on Aug. 24th, 1901. He was the only son of the late Lieut.-Col. Thomas Tryon, of Bulwick, was born in Oct., 1878, and educated at Eton (Mr. Austen Leigh's.) He entered the Grenadier Guards from the 3rd Batt. Northamptonshire Regt. in Nov., 1899. He accompanied his battalion to South Africa in March, 1900, and afterwards served throughout the war up to his death.

Tubman.—Capt. Robert George Tubman, 7th New Zealand M.I., died of enteric at Heilbron on April 11th, 1902.

Tucker.—Capt. Sydney Norval Tucker, D.S.O., South African Constabulary, died of enteric on Jan. 6th, 1902. He had previously served as a capt. in the South African Light Horse, and saw much service during the war, being mentioned in despatches, L.G., April 2nd, 1901. He was awarded the D.S.O. for his services Nov. 29th, 1900, and afterwards joined the South African Constabulary.

Tupman.—Capt. Kenneth Lyon Tupman, 1st Batt. The King's Liverpool Regt., died in Ladysmith Feb. 4th, 1900. He was born in Nov., 1869, and entered the Liverpool Regt. Oct., 1890, being promoted lieut. Jan., 1892, and capt. Nov., 1898. Capt. Tupman was serving with his battalion in Natal at the outbreak of the war, and was in Ladysmith during the siege up to the time of his death.

Turner.—Lieut. George Turner, 35th Co., Army Service Corps, died of enteric at Kroonstad, on April 16th (one report mentions the 10th), 1902.

Turner.—Capt. Neville George Harry Turner, 2nd Batt. West Riding Regt., died of enteric at Wynberg, on May 25th, 1900. He was born in Dec., 1864, and entered the West Riding Regt. from the 3rd Batt. King's Shropshire Light Infantry, Dec. 1886, and was promoted capt. Nov., 1895.

Turner.—Capt. and Brevet-Major Henry Scott Turner, Royal Highlanders, was killed in action at Carter's Ridge, Kimberley, Nov,, 28th. 1899. He was the son of Major Scott Turner, formerly of the 69th Regt.; was born in May, 1867, and educated at Clifton College. He entered the Royal Highlanders as 2nd lieut. in Dec., 1887, and was promoted lieut. May, 1890, capt. May 24th, 1898, and brevet-major on the following day. He served in Matabeleland, 1893-94, and also in 1896, when he was adjutant and paymaster of the Matabeleland Relief Force. Major Turner was mentioned in despatches March 9th, 1897, and granted a brevet majority for his services. Previous to the South African War Major Turner was serving under the British South African Co., but in Oct., 1899, was seconded for special service, and proceeded to Kimberley and took part in the defence of the town. He had been wounded three days before he was killed while leading a sortie, which was most successful, thirty-three Boers being captured. Recovering, he again commanded a second sortie, and fell while directing his men. Col. Kekewich in his despatch of Feb. 15th, 1900, mentions Major Scott Turner's brilliant services, his energy, and courage; and adds, "in him the army has lost a most valuable officer." The De Beers Co. have erected, on Carter's Ridge, a monument consisting of a cairn 20 feet high with a slab in the centre, in memory of Major Scott Turner and others who fell in the sortie on Nov. 26th, 1899. On the slab are engraved the names of all who were killed.

Turpin.—Lieut. Cliff Turpin, Marshall's Horse, was killed in action at Dorignspoort, on March 24th, 1901.

Twigg.—Lieut. James Stuart Twigg, M.B., Royal Army Medical Corps, was killed in action between Clanwilliam and Calvinia, Dec. 22nd, 1901. He was born in Oct., 1874, entered the Royal Army Medical Corps April, 1900, and proceeded to South Africa in June, serving there until his death.

Twisleton. — Lieut. T. H. G. Twisleton, 7th New Zealand M.I., died of pneumonia at Losberg, on Aug. 26th, 1901.

Twyford. — Major Ernest Henry Samuel Twyford, D.S.O., p.s.c., 1st Batt. Royal Scots, was killed in action at Badfontein, in the Lydenburg district, April 13th, 1901. He was born Oct., 1863, and entered the Cameronians (Scottish Rifles) in Dec., 1883, being promoted lieut. Nov., 1887, capt. March, 1894, major April, 1899, and was transferred to the 1st Batt. Royal Scots in Feb., 1901. He had held the position of adjutant, Scottish Rifles, from Nov., 1887-91. He served with the Chin Lushai Expeditionary Force as transport officer in 1889, receiving the medal with clasp. In the South African War he was with the 2nd Batt. Scottish Rifles in the Natal Field Force, and was present at the battle of Colenso, the engagements at Spion Kop and Vaal Kranz, in the operations on the Tugela from Feb. 14th-27th, 1900, including the fighting at Pieter's Hill (severely wounded) and the relief of Ladysmith, being mentioned in despatches. Major **Twyford** also took part in the subsequent operations in the Transvaal, and was awarded the D.S.O., L.G., April 19th, 1901. When killed he was on his way to join the 1st Batt. Royal Scots, to which he had been appointed as second in command.

Tyler.—Lieut. Arthur John Tyler, West Riding Regt., serving with Col. Plumer's Force, was killed in action north of Mafeking, March 14th, 1900. He was born in June, 1871, entered the West Riding Regt. June, 1892, being promoted lieut. Sept., 1895. He was seconded in Sept., 1899, for special service in South Africa with Col. Plumer's M.I.

Tyndall Staines.—2nd Lieut. Bertram James Tyndall Staines, 1st Batt. East Lancashire Regt., died of dysentery at Heilbron on Dec. 1st, 1901. He first joined Thorneycroft's M.I. as a private, and was present at Colenso, Spion Kop, and the fighting on the Tugela, having had two horses shot under him. For his services he was granted a commission in the East Lancashire Regt. in Sept., 1901.

Umphelby.—Lieut.-Col. C. E. E. Umphelby, Australian Artillery, died of wounds received in action on March 10th, 1900, at Driefontein. He belonged to the Royal Australian Artillery, and had been attached to the Victorian Contingent in South Africa. He was mentioned in despatches by F.-M. Earl Roberts, L.G., Feb. 8th, 1901, for having "rendered conspicuously valuable service," and, had he survived, his name would have been brought prominently to notice. Lieut.-Col. Umphelby was again mentioned in despatches, L.G., April 16th, 1901, for meritorious service.

Urey.—Lieut. J. Urey, 2nd Batt. I.Y., died at Heilbron on Feb. 21st, 1902. He first served as a trooper, and was promoted lieut., with the rank of lieut. in the army, May 22nd, 1901.

Ussher.—Capt. Edward Ussher, D.S.O., 2nd Dragoons, died at the Nigel Mines on Feb. 20th, 1902, of wounds received in action at Klippan, near Springs, two days previously. He was the eldest son of John Ussher, Esq., of The Dene, Great Budworth, Cheshire, was born in Nov., 1869, and educated at Eton (Dr. Warre's and Mr. Wintle's). He entered the 2nd Dragoons from the Royal Military College in March, 1890, being promoted lieut. in Sept., 1892, and capt. in Sept., 1900. He had been adjutant from May 10th, 1900, and was present at all the actions in which his regiment took part since the commencement of the war, including the operations on the Orange River, the relief of Kimberley, the surrender of Cronje, and the advance on Bloemfontein and Pretoria. Capt. Ussher was mentioned in despatches, L.G., Sept. 10th, 1901, and was awarded the D.S.O.

Vallentin.—Brevet-Major John Maximilian Vallentin, p.s.c., Somersetshire Light Infantry, was killed in action at Onverwacht, Ermelo District, on Jan. 4th, 1902. He was the son of Sir J. Vallentin, was born in Feb., 1865, and educated at Haileybury. He entered the Somersetshire Light Infantry Feb., 1885, was promoted capt. June, 1892, and brevet-major Nov., 1900. In Aug., 1888, he married Helen Mary, daughter of Col. Carnegy. He served in the Burmese Expedition of 1886-87 with the 2nd battalion of his regiment, and received the medal with clasp. He graduated at the Staff College in 1897, and before the outbreak of the war in South Africa was brigade-major at Ladysmith, Natal. On the re-distribution of the brigades of the Natal Field Force, after the arrival of Sir George White, Major Vallentin was appointed brigade-major to Lieut.-Gen. Sir Ian Hamilton. At the battle of Elandslaagte, Major Vallentin behaved with conspicuous gallantry in rallying the flank attack during the most critical phase of the assault. He served throughout the siege of Ladysmith until Jan., when he had a severe attack of enteric. When convalescent, he elected to return to his chief, Sir I. Hamilton, and joined him at Bloemfontein just after his appointment to the command of a division. After the occupation of Heidelberg, Major Vallentin was appointed Commissioner of that town. In the autumn of 1900, while holding this position, he was sent out with one of F.-M. Earl Roberts' Proclamations to a commando in his neighbourhood, and lived with the Boers for a week as their guest while the object of his visit was under discussion. He then returned to military duty, and saw much service during 1901. He met his death while pursuing with about fifty men some Boers under Oppermann and Christian Botha, who were several hundreds strong; his party suffered severely, but Oppermann was killed. Major Vallentin was mentioned in despatches by Gen. Sir George White on Dec. 2nd, 1899, from Ladysmith, and again in the despatch of March 23rd, 1900, L.G., Feb. 8th, 1901; also in the despatches of Gen. Lord Kitchener, July 28th, 1901, and of Aug. 8th, 1901, this latter making the fourth occasion on which he was mentioned during the war. He was awarded a brevet-majority for his services.

Vandeleur.—Lieut.-Col. Cecil Foster Seymour Vandeleur, D.S.O., Scots Guards, was killed in a train which was wrecked between Isaterval and Hamman's Kraal, about fifteen miles north of Pretoria, Aug. 31st, 1901. The enemy, who lined the banks of the cutting, opened fire on the derailed carriages, and Lieut.-Col. Vandeleur was shot down. He was the eldest son of Hector Stewart Vandeleur, Esq., of Kilrush, was born in July, 1869, and educated at Eton (Dr. Warre's and Mr.

Donaldson's). He entered the Scots Guards in Feb., 1889, being promoted lieut. May, 1892, capt. and brevet-major in June, 1899, transferred to the Irish Guards, May, 1900, became major in the following Oct., and brevet-lieut.-col. a month later. He served with the Unyoro Expedition in 1895, being mentioned in despatches and receiving the medal. He took part in the Nandi Expedition, 1895-96, being again mentioned in despatches and receiving the D.S.O. He served in the Niger-Soudan Campaign under Major Arnold in 1897, including the expeditions to Egbon, Bida, and Ilorin, was mentioned in despatches, and received the brevet of major and the medal with clasp. Lieut.-Col. Vandeleur served in the Soudan Campaign under Lord (then Sir Herbert) Kitchener in 1898, and was present at the battles of the Atbara and Khartoum, being slightly wounded, was mentioned in despatches, and received the British medal and Khedive's medal with two clasps and the Fourth Class of the Order of the Medjidie. He was on special service in South Africa from Dec., 1899, to Jan., 1900, and was employed with transport from Jan. 20th, 1900, and was D.A.A.G. Lieut.-Col. Vandeleur is buried in Pretoria. He was mentioned in despatches, L.G., Feb. 8th, 1901, and promoted brevet-lieut.-col.

Vaughan.—Lieut. Esmæ Allen Peers Vaughan, 2nd Batt. Royal Lancaster Regt., died at the Base Hospital, Pietermaritzburg, March 7th, 1900, of wounds received on Feb. 27th in the operations on the Tugela. He was the youngest son of Charles Peers Vaughan, Esq., of Buch Lawn, Pendleton, was born in Aug., 1877, and educated at Harrow. He entered the Royal Lancaster Regt. in Feb., 1898, and was promoted lieut. Nov., 1899. Lieut. Vaughan accompanied his battalion to South Africa in Nov., 1899, and served with the Natal Field Force.

Veitch.—Major Quinten R. Veitch, Cape Volunteer Medical Staff Corps (Cape Mounted Rifles), died of heart disease at Cape Town on Feb. 2nd, 1902.

Venning.—Lieut. Gordon Ralph Venning, D.S.O., 4th Battery Royal Field Artillery, was killed in action between Tweebosch and Palmietkuil March 7th, 1902. He was the son of A. R. Venning, Esq., was born in June, 1880, and educated at Bath College, where he is well remembered for his notable athletic record. He entered the Royal Artillery in Dec., 1898, and was promoted lieut. Feb., 1901. He was one of the youngest wearers of the decoration of the D.S.O. Lieut. Venning accompanied his battery to South Africa in Nov., 1899, and had served throughout the war. At Tweebosch he and all his men were either killed or wounded round their two guns. He was mentioned in despatches, L.G., Sept. 10th, 1901, and was awarded the D.S.O. He was also mentioned in the despatch of Lieut.-Gen. Lord Methuen from Klerksdorp, March 13th, 1902, who called "attention to the gallant manner in which Lieut. Venning stuck to his guns" at Tweebosch.

Vernon.—Capt. Ronald James Vernon, King's Royal Rifle Corps, was killed in action at Game Tree in a sortie from Mafeking on Dec. 26th, 1899. He was the son of the Hon. Mr. and Mrs. Greville Vernon, and was born in Jan., 1866. He entered the King's Royal Rifle Corps from the Militia in Jan., 1889, was promoted lieut. Feb., 1891, and capt. May, 1897. He served in the Expedition to Manipur in 1891. Capt. Vernon was A.D.C. to the General Officer Commanding at the Cape of Good Hope from 1894-98, and at the time of his death was on special service in South Africa. In this sortie several gallant lives were lost in addition to Capt. Vernon; Capt. Sandford and Lieut. Paton being killed.

All three fell at the "very muzzles of the enemy's guns." The attacking party consisted of eighty, and of these twenty-four were killed and twenty-three wounded. The death of these officers is mentioned in the despatch of Major.-Gen. Baden-Powell of May 18th, 1900, from Mafeking, where Capt. Vernon is stated to have been "a most successful officer in command of a squadron," and to have "displayed the greatest gallantry in action." Major-Gen. Baden-Powell added, "Both officers and men worked with splendid courage and spirit," L.G., Feb. 8th, 1901.

Verschoyle.—Capt. Edward Greville Verschoyle, 2nd Batt. Grenadier Guards, died of wounds received in action at Thaba N'chu on May 5th, 1900. He was the second son of the late Lieut.-Col. Verschoyle, Grenadier Guards, of Killbery, co. Kildare, by his marriage with Lucy Clarissa, third daughter of Ambrose Goddard, Esq., of the Lawn, Swindon. Capt. Verschoyle was born in Nov., 1866, and educated at Wellington, where he was in Kempthorne's House, 1880-84. He entered the Grenadier Guards from the Royal Military College in May, 1885, being promoted capt. Oct., 1897. He served in the Nile Expedition of 1898, and took part in the battle of Khartoum, receiving the medal and the Egyptian medal with clasp. Capt. Verschoyle accompanied his battalion to South Africa in March, 1900, and served in the Cape and Orange River Colonies up to the time of his death.

Vertue.—Capt. Naunton Henry Vertue, p.s.c., East Kent Regt., was killed in action at Spion Kop, in the operations on the Upper Tugela, on Jan. 24th, 1900. He was born in Jan., 1863, educated at Clifton and entered the East Kent Regt. Feb., 1884, being promoted lieut. May, 1890, and capt. March, 1893. He was adjutant of his battalion from May, 1890, to May,

1894, and served as A.D.C. to the Brigadier-Gen. commanding in Ceylon from March, 1897, to Jan., 1899. At the time of his death, Capt. Vertue held the appointment of Brigade-Major to the 11th Infantry Brigade in South Africa, commanded by Major-Gen. Woodgate. Capt. Vertue was mentioned in despatches, L.G., Feb. 8th, 1901.

Von Schade.—Lieut. F. C. Von Schade, Commander-in-Chief's Bodyguard, died of wounds received in action in South Africa, Jan., 1901.

Waddell-Dudley.— Lieut. Bertram Barré Waddell-Dudley, 2nd Batt. North Staffordshire Regt., died of enteric at Bloemfontein on June 20th, 1900. He was the son of the Rev. W. D. Waddell-Dudley, of St. Stephen's Vicarage, St. Albans, was born in June, 1874, and educated at Haileybury. He entered the North Staffordshire Regt. from the Militia in June, 1896, being promoted lieut. Jan. 1899. Lieut. Waddell-Dudley accompanied his battalion to South Africa in Jan., 1900, and served in the Seventh Division under Lieut.-Gen. Tucker, taking part in the advance on Bloemfontein.

Wade.—Lieut. Alexander Price Conolly Herschel Wade, 2nd Batt. Royal Lancaster Regt., was killed in action at Spion Kop in the operations on the Upper Tugela, Jan. 24th, 1900. He was the second son of Sir Thomas Francis Wade, G.C.M.G., K.C.B., was born in August, 1870, and educated at Winchester. He entered the East Yorkshire Regt. in Jan., 1892, and was promoted lieut. Oct., 1895, and exchanged to the Royal Lancaster Regt. as a lieut. in Feb., 1897. Lieut. Wade accompanied his battalion to South Africa in Nov., 1899, and served with the Natal Field Force. At Spion Kop he ran out leading some men to reinforce the firing line, and was instantly killed.

Wadling.—2nd Lieut. John William Cottingham Wadling, 2nd Batt. Royal Berkshire Regt., died of enteric at Naauwpoort on March 5th, 1900. He was the only son of Lieut.-Col. J. Cottingham Wadling, late of the 5th Northumberland Fusiliers, was born in Sept. 1878, and educated at Rugby, where he was one of the rifle team when the school won the Ashburton Shield. He entered the 2nd Batt. Royal Berkshire Regt. from the 3rd. Batt. in June, 1898. 2nd Lieut. Wadling was with his battalion in South Africa on the outbreak of the war, and served with it in the operations in the north of Cape Colony.

Waldy.—Capt. Richard Wartyr Waldy, 2nd Batt. Bedfordshire Regt., died on Feb. 22nd, 1900, of wounds received in action at Paardeberg four days previously. He was born in Dec., 1868, and educated at Sherbourne from 1880-87. He entered the Bedfordshire Regt. from the 3rd Batt. Devonshire Regt. in Dec., 1889, being promoted lieut. March, 1892, and capt. July, 1899. He served with the Isazai Expedition in 1892, also with the Chitral Relief Force under Sir Robert Low in 1895, with the 1st battalion of his regiment, and received the medal with clasp. Capt. Waldy embarked with the 2nd battalion of his regiment for South Africa in Dec. 1899, and served with it until his death.

Walker.—Lieut. Charles Henry Walker, 3rd Batt. South Lancashire Regt., died of acute bronchitis at De Aar on Sept. 20th, 1901. He was appointed in Dec., 1900 as a lieut. in his battalion, which had been serving in South Africa since Feb. of the same year.

Walker.—Lieut. Charles James Reginald Walker, 1st Batt. Royal Inniskilling Fusiliers, was dangerously wounded near Lietgat on Feb. 19th, 1902, and died the same day. He was born in Feb., 1873, educated at Winchester, and entered the 1st Batt. Royal Inniskilling Fusiliers from the 4th Batt. (Royal Tyrone Militia) in April, 1900, being promoted lieut. July, 1901. He is buried at Lichtenburg. A marble stone has been erected over his grave by his comrades of the 1st battalion.

Walker.—Major Charles Pope Walker, M.B., Royal Army Medical Corps, died in Ladysmith on Jan. 5th, 1900. He was born in July, 1860, and was appointed to the Royal Army Medical Corps July, 1886, being promoted major July, 1898. Major Walker was serving in South Africa at the commencement of the war, and took part in the defence of Ladysmith up to the time of his death.

Walker.—Lieut. Claude Ernest Myln Walker, 1st Batt. Somersetshire Light Infantry, was killed in action in the engagement at Wagon Hill, Ladysmith, Jan. 6th, 1900. He was born in Dec., 1875, and entered the Somersetshire Light Infantry from the 3rd Batt. Yorkshire Light Infantry, Dec., 1897, being promoted lieut. July, 1899. He served in the operations on the North-West Frontier of India, 1897-98, with the Tirah Expeditionary Force, for which he received the medal with clasp. Lieut. Walker was mentioned in despatches by Lieut.-Gen. Sir G. White, March 23rd, 1900, L.G. Feb. 8th, 1901.

Walker.—Capt. George Stanley Walker, M.B., Royal Army Medical Corps, died of enteric in Ladysmith, Feb. 23rd, 1900. He was born in May, 1865, joined the Royal Army Medical Corps, 1892, and was promoted capt. July, 1895. Capt. Walker was serving in India in 1899, but went to South Africa in Oct., and was in Ladysmith till his death. He was mentioned in despatches by Lieut.-Gen. Sir G. White, March 23rd, 1900, L.G. Feb. 8th, 1901.

OFFICERS WHO FELL IN SOUTH AFRICA. 401

Walker.—Major John Charles Arthington Walker, 2nd Dragoon Guards (Queen's Bays), was killed in action in the engagement near Leeuwkop, April 1st, 1902. He was born in May, 1859, entered the 19th Hussars from the 4th Batt. Duke of Wellington's West Riding Regt. (6th West York Militia) July, 1882, was promoted capt. Jan., 1886, and major in the 2nd Dragoon Guards, May, 1897. He was Recruiting Staff Officer, London District from 1896-99. He served in the Soudan Expedition, 1884, with the 19th Hussars, and was present at the engagements at El Teb and Tamai, receiving the medal with clasp and the Khedive's star. He also served in the Nile Expedition, 1884-85, with the same regiment (clasp). Major Walker embarked with The Queen's Bays for South Africa, Nov., 1901. In the action in which he was killed three squadrons of the Bays first attacked a farm house at Holspruit, capturing Commandant Pretorius. They afterwards attacked Albert's commando, which was found encamped near and in very superior numbers. The fighting was most determined, Major Walker and Capt. Herron being killed.

Walker.—Lieut. J. Walker, Railway Pioneer Regt., died of tuberculosis at Johannesburg on Nov. 23rd, 1901.

Walker.—Lieut. T. G. Walker, late Rhodesia Field Force, died of abscess and syncope at Wynberg during the war.

Wallace.—Lieut. Augustus Robert Wallace, 1st Batt. Loyal North Lancashire Regt., was accidently killed by the explosion of a mine, at Zeerust, Jan. 13th, 1901. He was born in Jan., 1872, and educated at Marlborough. He entered the Loyal North Lancashire Regt. in Jan., 1893, being promoted lieut. May, 1895. Lieut. Wallace was with his battalion in South Africa when war was

Wallace.—2nd Lieut. Aylmer Willoughby Wallace, 2nd Batt. King's Own Yorkshire Light Infantry, was invalided home suffering from a broken leg, the effects of an accident in South Africa. He, however, developed symptoms of enteric the day after he joined the S.S. "Dunera," and died Oct. 9th, 1901, from this disease. He was the son of Col. N. W. Wallace, J.P., late of the King's Royal Rifle Corps, and now commanding the 4th County of London (King's Colonials) I.Y. 2nd Lieut. Wallace was born in Feb., 1880, and educated at Rugby. He first served in the Cape Mounted Rifles from the commencement of the war, and on the recommendation of the Field-Marshal commanding-in-chief, South Africa, he was granted a commission in the Yorkshire Light Infantry in May, 1900. He was then appointed to the M.I. of his battalion, and when invalided had taken part in some 30 engagements, among them the defence of Wepener during its siege by the Boers.

Wallis.—Captain Alexander Frederic Wallis, 1st Batt. The Duke of Wellington's (West Riding) Regt., was killed in action at Arundel, Feb. 24th, 1900. He was born in Jan., 1867, and educated at Derby School. He entered the West Riding Regiment in Feb., 1887, was promoted lieut. July, 1889, and capt. March, 1896. He had served in the operations in South Africa in 1896. Capt. Wallace accompanied his battalion on active service in Dec., 1899, and served with it in the North of Cape Colony until killed.

Wallis.—2nd Lieut. Clifton Edmund Percival Wallis,

OFFICERS WHO FELL IN SOUTH AFRICA. 403

2nd Batt. Royal Irish Fusiliers, was killed in action at Jaskraal, O.R.C., Aug. 28th, 1901. He was born in Oct., 1878, and entered the 5th Batt. Connaught Rangers as a lieut. in Dec., 1899, from the 5th Batt. Royal Irish Regt. In April, 1900, he was given a commission as 2nd Lieut. in the Royal Irish Fusiliers, which he then joined in South Africa, and served with it until killed.

Wallis.—Lieut. Henry Wallis, British South African Mounted Police, died of fever at Gaberones, on April 21st, 1900, while serving under Col. Plumer. He was the youngest son of Major H. B. Wallis, late of the Duke of Wellington's West Riding Regt.

Walsh.—Lieut. Frederick Lawrence Walsh, South African Light Horse, died of enteric at Kroonstad, on Jan. 14th, 1902. He was 33 years of age, and had formerly been in the 3rd Batt. The Buffs.

Walter.—Capt. Charles Walter, 1st Batt. The Cameronians (Scottish Rifles), was killed in action at Spion Kop, in the operations on the Upper Tugela, Jan 24th, 1900. He was the son of Gen. J. M. Walter, C.B., was born in Nov., 1872, and educated at Wellington (where he was in the Hopetoun), 1885 to 1890, whence he passed direct into the Royal Military College. He entered the Scottish Rifles in Oct., 1892, being promoted lieut. Dec., 1894, capt. Feb., 1899, and was serving with his battalion in India. Capt. Walter volunteered for active service, and was sent to Natal at the commencement of the war, and served there until killed.

Walter.—Lieut. Crespele Walter, Tasmanian Bushmen, was killed in action at Pietersburg, on April 8th, 1901.

Walton.—Lieut. Louis Alban Walton, 4th Batt. Royal Lancaster Regiment, died of enteric at Naauwpoort, Cape Colony, May 19th, 1901. He was the sixth son of Judge Walton, was born in June, 1880; educated at Stonyhurst College, and entered his regiment in Jan., 1900, being promoted lieut. Feb., 1901. His battalion had been embodied in Dec., 1899, and proceeded to South Africa in January, 1900, where Lieut. Walton joined it, and served with it till his death.

Ward.—Lieut. H. H. Ward, 24th Co., 8th Batt. I.Y., was killed in action at Dehoop, north-east of Calvinia, on Feb. 6th, 1902. He first served as a trooper, but was afterwards granted a commission and was appointed to the 8th Batt. I.Y., as a lieut. Oct. 12th, 1901, with the rank of lieut. in the army.

Wardlaw.—Capt. Edgar Penrose Wardlaw, Duke of Cornwall's Light Infantry, was killed in action on Feb. 18th, 1900, near Paardeberg. He was born in Nov., 1866, and educated at Wellington, where he was in the Anglesey, being then known as E. P. Mark, but afterwards took up the old family name of Wardlaw. At Wellington he was a Prefect and in the football XV. He entered the Duke of Cornwall's Light Infantry from the 3rd Batt. North Staffordshire Regt., in Nov., 1887, and was promoted lieut. in April, 1890, and capt. April, 1897. He had been adjutant of his battalion since May, 1897. Capt. Wardlaw was mentioned in the despatch of F.-M. Earl Roberts, from Paardeberg, Feb. 28th, 1900, L.G., Feb. 8th, 1901.

Waring.—Surg.-Lieut.-Col. Walter Waring, Militia Medical Staff Corps, died of dysentery at the Princess Christian Hospital, at Pine Town Bridge, South Africa, Oct. 6th, 1900. He was appointed surg.-capt. in June,

1902, and surg.-lieut.-col. the following Aug. Surg.-Lieut.-Col. Waring volunteered for active service, and proceeded to South Africa in Feb., 1900, and served during the war up to the time of his death.

Warren.—Lieut. Warren, Cape Mounted Rifles, was killed in action at Dordrecht, on Jan. 2nd, 1900.

Warren.—Capt. W. J. Y. Warren, Volunteer Co. King's Royal Rifle Corps, died of dysentery at Modder Spruit, May, 8th, 1900. He had held the rank of capt. in the 2nd City of London Volunteer Rifle Corps from Oct., 1895, and had qualified in all military subjects, having passed the School of Instruction, and examinations in musketry, signalling, etc. On March 28th, 1900, he was appointed to serve with the line battalion in South Africa with the rank of capt. in the army, and at once proceeded to South Africa and served there till his death. A tablet of brass and alabaster to his memory and that of his comrades who fell in the war, has been erected at the headquarters of the 2nd City of London Rifles, Farringdon Road.

Watney.—Lieut. Jack Southard Watney, 11th Batt. I.Y., was killed in action at Tweefontein, in De Wet's attack on Christmas morning, 1901. He was the eldest son of Mrs. Hattie Gilbey Watney, of 24, Clanricarde Gardens, and of the late Ernest Watney, Esq. He was born in March, 1882, and educated at St. Paul's School and at Eton (Mr. Alcock's). He volunteered for active service in South Africa, and first served in the ranks of the I.Y. He was quickly promoted sergeant, and appointed to the 11th Battalion in June, 1901, as machine gun commander, with the rank of lieut. in the army. In the action in which he fell he was in command of a maxim gun, and reported by Lord Kitchener to have been killed "while heading a charge." He died with all the men of his gun section around him either killed or wounded. Lieut. Watney is buried at Tweefontein, and his name is inscribed on an obelisk, which has been erected there in memory of all those who fell in this action.

Watson.—Lieut.-Col. Arthur John Watson, p.s.c., 1st Batt. Suffolk Regt., was killed in action near Rensburg, Jan. 6th, 1900. He was born in June, 1853, and entered the 12th Foot in Aug., 1873, being promoted capt. April, 1883, major Oct., 1886, and lieut.-col. Sept., 1898. He was instructor of musketry to his battalion from Feb., 1880, to Jan., 1883. He served with the Bechuanaland Expedition under Sir Charles Warren, 1884-85, as brigade-major, and was mentioned in despatches. He was employed with the Egyptian Army from Feb., 1886, to the following Sept. He took part in the Hazara Expedition in 1888 as brigade-major to the First Column, under Brigadier-General Channer, was mentioned in despatches and received the medal with clasp. He also served with the Chitral Relief Force under Sir Robert Low, in 1897, as road commandant on the lines of communications, receiving the medal with clasp. Lieut.-Col. Watson was D.A.A.G. in Bengal from July, 1889, to Feb., 1896. He obtained command of the 1st Batt. Suffolk Regt. in Sept., 1898, and took the battalion to South Africa in Nov., 1899. He fell in a night attack on the enemy who held a kopje which formed the key to their position round the town of Colesberg. The Boers, who were apparently well informed of our intended attack, opened fire and Lieut.-Col. Watson was killed early in the fight. A monument has been erected at Colesberg in memory of all those who fell in this engagement.

Watson.—Capt. Harry Augustus Ferguson Watson, 3rd Batt. Lancashire Fusiliers, attached to the Scottish Horse, died Oct. 2nd, 1901, of wounds received in action two days previously at Moedwill (7 miles east of Magota Nek). He was born in Feb., 1876, educated at Bedford Grammar School, and entered the Royal Dublin Fusiliers in March, 1896, being promoted lieut. March, 1898, and capt. in the Lancashire Fusiliers June, 1901. Capt. Watson had served throughout the War having accompanied the 1st Batt. Royal Dublin Fusiliers to South Africa in Oct., 1899. He had been employed with M.I., and had been severely wounded. He was afterwards appointed adjutant of the Scottish Horse, and held this position at the time of his death. He was mentioned in despatches, L.G., Feb. 8th, 1901.

Watson.—Capt. John Capron Watson, Royal Field Artillery, was killed in action near Wilman's Rust, Transvaal, June 12th, 1901. He was the eldest son of the late Col. William Henry Watson, Royal Artillery, of Minsted, Midhurst, Sussex, was born in Aug., 1867, and educated at Cheltenham. He entered the Royal Artillery in July, 1886, and was promoted capt. July, 1897. Capt. Watson went to South Africa in Dec., 1899, in charge of a special ammunition column, but on his old battery (the 9th), being ordered to the war in Jan., 1900, he rejoined it, and served with it until his death. His name is inscribed on the Eleanor Cross War Memorial at Cheltenham College.

Watson.—Lieut. William Watson, District Mounted Troops, was killed at Somerset East on Oct. 5th, 1901.

Wauchope.— Maj.-Gen. Andrew Gilbert Wauchope, C.B., C.M.G., was killed in action at Magersfontein Dec. 11th, 1899. He was the only surviving son of the late Andrew Wauchope, Esq., D.L., J.P., of Niddrie

Marischal, Midlothian, and was born in July, 1846. He joined the 42nd Foot in Nov., 1865, was promoted lieut. June, 1867, capt, Sept., 1878, major March, 1884, brevet-lieut.-col. May, 1884, lieut.-col. Aug., 1894, col. May, 1898, and maj.-gen. in Nov., 1898. He served in the Ashantee War from the 30th Nov., 1873, and commanded the Winnebah Company of Russell's Regiment as far as the Adansi Hills. He was then appointed staff officer to Sir J. M'Leod, commanding the advanced guard of F.-M. Lord Wolseley's force, and was present at the capture and destruction of Adubiassie, capture of Borborassie, battle of Amoaful, capture and destruction of Becquah, the advanced guard engagement of Jarbinbah (wounded slightly), skirmishes and ambuscade affairs between Adwabin and the river Ordah, the battle of Ordahsu (severely wounded), and capture of Kumassi, being mentioned in despatches and receiving the medal with clasp. He served with the 1st Batt. Black Watch in the Egyptian War of 1882, and was present at the battle of Tel-el-Kebir, receiving the medal with clasp and Khedive's star. He took part in the Soudan Expedition under Sir Gerald Graham in 1884, as D.A.A. and Q.M.G., and was present in the engagement at El Teb (severely wounded), being mentioned in despatches and receiving the brevet of lieut.-col. and two clasps. He also served in the Nile expedition, 1884-85, with the 1st Batt. of the Black Watch, and was with the river column under Maj.-Gen. Earle, and was present in the engagement at Kirbekan, being very severely wounded (two clasps). His next war experience was in the campaign in the Soudan under Lord (then Sir Herbert) Kitchener in 1898, when he was in command of the 1st Brigade British Division, and was present at the battle of Khartoum, being mentioned in despatches and promoted maj.-gen. for distinguished service in the field, and received the thanks of both Houses of Parliament, and the British medal and Khedive's medal with clasp. Gen. Wauchope had only joined the Kimberley Relief Force, under Lieut.-Gen. Lord Methuen, a few days before the battle of Magersfontein; at this action he was in command of the Highland Brigade, which in the early dawn was suddenly exposed to a terrific infantry fire at close range. "*The Times* History of the War" thus describes what took place: "At the first burst of fire Gen. Wauchope, at once realising the cause of the disaster, walked forward in front of the leading companies to ascertain, if possible, how far the advanced trenches extended. A glance at the line of flashes was enough. He immediately sent back his cousin to tell the Black Watch to reinforce on the right as quickly as they could. Young Wauchope ran back along the lines of prostrate men, gave the order to Col. Coode and to all the officers he could see, and then hurried forward again to the spot where he had left the general alone. But before he returned Wauchope had fallen, and a moment later his devoted A.D.C. fell wounded too." [Capt. Wauchope survived his wounds.] "Coode gallantly led his men forward, but was killed almost immediately. Next day all three were found close together within 200 yards of the trenches." Describing this battle, Sir A. Conan Doyle states he has been assured by a Boer who was present that "it was the sound of the tins attached to the alarm wires which disturbed" the enemy; and that "in an instant there crashed out of the darkness a roar of point blank fire." The storm of lead burst upon the column "which broke to pieces under the murderous volley." "Wauchope was shot, struggled up, and fell once more for ever." Major-Gen. Wauchope is buried at Magersfontein, close to, and in front of the graves of the fallen of his devoted Highland brigade. He was always known by his intimate friends as "Andy" Wauchope, and was universally popular and beloved.

Waudby.—Lieut. William Waudby, Leinster Regt., died at Netley Hospital of enteric, April 3rd, 1901. He was the son of the late Major Sidney James Waudby, was born on March 9th, 1876, and educated at Rossall. He entered the Leinster Regt. from the 4th Batt. Border Regt. in May, 1898, and was promoted lieut. Nov., 1900. He accompanied his battalion to South Africa in April, 1900, and served with it until invalided home. He was mentioned in despatches, L.G., Sept. 10th 1901.

Way.—Lieut. Arthur Strachan Way, D.S.O., 2nd Batt. Durham Light Infantry, was killed in action at Tabaksberg, south of Welcome, Jan. 29th, 1901, in the fighting with De Wet. He was the fourth son of the Rev. W. H. Bromley Way, late Rector of Warboys, Hants, was born in March, 1876, and educated at Marlborough. He was a keen sportsman and a good Rugby forward. He entered the Durham Light Infantry from the Royal Military College in Feb., 1896, being promoted lieut. July, 1897. He saw much service during the campaign and at Sanna's Post, and when surrounding Prinsloo, behaved with conspicuous bravery. Lieut. Way was awarded the D.S.O., Sept, 28th, 1901, and the medal with five clasps for Paardeberg, Wittebergen, Johannesburg, Diamond Hill, and Driefontein. He was mentioned in despatches, L.G., Sept. 10th, 1901. The following is an extract from the orders of his battalion (then stationed in Burmah), of Feb. 4th, 1901: "The Commanding Officer announces with great regret the death, in South Africa, of Lieut. A. S. Way, who was killed in action Jan. 29th. Lieut. Way was a most promising and zealous officer, and his death is a great loss to the battalion, where he was known and liked by all ranks as a good all round sportsman." His battalion has put up a marble cross in his memory at Welcome, and his name is inscribed on a tablet placed in Marlborough

College Chapel in memory of all Marlburians who fell in the war.

Webster.—Capt. Godfrey Vassall George Frederick Charles Webster, Bethune's M.I., was killed in an accident on the railway at Bethulie on Feb. 1st, 1901. He was the son of the late Sir Augustus Frederick Webster, Bart., by his marriage with Amelia Sophia, 2nd daughter of the late Charles Frederick Augustus Prosser-Hastings, Esq., Taunton, Somerset. Capt. Webster was born in 1872, and was educated at Eton (Mr. Hales').

Webster.—Lieut. Leveret Beverley Webster, 1st Batt. King's Own (Royal Lancaster Regt.), died in London, March 22nd, 1902. He was the only son of Barclay Webster, Esq., of Kentville, Nova Scotia, Canada, and was born in Sept., 1878. He entered the Royal Lancaster Regt. from the Local Militia Forces of Canada in April, 1900, being promoted lieut. Feb., 1901. He served with his battalion in South Africa for about eighteen months, in the operations in northern Natal, and the fighting around Dundee and Vryheid, and was invalided to England. He then entered one of Lady Dudley's nursing homes in Dec., 1901, but never recovered his strength. His body was conveyed to Canada for interment.

Wedd.—Lieut. Lawrence Dunkin Wedd, D.S.O., 2nd Batt. The Queen's Royal West Surrey Regt., died of enteric at Kroonstad, July 7th, 1902. He was born in Jan., 1878, entered the Royal West Surrey Regt, Feb., 1898, and was promoted lieut. April, 1900. He embarked with his battalion for South Africa in Oct., 1899, served with the Natal Field Force, and was present at the battle of Colenso and the operations on the Tugela, the action at Pieter's Hill, and the relief of Ladysmith. He was twice mentioned in despatches, L.G., Feb. 8th and Sept. 10th, 1901, for his services, and was awarded the D.S.O.

Welch.—Brevet-Major Norman Charles Welch, 2nd Batt. Hampshire Regt., died Nov. 10th, 1900, of wounds received in action near Bothaville four days previously. He was the youngest son of the late John D. Welch, Esq., of Herne Hill, Surrey, was born in July, 1865, and educated at Charterhouse. He entered the Hampshire Regt. from the 3rd Batt. The Queen's in Nov., 1886, being promoted capt. July, 1893, and brevet-major July, 1899. He served with the Burmese Expedition in 1887, and received the medal with clasp. He also served in the operations on the Niger, 1897-98, being mentioned in despatches, L.G., March 7th, 1899, and receiving the brevet of major for his services. He was employed with the West African Frontier Force from Feb., 1898, to Sept., 1899. Major Welch proceeded to South Africa in Jan., 1900, and served in Cape and Orange River Colonies. The author of "The Great Boer War," in writing of the action at Bothaville, states that four officers were killed, among them " Major Welch, a soldier of great promise, much beloved by his men." His name is inscribed on the tablet in the War Memorial Cloister erected at Charterhouse.

Weldon.—Capt. George Anthony Weldon, 2nd Batt. Royal Dublin Fusiliers, was killed in action at the battle of Talana Hill, Oct. 20th, 1899, while endeavouring to carry a wounded soldier to a place of safety. Capt. Weldon was the son of Col. Thomas Weldon, C.I.E., and grandson of the late Sir Anthony Weldon, Bart. His mother, Helen Rachel Louisa, was a daughter of General George William Young Simpson, R.A. Capt. Weldon was born in Feb., 1866, and educated at Cheltenham College. He entered the Royal Dublin Fusiliers from the Militia in Dec., 1886, and was promoted capt. Jan., 1896. He served in the Burmese Expedition, 1887-89, and received the medal with clasp. On the outbreak of the war he was serving at Maritzburg with his battalion, which was at once pushed on to Dundee. At the battle of Talana Hill, the first action of the war, E Company, commanded by Capt. Weldon, was lining the edge of a wood at the side nearest to the enemy, Capt. Weldon's servant, Private Crotty, was seen to fall a few yards in advance, and Capt. Weldon at once dashed forward to endeavour to carry him under cover, but was killed in the attempt. Thus master and man fell together. Three men of his company, under Corporal Foley, went out early next morning to bury Capt. Weldon, but could not find his body. After some further search, they heard his faithful terrier, "Rose," howling piteously. She was lying on his body, which she had apparently never left. At first,

"Their search seemed all in vain,
Till suddenly they heard a dog's heart break
In a long low wail of pain."

They buried Capt. Weldon in the cemetery at Dundee, just below Talana Hill, and "Rose" was taken back to E Company. Capt. Weldon was the first officer killed in the South African War. He was mentioned in despatches by Lieut.-Gen. Sir George White, Dec. 2nd, 1899, L.G., Feb. 8th, 1901. Memorials to Capt. Weldon have been erected at St. James's Church, Dundee, Natal, and at St. George's Church, Pietermaritzburg; also at St. Mary's Church, Blythe, at Athy, co. Kildare, and at Naas, the depôt of the Royal Dublin Fusiliers. On the memorial at Blythe are inscribed the words:—

"He hath well done, and so made good hys name."

Capt. Weldon's name is also recorded on the Eleanor Cross War Memorial at Cheltenham College.

Wellford.—Capt. Francis Wellford, M.B., 7th Batt. I.Y., died June 1st, 1901, of wounds received in action at Vlakfontein two days previously. He was the son of the Rev. John Francis Wellford, of Oakland, Sidmouth, and was born at Clevedon in April, 1863. He was educated privately and at Trinity College, Cambridge. From Jan., 1887, to Nov., 1892, he was at Guy's Hospital. He then went to New South Wales, and practised at Sydney, and was medical officer of the Winton District Hospital, Queensland, from 1893 to 1895. From the latter date to 1899 he was in the Straits Settlements, but in Dec., 1899, he volunteered for active service, and in Feb., 1900, joined the I.Y. as a medical officer with the rank of capt. He was mentioned by F.-M. Earl Roberts in his despatch of Sept. 4th, 1901, L.G., Sept. 10th, 1901. Capt. Wellford was a fellow of the Royal Colonial Institute, and his name is inscribed on a memorial tablet in the hall of the building in Northumberland Avenue, S.W.

Wellby.—Capt. Montagu Sinclair Wellby, 18th Hussars, died at Paardekop, Aug. 5th, 1900, of wounds received in action at Mertzicht, July 30th. He was the fourth son of John Henry Wellby, Esq., of 1, Sussex Place, Regent's Park, N.W., was born in Oct., 1866, and educated at University College School and at Rugby. He entered the 18th Hussars in Aug., 1886, being promoted capt. 1894, and was adjutant of his regiment from Feb., 1897, to Aug. 1898. He was a well-known traveller and explorer. He served with the Tochi Field Force in the operations on the North-West Frontier of India in 1897, receiving the medal with clasp. Capt. Wellby had served in South Africa from the commencement of the war in the operations in Natal, and the defence of Ladysmith. He is buried at Zandspruit.

West.—2nd Lieut. Archibald Vivian West, 2nd Batt. Royal Berkshire Regt., was killed in action at Rensburg,

Jan. 1st, 1900. He was the only son of Lieut.-Col. Frederick West, and grandson of Admiral Sir John West, G.C.B. He was born in June, 1876, and educated at Allhallowes School, Honiton. He served in the ranks for over four years, and was granted a commission in the Royal Berkshire Regt. in Aug., 1898. 2nd Lieut. West was with his battalion in South Africa when war was declared, and served in the north of Cape Colony until his death.

Whitaker.—Capt. Frederick Shewell Whitaker, Roberts' Horse, died June 24th, 1900, at Heidelberg, of wounds received in action the previous day. He had seen much service in South Africa previous to 1899, having been through the Galeka and Gaika Wars, the Bechuanaland Expedition, and the Matabele Campaign. He offered his services at the outbreak of the war, and was first given command of a squadron in the South African Light Horse, and afterwards in Roberts' Horse. Capt. Whitaker was a Fellow of the Royal Colonial Institute, and his name is inscribed on a memorial tablet in the hall of the building in Northumberland Avenue, S.W.

White.—Lieut. Cecil Arbuthnot White, 1st Batt. Suffolk Regt., was killed in action near Rensburg, Jan. 6th, 1900. He was the youngest son of Robert Holmes White, Esq., of 10, Devonshire Place, W., and Boulge Hall, Woodbridge. He was born Aug., 1874, educated at Eton (Mr. Durnford's), and entered the Suffolk Regt. from the 3rd Batt. Derbyshire Regt. in May, 1897, being promoted lieut. March, 1899. Lieut. White accompanied his battalion to South Africa in Nov., 1899, and served with it in the north of Cape Colony until killed.

White.—Lieut. R. J. L. White, New South Wales

Bushmen, was killed in action at Wonderfontein on Sept. 12th, 1900.

White.—Lieut. William Michael Joseph White, 2nd Batt. Cameronians (Scottish Rifles), was killed in action near Smithfield March 12th, 1901. He was the voungest son of the late J. White, Esq., D.L., of Nantenan, co. Limerick, was born in Sept., 1876, and educated at Stonyhurst, where he was in the cricket and football teams. He entered the Scottish Rifles, May, 1897, from the Royal Military College, and was promoted lieut. Jan., 1899. At the commencement of the war in Oct., 1899, he went out on special service with M.I., and saw much fighting. He is reported to have been seldom out of action for nearly eighteen months. He was present at Paardeberg, and took part in the advance on Bloemfontein and Pretoria. On many occasions his bravery is stated to have been very conspicuous. Shortly before his death he was sent as adjutant to some Yeomanry who had just arrived from England. While in action and carrying a message to one of the companies in heavy rain, Lieut. White is believed to have ridden by mistake into a party of Boers, and nothing was heard of him until the enemy reported him as killed in action. He was mentioned in despatches, L.G., Sept. 10th, 1901.

Whitehead.—Lieut. James Allan Whitehead, 5th Batt. Manchester Regt., attached 28th Co. Army Service Corps, died of enteric at Heilbron, May 28th, 1902. He was the son of Mr. Whitehead, of Ewood Hall, Todmorden, and was eighteen years of age. He entered the Manchester Regt. Jan., 1901, and was promoted lieut. the following May, and accompanied the 5th battalion to South Africa in June, 1901, and served as senior transport officer to the columns commanded by Colonels Dawkins and Nixon. He was wounded on three occasions, and was awarded the medal and five clasps.

OFFICERS WHO FELL IN SOUTH AFRICA.

Whitehead.— Major Randolph Edward Whitehead, 1st Batt. Royal Munster Fusiliers, was killed in action at Doornfontein, near Griquatown, on Jan. 13th, 1902. He was the youngest son of the late Rev. Thomas Whitehead, vicar of Shustoke, Warwickshire, was born in June, 1861, and educated at Winchester. He entered the 101st Foot from the Royal Military College in August, 1880, being promoted lieut. July, 1881, capt. Sept., 1889, and major March, 1901. He was adjutant of his battalion from May, 1887, to July 1891, and of the 1st Wiltshire Rifle Volunteers from Nov., 1891 to Nov., 1895. Major Whitehead had served in South Africa since June, 1900, and had been present with his battalion in many engagements. The day he was killed he had joined Col. Sitwell's Column at Doornfontein. He fell while leading his company, only eighty strong, to attack a ridge held by four hundred Boers, under De Villiers. The ridge was carried by a bayonet charge, but Major Whitehead fell within about fifty yards of the Boer entrenchments and died immediately. Those who saw this attack of Major Whitehead's company state that it was most gallantly carried out, the enemy being driven out of their position.

Wickham.—Capt. Edward David Provis Wickham, 84th Co., 22nd Batt. I.Y., was killed in action at Doorn River, O.R.C., Oct. 16th, 1901. He was the eldest son of the late Lieut.-Col. Thomas Wickham, of Fronwnion, North Wales, J.P., and D.L. for Monmouthshire, who served formerly in the 33rd Foot, and who died at Cheltenham on April 3rd, 1903. Capt. Wickham was born in 1857, and educated at Cheltenham College. He first served in the ranks of the I.Y., and gaining the rank of sergt. was, on the 8th March, 1901, granted a commission as 2nd lieut. On the 27th of the same month he was promoted capt. into the 22nd Batt., with which he served till killed. His name is inscribed on the Eleanor Cross War Memorial erected at Cheltenham College.

Wilde.—2nd Lieut. Brenchley Wilde, 2nd Batt. East Yorkshire Regt., died of enteric at Harrismith on Feb. 26th, 1902. He was born in Jan., 1882, and entered the East Yorkshire Regt. from the Royal Military College, May, 1901. He is buried in Harrismith military cemetery.

Wilford.—Col. Edmund Percival Wilford, 1st Batt. Gloucestershire Regt., was killed in action in the engagement at Rietfontein, near Ladysmith, Oct. 24th, 1899. He was born in May, 1846, joined the 8th Foot July, 1865, and was transferred to the 28th Foot in August of the same year. He was promoted lieut. June, 1868, capt. Sept., 1879, major July, 1882, lieut.-col. May, 1894, and col. July, 1899. He was adjutant of Auxiliary Forces from July, 1880, to July, 1885. Col. Wilford was serving in command of his battalion in Natal at the commencement of the war and fell while leading it. It had to advance down a ridge, and was suddenly exposed to a cross musketry fire. Col. Wilford and six men were killed and forty wounded.

Wilfred.—Lieut. Wilfred, Rhodesia Regt., was killed at Mafeking on May 16th, 1900.

Wilkins.—Capt. Francis Alfred Pressland Wilkins, Suffolk Regt., was killed in action near Rensburg, Jan. 6th, 1900. He was the only son of Alfred Wilkins, Esq., of 43, Earl's Court Square, S.W., and was born in April, 1871. He was educated at Westminster School, and at Paris, and passed into the Royal Military College at the head of the list. When leaving Sandhurst he passed out with Honours, and entered the Suffolk Regt. in May, 1892, being promoted lieut. June, 1895, and capt. August, 1899. He had been adjutant of his battalion since Jan., 1899, and was qualified as an interpreter in French, German, and Italian. Capt. Wilkins embarked for South Africa with his battalion in Nov., 1899, and served with it in the north of Cape Colony until killed.

Williams.—2nd Lieut. Arthur Cole Williams, Nottinghamshire (Sherwood Rangers) Yeomanry Cavalry, was killed in action at Boshof, April 5th, 1900, a victim to the abuse of the white flag by the Boers. He was educated at Wellington, where he was in Saunders House, 1887-91. He was for a time in the Surrey Militia; he then became a brewer. The loss of this officer is referred to "with regret" by Lieut.-Gen. Lord Methuen in his despatch of April 6th, 1900, L.G., Feb. 8th, 1901, who reports that "Lieut. Williams was killed deliberately after the white flag was held up." The Boer who killed Lieut. Williams was at once shot. 2nd Lieut. Williams had only entered the Nottinghamshire Yeomanry Cavalry in Feb., 1900, proceeding immediately after to South Africa.

Williams.—Capt. Edward Arthur Williams, 1st Dragoon Guards, was killed in action at Orebyfontein, O.R.C., Nov. 9th, 1901. He was born in June, 1869, and entered the 18th Hussars from the Lancashire Artillery (Southern Division, R.A.), in June, 1892, being promoted lieut. Nov., 1894, and capt. into the 1st Dragoon Guards in July, 1900. He had served in South Africa from the commencement of the war, and was employed with Bethune's Mounted Infantry.

Williams.—Major George Albanus Williams, 1st Batt. South Staffordshire Regt., was killed in action at Tweefontein, in De Wet's attack on Christmas morning, 1901. He was the third son of Gen. J. W. C. Williams, K.C.B., of Morelands, Purbrook, Hants, and was born in Sept., 1860. He entered the 80th Foot in Jan., 1879, was promoted lieut. Feb., 1881, capt. Aug., 1887, and major Nov., 1896. He was adjutant of his battalion from Aug., 1887 to April, 1891, and afterwards adjutant of a provisional battalion from May, 1891, to Nov., 1895. He served in South Africa in 1879, in the Zulu Campaign, and in the subsequent operations against Sekukuni, receiving the medal with clasp. He also took part in the Nile Expedition of 1884-85, and was present at the action of Kirbekan, and received the medal with clasp and the Khedive's star. He went on special service to Ashanti, with the Expedition under Sir Francis Scott, in 1895-96, being mentioned in despatches and receiving the star awarded. Major Williams was A.D.C. in India from Sept., 1897, to Dec., 1899, and was afterwards A.D.C. to the General Officer Commanding a Division in South Africa, from Jan. 2nd, 1900. At the time of his death, he was second in command of the 1st Batt. South Staffordshire Regt. At Tweefontein the Boers attacked the British force by moonlight about two o'clock in the morning. The enemy crept up without their boots on, and in the confusion which ensued some of our men killed each other. Two Boers who put on our helmets were shot by their own men. Major Williams was killed while rallying those under his command. He is buried at Tweefontein, and his name is inscribed on an obelisk which has been erected there in memory of all who fell in this action.

Williams.—2nd Lieut. John Condé Williams, 3rd Batt. Durham Light Infantry, died of enteric at Kroonstad

Jan. 15th, 1901. He was born in June, 1881, educated at the South Eastern College, Ramsgate, and entered the Durham Light Infantry Dec., 1899, and joined the 3rd Batt., which was then embodied. He accompanied it to South Africa in Jan., 1900, and served in the Cape and Orange River Colonies up to the time of his death.

Williams.—2nd Lieut. Raymond Henry Williams, 2nd Batt. Somersetshire Light Infantry, was wounded by the accidental discharge of his revolver while on outpost duty on Sept. 6th, 1901, and died the same day at Nigel. He was born in June, 1882, educated at Wellington, and entered the 4th Batt., Somersetshire Light Infantry in Oct., 1899. His battalion was embodied in Dec., 1899, and proceeded to South Africa in Feb., 1900. 2nd Lieut. Williams served with it for over a year and was then granted a commission in the Dorsetshire Regt. in Jan., 1901, being transferred to the 2nd Batt. Somersetshire Light Infantry in the following May and joined it in South Africa. He had thus served throughout the war from Feb., 1900.

Williams.—Lieut. William Arthur Glanmor Williams, D.S.O., 2nd Batt. South Wales Borderers, was killed in action near Bothaville Nov. 6th, 1900. He was the second son of the late Hugh Williams, Esq., of Ferry Side, Carmarthenshire, was born in Sept., 1873, and educated at Clifton College. He was fond of games and a good cricketer. He entered the South Wales Borderers in May, 1893, being promoted lieut. Oct., 1895. He served in the operations in the Niger Territories in 1898, including the Benin Hinterland and Siama Expeditions (wounded), being mentioned in despatches and receiving the medal with clasp and the D.S.O. For his services in the South African War he was mentioned in despatches, L.G., Sept. 10th, 1901. In the despatch of

Gen. Lord Kitchener of May 8th, 1901, the death of Lieut. Williams is mentioned.

Williams-Ellis.—2nd Lieut. John Roger Williams-Ellis, 1st Batt. Royal Welsh Fusiliers, was killed in action at Dwarsvlei, Oct. 9th, 1900. He was the third son of the Rev. J. C. Williams-Ellis, of Glasfryn, Carnarvonshire, sometime Fellow and Tutor of Sidney Sussex College, Cambridge. 2nd Lieut. Williams-Ellis was born in Dec., 1880, and was educated privately and at Rossall. He entered the Royal Welsh Fusiliers from the Royal Military College in Dec., 1899, and embarked immediately for Natal, joining the battalion soon after the relief of Ladysmith. He then served with Major-Gen. Barton's Brigade for the relief of Mafeking, and was present at the action of Rindam and the march to Krugersdorp. He fell while leading a section of his company against a Boer position. 2nd Lieut. Williams-Ellis is buried in the cemetery at Krugersdorp. A tablet has been erected in his memory in Llangybi Church, and bears these words:

" He reached by Duty's path.
A life beyond the life he lost."

Willis.—Lieut. T. Willis, 40th Co. I.Y., was killed in action near Wolmaranstad on Feb. 26th, 1902.

Willshire.—Major Ernest Maxwell Willshire, 2nd Batt. the Black Watch (Royal Highlanders), died at Boshof's Farm on July 25th, 1900, of wounds received in action at Retief's Nek two days previously. He was the second son of the late Lieut.-Gen. Sir T. Willshire, Bart., G.C.B., by his marriage with Annette Letitia, daughter of Capt. George Berkeley Maxwell, R.N. Major Willshire was born in May, 1856, and educated at Eton (Mr. James'). He entered the 73rd Foot from the Royal

Aberdeenshire Highlanders (Militia) in Oct., 1877, and was promoted lieut. in the Royal Highlanders May, 1878, capt. May, 1885, and major Aug., 1894. He was adjutant of Militia from Nov., 1886, to Jan., 1892. Major Willshire married in 1882 Lilian Gertrude Henrietta, eldest daughter of Major-Gen. James Davidson. At the time of his death he was 2nd-in-command of his battalion, to which he had been appointed in Dec., 1899, from the 1st battalion serving in India.

Wilmer.—Lieut. Altham Browning Wilmer, M.I. Co., Bedfordshire Regt., died on Oct. 23rd, 1901, of wounds received in action at Kafirstad, O.R.C., the previous day. He was the eldest son of Horace Wilmer, Esq., of Grove Hill, South Woodford, Essex; was born in Aug., 1876, and educated at Wellington. While only thirteen years of age he was awarded the certificate of the Royal Humane Society for saving a child from drowning at Woodford. He entered the Bedfordshire Regt., from the 4th Batt. Essex Regt., in Dec., 1897, being promoted lieut. in Jan., 1899. He accompanied his battalion to South Africa in Dec., 1899, and first served in the north of Cape Colony, and was severely wounded. Lieut. Wilmer subsequently was with the M.I. of his battalion under Col. De Lisle, until wounded at Kafirstad. He thus served in the war for nearly two years, and was awarded the medal with two clasps.

Wilson.—2nd Lieut. Harold Alfred Cobbe Wilson, 2nd Batt. Middlesex Regt., was killed in action at Spion Kop, in the operations on the Upper Tugela Jan. 24th, 1900. He was the second son of the Rev. Alfred Wilson, of the Vicarage, Bedford Park, Chiswick, was born in Sept., 1878, and educated at Marlborough, where he is still remembered in B.I. He entered the Middlesex Regt.

June, 1899, and proceeded with it to South Africa in Dec., 1899, serving with the Natal Field Force, and fell in his first battle. At Spion Kop he had taken a party of his company to a detached spur which was swept by the enemy's fire, and where there was very little cover. He made his men lie down, and was himself entreated to do so, but continued to walk up and down the line speaking to and encouraging those under his command. He then advanced quite alone, in order to better see how he should direct his men's fire, and while doing so was killed. 2nd Lieut. Wilson's name is inscribed on a tablet placed in Marlborough College Chapel in memory of all Marlburians who fell in the war.

Wilson.—Lieut. James Wilson, Military Pigeon Post (late Cape Colony Public Works Department), was killed in the Clanwilliam district on Oct. 31st, 1901.

Wilson.—Col. John Gerald Wilson, C.B., commanding 3rd Batt. York and Lancaster Regt., died March 8th, 1902, of wounds received in action between Tweebosch and Palmietkuil the previous day. He was the eldest son of the late Richard Bassett Wilson, Esq., of Cliffe, by his marriage with Anne, daughter of the late William Fitzgerald, Esq., of Adelphi, co. Clare. Col. Wilson was born in 1841, and educated at Cheltenham. He joined the 84th Regt. in 1858 from the Royal Military College as an ensign. After the death of his father in 1867, and his succession to the family estate of Cliffe Hall, Piercebridge, Darlington, he retired from the army as a capt., but subsequently accepted a commission in the volunteer force, and in 1873 was appointed to the command of the 1st North Yorkshire Rifle Volunteers. From the latter he was transferred in 1883 to the command of the 3rd West Yorkshire Militia, now the 3rd Batt. York and Lancaster Regt., and in 1889 he was appointed to the command of the West Yorkshire Volunteer Brigade. He was awarded the C.B. on the occasion of the Diamond Jubilee of Her late Majesty Queen Victoria in 1897, and was hon. col. of the 2nd Volunteer Batt. Prince of Wales's West Yorkshire Regt. His battalion was first embodied in Dec., 1899, being disembodied after twelve months' service. It was again embodied in Dec., 1901, and volunteering for active service proceeded to South Africa. In the course of the war, Col. Wilson lost a brother (Col. Richard B. Wilson) and a son (2nd Lieut. Richard B. Wilson). The name of Col. J. G. Wilson is inscribed on the Eleanor Cross War Memorial erected at Cheltenham College.

Wilson. — Lieut.-Col. and Hon. Col. Richard B. Wilson, C.M.G., commanding 3rd Batt. Durham Light Infantry, died of enteric at Kroonstad, March 21st, 1901. He was the third son of the late Richard Bassett Wilson, Esq., of Cliffe, and brother of Col. J. G. Wilson, C.B. Col. R. B. Wilson was educated at Rugby, and took his battalion out to South Africa in Jan., 1900, and served with it till his death. He was mentioned in despatches, L.G., Feb. 8th, 1901, and was awarded the C.M.G.

Wilson.—Lieut. Richard Bassett Wilson, 3rd Batt. I.Y., died at Rustenburg on July 26th, 1900, of wounds received in action five days previously at Oliphant's Nek. He was the eldest son of Col. John Gerald Wilson, C.B., commanding 3rd Batt. York and Lancashire Regt. He was born in 1874, and educated at Eton (Mr. Broadbent's) and New College, Oxford. He entered the Yorkshire Hussars (Princess of Wales's Own) Yeomanry Cavalry in Jan., 1900, and joining the I.Y. as lieut. went to South Africa on the 26th of the same month. Lieut. Wilson was a barrister, having been called to the bar on the day of his departure. A tablet has been erected to his memory in York Minster by his brother officers of the Princess of Wales's Own Yorkshire Hussars as a token of their sincere affection.

Wilson.—Lieut. W. C. Wilson, Northumberland I.Y., died of wounds received in action at Hartebeestefontein on Feb. 16th, 1901. He was educated at Eton (Mr. Cornish's).

Wiltshire. — Capt. Herbert Wiltshire, Reserve of Officers, was killed at Kaffir Kop Oct. 4th, 1900, while on patrol duty eighteen miles south-east of Lindley. He was born in Jan., 1855, and served for nearly eleven years in the ranks. He became lieut. in the 20th Hussars in Dec., 1886, being promoted capt. in 1895, when he retired. He saw service in the Egyptian War of 1882, and was present in the engagement at Mahsama, in the two actions at Kassassin, at the battle of Tel-el-Kebir, and the capture of Cairo, receiving the medal with clasp and the Khedive's star. He also served in the operations in the Soudan in 1889, including the engagement at Toski, and received a clasp. He had been on special service in South Africa from March, 1900, and was attached to the M.I. Co. of the Lincolnshire Regt.

Wiltshire.—2nd Lieut. Richard Clare Wiltshire, 1st Batt. Loyal North Lancashire Regt., died of abcess of the liver at Kimberley, March 21st, 1901. He was the eldest surviving son of C. P. B. Wiltshire, Esq., I.C.S. (retired), of Madeley Road, Ealing, was born in Oct., 1879, and educated at Tonbridge. He entered the Loyal North Lancashire Regt. in Aug., 1899, and joined the 1st Batt. at Capetown, where it was stationed. 2nd Lieut. Wiltshire had served throughout the war. He first joined the Kimberley Relief Force under Lieut.-Gen. Lord Methuen, and was present at the fighting up to

Modder River and Magersfontein. After the relief of Kimberley he took part in the subsequent operations in the O.R.C. and Transvaal.

Wimberley.—2nd Lieut. Charles Francis Irvine Wimberley, 2nd Batt. Welsh Regt., died March 12th, 1900, at Driefontein of wounds received in action two days previously. He was the youngest son of Col. R. J. Wimberley, late Bombay Staff Corps, was born in June, 1878, and educated at the Northern Counties Collegiate School, Inverness, and at Blundell's School, Tiverton. He entered the Welsh Regt. from the 4th Batt. King's Liverpool Regt., in May, 1899, and proceeded to South Africa early in the war. He was present at the relief of Kimberley and the battle of Paardeberg and the subsequent advance to Driefontein.

Winchester.—Major Augustus John Henry Beaumont Paulet, Marquis of Winchester, Earl of Wiltshire, and Baron St. John, 2nd Batt. Coldstream Guards, was killed in action at Magersfontein Dec. 11th, 1899. He was the eldest son of the 14th Marquis by his marriage with the Hon. Mary Montagu, the eldest daughter of the 6th Baron Rokeby, was born Feb., 1858, and educated at Eton (Mr. Marindin's). He entered the Coldstream Guards from the Militia in Sept., 1879, was promoted lieut. July, 1881, capt. July, 1890, and major April, 1897. The Marquis of Winchester was the hereditary Bearer of the Cap of Maintenance, a cap of dignity carried before the sovereigns of England at their coronation. He served in the Soudan Expedition in 1885, at Suakin as A.D.C. to Sir John McNeill, and was present at the actions of Hasheen, Tofrek, and Tamai, receiving the medal with two clasps and bronze star. The Marquis of Winchester embarked for South Africa in Oct., 1899, with his battalion, which on arrival joined the Kimberley Relief Force. He was present at the actions of Belmont, Graspan, and Modder River. At Magersfontein he showed conspicuous bravery, Lieut.-Gen. Lord Methuen in his despatch of Feb. 15th, 1900, stating that " Major the Marquis of Winchester was killed while displaying almost reckless courage."

Winder.—Lieut. Henry Winder, Midland Mounted Rifles (Colonial Defence Force), died of enteric at Cradock on Nov. 1st, 1901.

Wingate.—Capt. Allen Sievwright Wingate, 1st Batt. Gordon Highlanders, died of wounds received in action Dec. 11th, 1899, at Magersfontein. He was the son of J. B. Wingate, Esq., of Crown Terrace, Glasgow, was born in Dec., 1870, and educated at Loretto School, Musselburgh, where he played in the football XV. He was also a first-class cricketer and very fond of games. He entered the Gordon Highlanders in March 1891, being promoted lieut. Sept., 1893, and capt. May, 1899. He served with the Chitral Relief Force under Sir Robert Low, in 1895, with the first battalion of his regiment, including the storming of the Malakand Pass, receiving the medal with clasp. He saw service in the campaign on the North-West Frontier of India under the late Sir William Lockhart, in 1897-98, with the Tochi Field Force, when he was attached to the 3rd Batt. Rifle Brigade. He afterwards went through the campaign with the Tirah Expeditionary Force, with the 1st Batt. Gordon Highlanders, and was present at the capture of the Sampagha and Arhanga Passes, and in the subsequent operations in the Maidan, Waran, and Bara Valleys, receiving two clasps. Capt. Wingate embarked for South Africa in Oct., 1899, with his battalion, which joined the Kimberley Relief Force shortly before the battle of Magersfontein, in which he fell.

Wingrove.—Lieut. Arthur C. H. Sharpe Wingrove, 5th Batt. I.Y., was killed in action at Elandslaagte, near Klerksdorp, Feb. 25th, 1902. He entered the 3rd Batt. East Yorkshire Regt. (East Yorkshire Militia), in Oct., 1900, and joined the I.Y., May, 1901, with the rank of lieut. Lieut. Wingrove was mentioned in despatches by Gen. Lord Kitchener, March 8th, 1902, for "gallantry and good service at Otterfontein, Western Transvaal."

Wombwell.—Capt. Stephen Frederick Wombwell, B.A., 3rd Batt. I.Y., Lieut., Alexandra Princess of Wales's Own Yorkshire Hussars, died of enteric at Vryburg, Feb. 1st, 1901. He was the only surviving son of Sir George and Lady Julia Wombwell, and was thirty-three years of age. He was educated at Charterhouse and the Royal Agricultural College, Cirencester. Capt. Wombwell entered the I.Y. as lieut. in Feb., 1900, and was promoted capt. the following August. He saw much service during the war, and had been previously wounded. A tablet in his memory has been erected in York Minster by his brother officers of the Princess of Wales's Own Yorkshire Hussars as a token of their sincere affection; and his name is inscribed on the tablet in the War Memorial Cloister at Charterhouse.

Wood.—Lieut. Charles Carroll Wood, 1st Batt. Loyal North Lancashire Regt., died of wounds received in the reconnaissance made by Col. Gough, 9th Lancers, at Belmont, Nov. 10th, 1899. He was the youngest son of J. Taylor Wood, Esq., who served as a confederate capt. in the American Civil War, and was a grandson of Gen. R. C. Wood, U.S. Army, and a great grandson of Gen. Zachary Taylor, President of the United States. Lieut. Wood was born in March, 1876, and educated at the Royal Military College, Kingston. He entered the Loyal North Lancashire Regt. in Sept., 1896, being promoted lieut. May, 1899, and was serving with his battalion in South Africa on the outbreak of the war. He was then sent to Orange River with M.I., and was killed in his first action.

Wood.—Capt. G. E. B. Wood, 5th Batt. I.Y., was killed in action at Weltevreden, near Zeerust, Oct. 20th, 1900. He was the eldest son of Edward Wood, Esq., of Culmington Manor, Shropshire, and Hanger Hill, Middlesex. Capt. Wood was born in 1866, and educated at Elstree (Rev. T. Saunderson's), and Christ Church, Oxford. He joined the 3rd Batt. Royal Welsh Fusiliers in 1884, and afterwards entered the Shropshire Yeomanry Cavalry May, 1889, being promoted capt. May, 1898. Early in 1900 he raised and commanded the Shropshire Squadron of the 5th Batt. I.Y., and was gazetted as capt. on Feb. 2nd. He then proceeded to South Africa and served under Lieut.-Gen. Lord Methuen after the relief of Kimberley, and saw continuous fighting in the Lindley and Heilbron districts, and subsequently in the Western Transvaal. At Weltevreden, Capt. Wood was first wounded, and was being carried on a stretcher to have his wound dressed, when a second bullet passed through his heart killing him instantly. He was mentioned in Lieut.-Gen. Lord Methuen's despatch, and was described as "a splendid officer." A marble cross has been placed over his grave by his brother officers of the Shropshire Yeomanry, and at Culmington Church, Shropshire, a stained glass window, a marble cross, and a brass tablet have been erected in his memory. A stained glass window has also been placed in the church at Melton Mowbray by his hunting friends in remembrance of Capt. Wood.

Wood.—2nd Lieut. Hugh Maurice Wood, 1st Batt. Royal Sussex Regt., died of abscess of the liver at Springfontein, May 3rd, 1902. He was the eldest son of

OFFICERS WHO FELL IN SOUTH AFRICA. 431

Thomas Archibald Wood, Esq., of Eliot Park, Blackheath, and was twenty-two years of age. He served throughout the early stages of the war with the Cape Mounted Rifles, and from the ranks of that corps, on the recommendation of Gen. Lord Kitchener, was gazetted in July, 1901, to a commission in the 1st Batt. Royal Sussex Regt., with which he served until his death.

Wood.—Col. Oswald Gillespie Wood, C.B., M.D., Royal Army Medical Corps, died of internal inflammation at Kroonstad, Jan. 3rd, 1902. He was born in Nov., 1851, and educated at Edinburgh Academy. He entered the Army Medical Staff in Sept., 1873, being promoted surgeon-major March, 1886, surgeon-lieut.-col. March, 1894, brigade surgeon-lieut.-col. April, 1897, and col. (South Africa) Oct., 1899. He served in the Egyptian War of 1882, and was present at the battle of Tel-el-Kebir, receiving the medal with clasp and the Khedive's star. In the operations on the Nile of 1889, he was senior medical officer to the British troops. At the beginning of the South African War he was in charge of a general hospital, and afterwards was Principal Medical Officer at Kroonstad, being mentioned in despatches, L.G., April 16th, 1901, and was awarded the C.B., Nov. 29th, 1900.

Woodgate.—Major-Gen. Sir Edward Robert Prevost Woodgate, K.C.M.G., C.B., p.s.c., was wounded at Spion Kop, Jan. 24th, 1900, and died at Mooi River, March 23rd. He was the second son of the Rev. H. A. Woodgate, rector of Belbroughton, Worcestershire, was born in Nov., 1845, and educated at Radley. He entered the 4th Foot in April, 1865, being promoted lieut. July, 1869, capt. March, 1878, brevet-major Nov., 1879, major Nov., 1881, lieut.-col. June, 1893, col. June, 1897, and was given the local rank of major-gen. in

Nov., 1899. He served with the 4th regiment throughout the Abyssinian Campaign of 1868, and was present at the action of Arogee and capture of Magdala, receiving the medal. He accompanied F.-M. Lord (then Sir Garnet) Wolseley to the Gold Coast in Sept., 1873, on special service, and served throughout the Ashanti War 1873-74, including the actions of Essaman and Ainsa, repulse of the Ashanti army at Abrakrampa during the 5th and 6th of Nov., 1873 (in command of the Kossoos), reconnaissance in force of the 8th and 27th of Nov., and battle of Amoaful, and capture of Coomassie, being mentioned in despatches and receiving the medal with clasp. He served in the Zulu War 1879, and was present at the engagements at Kambula and Ulundi, was twice mentioned in despatches, and received the brevet of major and the medal with clasp. He again saw service in West Africa in 1898, in command of the forces against the Sierra Leone insurgents, and organised the Protectorate Expedition, being mentioned in despatches and received the C.M.G. Sir E. Woodgate was made a C.B. in May, 1896, and a K.C.M.G. Jan. 9th, 1900. He proceeded to South Africa in Dec., 1899, in command of the 9th Brigade of the 5th Division, and was specially selected to command the troops detailed to capture Spion Kop. He was mortally wounded early in the action, and was mentioned in despatches, L.G., Feb. 8th, 1901, by Gen. Sir R. Buller, who referred to the great loss the country had sustained by the death of Gen. Woodgate.

Woodgate.—Lieut. William Ernest Streatfield Woodgate, 2nd Batt. Royal Lancaster Regt., died Dec. 12th, 1900, of wounds received in action the previous day at Vryheid. He was the eldest son of the late Ernest Woodgate, Esq., solicitor, of Rochester, was born in Nov., 1877, and educated at Bradfield College. He entered the Royal Lancaster Regt. from the Royal

Military College in Sept., 1897, and was promoted lieut. June, 1899. He was fond of all games and a good Polo player. At Vryheid Lieut. Woodgate was in charge of a picquet which was suddenly attacked at 2.15 on a cold dark morning. A Boer called on him to surrender, but this he refused to do, although unarmed at the time. Lieut. Woodgate then seized a hammer and rushed at the Boer, who fired twice at him at close quarters, and Lieut. Woodgate fell mortally wounded. He is buried in the cemetery at Vryheid.

Woodhouse.—2nd Lieut. Henry George Wilkinson Woodhouse, 2nd Batt. Manchester Regt., died Nov. 10th, 1900, of wounds received in action near Vrede the previous day. He was the eldest son of Major S. H. Woodhouse, 4th Batt. Somersetshire Light Infantry, late of Norley Hall, Cheshire, and now of Heatherton Park, Taunton. 2nd Lieut. Woodhouse was born Dec., 1879, educated at Marlborough, and entered the 4th Batt. Somersetshire Light Infantry, Feb., 1899, being promoted lieut. the following Nov. In Dec., 1899, his battalion was embodied, and proceeded to South Africa in February, 1900. In the following April he was granted a commission as 2nd lieut. in the Manchester Regt., and joined the 2nd battalion then in South Africa. He was present at the surrender of Prinsloo, and when mortally wounded was on the march from Standerton to Vrede escorting a convoy. He fell while leading a flanking party. 2nd Lieut. Woodhouse is buried in the churchyard at Vrede. His name is inscribed on a tablet erected in Marlborough College Chapel in memory of all Marlburians who fell in the war.

Woodhouse.—Lieut. Robert Walker Woodhouse, 69th Co. 7th Batt. I.Y., was killed in action at Holfontein, Western Transvaal, Jan. 2nd, 1902. He was the eldest surviving son of Robert Hall Woodhouse, Esq., of

Ralsbury, Ealing, and 1, Hanover Square, W., and was nineteen years of age. He was educated privately and at Charterhouse, where he was in the school rifle team. He was also a good athlete and swimmer. He entered the Donegal Artillery in Oct., 1900, and joined the 69th (Sussex) Co. I.Y. in June, 1901 with the rank of lieut. He first served with the Dorset Co., and saw much fighting with Col. Dixon's column, being wounded on May 23rd, 1901. Lieut. Woodhouse afterwards joined the 69th Co. in Col. Kekewich's column. A brother officer reports Lieut. Woodhouse as having been always "cool and fearless in danger." He had been slightly wounded during the war. His name is inscribed on the tablet in the War Memorial Cloister at Charterhouse.

Woodman.—Lieut. C. Woodman, 2nd Regt. of Scottish Horse, died of wounds received in action near Brakenlaagte, twenty miles north-west of Bethel, on Oct. 31st, 1901.

Wright.—Lieut. Godfrey Charles de Cardonnell Wright, 12th Lancers, was killed in action at Diamond Hill, near Pretoria, June 11th, 1900. He was the eldest son of Charles Booth E. Wright, Esq., of Bolton Hall, Yorkshire, by his marriage with Edith de Cardonnel, second daughter of R. W. M. Nesfield, Esq., of Castle Hill, Bakewell, Derbyshire. Lieut. Wright was born in Dec., 1873, educated at Eton (Mr. Austen Leigh's), and entered the 12th Lancers, March, 1893, being promoted lieut. Oct., 1895. He proceeded to South Africa with his regiment in Oct., 1899, and served in Cape Colony. He was afterwards present at the battles of Paardeberg and Driefontien, and took part in the advance on Bloemfontein and Pretoria.

Wright.—Lieut. S. O. Wright, Kimberley Light Horse, died in Kimberley on Nov. 28th, 1899.

OFFICERS WHO FELL IN SOUTH AFRICA. 435

Wrottesley.—Major Alfred Edward Wrottesley, Royal Engineers, was drowned on passage to South Africa Oct. 26th, 1899. He was born in Dec., 1855, and entered the Royal Engineers in Aug., 1874, being promoted capt. Aug., 1885, and major in May, 1894. He had been an associate member of the Royal Engineer committee from June, 1898.

Wylam. — Lieut. Frederick Herbert Wylam, 8th Hussars, was killed in action between Machadodorp and Heidelberg Oct. 13th, 1900. He was the only son of Edward Wylam, Esq., of Runnymede Park, Staines, was born in Sept., 1876, and educated at Harrow. He entered the 8th Hussars in Feb., 1897, being promoted lieut. March, 1898. Lieut. Wylam accompanied his regiment to South Africa in Feb., 1900, and served in the O.R.C., taking part in the advance on Pretoria, and the subsequent operations in the Transvaal.

Wylie.—Lieut. C. H. B. A. Wylie, Indian Medical Service, died of enteric at Bloemfontein on June 2nd, 1900.

Yeatherd.—Major Ernest Walter Yeatherd, p.s.c., 2nd-in-command, 2nd Batt. King's Own Royal Lancaster Regt., died at the Base Hospital, Pietermaritzburg, Feb. 26th, 1900, of wounds received in action in the operations on the Tugela four days previously. He was born in March, 1852, and entered the 4th Foot Nov., 1872, being promoted capt. Oct., 1881, and major Feb., 1892. He was D.A.A. and Quartermaster-General, Dublin District, from March, 1885, to May, 1887, and D.A.A.G., Hong Kong, etc., from June, 1887, to April, 1890. Major Yeatherd accompanied his battalion to South Africa in Nov., 1899, and served with the Natal Field Force in the fighting on the Tugela.

Yockney.—Capt. T. Yockney, Imperial Light Horse, was killed in action at Naauwpoort, Jan. 5th, 1901. Capt. Yockney had seen much service during the war. He was in the fighting at Frederickstad in Oct., 1900, when the town was invested by De Wet, and on the 25th took part in the attack on the Boers. Sir A. Conan Doyle thus refers to an incident in this fight: "A small party of Imperial Light Horse, gallantly led by Capt. Yockney, came to close quarters with a group of Boers. Five of the enemy having held up their hands, Yockney passed them, and pushed on against their comrades. On this the prisoners seized their rifles once more and fired upon their captors. A fierce fight ensued with only a few feet between the muzzles of the rifles." Eight Boers were captured, and of these, three were shot next day for having resumed their weapons after surrender.

Young.—Capt. Edward Gordon Young, Royal Engineers, died of enteric at Kimberley, June 5th, 1900. He was the son of H. L. Young, Esq., was born in Feb., 1868, and educated at Haileybury. He entered the Royal Engineers in July, 1886, was promoted capt. in Feb., 1897, and went to South Africa in Jan., 1900. He married Isabella Maude, second daughter of C. P. Allix, Esq.

Young.—Lieut. Edward Maule Young, 1st Batt. King's Own Scottish Borderers, died of wounds received in action near Brandfort, O.R.C., March 29th, 1900. He was born in July, 1870, and educated at Cheltenham. He entered the King's Own Scottish Borderers in Jan., 1891, being promoted lieut. March, 1893, and proceeded to South Africa with his regiment in Dec., 1899, and was present at Paardeberg and the advance to Bloemfontein, then moving to the north to Brandfort, where he fell. His name is inscribed on the Eleanor Cross War Memorial at Cheltenham College.

Young.—Major Norman Edward Young, D.S.O., Royal Field Artillery, died of enteric at Bloemfontein, Feb. 26th, 1902. He was the eldest son of Major-Gen. C. M. Young, late R.A., was born in Oct., 1862, and educated at the United Services College, Westward Ho. He entered the Royal Artillery from the Royal Military Academy in July, 1882, was promoted capt. May, 1891, brevet-major Nov., 1896, and major Jan., 1900. He served with the expedition to Dongola in 1896, taking part in the operations of June 7th and Sept. 19th, being mentioned in despatches Nov. 3rd, 1896, and received the brevet of major and the Egyptian medal with two clasps. He took part in the Nile Expedition, 1897, and was present at the action of Abu Hamed, being mentioned in despatches, Jan. 25th, 1898, and receiving two clasps to the Egyptian medal. He also served in the Nile Expedition 1898, and took part in the cavalry reconnaissance of March 30th, and the battles of the Atbara and Omdurman, being mentioned in despatches, Sept. 30th, 1898, and was awarded the D.S.O., the Fourth Class of the Order of the Osmanieh, the medal, and two clasps to the Egyptian medal. Major Young went to South Africa in 1899 with the special ammunition column under Major May, and took part in Lieut.-Gen. Lord Methuen's advance and the action at Magersfontein and was present at Paardeberg and the capture of Cronje. When promoted major he was posted to the 75th Battery, Royal Field Artillery, which he commanded till Dec., 1901, and then became staff officer to Col. Dunlop's column of Royal Artillery Mounted Rifles, which post he held at the time of his death. When taken ill, he was first sent to Heilbron and thence to Bloemfontein, where he died. He was mentioned in despatches, L.G., April 19th, 1901. His name is inscribed on a memorial tablet in the United Services College at Westward Ho.

Younger.—Capt. David Reginald Younger, V.C., 1st Batt. Gordon Highlanders, was killed in action at Doornboschfontein, near Krugersdorp, June 11th, 1900. He was the eldest son of the late David Younger, Esq., and cousin of William Younger, Esq., M.P., of Auchen Castle, Dumfries. Capt. Younger was born in March, 1871, and educated at St. Ninians School, Moffat, Dumfriesshire and at Malvern College. He entered the Gordon Highlanders from the Duke of Edinburgh's Own Edinburgh Artillery, in Dec., 1893, being promoted lieut. Nov., 1896, and capt. Dec., 1899. He served with the Chitral Relief Force under Sir Robert Low in 1895, with the 1st battalion of his regiment, and took part in the storming of the Malakand Pass, receiving the medal with clasp. He next saw service in the North-West Frontier of India campaign, 1897-98, under the late Sir William Lockhart, taking part in the operations in the Maidan and Bara Valleys, and receiving two clasps. Capt. Younger proceeded to South Africa with his regiment in Oct., 1899, and joining the Kimberley Relief Force, was present at the battle of Magersfontein, and took part in the subsequent advance into O.R.C. and the Transvaal. In the action in which he was killed he took out a party and successfully dragged a Royal Artillery wagon under cover though exposed to a heavy fire. He then accompanied a second party to bring in a gun, but in this attempt he was mortally wounded and died shortly afterwards. His cool and gallant conduct is stated to have been the admiration of all who witnessed it. For his bravery he was awarded the V.C., L.G. Sept. 28th, 1900, and it was announced in the L.G., Aug. 8th, 1902, that His Majesty the King had been graciously pleased to approve of the decoration being delivered to the representative of Capt. Younger. He had been previously mentioned in despatches, L.G., Feb. 8th, 1901, for his services and having distinguished himself during the operations between Feb. 28th and March 13th, 1900. When Capt. Younger was lying mortally wounded, exposed to a terrific fire, Corporal McKay went out alone and carried him to a place of safety; and for this act Corporal McKay was awarded the V.C. Capt. Younger is buried in the cemetery at Krugersdorp, and a marble cross has been erected over his grave by his brother officers.

Younger.—2nd Lieut. Edward John Younger, 16th Lancers, was killed in action between Clanwilliam and Calvinia, Dec. 23rd, 1901. He was the second son of George Younger, Esq., of Valleyfield, Culross, Fife, N.B., was born in July, 1882, and educated at Harrow. He entered the 16th Lancers in August, 1900, and proceeded to South Africa, Jan., 1901, and served with his regiment in Cape and Orange River Colonies. The day he was killed 2nd Lieut. Younger behaved with great gallantry. The Boers had attacked a convoy with much determination on Dec. 22nd, but had been driven off. The next day, however, being most anxious to get supplies, they renewed the attack, and had taken possession of a ridge commanding the line of advance of the convoy. The 16th Lancers detachment charged with great dash and compelled them to retreat. It was in this charge that 2nd Lieut. Younger "while gallantly leading his men" was mortally wounded, dying almost immediately. He is buried close to where he fell. A chancel screen, a brass tablet in a slab of granite, and a stained glass window have been erected to his memory in St. John's Church, Alloa. The tablet bears the inscription: "In loving memory of 2nd Lieut. E. J. Younger, 16th Queen's Lancers, killed in action near Calvinia, Cape Colony, on Dec. 23rd, 1901, in his twentieth year. Erected by his Brother Officers."

APPENDIX.

WAR CORRESPONDENTS WHO LOST THEIR LIVES IN SOUTH AFRICA.

Adams.—Mr. Albert F. Adams, Exchange Telegraph Company, died of fever at Aliwal North.

Adams.—Mr. Albert Julian Adams, Exchange Telegraph Company, died of fever at Bloemfontein.

Calder.—Mr. James Innes Calder, Reuter's Agency, died of dysentery at Maseru.

Collett.—Mr. Frederick Slater Collett, *Daily Mail*, was killed at Schoeman's Farm.

Farrand.—Mr. George Alfred Farrand, *Morning Post*, was killed at Wagon Hill, Ladysmith, on Jan. 6th, 1900.

Inder.—Mr. William Sidney Inder, *Westmoreland Gazette*, who died of pneumonia at Bloemfontein, Jan. 7th, 1902, was the eldest son of Mr. W. S. Inder, Excise Officer, Kendal, was born in Dec., 1879, and educated at

Yeovil, and Kendal Grammar School. He was fond of all outdoor pursuits and games, and a very good football player. Mr. W. S. Inder formerly belonged to the 2nd Volunteer Batt. of the Border Regt., but when the war broke out was a member of the St. John's Ambulance Brigade. He offered his services, and being accepted he proceeded to South Africa in Nov., 1899, and served in the base hospital at Wynberg, and was quickly promoted to be sergeant. On completing six months service he returned with invalids; but as the war continued he again volunteered, and after spending one Sunday with his parents at Kendal he again embarked in June, 1900. Having served for twelve months at Wynberg and at Nourse Deep, near Johannesburg, he was appointed to the Imperial Military Railways at Bloemfontein with excellent prospects, but in Dec., 1901, was taken ill. He acted as war correspondent to the *Westmoreland Gazette* during the time he was in South Africa. He was in possession of the St. John's Ambulance medal and the South African War medal with three clasps. He is buried in the old cemetery at Bloemfontein.

Kingsley.—Miss Mary Kingsley, the African traveller, correspondent of the *Morning Post*, died at Simonstown on Whit-Sunday, 1900, of fever, and from the results of an operation. She had assisted to nurse the sick, &c., of the Boer prisoners of war. By her expressed wish she was buried at sea. The coffin, with her remains, was taken to the Pier at Simonstown on Whit-Monday, the procession being headed by the band of the West Yorkshire Regt. It was then placed on board Torpedo Boat No. 29, was taken out to sea, and committed to the deep.

Lambie.—Mr. W. J. Lambie, *Age*, Melbourne, was killed at Slingersfontein in Jan., 1900.

Mitchell.—Mr. Robert Mitchell, *Standard*, died of fever at Ladysmith. He was in Johannesburg, where he was well known, in Oct., 1899, and when war appeared imminent he decided on going to Natal, and arrived in Ladysmith a few days before the battle of Talana Hill. Thinking he would see more exciting work with Major-Gen. Sir W. P. Symons' column, he endeavoured to get to Dundee; but on the way the train he was travelling in was captured by the Boers. He was then made a prisoner, but during the battle of Elandslaagte he succeeded in escaping. He remained on the battlefield during the action, and later on returned to Ladysmith where he served until his death. The South African campaign was his first experience of active service as a war correspondent.

Parslow.—Mr. Edwin George Parslow, *Daily Chronicle*, was killed at Mafeking. He went to South Africa some years ago, and was engaged in journalism in Cape Colony. In Oct. 1899, he was at Mafeking, and remained there during the siege. This was his first experience of warfare. He is buried at Mafeking.

Scott.—Mr. E. D. Scott, *Manchester Courier*, was killed on the railway at Rietfontein, near Elandsfontein, July 26th, 1902. He belonged to a prominent Manchester family, was born in Feb., 1857, and for some years was a partner in the firm of G. F. Scott & Co., Mosley Street. He was fond of adventure and travelling and in 1894, giving up business, went to South Africa with Capt. J. A. Turner, of Winsford, Cheshire. They then went to Mafeking, to the Victoria Falls, and into the Barotse Country, and to King Lewanika's kraal. When the South African War broke out Mr. Scott placed his knowledge at the service of the *Manchester Courier*, and acted as their war correspondent. He first served with Lieut.-Gen. Lord Methuen's column, and was present at the actions of Graspan and Magersfontein. He subsequently accompanied the army under F.-M. Earl Roberts to Paardeberg, and was present at that battle and at Cronje's surrender. At Driefontein he was wounded in the leg, but recovering proceeded to Bloemfontein, and took part in the advance to Johannesburg and Pretoria. He then moved eastwards with the army under F.-M. Earl Roberts, and afterwards accompanied the force under Gen. Sir R. Buller, to Lydenburg. He subsequently saw much service up to the end of the war.

Spooner.—Mr. H. H. Spooner, *Evening News*, etc., Sydney, N.S.W., died of fever at Deelfontein.

Steevens.—Mr. George Warrington Steevens, the well-known correspondent of the *Daily Mail*, died at Ladysmith of enteric during the siege. He first made his mark as a member of the staff of the *Pall Mall Gazette*. After a connection of four years with that journal, he joined the *Daily Mail*, and as its correspondent, he wrote the series of articles " With Kitchener to Khartoum."

N.B.—It is intended by the Committee of the Institute of Journalists to erect a Memorial (for which the necessary permission has been obtained) in the Crypt of St. Paul's Cathedral to the above; also to Major G. L. Sidney Ray, Northumberland Fusiliers, and Lieut. T. J. Dunn, Scottish Horse, who, while serving in South Africa, acted as war correspondents.

NURSING SISTERS WHO DIED IN SOUTH AFRICA.

Boyd.—Nursing Sister M. S. Boyd died at Edinburgh Hospital, Naauwpoort, on May 15th, 1900.

Chown.—Nursing Sister Chown, Army Nursing Reserve, died on March 23rd, 1900.

Doran.—Nursing Sister Georgina Doran (Gena), died at the Officers' Military Hospital, Carnarvon, Cape Colony, on May 11th, 1902, of acute gastritis after two days' illness. She was the eldest daughter of Gen. Sir John Doran, K.C.B., and Lady Doran, Ely House, Wexford, and went to South Africa in Dec., 1901. She is buried in Carnarvon, and a cross has been erected over her grave.

Jones.—Nursing Sister Stuart Jones died in South Africa on May 15th, 1900.

Lloyd.—Nursing Sister Lloyd died of enteric at Pretoria in Oct., 1901. She went to South Africa with the Welsh Hospital, and when this hospital was broken up she was appointed matron of the officers' branch of No. 2 General Hospital in Pretoria. She is buried in the cemetery there.

Owen.—Nursing Sister Owen was accidentally drowned at Elandsfontein, Transvaal, on Jan. 24th, 1901.

Rose.—Nursing Sister M. C. Rose, Army Nursing Service, died at Durban on Jan. 3rd, 1900.

Sage.—Nursing Sister Sage, Army Nursing Service, died at Springfontein on June 12th, 1900.

West.—Nursing Sister M. J. West died at Pretoria on Oct. 20th, 1900.

Wood.—Mrs. O. G. Wood died at Kroonstad, O.R.C., Oct. 4th, 1901. She was known a few years ago in the Service as Sister Ireland. She joined the Army Nursing Service in 1882, and spent most of her time between Aldershot and Egypt. In 1885 she served as Superintending Sister with Miss Norman and Sister King at H Redoubt, Suakin, obtaining the Egyptian medal and Khedive's star, and the decoration of the Royal Red Cross. Many look back with gratitude to her gentle and capable nursing, and confess that to her ministrations, under Providence, they owe their lives. Always bright and cheerful, she was universally popular. She held the post of Superintending Sister of the Citadel Hospital, Cairo, from 1889-91, when she left the Service to be married to Col. Oswald G. Wood, Royal Army Medical Corps. Early in the war she volunteered her services as nursing sister, and followed her husband to South Africa, where she contracted a long and painful illness which ended in her death. Two little sons survive her, and their father, Col. Wood (*which see*).

FINIS.

PRINTERS: ARMY AND NAVY CO-OPERATIVE SOCIETY, LIMITED,
105, VICTORIA STREET, WESTMINSTER, LONDON, S.W.

www.ingramcontent.com/pod-product-compliance
Lightning Source LLC
Chambersburg PA
CBHW031129160426
43193CB00008B/80